Understanding Service Businesses

Applying Principles
of Unified Services Theory

Second Edition

Scott E. Sampson
Brigham Young University

WILEY
CUSTOM SERVICES

This custom textbook includes materials submitted by the Author for publication by John Wiley & Sons, Inc. The material has not been edited by Wiley and the Author is solely responsible for its content.

Published by John Wiley & Sons, Inc.

Sampson, Scott E.
    Understanding Service Businesses / Scott Sampson – 2nd ed.
    Includes bibliographical references and index.
    ISBN 0-471-21050-1
    1. Services management   I. Sampson, Scott   II. Title.

Printed in the United States of America.

Ordering Information

For information about ordering the workbook, contact John Wiley & Sons (**http://www.wiley.com/**) or see http://sampson.byu.edu/workbook/info/ordering/htm on the workbook website.

Many Thanks...

To Kristin, for providing ideas and time; to Giovanni, for expediting the original publication process, to Ben Dastrup, for assisting with the copyediting; to many SOMA members, for encouraging this work; and to all of my students, for providing the purspose.

Edition 2.13
7/9/2001

Understanding Service Businesses
Welcome to the Workbook!

What Is this Workbook About?

The following quotes are referenced in the Introduction section. Emphasis is added here.

☞ # Services are Predominant in Developed Economies.

"For far longer than most of us realize –for most of this century, in fact–services have dominated the American economy. They now generate 74% of gross domestic product, account for 79% of all jobs, and produce a balance-of-trade surplus that hit $55.7 billion last year vs. a deficit of $132.4 billion for goods." **"In the most advanced economies of the world, services account for two-thirds or more of output."**

☞ # Service Businesses Are Often Poorly Managed.

"Cause for concern is found in the observation that customer satisfaction in the U.S. is declining, primarily because of **decreasing satisfaction with services**." (Claes Fornell, chief researcher of the *American Customer Satisfaction Index*, an annual study of tens of thousands of U.S. consumers.)

"**Service quality**, while difficult to measure, is generally perceived to be **deteriorating**." (Gregory P. Hackett of Booz, Allen & Hamilton, Inc.)

"The **innovation** process [in studied service industries] is generally an **unsystematic** search-and-learning process." (Jon Sundbo, who studied innovation in twenty-one European service industry companies.)

"The primary reason why the **productivity** growth rate has **stagnated** in the service sector is *management*." (Researchers Michael van Biema and Bruce Greenwald)

☞ # Services Management is Largely Misunderstood.

"The service economy, despite its size and growth, remains extraordinarily *misunderstood*, *mismeasured*, and *mismanaged*." (Ronald Henkoff of *Fortune* Magazine)

"Most people (managers) still view the world through **manufacturing goggles**." (Fred Reichheld, head of the customer-loyalty practice at the consulting firm Bain & Co.)

"Old legends die hard. Many service firms have [imitated] the **worst aspects of manufacturing management**." (Professor Leonard Schlesinger of the Harvard Business School)

"Despite the steady expansion of the service economy, American management practices, accounting conventions, *business school courses*, and public policies continue to suffer from an acute **Industrial Age hangover**." "Service executives...[subject] their companies to management theories–both traditional and trendy–that were invented **in the factory**." (Henkoff)

This workbook is about improving how we *understand* and *manage* Service Businesses!

Understanding Service Businesses:
Applying Principles of the Unified Services Theory
Second Edition

Quick Start

This list is to help get you started with the workbook. I want the workbook to help you find answers to your Services Management questions. The following may help you find them a little faster.

Questions an Instructor May Have

☞"How do I use this workbook in an **Operations Management** course?"
  See the Preface section: Operations Management Context (starting on page vi).

☞"How do I use this workbook in a **Services Management** course?"
  See the Preface section : Services Management Perspective (starting on page viii).

☞"Can I use this workbook in a **Services Marketing** or **Services Strategy** course?"
  Yes. Units 5 and 6 cover important issues in Services Strategy. Units 8 through 14 are particularly relevant to Services Marketing.

☞"How do I **customize** the use of the workbook to my course needs and interests?"
  See the Preface section titled Instructor Selected Material (starting on page ix).

☞"What **text books** should I consider for assigning supplemental readings?"
  See page ix on Supplemental Text Readings. It is possible to use the workbook without additional supplemental readings, but good supplemental readings can be useful.

☞"Where can I get access to other instructor resources?"
  Teaching resources are available to instructors (with passwords) on the workbook website (http://sampson.byu.edu/workbook/instructor).

Questions a Student May Have about Using the Workbook

☞"Why is there a great need to study Services Management?"
  See the Introduction section starting on page 1.

☞"Why is there a great need for a **Unified Services Theory**?"
  See the Introduction sections on Defining Services (page 4) and The Need for a Unified Services Theory (page 5).

☞"What is meant by a **Service Business Principle** (SBP)?"
  See page 7 on the Organization of this Workbook.

☞"How are Service Business Principles organized in the workbook?"
  See Sections of Each Service Business Principle starting on page 9.

☞"How do I access the workbook **website**?"
  See Appendix A on using the workbook website.

☞"The *brief* Table of Contents is on the next page. Where is the *full* **Table of Contents**?"
  At the back of the workbook right after the topical Index. (It seems more convenient there.)

Preface
Intro
Unit 1
Unit 2
Unit 3
Unit 4
Unit 5
Unit 6
Unit 7
Unit 8
Unit 9
Unit 10
Unit 11
Unit 12
Unit 13
Unit 14
Apx A
Apx B
Apx C
Apx D
Index
T of C

Quick Start Questions about Services Management

☞"What exactly is a 'service business' anyway?"
    See Unit 1: Unified Services Theory Basics.

☞"What characteristics of services need to be considered in service process **design**?"
    See Unit 2: Services Fundamentals: Planning.

☞"What characteristics of services make the **day-to-day management** of services challenging?"
    See Unit 3: Services Fundamentals: Execution.

☞"What is important to understand about manufacturers (who may supply goods used in the service)?"
    See Unit 4: Understanding Non-Services (manufacturing).

☞"How might a service business attain and sustain **competitive (or contributive[1]) advantage**?"
    See Unit 5: Identifying Strategic Opportunities.

☞"What tend to be the biggest challenges to sustaining that advantage over time?"
    See Unit 6: Identifying Strategic Threats.

☞"How might a service increase process improve **efficiency**, and what limits that efficiency?"
    See Unit 7: Cost Issues.

☞"What causes **labor management** to be so difficult in services and how might labor be managed effectively?"
    See Unit 8: Human Resources Management.

☞"What are the keys to effective **marketing** of services, and why is service pricing often difficult?"
    See Unit 9: Marketing in Services.

☞"Why do so many services keep their **customers in inventory** (waiting), and what should they do about it?"
    See Unit 10: Production and Inventory Control.

☞"Why is **service quality** so hard to define, and how might we know what it is for a particular service?"
    See Unit 11: Defining Service Quality.

☞"What are the key forces that make it difficult to assure service quality on an ongoing basis?"
    See Unit 12: Challenges in Delivering Service Quality.

☞"When things do go wrong in a service process, how can service providers effectively minimize the damage?"
    See Unit 13: Service Recovery.

☞"How can we **measure the results** of a service to know if it is on track, and to motivate employees to do better?"
    See Unit 14: Measuring Service Quality and Productivity.

---

[1] Some services are successful not by competing, but by contributing. For example, government services are often judged on their ability to contribute to the nation or region, and generally do not compete with organizations in the same region. Even in competitive environments the companies that are the "most competitive" tend to be those who are most able to contribute by adding value and in other ways.

Brief Table of Contents

Preface for Instructors

(Students may skip forward to the workbook Introduction on page 1.)

I have developed this workbook so that it can be applied to two general course contexts. One is Operations Management courses of a general nature. This includes the Introductory Operations Management courses offered to undergraduate and graduate students at most universities.

The other context for using the workbook is Services Management courses, which are increasingly being offered at universities, often as an undergraduate or graduate elective.

These two contexts differ, but are complementary. In fact, a practical approach is to use the workbook in an Introductory Operations Management course, with an in-depth study of Units 1 through 3, followed by a Services Management elective, wherein Units 1 and 4 (or 5) through 14 would be studied. (I recommend that Unit 1 be read in every course, since it is foundational to all other units.)

The following two preface sections explain and justify the workbook applicability to each of these contexts. After that is a section titled "Instructor Selected Material," which describes how instructors can further customize a course around the workbook.

Preface: Operations Management Context

The tradition of Operations Management is rooted in manufacturing. In fact, "operations management" is assumed by many to be synonymous with "manufacturing management." This unjustified assumption ignores the fact that *most* business operations in the developed world are *not* manufacturing processes, but are service processes.

Despite the service operations predominance, most Operations Management courses and texts are founded in manufacturing perspectives and principles. Well-intended authors and instructors have sought to recognize the shift to a service economy by sprinkling service examples among the manufacturing material. Such action implies a bold assumption that service operations principles are simply an extension of manufacturing operations principles. The study of services is thus viewed as secondary to the study of the manufacturing contexts which are most familiar.

This treatment of service operations as subservient to manufacturing has led to a false perception by many that the study of operations issues in service contexts is shallow and unscientific. This is illustrated by the way services topics are introduced.

For example, a major topic in many Operations Management texts and courses is product layouts, which are assembly lines. Significant attention is paid to discussing assembly line balancing, which involves identifying and relieving bottlenecks in the process to increase overall throughput (i.e. the amount of production per time period). After discussing these ideas in manufacturing contexts, well-meaning authors and instructors attempt to tie this in to services with an example. The example we give is generally something like the food serving line in a cafeteria. We make all kinds of dramatic assumptions about the process times at each station (salad, entree, dessert, drinks, etc.) so that the manufacturing management techniques can be applied. To the student, such an example can easily come across as contrived and of little relevant value. Students may think "talking about managing cafeteria lines is of little value to me, since it is unlikely I will ever manage a cafeteria with significant throughput problems." Indeed, few business school graduates go to work in cafeterias, and it is unlikely that those who do will spend much time concerned about food-line throughput.

So why don't authors and instructors give more realistic service examples of assembly line balancing–examples from industries many students are interested in such as financial planning, accounting, marketing, consulting, etc.? The answer is that assembly line balancing, dare I say, is *virtually irrelevant in most service contexts!!!* How can it be that such a time-tested manufacturing topic could find weak application in service contexts? The answer is that, believe it or not, SERVICES ARE FUNDAMENTALLY DIFFERENT FROM MANUFACTURING.

The problems occur when we study services with an assumption that they are simply an extension of manufacturing, which they are not. For example, one inherent assumption of assembly line balancing is that there is relatively homogenous production. If every item in production had unique and random processing times, it would be difficult to characterize the capacity of various workstations, thus confounding the bottleneck identification issues. The occurrence of bottlenecks could be almost random, depending on the random nature of each product's requirements. Well, frankly, that is the case in most service processes. That is why we have to pick an isolated example like cafeteria lines when studying assembly line balancing.

I am afraid that such dramatic stretching to apply manufacturing principles to services contexts has led some to wrongly conclude that there is little place for Operations Management in services. For example, years ago I sat across the desk from a department chairman of what, at one point, had been a well-respected university department. I was interviewing for an Operations Management faculty position, and had expressed my interests in Service Operations Management teaching and research. After a little discussion, the department chairman made a statement to the effect of, "Come now, both you and I know that if there is anything interesting to study in Operations Management, it will be in manufacturing." At the time I thought he was just ignorant. Since then I have realized that his misconceptions may have been caused by the way services Operations Management had been forced into manufacturing molds.

If we falsely equate "operations management" with "manufacturing management," and observe that manufacturing principles do not drive most service business, then we may conclude that "operations management does not apply to service businesses." That is like saying "boxing is the sport of true athletes," and observe that "women are generally not good at boxing," then concluding that "women are generally not good athletes." Only a naive buffoon would make such a statement. Many women are great athletes, just not by the measure of boxing fanatics. Likewise, services processes are rich with Operations Management principles, just not by the context of traditional manufacturing management.

I do not mean to imply that there is nothing about service operations to be learned from manufacturing operations. In fact, many manufacturing concepts can benefit service operations managers. However, **what I propose is that we study Service Operations Management from the context and realities of service operations.** That is the design of this workbook.

You will also note that I have said nothing to imply that there is no value in continuing to study manufacturing management in business schools. In fact, in this edition of the workbook I have included sections titled "How manufacturing differs from services," which can be used as a lead-in to a discussion of manufacturing concepts. But, of course, I would recommend that the balance of class time between manufacturing principles and services principles be related to the percent of graduates who will go to work in these respective sectors.

> Examples of syllabi for Operations Management courses which use this workbook are found at http://sampson.byu.edu/workbook/syllabi/ on the workbook website. In mere minutes, the syllabus wizard will automatically create a syllabus for your course, which you can print out or save and modify with your word processor.

Preface: Services Management Perspective

This workbook originally evolved out of topics I have covered in my Services Management course. (Later I added material from my Operations Management course.) A few years ago I felt that I was teaching interesting and important Services Management topics, but that the material was somewhat disjointed. I attribute part of this to the relative newness of Services Management as a discipline. Academic fields that have evolved over many decades tend to develop staples and structure. The *staples* are the fundamental concepts every student of that discipline should know. (For example, net present value analysis is a staple of finance.) The *structure* of an academic field categorizes the major issues of the field and defines a logical ordering of the topics. Services Management as an academic field is so new that the staples and structure were still somewhat undefined, at least as I saw it. So, of course, I wanted to do something about it. That is why I developed this workbook.

One interesting thing about the Services Management discipline is that *of necessity* it integrates operations, human resources, and marketing. This is different from manufacturing management, wherein Manufacturing Operations Management, Product Marketing, and Human Resource Management are commonly taught as distinct disciplines (which is not ideal, but the result of traditional functional specialization).

With Services Management it is *impossible* to adequately talk about Operations Management without addressing major human resource issues. Further, it is *impossible* to do justice to services marketing without discussing operations design and execution.

I generally discourage any university from offering distinct courses in services marketing and services operations, unless the courses are tightly integrated. My preference for a single course title is "Services Management," which does not draw nonproductive barriers between functional areas. Given the approach of this workbook, such a course can be effectively taught by instructors from various functional specializations.

Therefore, using the workbook in a Services Management course will help clarify what to study (the "staples"), how to study it (the "structure"), and how the topics interrelate. Further, numerous examples and Application Exercises will assist the student in applying the material to decision making in real business situations.

> Also, examples of syllabi for Services Management courses which use this workbook are found at http://sampson.byu.edu/workbook/syllabi/ on the workbook website. The syllabus wizard will create a syllabus for your course which you can print out or save and modify with your word processor.

Instructor Selected Material

This workbook can be used in many different ways in various courses. The workbook has been designed to allow instructors to tailor study to meet the objectives of each particular course. Instructors can choose their preferred companion textbook, may choose to incorporate cases in the study, may elect to take a quantitative approach, and may incorporate the study of manufacturing principles. No one approach is necessarily better than the others in all situations, but the approach depends upon the curriculum needs as determined by the instructor. Ultimately, the instructor is the expert in making course composition decisions. The following are some elements he or she may elect to involve in the course, including supplemental text readings and cases, quantitative analysis, links to manufacturing, application questions, and Application Exercises.

Supplemental Text Readings

The workbook is not exhaustive in describing the material. I have no aspirations to reinvent the wheel. Throughout the workbook I will refer the student to other readings. At present the entire workbook is cross-referenced to the following excellent and popular Services Management book:

- **"Fitzsimmons2"** refers to *Service Management: Operations, Strategy, and Information Technology*, Second Edition, by James A. Fitzsimmons and Mona J. Fitzsimmons, Irwin/McGraw-Hill, 1998.

At this writing, we are in the process of compiling an "Essential Readings in Services Management" book that can be used for supplemental readings. Information about that book and its availability will be posted on the workbook website (http://sampson.byu.edu/workbook/updates/).

Units 2 and 3 contain quantitative analysis material and simulation exercises. Each principle in those units ties in to a specific section of Appendix C: Quantitative Tools. The Quantitative Tools section is intended to tie the service principles into relevant quantitative topics by introducing the student to the topic. The Quantitative Tools appendix sections is not intended to give a thorough coverage of the quantitative topics, but instead to refer the student to the latest editions of some of the best and most popular Operations Management textbooks:

- **"Chase8"** refers to *Production and Operations Management: Manufacturing and Services*, Eighth Edition, by Richard B. Chase, Nicholas J. Aquilano, and Hal Jacobs, Irwin/McGraw-Hill, 1998.

- **"Stevenson6"** refers to *Production Operations Management*, Sixth Edition, by William J. Stevenson, Irwin/McGraw-Hill, 1999.

- **"Heizer5"** refers to *Operations Management*, Fifth Edition, by Jay Heizer and Barry Render, Prentice-Hall, 1999.

The instructor will inform the students which readings they will be responsible for. In most cases, readings are specified at the start of each unit. Each unit again refers to appropriate unit readings.

(Instructors can obtain from the workbook website a list which summarizes readings corresponding to each unit. See http://sampson.byu.edu/workbook/instructor/ for more information.)

Supplemental Case Studies

Some courses are case-based or involve cases in the study. This often occurs in graduate level courses; however cases can also be effectively used in undergraduate courses. The "Supplemental reading" section of many units contains references to cases which are particularly effective for exploring particular Service Business Principles. Student preparation of the cases, such as writeups or in-class discussion, will be specified by the instructor.

Unless specified otherwise, cases listed under Supplemental Readings are from the Harvard Business School (HBS). Information about the cases can be found at the HBS website.

Other Supplemental Readings

In some instances, the "Supplemental reading" section of a unit will contain references to a published article. Again, the instructor will determine which, if any, of these readings students will be responsible for. At many universities, any specified cases or supplemental readings will be made available as a packet that students can purchase. This allows the university to obtain all copyright permissions necessary to distribute the material.

A few of the listed supplemental readings are not presently available from a published source, thus have been included in Appendix D.

Quantitative Analysis

Some courses are *not* quantitative in nature, and involve little to no quantitative analysis; this is how I choose to teach one of my courses based on this workbook. Other courses are mostly quantitative, with numerical analysis at every turn; this is the way I choose to offer another course based on this workbook. The point is that courses can be extremely effective with or without a quantitative focus. Again, it is the instructor who decides what is appropriate given curriculum requirements.

This workbook has been designed to allow instructors to either include or omit quantitative material. There are boxes throughout the workbook with the heading "Quantitative analysis" which describe approaches and tools relating to a particular Service Business Principle. The instructor may also choose to have students complete analysis assignments involving quantitative analysis.

Note that in the second edition of the workbook the quantitative material is concentrated in Unit 2 (Services Fundamentals: Planning) and Unit 3 (Services Fundamentals: Execution). In some cases, an entire quantitative course may only cover Units 1 through 3, taking extended time covering each of the types of quantitative analysis described in Units 2 and 3. A separate course may then build on this by covering the non-quantitative material in Units 4 through 14.

The "Quantitative analysis" sections that show up in Units 4 through 14 simply refer the student to quantitative topics, some of which were covered in Units 2 and 3.

Related Manufacturing Concepts

Earlier in this preface I emphasized the objective of this workbook of advancing the study of the *service sector*, which represents the vast majority of job growth and economic advancement in developed nations. But the preface also includes the statement "I have said nothing to imply that there is no value in continuing to study manufacturing management in business schools." Indeed, the study of manufacturing management has its place and importance, which in most cases is secondary to the study of Services Management.

Some courses will have little to no discussion of manufacturing management. However, even in my Services Management course we cover Unit 4: *Understanding Non-Services (Manufacturing)*. That unit contains principles which relate manufacturing paradigms to service paradigms and perspectives.

In some courses the instructor desires to involve a greater infusion of manufacturing management concepts. For this purpose, boxed sections titled "How manufacturing differs from services" are included throughout the workbook. Those sections briefly indicate how manufacturing organizations differ with regard to the current service principle, and can lead to a discussion of the issues which are relevant to manufacturing. Again, these boxes and the related manufacturing concepts should be covered at the instructor's discretion.

Questions and Application Exercises

The workbook material is most effectively studied with an applied focus. That is why it is a *workbook*, not just a readings book. The student will get much more out of the material by applying concepts and principles as they are learned.

To help students prepare their minds for new principles, nearly all Service Business Principles are preceded by "To consider" questions. The instructor may have students think through these issues before advancing to the principle. Those questions can also serve as a great basis for invigorating classroom discussion.

After the discussion of a Service Business Principle and description of examples, each student is responsible to apply what has been learned. "Analysis questions" sections are included to help the student discover how the principle applies to a particular industry of interest. It is always valuable to complete those questions, but each instructor may decide whether the questions are assigned and should be turned in. (In my Services Management course I leave it up to the students to decide if they want to complete the "Analysis questions," and do not ask them to turn them in. Students who choose to complete the questions report that it is a good use of time and very helpful in increasing the understanding of Service Business Principles.)

One of the most valuable ways to practice applying the material is to complete the "Application exercise" sections associated with most Service Business Principles. These are generally non-quantitative methods of analysis that draw insights about an industry relative to a particular principle. (In my Services Management course I require students to complete Application Exercises each week and be prepared to hand them in or share them with the class.) Again, the incorporation of Application Exercises in a particular course is left to the discretion of the instructor.

The study and interest of the material is greatly enhanced if each student completes the Analysis Questions and Application Exercise based on a service industry of particular interest to him or her. For this reason, students should be encouraged to select a Target Service Business early in the course, which will be discussed on page 8. In executive education, it is good for students to use their present employment as their Target Service Business.

Other Resources for Instructors

Other teaching resources that may be of interest to instructors are found at http://sampson.byu.edu/workbook/instructor on the workbook website. Some of those materials, such as course syllabi, are publically accessible. Other materials, such as the "Topics for Debate" questions are only viewable by instructors with passwords. (This prevents students from accessing them and getting ahead of the class.)

Understanding Service Businesses:
Applying Principles of the Unified Services Theory

Second Edition

Introduction

(References for this Introduction are listed at the end of Appendix D.)

The United States of America has become a service economy, meaning that the majority of economic output (approximately three-fourths of GDP) comes from service businesses. Services are predominant in the economies of other developed nations as well. Robert F. Kelly, Managing Partner for Andersen Worldwide, has pointed out that, "In the most advanced economies of the world, services account for two-thirds or more of output." (1997) Even countries known for their large manufacturing bases have much of their GDP output attributable to services. (e.g. Korea: 63 percent, Chinese Taipei: 56 percent, Thailand: 47 percent (Kelly 1997)).

Services dominate not only the *output* of developed nations, but also absorb much of the *inputs* of production, such as labor and capital. For example, the percentage of employment in service sector jobs in 1993 for a sampling of nations was Canada 75%, U.S. 74%, Australia 72%, Belgium 71%, Israel 68%, France 66%, Finland 66%, Italy 60%, Japan 60% (United.Nations 1993). This is not at all to imply that developed nations are *good* at managing services. In fact, it appears that generally they are *not*. The following are a few examples of the need for better service management.

The service sector is not very productive.

Services sector utilization of labor and capital has only improved slightly in recent decades (Productivity.Indexes 1988). While manufacturing sectors experienced a 3.3% productivity increase between 1980 and 1990, service sector productivity only increased a paltry 0.8% (van Biema and Greenwald 1997).

Service quality is not very good, and seems to be on the decline.

One author observed, "Service quality, while difficult to measure, is generally perceived to be deteriorating" (Hackett 1990). This observation is verified by the American Customer Satisfaction Index (ASCI), an annual survey which is sponsored by the American Society for Quality (ASQ) and the University of Michigan Business School. Each year tens of thousands of consumers are surveyed about perceptions of companies in various industries. The results are organized by economic sector according to Standard Industrial Codes (SIC).

In 1996, the chief researcher of the ASCI, Claes Fornell, and colleagues, observed, "Customer satisfaction is found to be greater for goods than for services.... Cause for concern is found in the observation that customer satisfaction in the U.S. is declining, primarily because of decreasing satisfaction with services" (Fornell, *et al.* 1997). ASCI reports finding that customer satisfaction is primarily quality-driven, implying that service quality is on the decline.

Unfortunately, the results for 1997 were worse in many respects, as shown in the figure below.

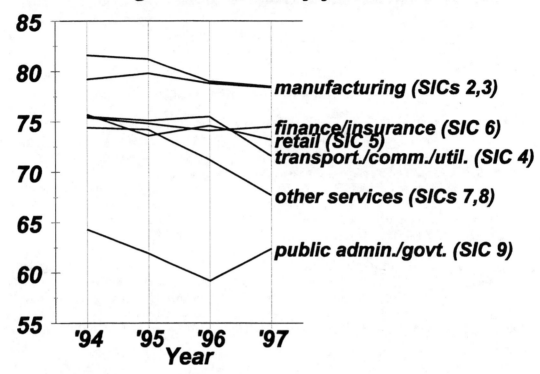

American Customer Satisfaction Index (CSI) Survey
Average CSI scores by year and sector

source: American Society for Quality (http://acsi.asq.org/results.htm)

Observe that both non-durable manufacturing (the top line) and durable manufacturing (the second line) are well above the various service sectors of the economy in average ratings. Further, the two areas of greatest decline in 1997 were transportation/communication/utilities, dropping 5.2 percent, and other services (hospitality, health care, movies) dropping 4.9 percent. Service quality is not generally improving, by any stretch of the imagination! (The notable exception is public administration/government, which actually *improved* in 1997, reflecting increased satisfaction with services such as law enforcement. Yet overall satisfaction levels are still quite low.)

Services are often managed by outdated paradigms.

A poignant article by Ronald Henkoff (1994) observes:

> "For far longer than most of us realize–for most of this century, in fact–services have dominated the American economy. They now generate 74% of gross domestic product, account for 79% of all jobs, and produce a balance-of-trade surplus that hit $55.7 billion last year, vs. a deficit of $132.4 billion for goods."

Nevertheless, he laments:

> "The service economy, despite its size and growth, remains extraordinarily *misunderstood*, *mismeasured*, and *mismanaged*." (italics added)

The service sector has grown in size, but not in managerial practice. Others, such as van Biema and Greenwald (1997), share this view. They assert that "The primary reason why the productivity growth rate has stagnated in the service sector is *management*" (italics added).

Henkoff continues:

> "Despite the steady expansion of the service economy, American management practices, accounting conventions, business school courses, and public policies continue to suffer from an acute Industrial Age hangover. 'Most people still view the world through manufacturing goggles,' complains Fred Reichheld, leader of the customer-loyalty practice at Bain & Co.

As an example of this mismanagement, Reichheld observes that the accounting systems currently in use were "designed to serve 19th-century textile and steel mills." More from Henkoff:

> "Service executives often behave much like belly dancers trying to march to a John Philip Sousa song, subjecting their companies to management theories–both traditional and trendy–that were invented in the factory. Says Leonard Schlesinger, a Harvard business school professor who has studied service companies for two decades: 'Old legends die hard. Many service firms have aped the worst aspects of manufacturing management. They oversupervise; they overcontrol.'"

We have thus far failed to make the shift in management practice to correspond with the shift to a service economy.

Few service companies are truly innovative.

Service innovation is often haphazard. Jon Sundbo (1997) conducted a study of innovation in twenty-one European companies from various service industries. He concluded, "The innovation process is generally an unsystematic search-and-learning process."

In fact, much of current practice in Services Management is unsystematic. There is a crying need to develop and study the science of Services Management, which is what this workbook is all about.

Defining Services Management

A real challenge in developing the science of Services Management is that people have a hard time defining what services are, and identifying what makes service businesses different from any other business. *Fortune* magazine seems to have felt the effects of this difficulty in defining service business when, after many years of publishing the Fortune Industrial 500 and the Fortune Service 500, they recently collapsed the two lists into one (Eiben and Davis 1995). It apparently became too difficult to sort the service firms from the manufacturers.

A serious problem occurs when the inability to understand services leads to treating them as a peculiar case of manufacturing. This cluelessness is illustrated by the practice of those who refer to services as "non-manufacturing" and/or who maintain that service businesses should be run by manufacturing paradigms. (Specific references available upon request. I deleted the references I had listed here to avoid making enemies.) Services are often treated by academics as a heterogeneous lump of leftovers. Since the unique aspects of Services Management are not understood, they are referred to simply by their relative proximity to what most people in academics do know: manufacturing management.

Authors Castells and Aoyama (Castells and Aoyama 1994) describe the prevalent confusion in defining services: (Citations listed in this quote are from their paper.)

> "the notion of 'services' is often considered at best ambiguous, at worst misleading (Gershuny and Miles, 1983; Daniels, 1993). In employment statistics, it has been used as a residual notion embracing all that is not agriculture, mining, construction, utilities, or manufacturing. Thus, the category of services includes activities of all kinds, with roots in various social structures and productive systems. The only feature common to these service activities is what they are not (Castells, 1976; Stanback, 1979; Cohen and Zysman, 1987; Katz 1988; Daniels, 1993)."

This definition of services as a disjointed "residual"–left over when all other sectors is accounted for–is peculiar. That "residual" is larger than *all other sectors combined* in advanced economies. The "residual" view has been perpetuated by the way governments have classified economic activities (Schmenner 1995). Attempts have been made to correct this confusion, such as with the new North American Industrial Classification System (NAICS). Such attempts more accurately capture the shift to a service-based economy, but provide little to our understanding of how businesses should be managed in the new economy.

Some authors and researchers have defined services in ways that are not "residual" per se, but still based on their distinction from manufactured goods. The following are a few examples.

- Gonçalves (1998, p. 1) sets forth the following definition: "a service business is one in which the perceived value of the offering to they buyer is determined more by the service rendered than the product offered."

- Ammer and Ammer (1984, p. 421) defined a service industry as "An industry that produces services rather than goods" (quoted in Riddle 1985, p. 9).

Such definitions can be less than fulfilling, and provide little insight into what services are. Other definitions focus on characteristics of services:

- Murdick, Render, and Russell (1990) identify services as intangible products, whereas (manufactured) goods are "tangible objects that can be created and sold or used later."

- Pearce defined services as follows: "[Services] are sometimes referred to as intangible *goods*; one of their characteristics being that in general they are 'consumed' at the point of production" (Pearce 1981, p. 390).

- Bannock, Baxter, and Reese put it this way: "[Services are] consumer or producer goods which are mainly intangible and often consumed at the same time as they are produced.... Service industries are usually labor-intensive" (Bannock, *et al.* 1982, p. 372).

Such definitions can provide insights into important issues of services. However, we might question whether a business is a service because it possesses such characteristics, or if it has those characteristics because it is a service. For example, software *manufacturing* produces a product that is very intangible (computer code) and the production process is very labor-intensive (computer programmers). Therefore, intangibility and labor intensity must not *define* a business as a service. We might conclude that if a business is a service it would tend to be intangible and labor-intensive, but not the other way around. This is a major problem with defining services by their characteristics. (Many characteristics of services will be discussed in Units 2 and 3: *Service Fundamentals*. The false idea of service intangibility will be rebuffed there.)

Other definitions of services focus on the service production process:

- **A service is a personal performance.** Levitt describes a service as being "invariably and undeviatingly personal, as something performed by individuals for other individuals" (Levitt 1972). Thomas disagrees with that conceptualization, since it denies automated services, particularly those acting on inanimate objects, such as an automated car wash service (Thomas 1978).

- **Service is to change a person or their belongings.** Hill (1977) defined a service as "a change in the condition of a person, or of a good belonging to some economic unit, which is brought about as the result of the activity of some other economic unit...."

- **A service is a product which is a process.** (Henkoff 1994; Shostack 1987)

- **Services are processes involving customer contact.** Chase (1978) introduced a classification system in which "pure service" involves high requirements for customer contact and manufacturing involves low contact. He defines "customer contact" as the physical presence of the customer in the system.

- **Services are "economic activities that produce time, place, form, or psychological utilities."** (Murdick, *et al.* 1990) Riddle (1985, p. 12) adds to this idea, "while bringing about a change in or for the recipient of the service."

There is a lot of truth in these conceptualizations. However, we still need to answer the fundamental question about why we are justified in studying disparate service industries under a single heading of "Services Management." For example, how are we justified in teaching a course on Services which encompasses health care and garbage collection, consulting and ski resorts, airlines and pawn shops, pet grooming and law firms, universities and butcher shops? They all seem to fit the conceptualizations above to one degree or another—but if we ran our university like a butcher shop, where would we be?

A major purpose of this workbook will be to define Services Management in such a way that the commonality of all service businesses will be captured, and important managerial implications will be revealed. The approach to accomplish this purpose is called the "Unified Services Theory."

The Need for a Unified Services Theory

Some time ago I studied and pondered the dilemma of defining services. I thought: "Would it be possible to define service businesses in a way that (a) justifies studying such a wide range of industries under one heading, and (b) will lead us to numerous managerial implications?" This question is similar to one Albert Einstein pondered for the last twenty years of his life. He felt driven to identify a "Unified Field Theory" which would describe how magnetism, gravity, radiation, light, and other energy fields were all part of a unified phenomenon. The implications of a Unified Field Theory were tremendous, for it would not only show what the various energy fields had in common, but led to insights about how each individual field type operates.

In like manner I concluded that what we need to hasten the development of the Services Management discipline was a "Unified *Services* Theory." After much study on the topic, I present The Unified Services Theory as described throughout this workbook. This Unified Services Theory clearly justifies the common consideration of various industries called "services."

The Unified Services Theory also unifies the distinctive characteristics of services by showing that they originate from a common cause. The various characteristics of services are generally described in the literature separately, even though the characteristics do not occur in isolation from one another. Fitzsimmons and Fitzsimmons (1998, p. 27) share the insight that, "many of the unique characteristics of services, such as customer participation and perishability, are interrelated." From this we may suppose that some characteristics are caused by other characteristics. That is an extremely reasonable assumption.

What if we went a step further? What if we assumed that there was a major factor that caused *almost every other characteristic of services to occur*? Proposing that factor is a fundamental purpose of the Unified Services Theory. This workbook describes dozens of service characteristics and Service Business Principles which are a direct result of that unifying factor. There is not a single Service Business Principle described in this workbook that is not a direct consequence of the Unified Services Theory.

The Workbook Premise

"The keys to successful management of Service businesses will be yours if you can learn and apply just two things: (1) the Unified Services Theory, and (2) its implications."

Everything in this workbook is centered on that objective.

In one sense, the Unified Services Theory is a descriptive model, and arguably so. However, perhaps in a larger sense it is a *prescriptive* model. I propose a standard of understanding that can help bring together the many diverse views of those who study Service industries.

Ideas and concepts that have gone into the Unified Services Theory and this workbook have been drawn from the best authors and researchers in Services Management. There is very little about this material that is new except for the packaging–the individual ideas have been written about in other places. The contribution of this workbook is in the way the principles are packaged in a unified whole that is more structured, more holistic, and more intuitive.

Be careful to not assume that the intuitiveness of the principles means they are commonplace. They are neither commonplace nor common practice. The power of the Unified Services Theory is in understanding how basic ideas, when fully understood and internalized by the service manager, can make a dramatic difference in how the service business operates and succeeds.

The Unified Services Theory will be introduced in Unit 1 of this workbook. The remaining units serve to draw managerial implications from the Unified Services Theory. This format is based on the idea that understanding how to best manage service businesses should be founded in an understanding of what service businesses are.

Organization of this Workbook

The workbook is organized into four major parts, each of which contain units:

Part I - Fundamentals
Unit 1: **Unified Services Theory Basics** (includes 6 Service Business Principles—SBPs)
Unit 2: **Services Fundamentals: Planning** (5 SBPs)
Unit 3: **Services Fundamentals: Execution** (5 SBPs)
Unit 4: **Understanding Non-Services (manufacturing)** (4 SBPs)

Part II - Service Business Strategy
Unit 5: **Identifying Strategic Opportunities** (5 SBPs)
Unit 6: **Identifying Strategic Threats** (6 SBPs)

Part III - Managing Service Processes
Unit 7: **Cost Issues** (3 SBPs)
Unit 8: **Human Resources Management** (3 SBPs)
Unit 9: **Marketing in Services** (4 SBPs)
Unit 10: **Production and Inventory Control** (3 SBPs)

Part IV - Service Quality and Value
Unit 11: **Defining Service Quality** (3 SBPs)
Unit 12: **Challenges in Delivering Service Quality** (3 SBPs)
Unit 13: **Service Recovery** (3 SBPs)
Unit 14: **Measuring Service Quality and Productivity** (3 SBPs)

Within each unit are Service Business Principles. (The number of Service Business Principles in each unit is listed in parentheses above.) The Service Business Principles are succinct concepts or observations from the Unified Services Theory that provide for more effective Services Management.

In the workbook I have outlined more than 50 Service Business Principles that follow directly from the Unified Services Theory. Nevertheless, I am confident that I have just scratched the surface of the potential for application of the Unified Services Theory. Therefore, the workbook will be revised and updated frequently. (If you have suggestions, such as great examples, e-mail them to comments@sampson.byu.edu. Please include the unit or Service Business Principle name in the subject line.)

Assignment #1: Selecting a Target Service Business

An important part of the workbook is the opportunity to apply each Service Business Principle. This is primarily accomplished through Analysis Questions and an Application Exercise listed at the end of each principle. The instructor will inform you about which of these you will be responsible for, including being prepared to present in class, to turn in, and/or to turn in at the end of the semester. To facilitate the application of the principles, each student must select a target service business process.

You are going to spend a lot of time contemplating and analyzing your target service business during the semester, so choose it with care. The following are some general guidelines:

- First, it should be a service business, which fact will be clear after the first few Service Business Principles. (Don't choose the General Motors auto assembly process.)

- Second, it should be of interest to you. Is there a service industry that you would be interested in working in? Is there a service industry that you are fascinated with?

- Third, you should select a service business that you can get information about. Is there an industry you have worked for, and would know a lot about? Some industries, such as health care, have had much information printed about them recently.

- Fourth, don't delay completing assignments while searching for the *perfect* target service business.

- Fifth, you cannot choose the commercial airline business, because I have.

Besides airlines, **other service businesses** that could be particularly interesting are: accounting, advertising agencies, animal care, architecture, appraising, arts, auto repair, banking, broadcasting, catering, cleaning, consulting, contractors, copy centers, cosmetology, counseling, custom home building, delivery, dentistry, distribution, education, employment agencies, engineering, entertainment, financial services, government, health care, health clubs, home inspection, hospitality, installation, instruction, insurance, Internet services, investments, junk yards, karate clinics, landscaping, law enforcement, leasing, legal services, marketing, money management, mortuaries, nursing homes, optometry, photography, printing, private investigation, product support, psychology, quick oil change centers, real estate, repair, research, resorts or other recreation, rest homes, restaurants, retail, sales, security services, service stations, shipping, ski resorts, sports organizations, storage facilities, surveyors, technology services, talent agencies, telecommunications, temp agencies, theaters, title companies, training companies, transportation, trash collection, underwriting, veterinaries, weight-loss clinics, window washing, x-ray labs, youth camps, and zoos. These are just some ideas for your target service business—or you can choose another if you would like.

After you select a service business, it is good if you can identify a particular service provider that you could study. This will help focus your application of Service Business Principles. For example, if you choose consulting as your target service business, you will find that there are a wide variety of consulting firms. You might choose to focus on human resources consulting, with a locally run HR consulting firm as your target company. The instructor will probably allow you, within reason and with approval, to complete application exercises with service companies outside of your target company or even outside of your target service business's industry. However, it is usually best to focus the application exercises on your target service business throughout the semester.

I have chosen airlines as my target service business, and particularly focus on Southwest Airlines as my target service company. I happen to know more about Southwest's operations than I do about other airlines. Also, it appears that more has been written about them in recent years than about other airlines. Nevertheless, in my application of Service Business Principles I will refer to other airlines as appropriate.

Intro

Sections of Each Service Business Principle

The various Service Business Principles follow the same general outline. Each has sections that describe the principle, give examples, etc. Each section of a Service Business Principle is identified by a heading. **The following few pages describe the sections that fall under each heading.** (Note that not all Service Business Principles have all of the same sections.) After covering the sections of Service Business Principles, we will begin the first unit: Unified Services Theory Basics.

Preparation for the next Service Business Principle (*number*)

To consider...   Before proceeding, consider the following and write thoughts and ideas below:

(This section will describe some important management issues for you to consider prior to studying the next Service Business Principle. **You should not read ahead to the Service Business Principle until you have answered the "To consider" question(s), since reading ahead would bias your thoughts about the question.** *This is why "To consider" sections always appear on odd-numbered pages. Sometimes you will be required to consider the questions on your own, sometimes in small groups, and sometimes as a class. In any case, you should write down some of your thoughts on the space provided.)*

_____

_____

_____

_____

_____

_____

_____

Service Business Principle *(number)*:
(NAME OF THE SERVICE BUSINESS PRINCIPLE)

Service Business Principle	*"(The descriptive text of the Service Business Principle shows up in this box. Reading or even memorizing a Service Business Principle will usually leave the student short of understanding it. Resist the urge to learn only the words of Service Business Principles without grasping the meaning.)"*

Why it occurs...   *(NAME OF THE SERVICE BUSINESS PRINCIPLE) occurs (This section describes why the Service Business Principle occurs with service businesses, and ties each Service Business Principle back into the Unified Services Theory. All of these Service Business Principles are founded in the Unified Services Theory.)*

Closely related to...   *(Some Service Business Principles are closely related to other Service Business Principles which have been or will be covered. This section will indicate some of these relationships. If the related Service Business Principle has not been covered already, please do not read ahead unless instructed to do so, since it may disrupt the ordering of the study.)*

Details...   *(More detailed explanations of the Service Business Principle are given in this section.)*

How it impacts decisions...   *(This section describes how the Service Business Principle impacts important decisions that must be made by service managers.)*

What to do about it...   *(This section discusses techniques that can be used to deal effectively with the decision issues and implications resulting from the Service Business Principle.)*

For example...   *(Examples from various service industries are given to aid your understanding of the application of the principle.)*

My airline application...   *(Throughout this workbook, I arbitrarily chose the airline business process as my target industry, and often identify Southwest Airlines as my target service business. I describe an example, or examples, of how the Service Business Principle is applied in the airline industry.)*

Supplemental reading...   *(This section lists readings from various sources which pertain to the Service Business Principle. The instructor will inform you as to which readings you are responsible for studying, and which are optional. If you already read this reading at the start of the Unit, review will be helpful in studying this Service Business Principle.)*

How manufacturing differs from services...

With manufacturing, *(This section describes how manufacturing organizations differ with regard to the particular Service Business Principle. Manufacturing processes can be a baseline for studying service processes, and they are used in this workbook to emphasize the added complexities of services management. Information in this box can lead to the study of manufacturing principles. In some courses, manufacturing principles are discussed, and in others, they are not. The instructor can tell you whether to cover or skip this box.)*

Quantitative analysis... (covered at the discretion of the instructor)

(The ability to manage some Service Business Principles is benefitted greatly by certain quantitative tools and techniques. This section lists those tools and possible reading. The instructor will inform you what, if any, quantitative tools you are responsible to learn, and whether quantitative assignments are required. Some courses do not involve quantitative analysis, so the Quantitative Analysis box can be skipped. **Note that since Analysis Questions always appear on odd-numbered pages, Application Exercises always appear on even-numbered pages.***)*

(Since analysis questions always appear on odd-numbered pages, they will sometimes be preceded by a blank page. You can use those blank pages for jotting down notes and ideas.)

SBP (number): (Name of the Service Business Principle)   Name (if turned in):_____

Analysis questions... To help apply this Service Business Principle, consider and answer the following questions about your specific service business process. (☐Check here if you are going outside of your target service business.)

Service company/business:_____

The service process:_____
(This section will contain questions which will help spur your thoughts about how the Service Business Principle applies in your particular industry. The instructor may or may not require you to complete any or all of these questions. Regardless, the questions are useful for uncovering the issues surrounding the Service Business Principle as it relates to a particular industry. If you are required by the instructor to complete the questions, and you feel the Service Business Principle does not apply to your particular target service business, then you may temporarily select another service business, and check the box above. **Analysis Questions always appear on odd-numbered pages.** *Why? Because, if your instructor asks you to turn the page in you will not have to remove text about the Service Business Principle that would be on the back of the page. The back of Analysis Question pages are Application Exercises, which may also be turned in.* **This means that sometimes there will be a blank page between the discussion of a principle and the analysis questions.** *You can use that blank page to take notes.)*

① _____

_____

_____

_____

_____

_____

_____

_____

_____

_____

_____

_____

_____

_____

_____

SBP (number): (Name of the Service Business Principle)   Name (if turned in):_____

Application exercise...   Also to help you apply this Service Business Principle, complete the following analysis with regard to your specific service business process, or another service process in your business. (❑Check here if you are going outside of your target service business, which was _____.)

Service company/business:_____

The service process:_____

(The workbook material will be much more valuable to you if you are able to apply it to actual business situations. That is why Application Exercises are included. The instructor will let you know which application exercise you are responsible for completing. The application exercises are an opportunity to actually apply the Service Business Principle to your target service business. If your are convinced that the Service Business Principle does not apply to your target service business, you may temporarily choose another and check the box indicating you have done so.)

Part I - Fundamentals
Unit 1:
UNIFIED SERVICES THEORY BASICS

There is no Service Business Principle which is more fundamental than the Unified Services Theory. In this unit we will introduce the Unified Services Theory (UST) and some fundamental definitions that will help us in applying the UST.

Unit reading...   The following reading pertains to Service Business Principles included in this unit. The instructor will let you know which of the readings you are responsible for studying.

Fitzsimmons2 chapter 1 on Services and the Economy

Preparation for the next Service Business Principle (1a)

To consider...   Before proceeding, consider the following and write thoughts and ideas below:

What are some differences between service businesses and manufacturing businesses that make a significant difference in the way each should be appropriately managed? One way to think of this is to answer the question: What are some reasons service businesses are particularly challenging to manage? Would it be possible to select *one* general way service businesses differ from manufacturing businesses that encompasses most or all of the other ways? If so, what might that *one* differentiation be?

_____

_____

_____

_____

_____

_____

_____

_____

Service Business Principle 1a:
THE UNIFIED SERVICES THEORY

Service Business Principle	*"With services, the customer provides significant inputs into the production process. With manufacturing, groups of customers may contribute ideas to the design of the product, however, individual customers' only part in the actual process is to select and consume the output. Nearly all other managerial themes unique to services are founded in this distinction."*

Why it occurs... THE UNIFIED SERVICES THEORY occurs as a fundamental defining principle. It serves to unify, or reveal commonality among all service businesses. In addition, it forms the basis for a myriad of Service Business Principles—principles which define good business practice in service industries. In other words, by understanding what makes a service business a service business, we gain insights into the critical success factors of such businesses. That is the role of the Unified Services Theory.

Details... Traditionally, the fundamental model of business operations is the following (called the I/O or Input/Output model):

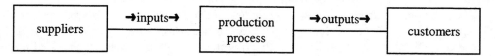

This, of course, is the fundamental model in its simplest form. The model makes perfect sense in non-service operations such as manufacturing. For example, the suppliers to bicycle manufacturing provide components, labor, energy, etc., which is converted into finished bicycle. The production process—also called the "transformation process," "conversion process," and "value adding process"—is to change inputs into outputs. The objective is to produce outputs with which the customer will ascribe value, and thus express "willingness to buy."

With service businesses, the model is somewhat different:

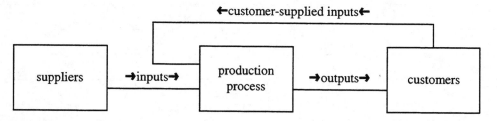

This distinction in fundamental operations models captures the essence of the Unified Services Theory. The distinction is that with services businesses, the *customer* provides significant inputs into the process. Therefore, the customer is more than merely the consumer of outputs.

Herein is the paradigm shift: It is not so much what a company does for the customer that makes it a service, but what the *customer does for the company*. Specifically, the customer provides essential inputs to the production process. (The next SBP, *Defining by Customer Content*, will discuss the types of inputs customers provide to service processes.)

Unit 1

Do customer inputs make a difference in the way a business should be appropriately run? It turns out, the involvement of customer inputs makes all the difference in the world. The purpose of this workbook is to explore the strategic and managerial implications of customer inputs. Each and every Service Business Principle covered in this workbook describes a direct consequence of customer inputs.

Technical note (ignore this paragraph if it is not clear to you): Scientists dealing with mathematical or logical proofs—proving that a relationship or condition exists—talk about "necessary" and "sufficient" conditions for something to be valid. "Necessary" means that the condition *must be met* in order for the proof to be true, but the condition could also be met in some cases where the proof is false. "Sufficient" means that if *the condition is met*, we *know* for certain that the proof is true. However, if the "sufficient" condition is not met, the proof could still be true. If a condition is both "necessary" and "sufficient," then if the condition is met, the proof is true; if the condition is not met the proof is not true. The Unified Services Theory defines customer content as a "necessary" and "sufficient" condition for a business process to be a "service" business process. In other words, if a business process is a "service" process, then it requires customer inputs ("necessary"), and if a business process requires customer inputs, then it is a "service" process ("sufficient").

One other technical note: The Unified Services Theory states that "nearly all" managerial themes unique to services are founded in the customer-input distinction. If the Unified Services Theory were given as a *purely* normative manner, it would include "all" managerial themes. However, for now we assume "nearly all" managerial themes are included.

For example...   The following are some service businesses from the front cover of the workbook, and examples of customer-inputs to that service process.

Service Business	Inputs from Customers
accounting	financial transaction records
airlines	selves and baggage
architecture	design preferences
auto repair	broken car
banking	savings, checks
consulting	business problems
custom home building	lot, colors and styles
delivery	packages
dental	teeth
education	mind
entertainment	attention
government	community issues
legal services	legal problems
medical	sickness or injuries
public services	burning house
real estate	property to sell
restaurant	empty stomach
retail	questions about products

Examples of how to *apply* the Unified Services Theory are listed under each of the subsequent Service Business Principles. When you come to the various Service Business Principles, with examples for each, it will be shown how they tie back into the Unified Services Theory.

It is not expected that you will fully understand the validity and the far-reaching significance of the Unified Services Theory based on the brief explanations given above.

The entire remainder of this workbook is devoted to explaining the implications of the Unified Services Theory. In fact, there is not a single Service Business Principle covered that does not tie back into the Unified Services Theory. As you proceed, you will be shown how the Unified Services Theory provides the foundation which uncovers the keys to successful service business management.

The remainder of this unit describes some fundamental concepts which will be helpful in subsequently applying the Unified Services Theory. Service Business Principles 1b through 1e are called "semantic" since they define basic terminology which will help the discussion and learning of other Service Business Principles.

How manufacturing differs from services...

With manufacturing, suppliers provide inputs and customers consume the production outputs. Individual customers provide no inputs, but simply select and pay for the outputs.

It is important to note in the Unified Services Theory that with manufacturing, "...groups of customers may contribute ideas to the design of the product,..." such as through market research studies. That information from groups of customers is not about a *specific* unit of production, but is about production in general. Therefore, we consider such general information to be an input in the design of the overall service or the overall service process, *not* an input into the process itself. Throughout this entire workbook, when we refer to "customer inputs" we are referring to inputs to be used in the *specific* customer's unit of production, not to general customer sentiment about the overall process or general product.

SBP 1a: The Unified Services Theory   Name (if turned in):_____

Analysis questions... To help apply this Service Business Principle, consider and answer the following questions about your specific service business process. (❑Check here if you are going outside of your target service business.)

Service company/business:_____

The service process:_____
    ① Are there customer-provided inputs in the process? What are they?
    ② Where do they enter the process?
    ③ Where are they kept and for how long?
    ④ How are these inputs transformed by the process?

① _____

_____

_____

_____

_____

_____

_____

_____

_____

_____

_____

_____

_____

_____

_____

_____

_____

_____

SBP 1a: The Unified Services Theory   Name (if turned in):_____

Application exercise... Also to help you apply this Service Business Principle, complete the following analysis with regard to your specific service business process, or another service process in your business. (❑Check here if you are going outside of your target service business, which was _____.)

Service company/business:_____

The service process:_____

To illustrate the significance of customer-provided inputs to service production processes, imagine the condition of your service business if there were no customer inputs whatsoever. First, list what the customer normally provides as inputs to the production process. For each of those inputs, indicate what the service provider does with the input. Finally, with each input also describe what the service provider would do if the customer selected the service but did *not* provide the input. (For example, airline passengers provide themselves as inputs into the air transportation process. Airlines transport passengers to a desired location. If an airline customer purchases a ticket but does not show up for the flight, the plane will fly but the passenger will not be transported. It is impossible to complete the passenger transportation process without a passenger to transport.)

Preparation for the next Service Business Principle (1b (semantic))

To consider...   Before proceeding, consider the following and write thoughts and ideas below:

According to the Unified Services Theory, the fundamental element of all service business processes is that they involve customer inputs. What are some general types of process inputs received from customers? (You might think of some specific customer-input examples, then consider how those examples might be generally categorized.)

_____

_____

_____

_____

_____

_____

_____

_____

_____

Service Business Principle 1b (semantic):
DEFINING BY CUSTOMER CONTENT

Service Business Principle	*"With services, an effective means of understanding, analyzing, and comparing processes is on the basis of customer content. There are three general types of customer inputs into service processes: the customer's self, the customer's belongings, and/or the customer's information."*

Why it occurs... DEFINING BY CUSTOMER CONTENT occurs because customer inputs are present in *all* services, in accordance with the Unified Services Theory.

How it impacts decisions... To effectively understand a service we need to identify customer inputs into production and how those inputs are processed.

For example... Is a hospital a service? What inputs do customers provide to the hospital process? Themselves as an ill, injured, or expecting patient. Their information, as medical history, description of symptoms, and list of allergies and special health conditions.

Is a bank a service? What inputs do customers provide to the banking process? Their belongings in the form of money. Also their check and credit card transactions, which can be considered information about desired payments.

Now for a more difficult example: Is a home builder a service? What customer inputs are involved in the home building process? The answer to that question determines whether a particular builder is a home manufacturer or a building service provider—home manufacturers build homes without the need for customer inputs. Does this designation matter? It certainly does. Custom home builders who ignore customer inputs, acting like home manufacturers, will soon find themselves liberated from their customers.

Another difficult example: Is a fast-food restaurant a service? Does the restaurant require customer inputs to begin the food preparation process? In fact, during busy times of the day the food is likely prepared prior to customer arrival—without any input from the customer. The customer order simply triggers the assembly of the order from items which were previously prepared. Thus we may observe that the cooking sub-process may at times be food manufacturing. Nevertheless, the front counter process—to take the order, answer questions, and accept payment— clearly cannot be accomplished without customer inputs. Thus we see that an overall operating process may have some elements which are service processes, and some elements which are manufacturing processes. (This idea will be discussed in "The Unit of Analysis" Service Business Principle.) These parts thus should be managed differently.

My airline application... The inputs to an airline "production process" are customers' selves, their luggage, and their seat requests. The outputs from that process are customers' selves and their luggage at a preferred location.

Supplemental reading... Fitzsimmons2 chapter 2 pages 25-27 on The Service Package.

How manufacturing differs from services...

With manufacturing, customers do not provide inputs to the main production process—non-customer suppliers provide all of the inputs. However, post-production elements may have customer inputs, making them service elements.

SBP 1b (semantic): Defining by Customer Content   Name (if turned in):_____

Analysis questions...   To help apply this Service Business Principle, consider and answer the following questions about your specific service business process. (☐Check here if you are going outside of your target service business.)

Service company/business:_____

The service process:_____
   ① Do customers provide themselves as an input to the service production process? If so, how does the service process act on each customer?
   ② Do customers provide their belongings as a service process input? How does the service provider manipulate those inputs? Are the customer-belonging inputs subsequently returned to the customer?
   ③ What information do customers provide as input to the service process? How is the information transformed or used by the service provider?

① _____

_____

_____

_____

_____

_____

_____

_____

_____

_____

_____

_____

_____

_____

_____

SBP 1b (semantic): Defining by Customer Content   Name (if turned in):_____

Application exercise...

Also to help you apply this Service Business Principle, complete the following analysis with regard to your specific service business process, or another service process in your business. (❑Check here if you are going outside of your target service business, which was _____.)

Service company/business:_____

The service process:_____

Draw a flowchart that describes the steps of a major processes in your company. Use rectangles for actions and diamonds for decisions, with arrows between to show the order of steps. (You should read Appendix B on Flowcharting Service Processes prior to completing this exercise.) For this exercise, choose a process that can be described in a dozen steps or fewer. Then, draw arrows identifying where customer inputs enter the process and **write what the customer inputs are at specific steps**. Put an "S:" before customer self inputs, a "B:" before customer belonging inputs, and a "I:" before customer information inputs. At the end of the process, identify how each of the inputs is likely to have been changed by the process. Where is most of the value added by the process?

Preparation for the next Service Business Principle (1c (semantic))

To consider... Before proceeding, consider the following and write thoughts and ideas below:

How might we identify a firm's "customers?" (Sometimes this is obvious and sometimes it is not. For example, who are the customers of a university? of the government? of a radio broadcaster?)

_____

_____

_____

_____

_____

_____

_____

_____

_____

Service Business Principle 1c (semantic):

IDENTIFYING THE CUSTOMER

Service Business Principle	*"With services, "the customer" is sometimes not clearly defined. Generally, the customer is the individual or entity who directly or indirectly decides whether or not the firm shall be compensated for production. The actual paying customer may desire a non-paying "critical audience" to be satisfied with production, qualifying the critical audience as an indirect customer."*

Why it occurs... IDENTIFYING THE CUSTOMER occurs because companies can have many stakeholders, some providing inputs and some merely consuming outputs. Since the Unified Services Theory is based on the idea of *customer* inputs, it is necessary to clearly define who the customer is.

Details... Some fields, such as marketing, distinguish between *primary customers* and *secondary customers*, which is similar to the distinction made in this service principle.

The value in defining different categories of customers is recognizing that sometimes the beneficiary of the service process is not the one to provide compensation to the producer. Both groups of customers are important, and either might provide inputs to the service process.

In some instances, different groups may each provide part of the compensation, such as state universities who are funded by the state (legislators or taxpayers), by the students (tuition), and by alumni and other donors. However, students are generally the only one of these groups to provide non-monetary inputs into the production process.

For example... In most cases, identifying the customer is a simple task. The following are less-obvious examples:

Who is the customer of higher education? I have yet to meet a student who was not sure they were the customer. In a sense they are direct customers, given that their tuition pays a portion of university expenses. However, at many universities and colleges most of the university budget comes from other entities such as governments or other sponsoring organizations. No doubt the state legislature (supposedly representing the taxpayers) is a primary customer of state university. Few legislators actually provide inputs to the education production process (thank goodness!), other than allocating taxpayer moneys. The legislators are concerned about the value being added to students, who are inputs to the process.

Are prospective employers and recruiters the customers of higher education? The education process can certainly operate without their inputs, and they do not usually provide compensation directly to the university. Nevertheless, they are a critical audience that is important to students and other university sponsors.

Is broadcast radio a service? Who is the customer of radio-broadcast companies? Listeners are a critical audience, but the actual paying customers are the advertisers. Broadcasters could certainly execute the broadcasting process without listener inputs. However, if their ultimate purpose is to sell and attract viewers of advertisements, it is impossible to accomplish that purpose without information from advertisers (i.e. the advertising material).

Are government agencies services? Who are their customers? Again, the paying entity is the legislature, who legislates the existence of agencies. Most legislators answer to the voters and taxpayers, who are a critical audience whose needs are supposedly served by the agency.

The following are some examples of groups that serve as critical audiences:

- **Regulators**. The County Health Department is a critical audience for restaurants. The State Professional Licensing Board is a critical audience for doctors, engineers, etc.

- **Certifying Organizations**. ASE (Automotive Service Excellence) certifies the skill of auto mechanics. The AACSB (American Association of Collegiate Schools of Business) accredits schools of business. The Bar Association certifies attorneys.

- **Special interest groups**. The American Association of Retired Persons (AARP) is a critical audience for hotels who want to be have AARP promotion. The Automotive Association of America (AAA) has tow-truck service affiliations to direct the business of AAA members.

My airline application...

The most obvious customer of airlines is passengers. However, some airlines are selected by the passengers' employers. For example, when I was teaching at a state university we had a thick contract that identified the carrier we were supposed to fly on for flights to specific destinations, and the contracted price. In that case the customer is whomever made that contract agreement with the airline. (Probably some legislator somewhere.) We the passengers did not pay for the tickets ourselves, but were "critical audience" customers.

The Federal Aviation Administration (FAA) is a critical audience–they do not compensate the airline, but paying customers demand that the FAA is happy with the way the airline does business.

How manufacturing differs from services...

With manufacturing, the customer definition is the same—the individual or entity who directly or indirectly decides whether or not the firm shall be compensated for production. In most cases, the manufacturing customer is the next step or the final stop of the product distribution chain.

SBP 1c (semantic): Identifying the Customer   Name (if turned in):_____

Analysis questions...   To help apply this Service Business Principle, consider and answer the following questions about your specific service business process. (❏Check here if you are going outside of your target service business.)

Service company/business:_____

The service process:_____
    ① Who is the direct customer—the one who actually provides compensation for production? Do they provide direct inputs to the production process?
    ② Are there any indirect customers or "critical audiences"—those whose satisfaction is of interest to the direct customer? Do the indirect customers provide direct inputs to the production process?

①_____

_____

_____

_____

_____

_____

_____

_____

_____

_____

_____

_____

_____

_____

_____

_____

_____

_____

SBP 1c (semantic): Identifying the Customer   Name (if turned in):_____

Application exercise...

Also to help you apply this Service Business Principle, complete the following analysis with regard to your specific service business process, or another service process in your business. (❑Check here if you are going outside of your target service business, which was _____.)

Service company/business:_____

The service process:_____

Diagram the relationship between the various customers of your service business. Start by drawing a circle representing your service business. Draw circles representing those who assure that you are compensated for the service, with arrows pointing to the service business circle. Draw circles representing those whom you serve (typically the ones whose inputs you act upon) with arrows coming from the service business circle. These latter circles might be the same as the compensating circles, or they might not. If they are not, identify which might be called the "critical audience." List other "critical audiences" who must be satisfied, such as regulators, certifying organizations, or special interest groups.

Preparation for the next Service Business Principle (1d (semantic))

To consider... Before proceeding, consider the following and write thoughts and ideas below:

How might we identify a service firm's production process? (Often this is obvious, however sometimes it is not. For example, the production process of medical surgery clearly includes operating on the patient, but does it also include the time the patient recovers at home?)

_____

_____

_____

_____

_____

_____

_____

_____

_____

Service Business Principle 1d (semantic):

IDENTIFYING THE PRODUCTION PROCESS

Service Business Principle	*"With services, the company's **production process** is defined as company effort to add value to customer inputs. Company effort in preparation for production is the **pre-production process**. When the production process concludes, and the customer may use the production outcome to continue to add value. This **post-production process** is primarily based on customer action. Often, well-designed service outcomes will enable the customer to create value in the post-production process."*

Why it occurs... IDENTIFYING THE PRODUCTION PROCESS occurs because the only ways companies can add value is through *efforts* and through *outputs*. Efforts can add value directly to customer inputs (given by the Unified Services Theory). Outputs, or outcomes, can allow customers to add value after the company's production efforts are complete.

For example... The production process of a hospital begins when a patient is admitted into the hospital. Pre-production activities include ordering supplies, cleaning facilities, and training the staff. Production activities include surgery and administering medications, which are intended to add value to a patient by improving the chances of recovery. Post-production processes include the patient taking medication and following other prescribed treatments (such as staying in bed).

The production process of a barber shop begins when the customer enters the facility. The barber adds value to the customer by transforming his or her hair from an undesirable state to a more desirable state. The production process ends when the barber is finished adding value to the customer's hair condition. The customer's post-production process may include washing his or her hair and following styling recommendations. In this haircut example, the barber's pre-production processes include cleaning the facility, ordering supplies, training the barbers, scheduling, etc.

My airline application... With airlines, pre-production efforts include procuring airplanes, maintaining airplanes, training pilots and flight attendants, procuring peanuts. These activities do not add value for customers, but enable the company to add value for customers.

The production process begins when the customer contacts the airline for flight information. Knowledge about flight schedules is valuable to customers, because it helps them with their planning. The production process continues when the customer arrives at the airport to check luggage. Shortly thereafter, the customers check themselves into the airplane. The flight is the major portion of the production process, adding value by transporting the customer to a location of value to the customer.

How manufacturing differs from services...

With manufacturing, the production process is more easily defined as company manipulation of goods from the stage of initial procurement of materials and resources through shipping of the finished goods.

SBP 1d (semantic): Identifying the Production Process   Name (if turned in):_____

Analysis questions...   To help apply this Service Business Principle. consider and answer the following questions about your specific service business process. (❑Check here if you are going outside of your target service business.)

Service company/business:_____

The service process:_____
 ① Where does the production process begin? In other words, what is the initial company effort towards directly adding value for customers?
 ② What is the pre-production process? In other words, what are company efforts which do not directly add value for customers, but prepare the company to add value for customers?
 ③ Where does the production process end? In other words, at what point does the company's efforts to add value for a particular customer cease?
 ④ After the end of this production process, in what ways does the customer use the process output to add value?

① _____

_____

_____

_____

_____

_____

_____

_____

_____

_____

_____

_____

_____

_____

_____

_____

_____

_____

_____

SBP 1d (semantic): Identifying the Production Process   Name (if turned in):_____

Application exercise...   Also to help you apply this Service Business Principle, complete the following analysis with regard to your specific service business process, or another service process in your business. (❏Check here if you are going outside of your target service business, which was _____).

Service company/business:_____

The service process:_____
   Draw (or redraw) a process flowchart.   (see Appendix B for information on flowcharting.) Are there process steps before and after those depicted in your flowchart? Draw dashed lines indicating where the production process begins and ends. Identify essential pre-production activities. What are the customer's post-production requirements? How is the customer prepared to perform post-production activities?

==

Preparation for the next Service Business Principle (1e (semantic))

To consider... Before proceeding, consider the following and write thoughts and ideas below:

Some people argue that the difference between service businesses and non-service businesses is so "gray" that it is difficult to make any meaningful distinction. Perhaps the reason for this confusion is a failure to adequately define the business process being analyzed. How might we look at business processes so that the distinction between services and non-services will be more clear? For example, is a fast food restaurant a service or a manufacturing business? Can there be different perspectives on this? What accounts for the difference? (Here is a useful analogy to help with that question: Find a newspaper showing a non-color photograph. Does the photograph show shades of gray, or is it all black and white? Look at the photograph up close. What do you see now? How might that be an analogy for how we look at service business processes?)

_____

_____

_____

_____

_____

_____

_____

_____

Service Business Principle 1e (semantic):

THE UNIT OF ANALYSIS

Service Business Principle	*"With services, the unit of analysis is a process segment. A **process segment** is a sequence of steps of production. When processes are dissected into smaller segments, the presence or absence of service principles becomes more pronounced."*

Why it occurs...   THE UNIT OF ANALYSIS occurs because customer inputs are present in some parts of a production process, but not present in others. By the Unified Services Theory, the parts that involve customer inputs identifies the process segment as a service process.

How it impacts decisions...   We should manage some parts of an overall production process differently than others depending on the presence or absence of customer inputs in each. It is often helpful to analyze the process at varying levels of detail.

What to do about it...   If a process step seems to be particularly challenging to manage, it is often useful to consider that step in greater detail—as a process segment. Often, the management challenge can be attributed to specific details of that process segment. This helps us isolate the specific sources of the challenge.

For example...   As mentioned previously, the fast food restaurant process includes preparation of food, taking orders, assembling orders, and processing payment. Each of these is a process segment. The process of taking an order can be described at various levels of detail, such as (1) greeting customer and asking for order, (2) answering customer questions, (3) describing current specials, (4) recording order, (5) reviewing order, and (6) indicating price. In the customer order process segment, appropriate customer information inputs are particularly crucial in steps (2) and (4).

My airline application...   There are indeed portions of the airline process—i.e. process segments—that are devoid of customer inputs. The airplane refueling process can be accomplished without any customer inputs. So can the preparation of beverages and so-called "food" for in-flight meals. Other process segments, such as boarding of passengers, cannot be accomplished without customer (self) inputs.

Two other airline process segments are ticketing and flights. Inputs to the ticketing process segment include customer information (day and destination), the flight schedule, seat availability, and ticket agent labor. The output is a reservation. Inputs to the flight process segment are the passengers and luggage, the plane, and the runway. Outputs are a transported passenger and luggage. The ticketing process can be considered part of the production process, or it might be considered a pre-production process relative to the primary process segment of transporting passengers and luggage.

How manufacturing differs from services...

With manufacturing, the major process segments are devoid of customer inputs.

Unit 1

SBP 1e (semantic): The Unit of Analysis   Name (if turned in):_____

Analysis questions...   To help apply this Service Business Principle, consider and answer the following questions about your specific service business process. (❑Check here if you are going outside of your target service business.)

Service company/business:_____

The service process:_____

① What are the major steps of production?

② At what point do customer inputs enter the process?

③ Can the process steps involving customer inputs be described in greater detail? (Think of an example or two.)

④ Can the process steps not involving any customer inputs be described in greater detail? (Think of an example or two.)

What you will usually find is that the process segments involving customer inputs are managed quite differently from the process steps devoid of customer inputs.

① _____

_____

_____

_____

_____

_____

_____

_____

_____

_____

_____

_____

_____

_____

_____

_____

_____

_____

SBP 1e (semantic): The Unit of Analysis   Name (if turned in):_____

Application exercise... Also to help you apply this Service Business Principle, complete the following analysis with regard to your specific service business process, or another service process in your business. (❑Check here if you are going outside of your target service business, which was _____.)

Service company/business:_____

The service process:_____
Redraw the flowchart you created in "Identifying the Customer." Identify one step of the process in which customer inputs are particularly prevalent or crucial. Also, identify a process segment involved in that process which is devoid of customer inputs, if there is one. Describe some of the ways the customer-input laden process segment is more difficult to manage than the customer-input-free process segment.

Preparation for the next Service Business Principle (1f)

To consider...   Before proceeding, consider the following and write thoughts and ideas below:

Given that services are composed of various process segments, it is reasonable to assume that all segments are not of equal importance. How might we differentiate the more important segments from the less important segments? If we needed to streamline a service process by eliminating one or more steps, how might we know which steps to eliminate?

_____

_____

_____

_____

_____

_____

_____

_____

_____

Service Business Principle 1f:
WEIGHTING THE MIXTURE

Service Business Principle	*"With services, different process segments have different degrees of customer input, and some may have none (acting as manufacturing). The weight, or significance, of specific process segments is most often determined by the amount of **value** in the overall service contributed by specific segments. This can be approximated by contribution to "willingness to pay." Some other segments are important for accounting, regulatory, or risk-control reasons."*

Why it occurs... WEIGHTING THE MIXTURE occurs because value of a service process or of individual process segments is judged by how well it adds value to customer inputs. The noted exception is process steps that protect the company's ability to remain in business by meeting regulatory or risk-control requirements, or by keeping an accurate accounting of production, revenues, and costs.

Closely related to... the "Identifying Key Production Elements" Service Business Principle and others which will be covered later under "Defining Service Quality and Value." (Again, since there is an ordering to this workbook, it is best to avoid reading in that unit until you get to it.)

Details... This Service Business Principle captures the idea that some components of a service process are more important than other steps. This knowledge can be helpful in understanding where to focus management attention, and where, perhaps, to simplify the process by eliminating steps.

How do we know how valuable each step of a service process is? One way is to ask about each process step: "How would the customer react if we eliminated this step? How much less would they be willing to pay for the service?"

In some cases, the customers are not willing to pay for the steps, but they are essential for other reasons, such as:
- accounting needs. Companies need to track revenues, costs, and other production-related data to assure they are in adequate control. For example, an essential step in medical offices is to collect and verify patient insurance information, to assure payment will be received. Companies also need to track production itself, which includes the ability to manage and replenish inventories. For example, an auto service process should include a parts ordering step—it would not be cost effective to keep a large supply of every part in stock at all times. Keep in mind that excessive administrative burdens placed on the customer as a result of the company's accounting needs can have an adverse affect.
- risk control. Some process steps may be in place to limit the risks to the company. For example, amusement parks have ways of keeping passengers with health problems off of dangerous rides, such as large signs at ride entrance. The customer step of reading the sign is essential in reducing the company's potential for lawsuits.
- regulatory requirements. Often, government regulation is risk control that some companies would not do otherwise. For example, bus transportation laws require that buses do not proceed until all passengers are a certain distance back in the bus (behind the "white line"). Of course, that makes sense anyway to reduce the likelihood of passengers losing their balance and falling through the front windshield. The regulation requires that all bus companies comply.

Unit 1

If a process step is not required for these types of reasons, and does not add any value in the eyes of the customer, it should perhaps be subjected to further scrutiny.

How it impacts decisions... By deciding where and how value will be added to customer inputs, the company is implicitly deciding the fundamental strategy question: What business are we truly in? The concept of "strategic alignment" means that the ways the service process adds value to customer inputs should be consistent with the business that the company claims to be in.

What to do about it... Assure that the service business is focusing efforts on process steps which are truly adding value, and be careful about allowing non-value-adding steps which are done simply because "that is the way we have always done it here."

For each process step or process segment, it is useful to ask the question "Why is this necessary?" Usually it will be obvious, but in some instances the answer will be very revealing about the unimportance of a particular step.

For example... Consider the process of movie theater service. From the customer perspective, the process is roughly as follows: Find a parking spot, walk to line, wait in line, purchase tickets, hand tickets to employee at door, wait in refreshments line, purchase refreshments, wait in line to enter theater (if prior showing is not out yet), enter theater, wait for movie to start, eat refreshments and watch movie, wait for crowd to clear enough to depart, walk to car. Where is value added in this process? Nearly all of the value is added in the process segment "eat refreshments and watch movie." Many of the other steps add little value. For example, why do we purchase a ticket and then immediately give it to the person at the door? Why can't they just put a cash register at the door? (for those who do not want to purchase tickets in advance) Why do we have to wait repeatedly? Why can't we buy refreshments from a cart positioned next to the line outdoors or next to the line to enter the theater or from an employee walking around the theater while customers are waiting for the movie to start? Even though such questions may represent an oversimplification of complex concerns, they do illustrate that some process segments are clearly more important and essential than others.

My airline application... What business are airlines in? An obvious answer is air transportation. However, many airlines spend a lot of effort on process steps not pertaining to air transportation. For example, many airlines offer full in-flight meals on relatively short (2-3 hour) flights. Granted, the cost of materials for airline food certainly could not be too great. The greatest cost is in additional airline process complexity. There is the process of forecasting meal requirements, the process of procuring and storing the meals in inventory, the process of "quality" control, the process of tracking customers with special dietary needs, the process of loading the meals onto the airplane, the process of heating and serving meals, the process of collecting trash and sorting out the utensils, the process of unloading the trash from the plane, the process of washing utensils and replacing those that accidentally wound up in the trash, the process of extra seat cleaning due to messy passengers, and so forth. From a procedural perspective it is *very costly* to offer in-flight meals. So why do some airlines do it when it is not absolutely necessary (such as on overseas flights)? The answer that airlines would probably give is: "because we have done it for years, and customers have come to expect it." Well, why don't you just cut the meals and pass the process savings on to us?! We will get a *real* meal before we get on the plane!

Some airlines have recognized that the in-flight meal process adds little value. As a result, some airlines have gone to offering a "snack" (a pre-packaged sandwich that is not heated) instead of a heated "meal." Southwest Airlines offers no meals, but only peanuts and a drink. (The length of their flights lends itself to that.) If airlines were concerned about starving customers, a more cost-effective approach would be to let passengers pick out a sandwich from a vendor's cart at the gate before boarding! Many passengers would eat their sandwich *before* boarding, which would turn the meal clean-up process over to the people who vacuum the terminal!

Supplemental reading...   case: USAA Business Process Review (HBS)

How manufacturing differs from services...

With manufacturing, the value of a product is found in the product features, which features are established at various manufacturing process segments. If features are eliminated, then the production steps to create those features can be eliminated.

Quantitative analysis... (covered at the discretion of the instructor)

One way to estimate customers' "willingness to pay" for various service features is to conduct *conjoint analysis*. With conjoint analysis, customers are presented with various service packages, and asked about how much they would be willing to pay for each package. Mathematical techniques are used to determine how much value might be ascribed to various service features. You can read about conjoint analysis in many marketing research texts.

SBP 1f: Weighting the Mixture   Name (if turned in):_____

Analysis questions...   To help apply this Service Business Principle, consider and answer the following questions about your specific service business process. (❑Check here if you are going outside of your target service business.)

Service company/business:_____

The service process:_____
   ① How is value added in the production process? In other words, how are the outputs from the production process more valuable to customers than the inputs? (If they are not, plan on going out of business.)
   ② How much more are customers willing to pay for outputs than they would be willing to pay for the inputs? (This gives an indication of the value added by the process.)
   ③ In the production process, *where* does this value creation occur? (This should indicate the weight of various elements.)
   ④ Are some process steps important because of regulatory or liability-control reasons, even though they are not valued by the customer?
   ⑤ How much of the value is added by changing customer inputs, and how much is added by manipulating non-customer inputs?

   ①_____

_____

_____

_____

_____

_____

_____

_____

_____

_____

_____

_____

_____

_____

_____

_____

_____

SBP 1f: Weighting the Mixture   Name (if turned in):_____

Application exercise...
Also to help you apply this Service Business Principle, complete the following analysis with regard to your specific service business process, or another service process in your business. (❑Check here if you are going outside of your target service business, which was _____.)

Service company/business:_____

The service process:_____
Redraw your service process flowchart. Identify the top three steps where value is added by writing ① ② ③. Identify steps that are necessary for tracking production (or customers) or for accounting with a circled "A." Identify any steps that are performed for regulatory reasons with a circled "R." Identified steps that occur to limit the company's liability or risk with a circled "L." If you had to eliminate one of the steps, which one would you eliminate first? Why?

Part I - Fundamentals
Unit 2:
SERVICES FUNDAMENTALS: PLANNING

Unit 2

Many authors have discussed characteristics of service businesses other than customer inputs. Ask yourself this question: Are there other relevant characteristics of service businesses that exist independently of the customer inputs which are specified in the Unified Services Theory? You will find that what many people consider the "characteristics of services" are in fact merely *symptoms* coming out of the Unified Services Theory. This is because the Unified Services Theory exists at a more basic level than other characteristics of services. We will see that if we ask why other characteristics of services exist the answer is generally "because of customer inputs." If we ask why customer inputs exist in a particular process, the answer is "because it is a service." Therefore, the Unified Services Theory is fundamental, and defines services.

The various characteristics of services are not generally present in manufacturing because of the lack of customer inputs. Nevertheless, in some manufacturing cases the characteristics (or symptoms) of services occur for reasons *besides* customer inputs. (This will be discussed later in the "Manufacturing in Sheep's Clothing" Service Business Principle.)

In this unit we will discuss various symptoms or characteristics of services which result from the Unified Services Theory. In particular, we will focus on those pertaining to planning.

Unit reading... The following reading pertains to Service Business Principles included in this unit. The instructor will let you know which of the readings you are responsible for studying.

Fitzsimmons2 chapter 2 on The Nature of Services.
Fitzsimmons2 chapter 13 on Capacity and Scheduling.

Quantitative analysis reading (covered at the discretion of the instructor)

Fitzsimmons2 chapter 16 on Forecasting
Fitzsimmons2 chapter 7 on Service Facility Location
Fitzsimmons2 chapter 18 on Linear Programming Models in Services
Fitzsimmons2 chapter 12 on Managing Facilitating Goods

Preparation for the next Service Business Principle (2a)

To consider...   Before proceeding, consider the following and write thoughts and ideas below:

With manufacturing processes, the company generally produces the product at a particular time, and the customer consumes (demands or takes delivery of) the product at some later time. With some manufacturing processes the time gap between production and consumption can be many months. For example, we often buy *new* books that were actually manufactured (printed) months or years ago. Let us now consider services businesses... What do you suppose is the nature of the time gap between service production and consumption (demand for the service or taking delivery of the service)? Why? Try to think of some specific examples of a service being delivered to the customer—when is that service produced?

_____

_____

_____

_____

_____

_____

_____

_____

Service Business Principle 2a:

SIMULTANEOUS PRODUCTION AND CONSUMPTION

Service Business Principle	*"With services, production (making the service "product") and consumption (customer demand or delivery) often occurs simultaneously, making the exact timing of production a critical issue."*

Why it occurs... SIMULTANEOUS PRODUCTION AND CONSUMPTION occurs because major portions of the service production process cannot begin until essential customer inputs are received. And, all services involve customer inputs, as per the Unified Services Theory.

Details... Note that this SBP has tied "consumption" to "demand" and "delivery," although those words can be used independently in other contexts. For example, imagine ordering a manufactured food item, such as an exotic cheese, from a mail order company. You may call up the company and place your order, which is "demand." The company retrieves the item you ordered from their inventory stock and ships it to you, which is "delivery." You receive the cheese and consume it—realizing the value or benefit of the cheese—which is "consumption." In this case you do not "consume" the cheese until after it has been "delivered," which does not occur until after you have "demanded" it. And in fact, the cheese was likely "produced" some unknown time prior to demand, delivery, and consumption. That time gap is generally unknown to the customer—Customers generally do not know, nor often care, when the manufactured product was produced (as long as it is in good shape when it is delivered and consumed). In summary, with manufactured products the following typically occurs:

1. Item is manufactured. (produced)
2. Item is stored until time of customer demand.
3. Customer places order. (demand)
4. Company fulfills order and gets item to customer. (delivery)
5. Customer receives value from item. (consumption) This value may continue to be realized for an extended period of time, until the product is completely "consumed." (An item which wears out and no longer provides value is "completely consumed.")

With service businesses, major portions of "production" *cannot* begin until after demand has been presented. Again, this is because the service cannot be produced until we have key production inputs that come from the customer. A doctor cannot produce a diagnosis or a treatment until *after* he or she has the customer's symptom and self inputs. An attorney cannot prepare a case until he or she has the client's legal issues and client information. Other examples will be listed below. The general situation with services is the following:

1. Perhaps part of the service-product is prepared. The rest cannot be produced until the company has customer inputs.
2. Customer places order (demand) and provides necessary inputs.
3. Right away, the company produces the service, often giving it to the customer (delivery) as it is being produced, with the customer immediately receiving value from the service (consumption).
4. Nevertheless, as with goods products, the customer is likely to *continue to receive value* from the service produced well after the time it is produced and delivered.

On this last point, services vary as to how long the value is realized after the service is delivered. Some services continue to provide value for a great deal of time, such as education, which provides value long after the student is out of school. Other services only provide value for a short time, such as restaurant food, which generally only provides value up through the time of the next meal. This important issue of the life of value will be revisited in the SBP: *Perishable Output Illusion*.

How it impacts decisions... We must carefully consider the exact timing of production. This implies that we need to carefully plan our production capacity, since capacity utilization will be determined by demand. Demand is uncertain to one degree or another, meaning that good forecasting is essential. In some situations, the uncertainty in demand can be mitigated to some degree by scheduling customers, such as through appointments.

What to do about it... Analysis and planning techniques can be employed to increase our ability to manage the need for simultaneous production and consumption. Fundamental techniques include forecasting, capacity planning, scheduling, and yield management. These will be discussed in the next Service Business Principle.

For example... "Production" for an architectural service firm is turning building ideas into blueprints and other information that can be used to actually construct a building. Ultimately, the architect cannot design a building for a specific customer without inputs from that customer, such as tastes, spacial requirements, budget limits, etc. Those essential inputs are provided as the architectural services are demanded. As the architect produces the building design, the customer is often given suggestions and ideas which are expected to be of value in making further design decisions. The further design decisions are additional inputs into the architectural design process. Thus, the customer often begins "consuming" the architect's service even before the final drawings are complete, and "demanding" additional service based on design decisions. Therefore, we have demand, production, and consumption occurring relatively simultaneously.

My airline application... The primary "production" process for an airline is transporting passengers and luggage from one location to another. Pre-production processes (see SBP: *Identifying the Production Process*) include preparing planes for travel. When does a customer "demand," or require, air transportation? In fact, customers indicate their demand *prior* to the time of production—by making flight reservations—with the actual demand taking place on the day of the requested flight. Likewise, *delivery* of the transportation service does not take place until it is actually produced—the day of the specific flight. The customer *consumes* the transportation while being transported, as well as after they arrive at the destination.

This is why scheduling is so important with airlines, since the airline can only produce when the customer is presenting demand. (Flying an empty plane is not producing—but is like running a drill machine when there is no item to be drilled.)

Supplemental reading... Fitzsimmons2 chapter 13 on Capacity and Scheduling.

How manufacturing differs from services...

With manufacturing, production and consumption are usually separated by time. Therefore, the exact timing of production is less of a critical issue.

Quantitative analysis... (covered at the discretion of the instructor)

Forecasting

One of the most fundamental and important elements of planning for service or manufacturing firms is *forecasting*. In manufacturing firms, product demand is forecast over a period of time, and production is planned to approximate the forecast. If demand is greater than the planned production, then backorders can occur and extra product needs to be produced. If demand is less than the forecast, then the company may be stuck with excess inventory. The company may likely reduce future production and may have to reduce the sales price to clear inventories.

Simultaneous production and consumption implies that good forecasting is even more essential for service firms. Service companies do not have the luxury of holding inventories if they over forecast–they are instead stuck with idle capacity. For example, a restaurant that over-forecasts demand for a particular evening may find itself with employees standing around, or being sent home.

Under-forecasting service demand can be extremely detrimental since the result is usually deterioration of service quality. When customers arrive wanting to be served, and normal capacity has been exceeded, waits for service can be intolerable and the attention of the server can be deplorable.

Forecasting demand for services is further confounded by the need to forecast not only *how many* customers to expect, but also the *complexity* of each customer's requirements. For example, a doctor's office may be able to accurately forecast how many patients will arrive on a given day, and in fact control the number of patients to some extent through appointment scheduling. However, it is much more difficult to forecast or control for the amount of time that will be needed for each patient. It is this difficulty that explains why doctor's offices tend to be behind schedule most of the time. If each patient took the exact time allotted in the appointment schedule it would be easier to stay on schedule.

(With manufacturing, it is usually not necessary to forecast the complexity of each unit of production, since production is more homogeneous and controlled.)

Forecasting Simulation Exercise

If this is your first simulation exercise, then read the "Running Simulation Exercises" section (and subsequent subsections) in Appendix A.

You will start by running the service simulation file *autoshop.mod*. This model will allow you to practice forecasting. Your objective will be to forecast the number of customers to arrive each day. That forecast will be helpful in labor planning and in ordering needed materials. Although each customer might come in for a different service, for simplicity we will only forecast customers in aggregate (i.e. in total).

After each day of the simulation, the computer will report to you your results thus far. This report will show you what your forecast was, what the actual number of customers was, and the error which is the actual minus the forecast. The formula for forecast error is $error_t = A_t - F_t$. (The mathematical notation F_t means the forecast for period t, where t is the number of a given period. A_t is the actual value for period t.)

At the bottom of the error column is the average error, or AE. AE tells us the direction of *bias*, of the forecast. A *biased* forecast is one that tends to either over-forecast (when AE is negative) or under-forecast (when AE is positive).

Next to the error column is an *absolute error* column, which simply contains the absolute value of the errors. The absolute error tells the *magnitude* of the errors, without regard for the sign (or direction) of the errors. At the bottom of the absolute error column is calculated the *Mean Absolute Deviation*, or MAD, which is the average of the absolute errors. The MAD value is a measure of forecast *precision*, or how precise the forecast is. The most precise forecasts will have small MAD values, and a perfect forecast will have a MAD value of zero. (When the forecast errors are normally distributed, which they usually are, then the standard deviation of the errors is approximately $1.25 \times$ MAD.)

It is bad for a forecast to have bias, since it tends to mis-forecast in a *given* direction. Nevertheless, if we know that a forecasting technique is biased we can *compensate* for the bias, such as by adding the AE value back in. It is *much worse* for a forecasting technique to be imprecise, as would be seen in a large MAD value. We cannot compensate for imprecision. If a forecasting technique is imprecise, we should probably look for a better forecasting technique.

Your objective in running the *autoshop.mod* simulation will be to come up with a low MAD value.

How to Proceed

Run the simulation *autoshop.mod*. (Instructions about running a simulation are found in Appendix A.) For your first tries you should run the simulation at the lowest "level" (easiest to solve).

Print your final results and submit them as directed by your instructor (either on paper, or electronically if your course is registered on the workbook website).

After you have run the simulation, read the section titled "Forecasting: Basic Time-Series Methods" in Appendix C. Do not read that appendix section until *after* you have tried the *autoshop.mod* at least once. If your results are not very good you should submit them anyway (if the instructor has asked you to), since you will have a chance to run the simulation again later and submit improved results.

SBP 2a: Simultaneous Production and Consumption   Name (if turned in):_____

Analysis questions...   To help apply this Service Business Principle, consider and answer the following questions about your specific service business process. (❑Check here if you are going outside of your target service business.)

Service company/business:_____

The service process:_____
   ① When does production occur?
   ② When do customers indicate their demand for the product?
   ③ When do customers take delivery of the product?
   ④ What is the temporal (or time) relationship between these three?
   ④ What are the factors that limit the temporal gap between these three?

① _____

_____

_____

_____

_____

_____

_____

_____

_____

_____

_____

_____

_____

_____

_____

_____

_____

SBP 2a: Simultaneous Production and Consumption   Name (if turned in):_____

Application exercise...   Also to help you apply this Service Business Principle, complete the following analysis with regard to your specific service business process, or another service process in your business. (❑Check here if you are going outside of your target service business, which was _____.)

Service company/business:_____

The service process:_____

Characterize the nature of demand. In what ways is it seasonal? In what ways is it cyclical? In what ways is it predictable? In what ways can demand be controlled? In what ways is it unpredictable and uncontrollable? Given these ideas, develop a method of forecasting demand by identifying factors and data on which the forecast would be based and the general method for coming up with forecasted values. Give some justification for the use of that forecasting method. Indicate limitations of that forecasting approach. Assuming that your forecasting approach is adequate, how would the resulting forecasts be used to plan production?

Preparation for the next Service Business Principle (2b)

To consider...   Before proceeding, consider the following and write thoughts and ideas below:

A common way to think of production capacity is in terms of number of units of production per time period. In manufacturing situations, we attempt to plan production capacity so that we will be able to produce enough items for upcoming demand. For example, companies that manufacture snow blowers might make as many in July as in December, with the objective of making enough throughout the year to meet the winter demand. The fixed capacity of snow-blower production facilities is not wasted in July nor in December. Would this be true for snow-blower repair services with a fixed capacity? Would capacity be "wasted" in July? What about some of the time in December? Why or why not?

_____

_____

_____

_____

_____

_____

_____

_____

Service Business Principle 2b:

TIME-PERISHABLE CAPACITY

Service Business Principle	*"With services, capacity is usually time-perishable, meaning that capacity without corresponding demand is lost forever. This is true even though the service product is often not perishable."*

Why it occurs...   TIME-PERISHABLE CAPACITY occurs because much or all of the service production cannot occur until after customer inputs are provided. The Unified Services Theory describes the essential nature of customer inputs in service processes.

Closely related to...   SBP: *Simultaneous Production and Consumption*

Details...   The perishability of services is often misunderstood. It is not the service product itself that is perishable, but rather the capacity to produce the service. What is capacity? In the production sense, it is the ability to meet a certain amount and type of demand.

Generally, service capacity can only be utilized to meet demand at the given time. This means that today's capacity cannot be used to meet tomorrow's demand. This is unfortunate, since today's demand may be low but tomorrow's demand may be high. Things would be a lot easier if we could meet some of tomorrow's high demand with today's extra capacity. That is what manufacturers do–it is called production smoothing. They simply produce more product today with the extra capacity and store it in inventory for sale tomorrow.

Service companies cannot generally produce with the extra capacity today since major portions of production require first getting inputs from customers. If a service provider wants to use extra capacity on a given day the either have to (a) pursue production activities that do not require additional customer inputs, or (b) convince customers to provide their inputs on the day of extra capacity. This latter option is actually to shift demand to more closely match capacity. For example, a movie theater may offer discounts for non-weekend movies to shift demand to times of lower capacity utilization.

As a result of time-perishable capacity, the capacity utilization of service firms can be relatively low, even under good conditions. For example, at the start of 1998, the average airline "passenger load factor" (the seat utilization rate) was 71 percent, up from about 60 percent at the start of the decade.[2] Even though 71 percent utilization is outstanding for service companies, it would be considered quite low for most manufacturing plants. Other services will have even lower utilization. An example is restaurants, where capacity utilization is high during mealtimes but mostly idle during interim times.

If a hypothetical restaurant which is open from 11:00 a.m. until 9:00 p.m. has 100 seats and each customer takes one hour to eat, then the daily capacity is 100 customer x 10 hours / 1hour per customer = 1000 customers per day. The restaurant might be full from noon to 2:00 and from 6:00 to 9:00, but have only a few customers between that time. The result is a capacity utilization of perhaps 50 percent. To make matters worse, the restaurant may actually turn customers away for dinner, or lose customers due to long wait times. If the restaurant could just serve dinner customers from 2:00 to 6:00, when there is a lot of extra capacity, the overall utilization would be much better. However, it would be a difficult task to convince many people to have dinner between 2:00 and 6:00.

---

[2] Meyer, M. (April 27, 1998). "Tales From the Sardine Run." *Newsweek*, pp. 58-60.

When there is uncertain demand, service companies need to "inventory" capacity for potential demand. This inventory of capacity represents relatively idle resources waiting for customers to present their inputs. For example, most emergency rooms have much more capacity than is typically needed–they keep the extra capacity just in case.

Who pays for the idle capacity? Ultimately the customers! Idle capacity is a form of overhead that needs to be paid for by revenue-generating production.

Unit 2

How it impacts decisions...   Capacity scheduling is difficult but essential. This scheduling requires forecasts of demand, not only in aggregate but period by period. Given a forecast, the service provider must still decide on the appropriate capacity to plan for at each time period. Even if the capacity is set exactly at the forecast level, uncertain forecasts can still result in unmet demand or idle capacity. The service provider must decide on the relative importance of avoiding insufficient capacity vs. avoiding idle capacity.

Other decisions include strategies for shifting demand to times of extra capacity.

What to do about it...   There are a number of ways to adjust capacity to more closely match demand. For example, companies can employ part-time workers or cross-train employees to help out where demand is higher than expected. Such strategies can make capacity more flexible and thus more able to match uncertain demand.

Various strategies also exist for influencing demand to more closely match capacity. Movie theaters might offer discounts for matinee or non-weekend movies. In some services it is appropriate to have reservation systems to assure that customers will arrive when there is available capacity.

A more complex system known as Yield Management dynamically adjusts capacity and influences demand to maximize revenues. Yield Management is used in situations where customers make reservations for future service where there is relatively fixed capacity (such as hotels or airlines).

Demand is influenced by adjusting price–if demand seems higher than usual then the price can be raised, but if it appears that demand will be below capacity then the price can be lowered. Capacity is adjusted by allocating capacity between service-price categories. For example, a given airplane may have a certain number of seats reserved for business-fare passengers (who typically pay more) and other seats available for coach-fare passengers who are more price conscious. If an extra number of business passengers make reservations, the airline might switch some of the coach-fare seats to be held for other business passengers, thus reducing the number of coach-fare seats. (Yield Management will be revisited in the *Price Guessing* Service Business Principle.)

(Fitzsimmons2 chapter 13 discusses a number of strategies for managing capacity and demand.)

For example...   At a hair salon, capacity is defined by the number of seats and the number of hairstylists. When a customer is not present in a hairstylist's chair, that capacity is lost forever. The hairstylist cannot (or at least should not) cut someone's hair that has not "demanded" to have it done. There are various ways a hair salon might bring capacity and demand more in line.

They might have more employees come in during busy times, might offer a price discount during consistently slow days, or have reservation systems.

My airline application... With an airline, capacity in a given flight is primarily defined by airplane seats. If no one is sitting in a particular seat during a flight, the capacity on that flight cannot be held until later demand. If there are 50 vacant seats on a morning flight to Dallas, but the evening flight were oversubscribed by 50 people, it is impossible to inventory the 50 vacant morning seats for use on the evening flight. Perhaps demand may be moved back from the evening flight to the morning flight, but it is impossible to recover the unused morning capacity to meet strictly evening-flight demand.

Supplemental reading... Fitzsimmons2 chapter 13 on Capacity and Demand Management.

How manufacturing differs from services...

With manufacturing, capacity is not time-perishable, for if no demand is present we can still produce and then store the product in inventory for future demand.

Quantitative analysis... (covered at the discretion of the instructor)

Capacity Scheduling

Capacity planning is extremely important in service businesses because of the high costs of poor planning. The costs of planning insufficient capacity include costs to the customer, such as slow service and poor quality, and costs to the service provider, including service employee burn-out. The costs of planning excessive capacity include employee idleness and boredom. (Believe it or not, most service employees prefer to have something to do than to be idle waiting for customers.)

Simulation Exercise

The simulation exercise called *bakery.mod* will allow you to practice the sale of cakes. Each day you will forecast the number of cakes you will need for the next day. The cakes are made early in the morning, before the bakery opens for business. Once the bakery opens no more cakes are made that day (the bakery is open for 8 hours). Therefore, the number of cakes made defines the capacity to sell cakes for a given day.

Your objective will be to sell cakes and maximize profit. The simulation will begin by telling you the forecast for the first period, and the standard deviation of demand. Demand for day 1 is random from a normal distribution, with a mean of the given forecast and a standard deviation of the given standard deviation. The simulation will ask how many cakes should be made for the first day.

Your objective will be to maximize profit. The amount it costs to make each cake and the amount you charge customers will be given at the start of the simulation.

How to Proceed

Run the simulation *bakery.mod*. (Instructions about running a simulation are found in Appendix A.) For your first tries you should run the simulation at the lowest "level" (easiest to solve).

Print your final results and submit them as directed by your instructor (either on paper, or electronically if your course is registered on the workbook website).

After you have run the simulation, read the section titled "Capacity Scheduling: The Critical Fractile Rule" in Appendix C. Do not read that appendix section until *after* you have tried the *bakery.mod* at least once. If your results are not very good you should submit them anyway (if the instructor has asked you to), since you will have a chance to run the simulation again later and submit improved results.

SBP 2b: Time-Perishable Capacity   Name (if turned in):_____

Analysis questions... To help apply this Service Business Principle, consider and answer the following questions about your specific service business process. (❑Check here if you are going outside of your target service business.)

Service company/business:_____

The service process:_____
   ① What happens at our production facility when customers are not present?
   ② How does this affect our utilization of capacity? What percent of our capacity do we reasonably expect to be used at different times? (i.e. busy times, slow times, etc.)
   ③ How does that utilization affect our cost structure? In other words, are customers who utilize capacity subsidizing, or paying for, the times that capacity is not utilized?

①_____

_____

_____

_____

_____

_____

_____

_____

_____

_____

_____

_____

_____

_____

_____

_____

_____

SBP 2b: Time-Perishable Capacity   Name (if turned in):_____

Application exercise...   Also to help you apply this Service Business Principle, complete the following analysis with regard to your specific service business process, or another service process in your business. (☐Check here if you are going outside of your target service business, which was _____.)

Service company/business:_____

The service process:_____

Estimate the percent of time service-production resources are idle waiting for customer inputs. List two major resources, such as a particular type of labor, customer seating, a production machine, etc. For each, estimate what percent of the time that resource is producing, and what percent of the time the resource is idle. Comment on why the idleness occurs and what the cost of that idleness might be to the company and to the customers. Also for *each* of the resources, describe an appropriate strategy for more closely matching capacity and demand, such as by adjusting capacity to meet demand or by influencing demand to meet capacity.

(One example of a airline resource is ticket counter agents. At a typical airport, ticket counter agents probably serve customers 70 percent of the time, implying that they are idle perhaps 30 percent of the time. This idleness occurs because fewer agents would mean longer lines during the busy times, which would upset customers and might make them miss flights. Ticket agent labor costs would be 30 percent higher than if capacity exactly equaled demand and no idleness occurred, but that probably has a relatively small impact on the overall cost of an airline ticket. Airlines could help make capacity more in line with demand by partitioning demand into passengers who simply want to check baggage and those who have other transactions, such as purchasing or changing tickets. The former is likely more cyclical during the day. When numerous flights are nearing departure, and ticket counters may be backed up with customers wanting to check in, employees could be brought in to help with "check baggage only" stations.)

Preparation for the next Service Business Principle (2c)

To consider...   Before proceeding, consider the following and write thoughts and ideas below:

If you were going to locate a factory that manufactures a clothing item anywhere in the world, where would you locate it? (Where do such factories tend to be located?) Why? What if you were going to locate a service facility that cleans clothing items—where would you locate it? How is your criteria for location decisions different between manufacturing and service facilities?

Service Business Principle 2c:
CUSTOMER PROXIMITY

Service Business Principle	*"With services, the production location is often dictated by the location of the customers who supply their inputs. To keep inconvenience costs down, the location where customer inputs enter the production process needs to be near the customer."*

Why it occurs... CUSTOMER PROXIMITY occurs because customers need to get their inputs to the location in order for production to begin (by the Unified Services Theory). Customer-suppliers cannot usually bulk-ship their individual inputs to the service production location.

Details... If information is the only input needed from customers, then much of the production process can be performed far from the customer, and telecommunications or mail can be used to bring the customer information to the production process. An example is the phone company, which processes telephone calls at centralized switching locations, but the "information portal" gathers customer inputs (i.e. voice signals) at locations very near the customers (i.e. telephones).

Some customer belongings can be shipped, implying that we could centralize production. It might be possible to centralize a shoe repair service—have customers send their shoes to a location that services a huge geographical area. However, having the customers ship their inputs to the production location can be very expensive since they are unlikely to take advantage of bulk rates or other economies of scale.

An example of a service that has successfully centralized is film processing. Customers mail their rolls of film to centralized processing facilities, and the developed prints are mailed back. The result is dramatic cost savings to the customer when compared with less-centralized film processing. Some cost savings come through economies of scale in film processing. Other cost savings come through low inconvenience to the customer: The "portal" (i.e. location) where the customer inputs (i.e. rolls of film) are provided to the service process is as near as the closest mail box.

How it impacts decisions... Service providers must pay close attention to location factors, particularly considering costs of location decisions to the customer. (As a hotel executive supposedly once said, the three most important success factors in his business were location, location, and location.)

Realize that there are many challenges in decentralized production such as limited scale of economies (a cost factor) and maintaining process control (a quality and productivity factor).

What to do about it... Conduct location analysis. This often means estimating where customers are located and the costs of getting customer inputs to the service production facility.

For example... Electronics manufacturing can be very labor-intensive, causing many companies to locate their production facilities in regions of the world with low labor costs—even though most of the present customers are in other regions of the world. Restaurant services are also quite labor-intensive. However, we would consider it absurd to locate a restaurant in an area of low labor costs when most of the potential customers are very far from there. In fact, many restaurants are located in high rent districts with expensive labor markets because those locations are very convenient to customers.

McKesson is a large drug distributor, with a number of centralized warehouses. Customers of McKesson are hospitals and pharmacies, which are dispersed around the world. Rather than locate a distribution facility near every customer, the company places computer terminals at many customers' locations. That way the customer inputs—order specifications—can be quickly sent to a centralized distribution location.

My airline application... A major decision for any airline is where to locate the facilities—which is where to locate a station with incoming and outgoing flights. The primary factor in deciding where to locate a new station is where the customers are coming from or want to go to. It is pointless to locate a station at a particular location for any other reason, if customers do not desire to fly from or to that location.

Supplemental reading... Fitzsimmons2 chapter 7 on Service Facility Location.
case: Southwest Airlines 1993 (A), which involves a location selection decision. (HBS)

How manufacturing differs from services...

With manufacturing, the production location is generally dictated by other factors. Non-customer suppliers can often bulk-ship their inputs. Customers generally do not need to even know where the production location is, or where inputs enter the process.

Quantitative analysis... (covered at the discretion of the instructor)

Location Planning

When customers need to travel to get their inputs to the service provider that represents a cost of the service. That is why a $12 pizza that is delivered is less expensive than the exact same pizza for $9 when it has to be picked up–when the convenience cost of driving to the restaurant is considered at least $3 greater than walking to the front door. It is not practical for many service providers to provide the service at the customers' location. Therefore, service providers need to consider the customers' costs of transportation to and from the service location.

The actual location planning decision can be influenced by many factors, such as the following:
- traffic levels along various roads,
- location of competitors,
- location of complementary services,
- accessability,
- and others.

Such factors may involve some objective analysis, but often are subjectively analyzed. One other factor that must be considered is the proximity to customers. When service providers are limited to a finite number of locations, they should select locations that are centrally located to the target market.

For example, consider the case of locating a new fitness center. Customers prefer to join a fitness center that is convenient to wherever they are coming from–home, the office, etc. The company may have survey or census data that reveals where fitness center customers are likely to come from throughout the area. Locating the fitness center in a heavily populated neighborhood may be good for that neighborhood, but may reduce the number of customers coming from adjoining neighborhoods.

Simulation Exercise

The simulation model *fitness.mod* will allow you to experiment with the location planning decision. When you run the model, the computer will show you the neighborhoods that might be served by the fitness club, with a forecast of how many fitness club customers would come from each neighborhood. You will be asked to decide where to locate your fitness center on the community grid. You will want to locate the fitness center where it will be convenient to many customers. One reason that you need to choose a good location is because your competitor will attempt to select a more convenient location, which will draw customers away from your facility. (In fact, the model is set up such that the probability of a customer joining a particular fitness club is an inverse function of the distance to that club.)

How to Proceed

Run the simulation *fitness.mod*. (Instructions about running a simulation are found in Appendix A.) For your first tries you should run the simulation at the lowest "level" (easiest to solve).

Print your final results and submit them as directed by your instructor (either on paper, or electronically if your course is registered on the workbook website).

After you have run the simulation, read the section titled "Location Planning: The Center of Gravity Method" in Appendix C. Do not read that appendix section until *after* you have tried the *fitness.mod* at least once. If your results are not very good you should submit them anyway (if the instructor has asked you to), since you will have a chance to run the simulation again later and submit improved results.

SBP 2c: Customer Proximity   Name (if turned in):_____

Analysis questions...   To help apply this Service Business Principle, consider and answer the following questions about your specific service business process. (☐Check here if you are going outside of your target service business.)

Service company/business:_____

The service process:_____
   ① Where do service (production) facilities tend to be located?
   ② How much of the production process must be near the customer?
   ③ How much of the production is centralized?
   ④ If production can be centralized, how do customers get their inputs to the central location?
   ⑤ What advantages would be gained by improving the proximity of the service location to the customer? What would the fixed and variable costs be?

① _____

_____

_____

_____

_____

_____

_____

_____

_____

_____

_____

_____

_____

_____

_____

_____

_____

_____

SBP 2c: Customer Proximity   Name (if turned in):_____

Application exercise...   Also to help you apply this Service Business Principle, complete the following analysis with regard to your specific service business process, or another service process in your business. (❑Check here if you are going outside of your target service business, which was _____.)

Service company/business:_____

The service process:_____
  If you were going to locate another entire production facility, where would you locate it? Why? What data would you need to make such a decision? What are the cost factors involved?

Preparation for the next Service Business Principle (2d)

To consider... Before proceeding, consider the following and write thoughts and ideas below:

Some production processes are very labor-intensive, implying that a large portion of the direct cost of production is attributed to labor. In many manufacturing industries, labor intensity tends to be decreasing over time. The manufacturing industries that continue to be labor-intensive often move production facilities to locations with cheap labor. What do you suppose is the trend in labor intensity of many services—does it also seem to be decreasing over time? Why or why not?

_____

_____

_____

_____

_____

_____

_____

_____

Service Business Principle 2d:
LABOR INTENSITY

Service Business Principle	*"With services, there are often forces that restrict automation. Therefore, the service production process tends to be more labor-intensive than manufacturing processes."*

Why it occurs... LABOR INTENSITY occurs because customer inputs can very widely, making it difficult for automation to adapt to the input variation. Also, customer-self inputs are resistant to automation and often prefer a personal touch. (This will be discussed later in SBPs: *Technological Depersonalization* and *Capricious Labor*)

Details... This Service Business Principle simply observes that service businesses tend to be labor-intensive. In other Service Business Principles, namely *Technological Depersonalization* and *Capricious Labor*, the causes and implications of labor intensity will be discussed in more detail.

One way to consider labor intensity is to use Schmenner's "Service Process Matrix" (which is described in the supporting reading). Schmenner graphs service businesses along two dimensions: labor intensity and degree of interaction and customization. A two-by-two graph might be depicted as follows:

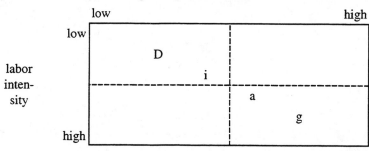

The line marked "Diag" represents the diagonal. There is a propensity for service businesses to move to the diagonal or up the diagonal. This implies that there is a relationship between interaction and customization, and labor intensity. This relationship is alluded to in this Service Business Principle: customer inputs (particularly those involving interaction and customization) limit the potential for automation, which therefore increases the labor intensity of the process.

In the Service Process Matrix, labor intensity is defined as the ratio between labor costs and capital costs, which is a cost-based view. That definition of labor intensity skews labor intensity measures based on capital intensity. An alternate way to view labor intensity is from a production process intensity perspective—defining "labor intensity" as percent of process effort which is accomplished by labor (as apposed to machine effort). I consider this latter definition of labor intensity more appropriate, but not as easy to estimate.

How it impacts decisions... We must not neglect labor development, since labor may ultimately be the limiting factor for our production capabilities.

● **What to do about it...**   The "move up the diagonal" idea of the Service Process Matrix implies that labor intensity can be reduced when interaction and customization are reduced.

In some cases it is possible to control the customer interaction, such as by standard procedures and customer involvement in the process. For example, when a new patient visits a doctor's office for the first time, they are given a myriad of forms for medical history and insurance information. Having those standardized forms is less labor-intensive than interviewing each patient personally.

Customization can be reduced by providing a standard "menu" of service options. Automatic teller machines only allow a fixed set of bank transactions, but those that are most commonly needed. More customized transactions, such as mortgage planning, are less automated and thus more labor-intensive.

With most services there are clear limits to the ability to reduce labor intensity. Much of the value of many services is in the interaction and customization. Rather than attempting to reduce labor intensity, such service providers must consider effective ways of developing labor into a serviceable and productive resource. Effective ways to manage labor include training and job design, which will be discussed in Unit 8: Human Resource Management.

For example...   Many companies, such as Marriott Hotels and Resorts, esteem labor as *the key* to providing excellent customer service. Despite the introduction of technologies (such as in-room check-out), the overall process continues to be very labor-intensive. Therefore, the company expends great effort in employee selection and training.

●   A company that has a well-thought-out system for labor management is Disney World. Their operations are extremely labor-intensive, and much of the Disney experience is defined by the quality of labor. Disney has a system for hiring college students on "internships" that involve a semester or two at a Disney park operation—doing anything from operating an attraction to sweeping the streets. In addition to their work responsibilities, the interns are required to attend extensive training courses about the company's culture and operations. (Including their legendary "traditions" course where the students learn, among other things, the names of the Seven Dwarfs.) Students who do well during that internship can apply for an "advanced internship" in more meaningful functional areas. Thus, through these programs Disney maintains high-quality, low-cost labor, and accomplishes much in the way of career employee selection.

My airline application...   Despite the large investment in capital equipment and technology, much of the airline production process still tends to be labor-intensive. The fortunes of airlines tend to be highly correlated with the relationships between labor and management. Airlines that have had labor problems, such as USAir, have also had profitability problems. Airlines known for good labor practices, such as Southwest Airlines, tend to be quite profitable.

Supplemental reading...   Fitzsimmons2 chapter 2 pages 32-33 on Labor-Intensiveness.
Fitzsimmons2 chapter 2 pages 24-26 on Service Classification (the Service Process Matrix).
Sloan Management Review article "How Can Service Businesses Survive and Prosper?" by Roger W Schmenner, Vol. 27, No. 3, Spring 1986, p. 25 (this article is the source for the material in the Fitzsimmons2 section on the Service Process Matrix).

●

How manufacturing differs from services...

With manufacturing, production is often standardized, and inputs do not care who or what is working on them, therefore technology can often easily replace labor.

Quantitative analysis... (covered at the discretion of the instructor)

Labor Planning

One challenge presented by labor intensity is planning labor requirements that continually shift over time. One advantage of the labor resource is that it is quite flexible. Other resources are not as flexible. When a service provider needs a facility, they typically need to acquire it for 100 percent of the time, not just when they need it. This is also true of equipment. For example, a restaurant must purchase ovens and tables for both busy and slow times. If demand is expected to be slow for a particular period of time, it is difficult to get out of the equipment and facilities expenses during that time.

With labor, if future demand is expected to be slow for a period of time in the future, then labor resources can be temporarily reduced to avoid unnecessary expense. In some cases, fewer of the hourly wage employees can be called in or full-time employees can be temporarily assigned to other work.

Another advantage of labor flexibility is being able to fairly quickly adjust to increases in demand. Employees can be "on call" for helping handle extra demand. There are also numerous temporary employment agency (temp agencies) that can provide short-term labor on little notice.

The first step in labor planning and scheduling is coming up with an estimate of labor requirements, which are a function of the demand forecast. Previously we looked at forecasting. Of particular concern in labor planning is the repeating patterns of demand, called seasonality. *Seasonality* is a pattern of demand movement that repeats at a particular interval. Seasonality can be yearly, such as the demand at a ski resort. Seasonality can be monthly, such as the demand for check deposits at a bank. Seasonality can be weekly, such as the demand at a movie theater. Seasonality can be daily, such as the demand at a restaurant throughout the day. In this last example, we see that demand would be typically be high during meal times and lower in between meal times.

For each of these seasonality examples it is advantageous to plan the labor schedule according to the expected demand. Ski resorts would want to bring on more employees during the ski season than during the off season. Banks might want have the most tellers on staff the last day of the month, or whenever customers tend to deposit their pay checks. Movie theaters want to have more concession counter staff available on weekends when many customers are likely to come. And restaurants might want to have extra part-time employees available during the lunch and dinner rush.

Simulation Exercise

In this exercise, you will forecast seasonal demand so that restaurant labor requirements can be planned.

The model to explore forecasting with seasonality involves a pizzeria. The manager of the pizzeria needs to plan the number of employees to schedule for each 2 hour shift. Most employees work part-time, and can be scheduled for one or more shifts in a day. By providing the manager with a shift-by-shift demand forecast, he can then determine how many employees to schedule for each shift.

The simulation will begin by telling you the demand for the previous few days. Then, you will be asked for demand forecasts for each of the shifts of subsequent days, which can be used to plan labor requirements.

There will probably be some seasonality throughout the day. In addition, external factors may make demand move up or down from day to day and throughout the day.

How to Proceed

Run the simulation *pizza.mod*. (Instructions about running a simulation are found in Appendix A.) For your first tries you should run the simulation at the lowest "level" (easiest to solve).

Print your final results and submit them as directed by your instructor (either on paper, or electronically if your course is registered on the workbook website).

After you have run the simulation, read the section titled "Labor Planning: Forecasting with Seasonality" in Appendix C. Do not read that appendix section until *after* you have tried the *pizza.mod* at least once. If your results are not very good you should submit them anyway (if the instructor has asked you to), since you will have a chance to run the simulation again later and submit improved results.

SBP 2d: Labor Intensity   Name (if turned in):_____

Analysis questions...   To help apply this Service Business Principle, consider and answer the following questions about your specific service business process. (❑Check here if you are going outside of your target service business.)

Service company/business:_____

The service process:_____
　　① What percent of operating costs is labor?
　　② Has labor content changed over time?
　　③ How might customers respond if production labor was replaces with automation?

① _____

_____

_____

_____

_____

_____

_____

_____

_____

_____

_____

_____

_____

_____

_____

_____

SBP 2d: Labor Intensity   Name (if turned in):_____

Application exercise...
Also to help you apply this Service Business Principle, complete the following analysis with regard to your specific service business process, or another service process in your business. (❑Check here if you are going outside of your target service business, which was _____).

Service company/business:_____

The service process:_____

For a Service Process Matrix, estimate the degree labor intensity of your business process. Does the process tend to be a labor-intensive? Identify the location of your business on the Service Process Matrix below. (Students submitting over the Internet should see instructions at the bottom of the Application Exercise Submission form.) Mark the area where other companies in that industry tend to be on the matrix. Identify a few companies in the industry that are positioned elsewhere. (Put letters on the matrix and tell what company each letter represents.) How do these other companies differ in terms of labor intensity? Why do they differ? What advantages or disadvantages are there to the alternate positioning?

(For this exercise, you might estimate "labor intensity" as the portion of production costs attributed to labor, and "degree of interaction and customization" as the extent employees interact with individual customers so that the service can be customized.)

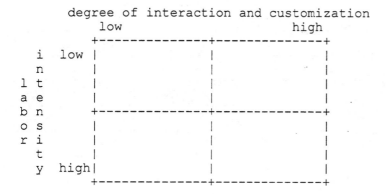

===

Preparation for the next Service Business Principle (2e)

To consider...   Before proceeding, consider the following and write thoughts and ideas below:

The "output" of a production process is what results when the process is complete. Some manufacturing outputs are durable, implying that they continue to be of value to the customer for a long time. Examples are washing machines and cars. Others are more perishable, meaning they lose their value quite soon. Examples are baked goods and computers. Now think about the output of various service processes. Some have proposed that the output of service processes tend to be perishable, implying that the value to the customer is fleeting. Do you agree? Why or why not?

_____

_____

_____

_____

_____

_____

_____

_____

_____

Service Business Principle 2e:

PERISHABLE OUTPUT ILLUSION

Service Business Principle	*"With services, "perishable output" is often an illusion not because the output perishes, but because the customer need is changing over time. Some needs increase over time and others become obsolete."*

Why it occurs... PERISHABLE OUTPUT ILLUSION occurs with some services because customers regularly return for service—the illusion is that this is because the previous output perished when often the return for service is actually because the customer needs have advanced.

Details... On occasion, people are confused about the perishable nature of services. In a sense, perishability is something that fundamentally differs between services and manufacturing. This was described in the *Time Perishable Capacity* Service Business Principle: production capacity without present demand is lost forever. It is the *capacity* of the service that perishes. However, sometimes *capacity* is confused with *output*. Capacity is a potential for production. Output is the end result of a process–what is ultimately delivered to the customer.

It is not a general truism that service *output* perishes. Further, it is not generally correct to differentiate manufacturing processes from service processes by claiming that the service output perishes. The fact is, as with manufacturing output, some service output is perishable and some is quite durable. Dr. Dorthy Riddle reminds us that "...differing degrees of [output] perishability exist in all three economic sectors."[3] (i.e. services, manufacturing, and agriculture/extractive) Manufactured goods can be perishable (e.g. bread), semi-durable (e.g. high-tech equipment), and durable (e.g. low-tech equipment). So also, service output can be perishable (e.g. cleaning, transportation, or communications), semi-durable (e.g. maintenance), or durable (e.g. research or education).[4]

Nevertheless, there is a key element of perishability that does differ between services and manufactured goods: The primary *cause* of the apparent perishability. The most common cause of manufactured goods perishing is when they deteriorate and thus fail to meet their original design. On the other hand, the primary cause of perishability in services is the changing customer requirements.

Think of it this way: What perishability complaint might you have about a manufactured television set you purchased? If the television set worked fine when you purchased it, but only lasted one year before it completely broke down, you would blame the manufacturer, would you not? So also for a car that only lasts two days after the warrantee period expires, for a clothing item in which the buttons fall off after two washes in the washing machine, or the book whose pages fall out on the first reading. When manufactured items perish prematurely, we blame the manufacturer.

What about with services? What perishability complaint might we have about a service we receive? If you eat a meal at a restaurant and you are full, then you are hungry again in two hours, do you blame the restaurant? If you attend a comedy play and leave amused, but are sad again in a few hours, do you blame the actors or the theater? If your dentist fills your cavity, then you get another cavity in a different tooth, do you blame the dentist? In all of these cases, the appearance of perishability was not the fault of the service provider as much as it was caused by the changing and advancing needs of the customer.

---

[3] Riddle, D. (1985). *Service-Lead Growth*, Praeger Publishing, New York, p. 9.

[4] Adapted from Kuznets, S., *Commodity Flows and Capital Formation*, Vol. 1, (New York: National Bureau of Economic Research, 1938). Cited in Riddle, D. (1985). *Service-Lead Growth*, Praeger Publishing, New York, p. 10.

Therefore, as with manufacturing output, some service output is perishable and some is quite durable. In either case, it is important to understand the advancing and changing needs of customers and to pay careful attention to customer retention.

How it impacts decisions... We must carefully consider how the needs of customers change over time. Service companies often underestimate the value of customer retention and loyalty. In fact, one loyal customer can be more profitable than multiple one-time customers. After evaluating the value of customer loyalty, companies must decide on effective approaches to customer retention.

Unit 2

For example... A service in which the output does in fact perish is a restaurant. However, over time people tend to get hungrier and hungrier, implying that the need for food is continually increasing.

There are a number of services which restore things to a previous state of better functionality. Dental services restore teeth to better condition. Auto repair restores vehicles to prior level. Dry cleaners restore clothing to a cleaner state. Even after a problem is solved by these restoration services, we are still likely to return since our needs for such services increases over time. (I.e. cars tend to deteriorate in the course of normal use, even if the previously repaired parts maintain their integrity.)

An example of a service that is extremely durable (even more than a washing machine) is education. Once a person has education, they can receive value from it for a great deal of time. If the output from education is so durable, then why do people go back for more education? It is because their needs are continually increasing over time. They may need more education to take advantage of more opportunities. In some instances, their prior education may become obsolete, meaning that in fact it is perishable.

Tax accounting is also very durable. Once the tax documents for a given year are complete, they function forever. However, each new year presents an entirely new need for tax accounting, which keeps tax accountants employed in perpetuity.

If photographs are printed on the correct type of paper they are extremely durable and will last a lifetime or more. But, of course, families continually return to photographers for family portraits. It is not because the "output" from the prior visits perished, but because of the changing "look" of the family, especially when new children arrive. (Example given by BYU student Jeff Watts.)

My airline application... When a person flies to Seattle, the output (or result) of the transportation service is being in Seattle. People fly to Seattle because there is some value in being in Seattle at that time. Will they ever fly again? Certainly. It is not because the result of the flight perishes—for the passenger would *still* be in Seattle for a long time unless they go somewhere else. The reason people who fly to Seattle fly somewhere else is because they see that there is greater value in being somewhere else at a later time.

How manufacturing differs from services...

With manufacturing, outputs can be perishable (e.g. foodstuffs) or durable (e.g. large appliances). Nonperishable manufactured goods can serve changing needs (which will be addressed later under SBP: *The Server-Ownership Perspective*)

Quantitative analysis... (covered at the discretion of the instructor)

Optimization

The fact that customers tend to return to service businesses means that decisions need to be made about the level of service to be given to all customers. Naive managers and educators say that the service provider should do "whatever it takes" to keep the customers coming back. "Whatever it takes" can be cost prohibitive, and the customers will greatly regret when the benevolent service provider goes out of business.

In most cases, service providers need to strike an appropriate balance between the costs of providing service and the benefits of the service to the customer. Too much focus on costs is likely to make the customer upset, preventing them from ever returning. Too little consideration of costs can make the service so expensive that it is priced out of the market, causing customers to go to less expensive competitors.

The idea of striking a balance implies that a "best" level or levels of service exits. Finding a "best" level for specific parts of a service is the objective of *optimization*. With *optimization*, we seek to determine the optimal value for various service system parameters.

Simulation Exercise

Snow skiing is a popular sport in some regions of the world. We will simulate a ski resort with one ski lift—the automated chairs that lift skiers from the bottom to the top of the hill. The company needs to decide how fast to run the ski lift so as to maximize profits. That speed of the lift will be called **LiftSpeed**, and it will be measured in *feet per minute*. (Apologies to international students for using feet instead of meters. The U.S. is still behind the times in measurement systems.)

The following is a list of parameters that will be used to solve this problem: (A *parameter* is a value which helps define a problem.)

- **RunFee**: The amount of revenue generated per ski run (measured in *dollars per run*).
- **LiftDistance**: The distance a lift chair travels from the bottom to the top of the lift (measured in *feet*).
- **MinLiftSpeed**: The minimum speed a lift chair can travel (measured in *feet per minute*).
- **MaxLiftSpeed**: The maximum speed a lift chair can travel (measured in *feet per minute*).
- **LiftSpeedCost**: The cost to run the lift at a given LiftSpeed for one hour (measured in *dollars per feet per minute per hour*). For example, if LiftSpeedCost was $10 and the LiftSpeed was 100 feet per minute, then it would cost $1000 to run the lift at that speed for one hour.
- **Skiers**: The number of skiers on the hill or waiting to ski.
- **ChairSpacing**: The distance between each chair on the lift (measured in *feet*).
- **ChairSeats**: The number of seats on each chair.
- **MaxRunsPerHour**: The maximum number of runs *an individual skier* will ski in an hour, given fatigue.

Following are more detailed descriptions of the parameters and how they impact the decision.

- Each time a skier begins a run they have their ticket punched. (A "run" means a ride up the lift and a ski down the hill.) The cost of a 10-run ticket is **10 x RunFee**, meaning that the ski resort makes **RunFee** for each ski run. Assume that if a skiers ticket runs out, they will simply purchase another.
- **Runs** is the number of runs skied by all skiers per hour. Therefore, the revenues per hour is **Runs x RunFee**.
- **LiftDistance** is the distance a lift chair travels from the bottom of the lift to the top of the lift.
- **LiftSpeed** is the speed at which the lift chairs travel up the hill, in feet per minute. **LiftSpeed** must be between **MinLiftSpeed** and **MaxLiftSpeed**.

- The lift is run by a diesel engine with a gear box to determine the **LiftSpeed**. The **LiftSpeed** takes two hours to adjust, so it is not adjusted very often.
- The faster the **LiftSpeed**, the more it costs for diesel fuel to run the lift. The incremental cost of a higher **LiftSpeed** is **LiftSpeedCost** which is an hourly cost. Therefore, the cost to run the lift for one hour is **LiftSpeed × LiftSpeedCost**.

- **LiftTime** is the number of minutes it takes for a chair to go from the bottom of the lift to the top of the lift. **LiftTime = LiftDistance / LiftSpeed**.
- When a skier sits down on a lift chair, the time it will take to complete the run will include the **LiftTime** and the **SkiTime**. The **SkiTime** is the number of minutes it will take the skier to ski from the top of the hill to the bottom of the hill. For simplicity, assume that **SkiTime** is exactly the same as **LiftTime**. (This implies that if you get them to the top faster they will come down faster–a dubious assumption, but one which simplifies the problem dramatically.)
- If a skier never waits in line to get on a lift chair, she can ski **60 / (LiftTime + SkiTime)** runs per hour.
- **Skiers** is the number of skiers on the hill at a given time (skiing or waiting to ski). If no skiers ever wait in line to get on a lift chair, the total number of runs they can all ski in an hour is **Skiers × 60 / (LiftTime + SkiTime)**,which equals **Skiers × 60 / (2 × LiftDistance / LiftSpeed)**, since we are assuming **SkiTime = LiftTime**. This total number of ski runs per hour can be algebraically simplified as:

$$\text{LiftSpeed} \times \text{Skiers} \times 30 / \text{LiftDistance}$$

- If skiers are waiting to ski, then the number of runs skied per hour will be limited by the rate of the lift.
- **ChairSpacing** is the number of feet between each lift chair. Chairs move at **LiftSpeed**. Therefore, a chair departs the bottom of the lift every **(ChairSpacing / LiftSpeed)** minutes. This means that **60 / (ChairSpacing / LiftSpeed)** chairs depart the bottom of the ski lift every hour (since there are 60 minutes in an hour).
- **ChairSeats** is the number of skiers that can sit on a single lift chair at the same time. Therefore, if skiers are waiting to ski, then the number of runs skied per hour will be limited by **ChairSeats × 60 / (ChairSpacing / LiftSpeed)**, which can be algebraically simplified as:

$$\text{LiftSpeed} \times \text{ChairSeats} \times 60 / \text{ChairSpacing}$$

- Each skier will ski a maximum of **MaxRunsPerHour** runs in an hour. Therefore, the most skiers that will ski in a given hour will be **MaxRunsPerHour × Skiers**.

Your objective will be to maximize your contribution to profits defined as the lift ticket revenues minus the fuel expense to run the lift. Remember that if you run the lift too slowly, you will limit the number of Runs and thus limit the revenues. However, if you run the lift too rapidly, you may waste fuel and incur unnecessary fuel expense.

How to Proceed

Run the simulation *ski.mod*. (Instructions about running a simulation are found in Appendix A.) For your first tries you should run the simulation at the lowest "level" (easiest to solve).

Print your final results and submit them as directed by your instructor (either on paper, or electronically if your course is registered on the workbook website).

After you have run the simulation, read the section titled "Optimization: Linear Programming" in Appendix C. Do not read that appendix section until *after* you have tried the *ski.mod* at least once. If your results are not very good you should submit them anyway (if the instructor has asked you to), since you will have a chance to run the simulation again later and submit improved results.

SBP 2e: Perishable Output Illusion   Name (if turned in):_____

Analysis questions...   To help apply this Service Business Principle, consider and answer the following questions about your specific service business process. (❑Check here if you are going outside of your target service business.)

Service company/business:_____

The service process:_____
    ① Do customers repeatedly return for the same service? If so, what is happening to the purchase-motivating need over time?
    ② Do customers repeatedly return for a different service? If so, how is their need changing over time?

① _____

_____

_____

_____

_____

_____

_____

_____

_____

_____

_____

_____

_____

_____

_____

_____

SBP 2e: Perishable Output Illusion   Name (if turned in):_____

Application exercise...   Also to help you apply this Service Business Principle, complete the following analysis with regard to your specific service business process, or another service process in your business. (❑Check here if you are going outside of your target service business, which was _____.)

Service company/business:_____

The service process:_____

Do analysis of repeat business. List what is involved in gaining new customers. What are the customer *recruitment* activities (such as advertising, promotions, etc.) and what might they typically cost? What would it cost to increase *retention* of current customers? How frequently would a loyal customer typically come back? Why would they come back (i.e. how do their needs advance over time)? Estimate how many one-time customers would equal the revenues or profits of one loyal customer? Currently, what percentage of customers would you estimate are repeat customers? Comment on that percentage–is it high or low, avoidable or unavoidable, etc..

Part I - Fundamentals
Unit 3:
SERVICES FUNDAMENTALS: EXECUTION

This unit continues the discussion of various symptoms of service businesses which result from the Unified Services Theory. In particular, we will look at some symptoms that pertain to the day-to-day production of services.

Unit reading... The following reading pertains to Service Business Principles included in this unit. The instructor will let you know which of the readings you are responsible for studying.

Fitzsimmons2 chapter 2 on The Nature of Services.
Fitzsimmons2 chapter 11 on Managing Queues

Quantitative analysis reading (covered at the discretion of the instructor)

Fitzsimmons2 chapter 17 on Queuing Models and Capacity Planning
Fitzsimmons2 chapter 8 on Managing Service Projects
Fitzsimmons2 chapter 6 on The Supporting Facility
Fitzsimmons2 chapter 10 on Service Quality

Preparation for the next Service Business Principle (3a)

To consider... Before proceeding, consider the following and write thoughts and ideas below:

Manufacturers typically produce goods then keep them in inventory until they are demanded by the customers. That is called "finished goods" inventory. Also, manufacturers often keep inventories of work-in-progress for various reasons. It is obvious that service businesses can keep inventories of supplies, such as paper, bandages, cleaning chemicals, etc. But, can service companies typically keep inventories of *finished production* or of *work-in-progress*? What would an inventory of finished services look like? Are they common? Why or why not?

_____

_____

_____

_____

_____

_____

_____

_____

_____

Service Business Principle 3a:

CUSTOMERS IN INVENTORY

Service Business Principle	*"The idea of being unable to inventory services is a common misconception. The correct concept is that it is impractical to inventory service production. With services, keeping work-in-progress inventory for extended periods of time will enrage the customer, and we rarely need to keep finished good inventory. Therefore, with services, managers do not generally assume the luxury of hiding poor management practice under inventory, as manufacturing managers do."*

Why it occurs...   CUSTOMERS IN INVENTORY occurs because of simultaneous production and consumption—production occurs after customer has indicated demand and presented inputs. The customer may be impatient if work-in-progress inventory is kept for a period of time. Also, there is usually no practical need to keep finished goods inventory, since the customer has already expressed willingness to take delivery *prior* to the time production is complete.

Closely related to...   The *Inadvertent JIT* Service Business Principle.

Details... Inventory is stored items. Why do inventories occur? There are a number of reasons. However, the most fundamental reason inventories occur is because there is an intentional or unintentional mismatch between production timing and demand timing.

Manufacturers intentionally keep inventories for various reasons, some of which are listed below. However, most of these reasons are not directly applicable to services:

(1) Production Smoothing.

Product demand rates are rarely level and stable–customers purchase whenever they want to. Manufacturers, however, desire to produce at stable rates. Demand for lawn mowers may go up and down with the seasons, but the factory may want to produce the same number each month, putting them in inventory in the winter for sale in the summer.

Service business generally cannot implement production smoothing through inventories. It is not practical for lawn mowing services to "inventory" mowed lawns in the winter so that they will have fewer to mow in the summer.

(2) Buffer Stock

Sometimes the big concern about forecasted demand is not *foreseeable* swings in demand, but *unforeseeable* demand. Manufacturers may inventory some extra product just in case demand is greater than expected. They may scale back future production to use up excess buffer stock, or produce extra when the buffer stock is running low.

Due to customer inputs, services typically have a one-to-one correspondence between demand and production. This means that the service only produces for demand, not extra just-in-case. The service may have buffer *capacity*, but cannot generally complete the service in anticipation of unforseen future demand.

(3) Material Handling

It can be impractical to handle or move one item of manufactured production. Imagine the shipping cost if a paper manufacturer shipped one roll of toilet tissue at a time. Instead, paper manufacturers produce a large inventory of toilet tissue, put it in huge creates, and ship it is bulk to the customers (i.e. distributors and retailers).

Every service customer represents a unique unit of production. Most of the time it is not possible to inventory large numbers of customer inputs to simplify "material" handling.

(4) Economies of Scale

Manufacturers often find it is less expensive to produce large production runs of an item than to produce individual items. For example, microchip fabricators will produce tens or hundreds of microchips on a single silicon wafer–it would be very expensive to etch each tiny microchip on its own wafer. The manufacturer will sell what has been ordered, and inventory the unsold portion of a batch for future sale.

Since service customers are individual and provide unique inputs, economies of scale are extremely difficult to realize. (This issue will be discussed further in the *Lowered Entry Barriers* Service Business Principle.)

We see that the reasons manufacturing companies keep inventories are not too relevant for service businesses. One might assume that service companies would thus not keep inventories. The reason service companies keep inventories is also a reason manufacturers often have excess inventories:

(5) Imprecise Planning

Manufacturers may just have poor planning which results in a excess inventories. The poor planning may be avoidable, such as planning production without seriously considering the implications of forecasted demand. (As ludicrous as that sounds, it is quite common.) Manufacturers can and often do use inventory to hide the effects of poor management practice. When production managers do not have a clue what they are doing, the just produce so much excess inventory that the customers are not aware of the problem. The company is aware, though, because of the high costs of unnecessary inventories.

With services companies, poor management practice is not so easily hidden. (This Service Business Principle states: "Therefore, with services, managers do not have the luxury of hiding poor management practice under inventory, as manufacturing managers do.") If the service providers do not have a clue what they are doing, the customer generally suffers. For example, have you ever had an experience trying to check in at an airport when they are clearly understaffed? The result is angry customers who have to wait an unacceptable amount of time!

This is the key to understanding the most significant inventories in services: the inventories of *customer inputs*. (Inventories of non-customer inputs will be discussed in the next Service Business Principle.) Post office customers are inventoried behind the ropes waiting for the next available service employee. Patients are inventoried in waiting rooms waiting for the production process of the doctor or dentist to catch up. Shoes are inventoried at the shoe repair shop waiting for the repair person to get to them. Loan applications are inventoried on the loan officer's desk waiting for the approval process to catch up to it. And, we even inventory our garbage in trash cans until the garbage collection process makes the weekly visit.

Such customer inventories are generally called a **queue**, which is a waiting line. Queues exist in many forms. The postal customers form a single-file, first-in-first-out queue called a "snake" (it often forms a path back and forth like a snake). The patients in the waiting room form a queue, even though they are not sitting in a straight line and are not always served by the first-in-first-out rule. People calling in to a busy doctor's office may be placed on hold, which is also a queue. People can be placed in a queue, as can their belongings or their information.

Customers do not like to be inventoried, or left in a queue, due to poor planning, and they do not like their belongings or information to be inventoried for more than a brief time. Think of how you react when you call the shop who is fixing your car and they say, "Sorry, we have not gotten to your car yet but should by the end of the week." That is to say, "our demand for auto repair has exceeded our production rate; therefore we are keeping your car in inventory until production can catch up with it." (Or, think how upset you are when the garbage collection people get behind and force you to inventory two weeks worth of garbage in a bin only big enough for one week.)

In fact, imprecise planning of service production is usually unavoidable, since production is so directly tied to actual demand. (recall the *Simultaneous Production and Consumption* Service Business Principle) The results is that some amount of production inventory is generally *inevitable*. Since it is *impractical* to keep service production inventories for an extended period of time, it is essential to carefully plan and manage the service production process

How it impacts decisions... Service providers must carefully consider the costs of customer provided inventories and plan service production capacity to control those costs. When inventories are inevitable, the service provider may implement strategies for reducing the cost of inventories to the customer.

What to do about it... Information about how to manage customer-inventory costs will be discussed later in the *Inadvertent JIT* and *Customer Inventory Costs* Service Business Principles.

For example... With dental care, many goods such as cleaners and x-ray film are kept in inventory. However, once the production process starts, meaning that a patient has provided his teeth to the dentist for care, it is impractical to keep that production (the patient's teeth) in inventory for any extended period of time. It would be absurd for a dentist to inventory a work-in-progress patient in a dental chair for a few hours while the dentist catches a game of golf. It would be even more absurd for patients to be inventoried in the dental office for an extended period of time after their dental care is finished. (Which is why the patient inventory in the dentist's waiting room tends to be incoming, not outgoing, patients.)

My airline application... Airlines do in fact keep a form of in-progress inventory in the form of layovers, or stops at a different airport on the way to the final destination. Layovers exist because part of the production process, the flight into the layover city, is not in perfect sync with the production process out of that city (the outbound flight). It is certainly possible for airlines to deal with poor flight scheduling by keeping huge inventories of passengers at layover cities. However, it is not practical to do so, since many customers would be angered by such inconvenience.

Another situation involving work-in-progress inventories in airlines is what occurs at the time a supporting facility (airplane) breaks down. If a factory breaks down for a couple of hours, we use inventories to buffer the production needs of dependent processes. However, if an airplane brakes down for a couple of hours, the impact on the customer can be quite dramatic. The typical response is to inventory passengers in the airport terminal for a period of time and often attempt to clear that inventory by channeling people on other flights. Even though an airline may attempt to inventory passengers in the airport for extended periods of time, it is not practical to do so.

The finished product of airline production is passengers and their baggage at the destination airport. Airlines have no desire to keep passenger and baggage inventories in planes that have landed at their destination. Usually, passengers are even more eager to be out of the airline supporting facility.

How manufacturing differs from services...

With manufacturing, since production usually occurs well before consumption, the product can easily be kept in inventory.

Quantitative analysis... (covered at the discretion of the instructor)

Queuing

How long will a customer or their inputs remain in inventory? In other words, how long will a customer or their inputs have to wait in a queue to receive service? The amount of waiting required of customers will be a function of various factors, including:

- the rate at which customers arrive,
- how fast the servers serve, and,
- the way the service system is configured.

If we have an idea of the customer arrival rate, that information might be used to determine service system configuration. This may involve some degree of optimization. If we have too much capacity, such as with too many servers working at too fast of a collective rate, then the servers could wind up spending most of their time idle. However, if we have too little capacity–with too few servers–then customers may spend much of their time idle, waiting to be served.

For example, think of the last time you visited a grocery store. Do you recall how many of the cash registers had cashiers to operate them? Although modern grocery stores typically have numerous check-out lanes, they are rarely, if ever, all utilized at the same time. Why is that the case? Because the grocery store does not want to pay cashier labor when no customers are present. What if one or two customers are "inventoried" in a cashier waiting line? Should capacity be increased by bringing on additional cashiers? Probably not, since it is not unreasonable to have customers wait a few minutes to be served. But, what if customers wait ten minutes or more? Then, the cost of customer waiting is likely larger than the cost of an additional cashier or two. These are not easy tradeoffs.

Simulation Exercise

For this exercise you will run the *carwash.mod* simulation model. In this simulation you are the manager of one location of a chain of car wash companies. The lease on your old automatic car wash machine just expired, and you are about to lease a new automatic car wash machine. There are various models available, with the more expensive models being able to wash cars at a greater speed. The least expensive machine has a small water pump and spray nozzle that moves around to wash various portions of the car. That machine takes ten minutes to wash a car. The most expensive machine has a large water pump and many nozzles that can wash the entire care at the same time. That machine takes only one minutes to wash a car. Assume that either machine does as good a job washing a car. Also assume that machine configurations are available to wash at *any* speed between one and ten minutes, including rational numbers like 5.86 minutes.

For simplicity, you will be asked to specify the wash speed (the variable "**WashTime**") in minutes per car. The daily lease cost will be five-hundred divided by WashTime. Therefore, a machine that washes cars in five minutes would cost $100 per day, and a two minute per wash machine would cost $250 per day.

The advantage of leasing an expensive model is that you will be able to serve your customers more quickly, so that customers will spend less time waiting in line. However, if you lease a machine with too much capacity, the expensive machine may sit idle much of the time.

At the start of the simulation you will be told how many customers per hour are expected to arrive (ArrivalRate), based on a good forecast of prior data. (Assume that the number of customers will not be impacted by the leasing of the new machine, at least during the time of the simulation. Also assume that this ArrivalRate will continue throughout the lease period.)

At the start of the simulation you will also be told **PullUpTime**, which is the amount of time (minutes) it takes them to pull up into the machine when it is their turn for service. PullUpTime is a very small amount of time, but may influence your decision in some way. Assume that when a customer is done being served, they will depart immediately, freeing the machine for the next customer.

The owner of the company wants you to make a good decision about which machine to lease. She recognizes that customers do not mind having a long wait every now and then, but that if the wait is consistently long, then customers will eventually find somewhere else to have their car washed.

To prevent unreasonable waits, the owner will specify a **TargetWait**, which is the number of minutes customers should wait *on average*. The owner commissioned an extensive customer survey and found that if their customers have to wait TargetWait or less for service, they are happy. The company wants customers to be happy, but also wants to maintain a reasonable profit, which means not paying for machine capacity that is not needed. To strike a balance between customer wait satisfaction and machine cost, the company has dictated that all locations should strive to have an average customer wait be exactly TargetWait.

To reward this effort, your bonus will be based on how far the average customer wait is from the TargetWait. When a customer arrives in line they are immediately clocked in on the computer. When service begins for that customer, the amount of time they spent in line is recorded on the computer. This way it is quite easy to calculate the average number of minutes customers wait.

Your bonus is proportional to the relative percent that the actual average customer wait (**ActualWait**) is from the TargetWait. The bonus factor score is calculated as

$$100 - 100 \times |\text{ActualWait} - \text{TargetWait}| / \text{TargetWait}$$

where we are taking the absolute value of the difference between ActualWait and TargetWait.

Therefore, if you're the ActualWait is exactly the TargetWait, then your score will be 100 and you will get 100% of your bonus. If your ActualWait is 20 percent higher or lower than the TargetWait, then the score will be 80 and you will get 80% of your bonus.

Your goal should be to have an ActualWait as close to the TargetWait as possible. You do this by specifying the appropriate washing speed (WashTime) of the machine you wish to lease.

When you run the *carwash.mod* simulation, the you will be asked how many services you will provide (the levels). For now, you should specify **1**, since all you will be doing is washing cars. Later you may have the opportunity to offer three services–washing, waxing, and buffing–to meet more customer needs and earn more money.

How to Proceed

Run the simulation *carwash.mod*. (Instructions about running a simulation are found in Appendix A.) For your first tries you should run the simulation at the lowest "level" (easiest to solve).

Print your final results and submit them as directed by your instructor (either on paper, or electronically if your course is registered on the workbook website).

After you have run the simulation, read the section titled "Queuing: Analytical Queuing Theory" in Appendix C. Do not read that appendix section until *after* you have tried the *carwash.mod* at least once. If your results are not very good you should submit them anyway (if the instructor has asked you to), since you will have a chance to run the simulation again later and submit improved results.

Unit 3

SBP 3a: Customers in Inventory   Name (if turned in):_____

Analysis questions...   To help apply this Service Business Principle, consider and answer the following questions about your specific service business process. (❑Check here if you are going outside of your target service business.)

Service company/business:_____

The service process:_____

① It is common to keep inventories of goods provided by non-customers. What are some examples? How long are they kept in inventory before they are used in production?

② Are customers kept in "inventory" (i.e. stored somewhere)? Where? How long are they kept in inventory?

③ What customer belongings are kept in inventory? Where? For how long?

④ What customer information is kept in inventory? Where? For how long?

⑤ After service production is complete, *could* the finished result be kept by the company for a period of time? If it *could* be kept by the company, would it be practical to do so? Why or why not?

Unit 3

①_____

_____

_____

_____

_____

_____

_____

_____

_____

_____

_____

_____

_____

_____

_____

_____

_____

SBP 3a: Customers in Inventory   Name (if turned in):_____

Application exercise...   Also to help you apply this Service Business Principle, complete the following analysis with regard to your specific service business process, or another service process in your business. (☐Check here if you are going outside of your target service business, which was _____).

Service company/business:_____

The service process:_____

    Draw a service business process flowchart (see Appendix B for information on flowcharting). Indicate where customer-inputs are stored, or kept waiting in inventory (the standard symbol is a small triangle pointing down). Write the reasons the company allows these inventories. Indicate the typical amount of time an item is kept in these inventories. What limits the amount of time customer inputs are kept in inventories?

Preparation for the next Service Business Principle (3b)

To consider... Before proceeding, consider the following and write thoughts and ideas below:

Probably the most often cited distinction between manufacturing and services is the issue of tangibility. Tangibility implies being "touchable" or "physical." It is recognized that manufacturing is tangible and services are intangible. Do you agree? Do services processes tend to be more or less tangible than manufacturing?

Unit 3

_____

_____

_____

_____

_____

_____

_____

_____

_____

Service Business Principle 3b:

INTANGIBILITY MYTH

Service Business Principle	*"With services, the delivery and "product" are generally no less tangible than produced goods. In fact, substantial supporting facilities and facilitating goods can render the service more tangible than a substitute manufactured good."*

Why it occurs...   INTANGIBILITY MYTH occurs because some people confuse the lack of ownership of the service provider with intangibility (this will be discussed later in SBP: *Server-Ownership Perspective*)

Details...   Perhaps the greatest fallacy authors and academics make about services is that they are intangible, whereas manufacturing is a tangible process. This fallacy is rebuffed by examples such as the following:

- On part of the Toyota auto manufacturing process is to paint the cars coming through the assembly line. This is a manufacturing process and involves paint, equipment, and the car being painted–all tangible elements. Other companies will paint used cars as a *service* to customers. This auto-painting process also involves paint, equipment, and the car–all tangible elements!

- Stoffers produces TV dinners at manufacturing facilities around the country. This may include cooking chicken and potatoes, and placing the items in packaging. The food, stoves, and packaging are all tangible. KFC (formerly Kentucky Fried Chicken) also involves food, stoves, and packaging, but is considered a service provider.

- Some companies manufacture artificial hips. This involves machining metal parts and injection molding of plastic or vinyl parts–tangible processes. The surgical procedure to install an artificial hip is considered a service, but is extremely tangible, especially from the perspective of the customer.

- Can we say that manufacturing airplanes is more tangible than flying on airplanes? that making snow skies is more tangible than skiing down a hill at a ski resort? that manufacturing a lawn mower is more tangible than having a landscaping company mow your lawn? Is the lawn mower assembly process more tangible than the lawn mowing process? I don't think so.

Why, then, do so many seem to think that services are intangible, and manufacturing tangible? The confusion is not in the tangibility, but in *who provides the tangible elements that the customer takes away with them.* With manufacturing, the manufacturer provides all of the elements that the customer takes away, since customers provide no inputs to the manufacturing process. (see the Unified Services Theory) With services, many of the tangible elements that the customer takes away with them *were already owned by the customer* prior to the production process. The auto-painting customer already owned their car, a major tangible element of the service. The KFC employee already owned their stomach. The artificial hip recipient already owned their body. The airline passenger already owned their selves and baggage, etc.

In fact, services are extremely tangible in process and often in output. It is a major Services Management mistake to minimize the importance of the tangible elements, such as the "supporting facility" (where the service takes place) and the "facilitating goods."

"Facilitating goods" are those physical items, generally manufactured items, that facilitate or make it possible to deliver the service. Sometimes the customer provides facilitating goods, but often they are obtained by the service provider prior to the time the customer demands service.

In some cases the customer takes facilitating goods with them, and in others, the company uses the facilitating goods on multiple customers.

Thus, facilitating goods can play a variety of roles in the service production process. In fact, most service involve some facilitating goods. It is essential to pay attention to the role of facilitating goods in services for a number of reasons, including the following:

- The quality of the facilitating goods can be a chief indicator of the quality of service. This is because it is often much easier for customers to judge the quality of physical goods than the quality of action or informational components of the service. For example, why do real estate agents typically drive expensive cars? A customer may not be able to judge the quality of the agent's advice, but might (rightly or wrongly) assume that the fancy car indicates that the agent must be able to know good quality. (If the fancy car is viewed as a supporting facility—described below—the observation is the same.)

- The availability of facilitating goods may define the capacity of production. Even though facilitating goods may represent a relatively small portion of costs of production, their absence can cause serious problems in production. Imagine a law firm that runs out of printer paper. Paper costs only a few dollars per ream, but if they run out they cannot print and deliver documents that represent thousands of dollars of billings.

- Some service industries, most notably retail, have the delivery of facilitating goods as the core focus of the service process. In one sense retail is the tail end of a long manufacturing process, with the purpose of inventorying goods for distribution to customers. In a service sense, retail is a process of exchanging information with customers regarding their needs and available ways of meeting their needs, providing products (facilitating goods) to meet customer needs, and receiving customer payment inputs that are processed by the cashier. The difference between these two senses is that the first focuses on the movement of goods from distributor to customer, whereas the second focuses on the interactions with customers which help to meet their needs through appropriate facilitating goods. In the latter view, we realize that actual delivery of the facilitating goods is just one component of complex exchange process.

In addition to facilitating goods, nearly all services involve a *supporting facility*, which is the physical structure that provides a setting for service delivery. And, as you would imagine, supporting facilities are extremely tangible!

Much of what we observe about facilitating goods is also true of supporting facilities: Customers often judge overall service quality based on the perceived quality of the supporting facility. The capacity of the supporting facility can be the factor which limits the overall capacity to deliver the service. Supporting facilities differ from facilitating goods in that they are not generally given to customer (although they may be owned by the customers) and they are less likely to be replenished over time.

How it impacts decisions... Carefully consider the tangible nature of service delivery. Supporting facility and facilitating goods can be evaluated by the customer and used for estimating service quality. We must be careful about the tangible aspects of the service production, since they are evidences the customer uses to evaluate the quality of the service.

For example... Is an automobile a good or a service? The question may be whether it is considered a vehicle (tangible) or transportation (intangible)? Is the tangibility of an automobile influenced by whether the customer is driving it or whether a taxi driver is driving it? The answer is no—the automobile is just as tangible in either case, even though the former is considered a good, and the later is considered a service.

Which is more tangible, a plunger or a plumber? A plunger is a device one can purchase to unstop a clogged drain. A plumber is a person who can be hired to unstop a clogged drain. The plunger is a manufactured good. The plumber provides a service. In fact, a plumber may use a plunger to do the job—the plunger is a *facilitating good*. The plumber's service using a plunger is seen to be just as tangible as a plunger that the customer uses. The difference is not one of tangibility, but one of ownership.

My airline application... An airplane is very tangible whether it is owned by the airline or by a private individual. The airplane is a supporting facility. The physical condition of plane may be the customers chief indicator safety and perceived quality of air travel. The capacity of the plane limits the capacity to serve, since each customer requires a seat.

Facilitating goods on an airline include tickets and boarding passes, peanuts, magazines, and what some call airline food.

How manufacturing differs from services...

With manufacturing, the product is also quite tangible, although the "value" or "service" we receive from manufactured goods may be considered intangible. In fact, many manufactured goods have almost all of their value in intangible components–music CDs, computer software, books and other published products, etc.. (How much would you pay for a book in an unknown language?) Manufacturers need to carefully manage intangibles as do service providers. (see SBP: *Manufacturing in Sheep's Clothing*)

Quantitative analysis... (covered at the discretion of the instructor)

Inventory Theory

In the *Customers in Inventory* Service Business Principle we considered the management of customer inventory, which are typically called queues. Non-customer inventories of facilitating goods are also important to manage–not because the customer cares how long they sit in inventory but because the production can be hindered or halted if they are not present.

With the exception of retail, facilitating goods inventories can represent quite a small cost of production. Labor is often more costly that the facilitating goods. The biggest cost of facilitating goods is the problems that occur when they are not available when needed. Think of a law firm who has written up a contract for a corporate client. Just as they are about to print the contract to express mail it to the client, they realize they are completely out of printer paper. How much would they be willing to pay for a emergency supply of paper? Imagine that it is on a Saturday and the only other open business for some distance is a loan shark who has some extra paper. The loan shark says the 30 sheets requested will cost $10. Would the law firm pay it? If it means getting the contract out on time or not, they probably would.

How much would a hospital pay for an emergency supply of needles if they inadvertently ran out?

How much would a ski resort pay for diesel fuel to run the ski lift if they accidentally ran out?

How much would an airplane pay for a case of soft drinks if they find they are out just before a long flight?

All of these facilitating goods–paper, needles, fuel, soft drinks–are a very small portion of the overall production process, but essential none the less. The following is a procedure that can be used to manage such inventories:

- Step 1: Determine how much inventory of the facilitating goods you will need between now and the next expected shipment.
- Step 2: Order twice as much. (Or some other extremely safe amount.)

Sales Inventory Approaches

Now, that seat-of-the-pants approach will be less effective if the cost of the facilitating goods is a significant portion of the overall service process cost. Sales services, such as retail or wholesale, have inventory as a major portion of cost. In such cases, some of the more traditional inventory management models come into play.

(Another way to view sales services is as a link in a manufacturing supply chain. Manufacturing sales can involve little or no customer inputs, other than the customer selection of the manufactured product. Other sales situations involve more customer inputs, such as real estate sales. Managing inventories of real estate properties is quite different from managing inventories of manufactured auto parts.)

Inventory is a function of how frequently orders are placed and how much is ordered. These two items constitute the company's *ordering policy*. There are two general categories of ordering policies:
- *Fixed quantity systems*, where the company orders the same amount each time but the time between orders varies.
- *Fixed period systems*, where the company orders at fixed intervals, and orders as much as is needed.

Simulation Exercise

The simulation model *shoes.mod* allows you to manage the shoe inventory of a retailer. The shoe delivery truck arrives once per week, therefore you will use a fixed-period inventory system. Your shoe store is open Monday through Friday, and orders placed at the end of the day on Wednesday are delivered at the end of the day on Friday. The order lead time, which is the time from placing an order until it is filled, is two days. The order cycle, or order interval, is five days.

Your job is to order shoes each week for a certain number of weeks. For simplicity, you will only order one type of shoes. Each week you will be given the following information about that one type of shoes:
- the daily demand forecast,
- standard deviation of the daily demand forecast,
- the wholesale cost of a pair of shoes,
- the retail cost of a pair of shoes,
- the customer goodwill cost of a stockout (the cost impact when a customer comes to buy a pair of shoes, but you are out), and
- the cost of unnecessarily keeping a pair of shoes in inventory for a week.

The simulation will stop at the end of the day each Wednesday to let you place an order to be delivered at the end of the day on Friday. You need to order enough to last through the next week, considering the fact that demand may be greater or less then the forecasted amount. Your objective will be to make as much profit as possible.

How to Proceed

Run the simulation *shoe.mod*. (Instructions about running a simulation are found in Appendix A.) For your first tries you should run the simulation at the lowest "level" (easiest to solve).

Print your final results and submit them as directed by your instructor (either on paper, or electronically if your course is registered on the workbook website).

After you have run the simulation, read the section titled "Inventory Theory: The Economic Order Quantity and Safety Stock Approaches" in Appendix C. Do not read that appendix section until *after* you have tried the *shoe.mod* at least once. If your results are not very good you should submit them anyway (if the instructor has asked you to), since you will have a chance to run the simulation again later and submit improved results.

SBP 3b: Intangibility Myth   Name (if turned in):_____

Analysis questions...   To help apply this Service Business Principle, consider and answer the following questions about your specific service business process. (❑Check here if you are going outside of your target service business.)

Service company/business:_____

The service process:_____
   ① What is the supporting facility?
   ② What are the facilitating goods?
   ③ What role do they play in the process?

① _____

_____

_____

_____

_____

_____

_____

_____

_____

_____

_____

_____

_____

_____

_____

_____

_____

SBP 3b: Intangibility Myth   Name (if turned in):_____

Application exercise...

Also to help you apply this Service Business Principle, complete the following analysis with regard to your specific service business process, or another service process in your business. (❑Check here if you are going outside of your target service business, which was _____.)

Service company/business:_____

The service process:_____

What are the tangible elements of this business. How are they maintained? What are procedures for maintaining the supporting facility? What are the systems for maintaining the replenishment of facilitating goods? How is the quality of the facilitating goods assured?

Preparation for the next Service Business Principle (3c)

To consider...   Before proceeding, consider the following and write thoughts and ideas below:

With a manufacturing process, especially in mass production, the final products tend be consistent one to the next. Often the capability of the manufacturing process is judged by its ability to produce consistent output. How consistent are the outputs of a service process? How similar would you expect one unit of output from a service process to be relative to another output from the same service process? Why?

Unit 3

_____

_____

_____

_____

_____

_____

_____

_____

Service Business Principle 3c:

HETEROGENEOUS PRODUCTION

Service Business Principle	*"With services, the output (or service-product or service-result) is often heterogeneous, meaning each unit of production is somewhat unique."*

Why it occurs... HETEROGENEOUS PRODUCTION occurs because there is often wide variance in customer inputs and their service-production specifications.

Details... Previously we considered the "output" of a service process–that it appears to be perishable when often it is not. Service "output" has also been characterized as being *variable* and *nonstandard*. This implies that every unit of production is potentially unique, even from the same production process. Think of a movie theater. The output is a customer with a manipulated emotional state. Two hundred customers can sit through the same movie and have completely different responses from one another.

More often than not the output of a service process is simply the transformed customer-input to that process. Since customer inputs are usually heterogeneous, it makes perfect sense that the output will be heterogeneous as well.

Not only is the *output* of the service production process nonstandard (i.e. heterogeneous) but often the *process* itself is nonstandard. A consultant with twenty clients in a year is likely to have twenty unique experiences with the clients. A doctor may see twenty patients in a day and utilize twenty different diagnostic procedures. An auto shop may repair twenty cars in a week with no two requiring the same repair procedure. Sure, elements of the repair, medical diagnosis, or consulting procedures may be relatively standard. But the overall procedure changes depending on the needs of the customer inputs.

How it impacts decisions... Be cautious about defining output in homogeneous terms, since each output may be unique. Avoid the temptation to make rigid production process decisions based on the "average customer," since it is likely that no customer will be truly average, nor provide truly average inputs.

What to do about it... Design sufficient flexibility into the service production process to handle the necessary variability in customer inputs and production outputs.

For example... Tax accounting may seem to the uninformed to be a relatively routine and standardized production process. The output from the process includes, among other things, completed tax documents. It is clear that every tax document produced is different from every other one produced. Although the forms may be standardized, the data recorded on the forms is (or should be) completely contingent upon the information provided by the customer. Thus, no two tax forms will be completed in exactly the same manner.

My airline application... On the surface, it would seem that airlines produce a relatively standardized service—every coach-class passenger on a given flight arrives at the same destination at the same time. However, airlines recognize that too much standardization would adversely affect the ability to meet passenger's varying needs. Instead of offering one flight per day to Albuquerque with a 600-seat jumbo jet, the airline offers perhaps four 150-seat flights at various times. Passengers recognize that arriving at 8:00 a.m. is very different from arriving at 8:00 p.m. Airlines offer first-class for passengers who are willing to pay for larger seats and more attention in flight. They offer direct flights and some less convenient indirect flights. They provide window and aisle seats. Movies and drinks are optional. Further, passengers can choose to redefine the production process to meet their specific needs for sleep, for reading, or for casual conversation with perfect strangers. This heterogeneous production of air travel makes relevant the commonly asked question "So, how was your flight?" (The answer is <u>not</u> "Exactly like every other flight.")

Unit 3

How manufacturing differs from services...

With manufacturing, inputs and specifications are relatively standard, resulting in standardized outputs. The standards and specifications generally come from engineers, not from individual customers.

Quantitative analysis... (covered at the discretion of the instructor)

Project Scheduling

Production processes of services vary in heterogeneity. Some services are somewhat standardized, such as the process of changing the oil in a car. The oil change service provider pretty much does the same procedure on every car, although some peculiar cars may cause the procedure to vary.

Other services are so homogeneous that each customer receives a somewhat unique procedure. In fact, sometimes the procedure needs to be redesigned for every customer. An example is many consulting projects, where the consultant first evaluates the client's needs and then develops an entire plan of action based on those needs.

Services of this nature generally require *project scheduling*. Each step of the custom procedure needs to be considered in a master schedule. That master schedule then guides the coordination of people and other resources towards the completion of the project.

Simulation Exercise

Custom home construction is an example of a service with relatively heterogeneous production—each custom home is somewhat different from every other custom home built by a builder. As a result, the home construction schedule can differ from one home to the next.

In this simulation exercise, *home.mod*, you will schedule the subcontractors, who are the experts at each step of home construction. At the start of the simulation you will be given the list of subcontractors to schedule. You will also be told how many days the work of each subcontractor is expected to take.

The following are some of the subcontractor activities you may have in the process: (The list you are given at the start of the simulation may differ from this list.)

- **excavate**: dig the basement hole.
- **pour**: lay the cement foundation.
- **frame**: put up the wood superstructure.
- **roof**: install the tar paper and shingles.

- **brick**: install the primary exterior covering.
- **electrical**: install the wiring.
- **plumbing**: install water, gas, and sewage pipes.
- **HVAC**: install heating and air conditioning systems.
- **drywall**: form the interior walls.
- **paint**: paint walls and moldings.
- **cabinets**: install cabinets in kitchen and bathrooms.
- **fixtures**: install light fixtures and switches.
- **flooring**: install carpet and other floor coverings.

Since the subcontractors are all different from one another, it may be possible to have two or more subcontractors working at the same time. However, some subcontractors' activities cannot begin until other subcontractors' activities are completed. These are precedence relationships. For example, you cannot pour the foundation cement until after the foundation space has been excavated. Therefore, excavation is a *predecessor* activity to pouring the foundation cement.

At the start of the simulation you will be told which activities are *immediate predecessors* (I.P.) to other activities. An *immediate predecessor* is a predecessor activity that comes right before a given activity, although there may be a time gap between the time one activity is finished and the next activity starts.

If "pour" has "excavate" as an I.P. then we cannot pour until after excavation is done. If also "frame" has "pour" as an I.P. then we cannot frame until the pouring is done. These precedence relationships imply that "frame" has "excavate" as a predecessor (must be completed before) even though it is not listed as an I.P..

Your scheduling job will be to tell each subcontractor what day they are to arrive. The excavator is already scheduled to start at day *zero*, which is the "groundbreaking" day. You must identify what day each subcontractor should arrive. For example, if the excavation takes *three* days then the cement contractor should arrive to pour the foundation on day *three*. All work days are numbered, and non-work days such as weekends and holidays are not numbered.

The following are financial conditions associated with this simulation, which will be defined at the start of the simulation:

- The construction contract says you will pay a penalty amount of **ProjectDelayPenalty** dollars for every day you are delayed beyond the optimal completion date. (The optimal completion date will be revealed at the end of the simulation.)
- You can reschedule a subcontractor to come earlier than the originally scheduled day by paying them **RescheduleFee** dollars. Whether this is a per-day amount or not depends on the level of simulation, and will be told you at the start.
- If a subcontractor arrives and the Immediate Predecessor activities are not yet completed, then the activity will be delayed. When an activity is delayed you must pay the subcontractor **ActivityDelayPenalty** dollars. Also, whether this is a per-day amount or not depends on the level of simulation, and will be told you at the start.
- You will be given the opportunity to "**crash**" some activity, which is to speed them up by bringing on additional workers. The cost for crashing a particular activity will be told you, and the maximum number of days you can speed up an activity will be told you. For example, you may be told that you can crash the framing activity up to three days at a cost of $50 per day. If you enter two days to crash then the framing activity will be accomplished in two fewer days at a total cost of $100. The result is that the framing will be completed two days faster than it would otherwise.

As you run the simulation, you will first need to determine your subcontractor starting date schedule based on the projected activity durations you will be given. Then, you will run the simulation day by day, and will be occasionally given project updates and opportunities to make decisions.

How to Proceed

Run the simulation *home.mod*. (Instructions about running a simulation are found in Appendix A.) For your first tries you should run the simulation at the lowest "level" (easiest to solve).

Print your final results and submit them as directed by your instructor (either on paper, or electronically if your course is registered on the workbook website).

After you have run the simulation, read the section titled "Project Scheduling: The Critical Path Method (CPM)" in Appendix C. Do not read that appendix section until *after* you have tried the *home.mod* at least once. If your results are not very good you should submit them anyway (if the instructor has asked you to), since you will have a chance to run the simulation again later and submit improved results.

Unit 3

SBP 3c: Heterogeneous Production   Name (if turned in):_____

Analysis questions...   To help apply this Service Business Principle, consider and answer the following questions about your specific service business process. (❑Check here if you are going outside of your target service business.)

Service company/business:_____

The service process:_____
    ① What is a "unit of output?"
    ② Is output standard, or does it vary?
    ③ What percent of our production output is unique?
    ④ What percent of each product is unique?
    ⑤ Is each output composed of different amounts of production resources? (Does each output cost differing amounts to produce?)
    ⑥ Does each output command a different amount of "willingness to pay?" (Does each output generate differing amounts of revenue?)

① _____

_____

_____

_____

_____

_____

_____

_____

_____

_____

_____

_____

_____

_____

_____

_____

Unit 3

SBP 3c: Heterogeneous Production   Name (if turned in):_____

Application exercise...

Also to help you apply this Service Business Principle, complete the following analysis with regard to your specific service business process, or another service process in your business. (❑Check here if you are going outside of your target service business, which was _____.)

Service company/business:_____

The service process:_____

Analyze the output variety resulting from the service process in terms of standardization versus variability. List some ways (or characteristics) in which the output from the service process is relatively standardized. List some typical ways the output varies from one unit to the next. What factors explain why some output characteristics are on the "standardized" list and others are on the "varying" list?

Preparation for the next Service Business Principle (3d)

To consider... Before proceeding, consider the following and write thoughts and ideas below:

In manufacturing, the way to know if a process was more productive one day than another is to compare how much output was produced on each day—the most productive days are the ones in which more is produced. With services, how do we know the difference between a productive day and a less productive day? Think of a service that involves highly variable output, such as healthcare, education, or legal services. In such a process, how would we know if we are producing more at one time than at another?

_____

_____

_____

_____

_____

_____

_____

_____

Service Business Principle 3d:
DIFFICULTY IN MEASURING OUTPUT

Service Business Principle	*"With services, although the output can be identified, it often cannot be easily quantified. Therefore, it can be hard to measure productivity."*

Why it occurs... DIFFICULTY IN MEASURING OUTPUT occurs because output is variable and nonstandard, as discussed in SBP: *Heterogeneous Production.*

Details... Most companies want to be productive. In general terms, *productivity* is what we get out of a process given the resources we put in. Thus, if we desire to measure changes in productivity over time, or compare the productivity of various service providers, we need to have some way of measuring output. Manufacturers of standard items can simply count the number of items produced. For a service company, counting items produced is a rough measure of output. The service business may handle fewer customers over time, but the processing requirements may be much more complex. For example, a consulting firm may originally handle simple jobs with a lot of clients, but as the firm's specialized expertise develops, they may handle more time-consuming projects involving fewer customers. Measuring time expended is to measure an input, not output. The primary output of most consulting firms is advice. How does one quantify the magnitude of advice? How do we tell if one consulting office is capable of producing "more" advice than another?

How it impacts decisions... Be careful in selecting productivity measures, since these measures tend to define what employees focus on in the production process. (This will be discussed later in the *A Measure of Motivation* Service Business Principle.)

For example... In education, how do we measure productivity? One way is to count the number of graduates. The problem with counting graduates is that it fails to capture the knowledge they have gained—it would be easy to "crank out" graduates with little competency (as is done in many highschool programs in the U.S.). Another way to measure education productivity is to count the number of courses taken or grade point averages. Yet, those are only vague surrogate measures of knowledge. Another means of measuring productivity is to tabulate job placement statistics or starting salary statistics. Yet, how many of those graduates could have gotten just equally good jobs by skipping class and "cramming" for exams—knowing little but being able to give a great job interview. Another way of measuring education productivity is to ask graduates who have been out a few years how much useful knowledge they thought they received from various courses. That is, unfortunately, a very delayed measure of education productivity. The bottom line is that measuring the output of education is no trivial matter.

My airline application... A common way to measure productivity of airlines is to calculate the "passenger load factor," which is the percent of available flight seats which are occupied. The problem is that such a measure almost discourages increasing capacity even when it might be warranted. (Over-booked flights show high passenger load factor, but may reflect many passengers lost to other airlines.) Another measure of productivity that is used is "passenger seat miles," which captures the idea that a passenger who flies 1000 miles represents twice as much production as a passenger who flies 500 miles.

Yet this measure does not really capture a concept of cost of production nor value to the passenger. (Is a 1000 mile flight twice as costly or twice as valuable as a 500 mile flight? Probably not.) Another measure of airline output is to count the raw number of passengers, which measurement is no panacea. We wind up having to measure output in a number of different ways.

How manufacturing differs from services...

With manufacturing, output is often relatively uniform, allowing clearly numerical output measurement (i.e. counting units of output).

Quantitative analysis... (covered at the discretion of the instructor)

Facility Layout

Output may be thought of as work accomplished. Indeed, with service companies it can be difficult to quantify how much is accomplished over a given time period. This implies that it can be difficult to know if productivity is going up or down over time.

Despite the challenges in measuring service output and productivity, it is often possible to model service production systems and determine ways of improvement. Sometimes these models require making simplifying assumptions. Even with such assumptions, models can help reveal ways of improving productivity in actual systems.

One concern in any system is idleness, which is the opposite of productivity. Idleness can be employees without work to do, or employees engaged in activities which do not contribute to the desired service output. Some idleness is avoidable and some is not. One common way to avoid some degree of idleness is to improve the process layout.

The "Process Layout" Problem

If a service facility has a poor arrangement of machines, employee stations, etc., employees can spend a lot of time walking from one location to the next. For example, if a copy center places the most frequently used machine at the back of the store, employees may spend a lot of time walking back and forth to that machine. By moving the machine to a more accessible location, employees can spend less time in "unproductively" walking around, and can spend more time actually serving customer needs.

This problem of figuring out how to arrange a service production facility is called the "process layout" or "relative location problem." The name "process layout" implies that we want to pick the best layout given the types of processes that take place at the service facility. Process layouts recognize that production tends to be heterogeneous. Process layouts assume that there is a cost associated with work flow moving from one location to the next, based on the distance moved. This does not typically apply to moving information over computer networks, but does apply to moving customers or their belongings.

The "Product Layout" Problem

Another type of layout problem pertains not to how the facility is physically laid out, but to how the steps of the process are managed. If a service process involves a number of steps, with specific employees assigned to each step, an objective may be to plan the capacity of each step so that there will be a good flow of work through the system. This problem is commonly called the "product layout" or "line-balancing problem." The primary objective of this problem is to identify and remove bottlenecks–those steps in the process with low capacity which slow down the entire system.

Issues such as heterogeneous production make it extremely difficult to analyze the product layout of service organizations. It is actually quite easy to identify bottlenecks in a process *if* the process is unvarying in the steps and each step is performed at an extremely constant rate. Heterogeneous production implies that both the set of steps to perform the service process and the time to accomplish each step will likely vary. Further, because customers deliver their inputs at random intervals demand itself can go in and out of being the bottleneck.

Simulation Exercise

A community is building a new hospital to serve the local population. Although the design of the building is mostly complete, it is yet to be determined which departments will be located in which sections of the building. The emergency room must be located at the emergency entrance. However, the other departments can be placed on any floors as desired.

A study of the old hospital revealed that there was potentially a lot of employee and customer travel between some of the departments. For a period of time, logs were kept to indicate the amount of travel between each location. Obviously, departments with a lot of travel between them should be closer together. However, space constraints made this a challenging problem.

When you run the simulation *hospital.mod*, you will be given an array that shows the typical amount of travel between each of the six departments, based on logs of work requirements taken over an extended period of time. You will also be shown the hospital building. The hospital has two wings with three floors each. Each department will go on one floor of one of the wings. The approximate distance between department locations (in this case, hundreds of feet) is as follows: (E=east wing, W=west wing. E1 is the first floor on the east wing.)

	E1	E2	E3	W1	W2	W3
E1	0	1	2	1	2	3
E2	1	0	1	2	1	2
E3	2	1	0	3	2	1
W1	1	2	3	0	1	2
W2	2	1	2	1	0	1
W3	3	2	1	2	1	0

For example, it is approximately 200 feet from department location W1 to E3. (The actual scale of distances will be given to you at the start of the simulation.)

The simulation will ask you what department to put in each location, beginning with E1 and ending with W3. Each department will be identified by a number. An example *might* include the following: (Actual departments will be given to you at the start of the simulation.)

Dept. No.	Department
1	Surgery
2	Regular Care
3	Intensive Care
4	Lab
5	Obstetrics
6	Radiology

Your objective will be to minimize the amount of time employees from each department spend walking from one department to the next.

How to Proceed

Run the simulation *hospital.mod*. (Instructions about running a simulation are found in Appendix A.) For your first tries you should run the simulation at the lowest "level" (easiest to solve).

Print your final results and submit them as directed by your instructor (either on paper, or electronically if your course is registered on the workbook website).

After you have run the simulation, read the section titled "Facility Layout: Process Layouts" in Appendix C. Do not read that appendix section until *after* you have tried the *hospital.mod* at least once. If your results are not very good you should submit them anyway (if the instructor has asked you to), since you will have a chance to run the simulation again later and submit improved results.

SBP 3d: Difficulty in Measuring Output   Name (if turned in):_____

Analysis questions...   To help apply this Service Business Principle, consider and answer the following questions about your specific service business process. (❑Check here if you are going outside of your target service business.)

Service company/business:_____

The service process:_____
  ① How do we measure output? In terms of number of customers served? In terms of value provided to each customer? In terms of revenue generated?
  ② In what way might the way we measure output vary customer to customer? Do some customers use one measure and other customers use another?

① _____

_____

_____

_____

_____

_____

_____

_____

_____

_____

_____

_____

_____

_____

_____

_____

SBP 3d: Difficulty in Measuring Output   Name (if turned in):_____

Application exercise...

Also to help you apply this Service Business Principle, complete the following analysis with regard to your specific service business process, or another service process in your business. (❑Check here if you are going outside of your target service business, which was _____.)

Service company/business:_____

The service process:_____

Describe three *different* ways "output" could be measured for your business process. Are the three exactly correlated with one another? In other words, is one measure of output simply a constant times another measure of output? Describe what each of the measures of output might be interpreted, and how each might be used to monitor productivity over time. Comment on which of the three you think is the most appropriate measure of output, and why.

Preparation for the next Service Business Principle (3e)

To consider...   Before proceeding, consider the following and write thoughts and ideas below:

In the last Service Business Principle, we considered how difficult it is to measure the *amount* of output that is produced. Things are complicated further by attempting to measure *how well* the output was produced. This is an issue of quality. With manufacturing, we measure specific features of the product, such as size or speed or strength, and compare those measurements with engineered specifications. The quality objective is to manage the production process to meet those specifications consistently. With service processes, how do we know *if* quality is being produced? How do we assure that quality is produced on a consistent basis? Since customers differ, should the specification of quality also differ from one customer to the next?

_____

_____

_____

_____

_____

_____

_____

_____

Service Business Principle 3e:

DIFFICULTY IN MAINTAINING QUALITY

Service Business Principle	*"With services, quality measurement tends to be subjective and difficult to scale. The standards by which quality is defined are often ambiguous. These unique specifications of quality, coupled with labor-intensiveness and inconsistent customer inputs, make it difficult to provide consistent quality."*

Why it occurs... DIFFICULTY IN MAINTAINING QUALITY occurs because each customer may present different inputs–of varying–quality to the process. Customers also specify different quality measurement standards, making the measurement of quality difficult.

Details... Quality has many definitions, although almost all capture some idea of "goodness." What is "good" production? Who says what is "good" and what is "not good?"

In manufacturing processes, the ultimate customer is often not identified until well after the production is complete. Therefore, the manufacturer has to estimate what customers will deem "good" and what they will consider "not good." Market researchers survey customers to determine what these designations might be, and give that information to product engineers, who interpret survey results into product specifications. These specifications are generally numerical in nature, based on objective quality measurements.

Service businesses have both the luxury and the challenge of having the customer involved in the quality measurement process. They do not have to estimate what the customer deems as "good" or "not good," but can directly *ask the customer*, if they choose to do so. The problem is that each customer may have a different scale for comparing good and not good, as well as unique standards by which the service is evaluated! Service that may be more than good for one customer may be worse than bad for another. Every customer may represent a unique quality measurement system! (These ideas will be discussed in more detail in the *Measuring Service Quality and Productivity* Unit.)

Even if we have a reliable and valid measure of service quality, achieving good quality can still be a difficult task. The best service processes and the best employees can only do so much if customers provide inputs of low quality. Therefore, much of the quality assurance process in service businesses involves managing customer inputs and customer involvement. (There will be more discussion on this in the *Challenges in Delivering Service Quality* Unit.)

How it impacts decisions... Service providers need to decide when and how to measure quality in the service process. Some measures may be objective, relying on service standards set by the company. Other measures might be subjective, based on customer evaluations of the service. Too frequent measurement can be a burden on employees and customers, but too little measurement can provide insufficient information.

Service providers also need to determine how best to approach the quality of customer-provided inputs. Too little control of customer inputs can lead to unacceptable quality of production, and too much control can be an annoyance to customers.

What to do about it...   Since quality measurement in services is less than an exact science, it is often good to improve measurement validity by using multiple measures. The service provider may base the service on internal standards which are justified and updated by quality assessments given from customers. Detailed information about service quality measurement techniques will be presented in the *Measuring Service Quality and Productivity* Unit. Issues about service quality assurance will be discussed in the *Challenges in Delivering Service Quality* Unit.

For example...   How can a bank measure quality? Some measures are quite objective, such as whether transactions balance or are accurately recorded. Others are extremely subjective, such as the cordiality of loan officers and other employees. Cordiality is extremely difficult to measure, and measurements are subject to customers' individual attitudes. What about the measure of wait time at the teller windows? One may think that is an objective measure, since it can be accurately recorded with a stop watch. However, the actual wait time is much less important to service quality than the customers' *perceptions* and *acceptance* of the wait times, which is more difficult to measure.

How can a law firm measure quality? A seemingly objective measure would be the number of cases won (for trial lawyers). However, heterogeneous production and variable customer inputs (i.e. cases) probably has as much or more of an influence on case winning than the "quality" of the legal service. (At least I would hope that would be the case, although it probably is not in many instances.) In fact, even poor quality lawyers win cases in which the client is clearly in the right.

This is similar to measuring quality of investment banks, who often publish statistics about their ability to generate a financial return over some past time period. U.S. law requires disclosure that "past performance does not guarantee future earnings," or something like that. Poor investment bankers can be lucky picking stocks, and good investment bankers can have portfolios go bad. In fact, even a "quality" measure of a 10 percent return is relative–is 10 percent a good or a bad return? Most would say that depends on what alternate investments are doing.

For each of the above examples, the fact that it is difficult to measure quality makes it more difficult to manage quality. Further, quality assurance may be influenced by the quality of customer inputs: Banks require correct and legible information on forms and checks. Law firms prefer cases with quality evidence. And investment bankers need customers' investment funds and preference information in a timely manner.

My airline application...   A 1996 Southwest Airlines advertisement proclaims that they won the "Triple Crown," which is that they were #1 in On-time performance, #1 in Baggage Handling, and #1 in Customer Satisfaction. What exactly is "on-time" performance? What denotes good baggage handling? How is customer satisfaction measured? And who defined these measures as such? Coming up with such measures is easier said than done.

Think about how much customers can influence on-time performance. Customers who violate procedures by being late, not checking in, or having too many carry-on bags can make it difficult to always have planes depart on time. One alternative is to not let such passengers on the plane, which can have a negative effect on those customers' perceptions of "quality."

Unit 3

How manufacturing differs from services...

With manufacturing, quality measurements tend to be relatively standard for a given product. Maintaining quality in a manufacturing process is often considered equal with meeting product design standards.

Quantitative analysis... (covered at the discretion of the instructor)

Statistical Process Control (SPC)

One major challenging in maintaining service quality is identifying when quality has drifted away from that which is acceptable. When a service is heterogeneous, each incident of service can present different standards of quality. Further, these quality standards can be very subjective, measured by the opinions of the customers.

When service quality standards (a) are expected to be consistent over time, and (b) are quantitatively measured, then statistical techniques can be used to help identify service quality drift. Examples of quality measurements and standards that may fit this criteria include:

- transaction error rates at banks
- on-time departure for airlines
- recurrence rates for repair services
- scaled service ratings on customer comment cards

If we look at the quality measurements over time, we may find that they may be mostly consistent, with only occasional random variation. In other situations, measurements may change with a pattern that results from a fundamental flaw in the service delivery process. Unfortunately, it can be quite difficult to tell the difference between a flaw in the service delivery process and a mere random variation.

For example, imagine a hotel that measures customer satisfaction with a survey that records a rating from 1 (worst quality) to 10 (best quality). Every week the hotel calculates average ratings for the week. The manager desires to know if quality is consistent or changing over time. Imagine that weekly ratings for a series of weeks are 8.8, 8.1, 8.9, 9.2, 8.2, 8.5, and 7.6. The manager is concerned about the last week's rating of 7.6. Does it represent a statistical anomaly, or is it simply a result of random variation. The fact is, customers assign different meaning to different points on the scale, and quality could have actually *improved* that week but the customers were simply frugal in giving high ratings. So, one thing the manager may want to know is if that 7.6 fits the random pattern of the other data, or if it does not.

Simulation Exercise

The *cookie.mod* simulation exercise will allow us to investigate a random process and try to determine if there is a problem or not.

You have an oven that bakes cookies. The oven is mostly reliable, but sometimes breaks down. The thermostat or a heating element might have a problem, causing the temperature to vary and the cookies to be poorly cooked.

Fortunately, the oven repairman will come right away whenever you call him. Unfortunately, he charges $50 for each repair visit, even if nothing was wrong. The way you can know if something is wrong with the oven is by inspecting sample batches of cookies.

When a batch of cookies comes out of the oven, you can check their doneness by running them under an optical inspector. The optical inspector gives a rating value in the range of 0 to 10. A perfect cookie will have a rating of 5.

Every day the system will give you a sample measurements for 5 batches of cookies.

At the end of the day, you will be asked whether you should have the repairman come at the start of the following day.

You begin the simulation with 100 points. You will lose 10 points each day the repairman comes but the oven was not broken. You will also lose 10 points for each day the oven was broken and you did not call the repairman. The simulation will run for 20 days, however you are only responsible for the profits of the last 10 days. After days 10 through 19 you will be asked whether to call the repairman or not. Therefore, the most you can lose is 100 points.

How to Proceed

Run the simulation *cookies.mod*. (Instructions about running a simulation are found in Appendix A.) For your first tries you should run the simulation at the lowest "level" (easiest to solve).

Print your final results and submit them as directed by your instructor (either on paper, or electronically if your course is registered on the workbook website).

After you have run the simulation, read the section titled "Statistical Process Control (SPC): Control Charts for Variables" in Appendix C. Do not read that appendix section until *after* you have tried the *cookies.mod* at least once. If your results are not very good you should submit them anyway (if the instructor has asked you to), since you will have a chance to run the simulation again later and submit improved results.

SBP 3e: Difficulty in Maintaining Quality   Name (if turned in):_____

Analysis questions...   To help apply this Service Business Principle, consider and answer the following questions about your specific service business process. (❏Check here if you are going outside of your target service business.)

Service company/business:_____

The service process:_____
　　① What product features denote quality?
　　② How would we know if we were providing quality?
　　③ How are we able to identify when quality is a problem? Can we measure quality problems before they come to the attention of customers? How or why not?
　　④ What are some methods used to assure quality?
　　⑤ What are the issues that may tend to undermine quality assurance?

① _____

_____

_____

_____

_____

_____

_____

_____

_____

_____

_____

_____

_____

_____

_____

_____

Unit 3

SBP 3e: Difficulty in Maintaining Quality   Name (if turned in):_____

Application exercise...   Also to help you apply this Service Business Principle, complete the following analysis with regard to your specific service business process, or another service process in your business. (❏Check here if you are going outside of your target service business, which was _____.)

Service company/business:_____

The service process:_____
  Imagine that your service company wants to implement a system which rewards individual employee based on their ability to provide quality. Describe how you would design such a system. What would the quality measures be? How might these quality measures by tied into rewards or compensation? Would they be a fair basis for allocating employee bonuses? How or why not? What are factors outside of the control of employees that would hinder quality assurance? In other words, what are ways that employees might do good work yet achieve results of unacceptable quality? Give a few examples.

Part I - Fundamentals
Unit 4:
UNDERSTANDING NON-SERVICES (MANUFACTURING)

Many non-service (manufacturing) processes can be better understood in light of service process concepts. By understanding what makes non-services different from services, we can identify different ways of looking at non-services to potentially apply service management principles.

Preparation for the next Service Business Principle (4a)

To consider... Before proceeding, consider the following and write thoughts and ideas below:

When we speak of a "supply chain" we refer to the idea that suppliers have suppliers, who have suppliers, etc. Recently there has been a trend in some industries to share production information with suppliers and the suppliers of suppliers to help them do their jobs better. What types of information would be helpful to share with suppliers? Are there risks to sharing such information with suppliers?

_____

_____

_____

_____

_____

_____

_____

_____

_____

Service Business Principle 4a:

SUPPLY CHAIN LINKAGES

Service Business Principle	*"Manufacturing supply chains include the firms that participate in the process of converting raw materials to finished goods and getting those finished goods to the end customer. A supply chain can involve raw material processors, component manufacturers, assemblers, distributers, and retailers. Service processes often occur at the interfaces between the various firms. An integrated supply chain is one where the different firms work together to increase responsiveness and synchronize efforts. This necessitates a continual flow of information from customers to suppliers, causing the supply chain to take on more Services properties. In a pure Service setting, customers and suppliers have multiple roles in the supply chain."*

Why it occurs... SUPPLY CHAIN LINKAGES occurs because of the coordinating efforts that occur between stages of a supply chain. Customer information can be a form of process input. When suppliers use customer information to guide their production processes, those processes assume service properties to some degree.

Closely related to... the *Mass Alliances* SBP.

This principle introduces the concept of the "supply chain." The field of supply chain management is relatively new, but very important in today's economies. Supply chain management has been defined as "the configuration, coordination, and improvement of a sequentially related set of operations."[5] As such, supply chain management involves considering the needs and linkages between various players in a production process. In this section, the concepts of supply chains and supply chain management will be applied to services. For more information on the topic, see: "Customer-supplier Duality and Bidirectional Supply Chains in Service Organizations" by Scott E. Sampson (yes, me), *International Journal of Service Industry Management*, Vol. 11, No. 4, 2000, pp. 348-364.

Details... A significant way to look at manufacturing processes is in terms of a "supply chain," which captures the idea of a link between supplier and customers. Very often, a manufacturer's suppliers have suppliers, and the customers have their own customers. The product or product components "flow" down a chain of suppliers to customers.

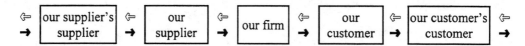

The filled arrows (→) represent the "downstream" movement of product from suppliers to customers. The hollow arrows (⇐) represent the "upstream" flow of requirement information from customers to suppliers. The other thing that flows upstream is money. For example, a product manufacturing and distribution supply chain may include stages such as the following:

---

[5] Hanna, Mark & Newman, Rocky, *Integrated Operations Management: Adding Value for Customers*, First Edition (2001), Prentice-Hall, Upper Saddle River, New Jersey, p. 45.

A furniture retailer may sell desks to end consumers. The desks may be supplied by a furniture distributor, who receives desks from a desk assembly plant. The metal parts of a desk may be provided by a steel fabrication company, who gets sheet metal material from a steel mill. (The steel mill possibly gets iron ore from an ore mining company, which is an "extraction" industry–extracting raw materials from the earth.)

In this example, note that the assembler wants to meet the needs of the distributer, who is trying to satisfy retailers, who serve end consumers. The assembler is reliant on parts suppliers, who are reliant on material suppliers, who count on their suppliers. This is like a chain, where each link is important. If a material supplier fails to perform, ultimately the end consumer is likely to suffer.

An example of this supply chain linkage was seen a few years ago when an Asian factory that made resin was destroyed by a fire. That resin was an important material in the production of integrated circuits such as computer memory chips. The memory chips went into new computer systems that were being assembled by various companies. Memory chip prices skyrocketed, which had a dramatic effect on prices down the supply chain. Ultimately, consumers suffered the consequences of higher computer prices.

In this section we will consider three types of supply chains. The first two are manufacturing situations, such as that just described. The third is a service situation.

Traditional Manufacturing Supply Chains

Traditional supply chain management is only concerned with the flows from and to our immediate suppliers and customers. Our firm provides requirements to (i.e. selects the output from) our immediate suppliers. We receive the filled order from our suppliers. We process those inputs to make them more valuable to our customers (a "value-adding process"). Our customers provide product requirements, which hopefully can be met by our output.

Service processes are often found in traditional supply chains at the *interfaces between suppliers and their customers*. The following are some common examples:

- The responsibility for interfacing with suppliers typically falls under a purchasing department or functional area. Purchasing departments receive requisitions for items from various company departments, locate the "best" suppliers, initiate orders, receive items, and initiate payment. All of this is dependent on requisitions from "customers" within the company (called "internal customers"). Since requisitions can be considered a "customer input," purchasing can be viewed as a service function.

- Suppliers may hire logistics companies to transport goods and materials to customers. ("Logistics" deals with the movement of items from one location to another.) Logistics companies receive the input (goods or materials) from their customers and transport them to their customers' customers. This reliance on customer-inputs classifies logistics companies a part of the service sector. In fact, logistics companies are a very large part, estimated at about ten percent of GNP in the United States.[5]

- When supplied items fail to perform, customers may require the suppliers to repair or replace the items. Repairing means fixing an item that already belongs to the customer–a customer input to the repair process. Manufacturers may have "Field *Service* Technicians" whose job it is to work on customers' products at the customer location (the "field"). Field Service Technicians

---

[5] Millen, Robert, "JIT Logistics, Puting JIT on Wheels," *Target* 7, no. 2, (Summer 1991), 4. also Heizer5 p. 429.

may be a part of a "Customer Service Department," which department is responsible for acting on customer inputs.

Integrated Supply Chains

A current trend in supply chain management is to create integrated supply chains. Integrated supply chain management involves sharing information throughout the supply chain and using that information to work in sync with all of the other parts of the supply chain.

What types of information might customers share upstream in an integrated supply chain?
- Current sales information.
- Future requirements and forecasts.
- Anticipated timing of future orders.
- Changes in marketing or product promotion which will influence future requirements.
- Anticipated changes in product design that will influence supplied parts and materials.
- Quality control information.

This information may be not only shared with our immediate suppliers but also with our suppliers' suppliers, who are called the "second-tier" suppliers. This implies that as a supplier we may need to interact with out customers' customers ("second-tier" customers) so that we can help assure that their needs are being met by our immediate customers. In fact, the information can be shared across the entire supply chain, as depicted in the following figure:

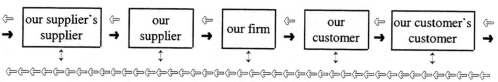

(information flowing "upstream" from customers to suppliers)

Working with second-tier (or third-tier, etc.) suppliers and customers is no easy task. Technology can help, such as Electronic Data Interchange (EDI), in which demand requirements are continually communicated up the supply chain. For example, when a customer purchases a can of creamed corn at a grocery store in Maine, the canned-corn distributor, the wholesaler, the packing plant, and even the corn farmer can be informed of the demand. The purchase of one can might not make a big difference, but an aggregate surge in demand for creamed corn in Maine can affect the planning and allocation of product and production capacity throughout the supply chain.

Suppliers can use the customer-provided information to help increase responsiveness. For example, the information may be used to adjust the design and production of a supplied product so that it meets changing customer requirements. The increased presence of customer-information inputs, and the influence of that information on production, causes stages of the integrated supply chain to assume some properties of Services.

Service Supply Chains

With integrated supply chains the customer inputs to the production process are customer *information*. The customers would typically not provide any *physical self* or *belonging* inputs into the production process. Processes involving customer-self and customer-belonging inputs are Service processes in a more pronounced way.

Do supply chains exist in service processes where the major inputs come from customers? The supply chain is a little different in these service situations, since the *customer* is a supplier of physical items and information. The customer is a supplier of inputs to the service supplier, then receives those transformed inputs back from that supplier. In other words, the customer is their own second-tier supplier! This is depicted as follows:

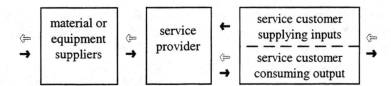

For example, a customer supplies a broken television to the television repair shop. The shop also receives replacement parts inputs from other suppliers. After repairing the shop returns the television to the customer. In this process the television was supplied by the repair shop, who got it from the customer.

Things get even more complicated when the service provider employs another service provider to assist with the processing of customer inputs. For example, a photographer may not process exposed film herself, but may send the film to a film processing company. The major input to the film processing company process is the film from the photographer which is from the photographs of the end customer. Therefore the end customer is a second-tier supplier to the film processing company. The film processing company supplies completed prints back to the photographer, who makes them available to the end customer. Therefore, the film processor is a second-tier supplier to the end customer. By providing the subjects to be photographed, and by receiving the finished prints, the end customers are in fact fourth-tier suppliers to themselves!

In this example, the initial service provider is an interface between the service customer and the service supplier, as depicted in the following figure:

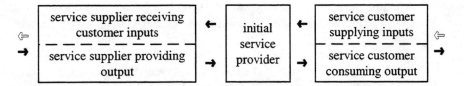

These types of service supply chains are circular in that inputs flow first in one direction–from customers to service suppliers–then in the other direction–from the service suppliers back to the customers. The initial service provider functions as a value-adding go-between in the process.

How does one *integrate* a supply chain that is circular in this manner? For one thing, communication needs to occur between customers and suppliers to prevent inadequate fulfilling of unrealistic expectations.

The concept of "garbage-in, garbage-out" implies that a company can only produce output that is as good as the supplied inputs. If a customer supplies lousy inputs, and that customer is subsequently upset with the shoddy outputs, who is to blame? In an integrated service supply chain everyone must take some responsibility, including the service provider and the customer. As appropriate, service providers need to inform customers about process capabilities and limitations. With the photography example, customers may need to be informed that certain color combinations will look bad, regardless of how well the photo processing is done. This implies that service providers need to understand the capabilities of *their* service suppliers, so that relevant conditions can be communicated to customers up front.

Customers do not want to hear a service provider blame a service failure on their supplier, even if it is that supplier's fault. For example, a photographer who blames the film processor for shoddy prints is like an auto dealer blaming the steel mill if a metal auto part breaks prematurely. Service providers are responsible for the work of chosen suppliers, and for choosing other suppliers when necessary.

Great advantage can be had by choosing suppliers and partnering with them as a team to meet customer needs, which helps integrate the service supply chain. However, the ability to integrate service supply chains is sometimes limited by the huge numbers of customer-supplier linkages. With the example

Unit 4

above, a film processing company may serve hundreds of photographers, who each serve hundreds of end customers. It can be difficult or impractical to form partnering relationships of those magnitudes. (see *Mass Alliances* SBP)

How it impacts decisions... Companies must decide when and to what extent it is appropriate to partner with various suppliers. Partnering implies communicating more information than just the current requirements. Usually, establishing a partnering relationship with a suppliers is only practical when purchase volumes justify the effort. (see *Mass Alliances* SBP)

What to do about it... As appropriate, get to know your suppliers. Recognize that if your suppliers do a better job, it can enable you to do a better job.

Also, seek to know what the needs and concerns of your customers are. If your customers have customers, it is valuable to know the needs of those second-tier customers as well. You will be more successful if you are able to help your customers meet the needs of their customers.

For example... An often-cited example of an integrated supply chain involves Wal-Mart, who has extensive communication with suppliers. Wal-Mart has a satellite system in which store sales data is transmitted to central locations. From there, vendors (suppliers) and manufacturers can access the data and use it to be more responsive to Wal-Mart customer demand.

A large auto repair chain was receiving complaints from customers that newly installed brakes were squeaking. At first, the company responded by reporting that brakes can squeak even when properly installed. This was little consolation to customers who did not want squeaky breaks. The company response could easily be perceived to be passing blame to the brake shoe suppliers. When the company realized their response was inadequate, they decided to change to a supplier of brake shoes that did not squeak.

Likewise, other service companies of necessity rely on suppliers for whom they are accountable. Bug exterminators rely on chemical companies for various sprays and poisons that may have harmful effects on customers' landscaping. Dentists rely on suppliers of teeth x-ray films that have been known to be quite painful in patients' mouths. Shoe repair shops rely on suppliers of replacement soles that may be uncomfortable to wear. Motel chains rely on suppliers of in-wall air conditioning units that have been known to operate loudly on warm summer nights. In each case, the customer blames problems with the supplied items on the service provider, not on the supplier of those items. Service providers need to be aware of problems with supplied materials, and communicate that information up the supply chain as appropriate. It can also be useful to communicate positive information about supplied products up the supply chain.

A major supplier to law firms is law schools, who supply graduates. Law firms want high quality graduates. If the admissions process at a law school is inadequate, the quality of students will likely suffer. Also, if there is a gap in the curriculum, and graduates are inadequately trained in a certain area, it can be detrimental to hiring firms. Thus it is advantageous for a law firm that frequently recruits at a particular law school to partner with that school in the specification of curriculum and other requirements of students.

An example of a service business employing a service supplier is a doctor's office. When blood tests are required, the doctor or nurse may draw the blood from the patient, but it is often an outside laboratory that conducts the tests. Then when the tests are complete, the test results are returned to the doctor or nurse, who reports the findings to the patient. The doctor's office is an intermediary between the patient and the laboratory, and is thus responsible for assuring that the various inputs are adequate for production capabilities. For example, some blood tests may be invalidated if the patient has eaten a sugary food just prior to the time blood is drawn. Someone at the doctor's office needs to relay that information to the patient in a timely manner.

Various types of retailers employ process-suppliers. For example, customers can purchase home improvement materials at Home Depot types of stores and at the same place arrange to have them installed. Home improvement stores generally do not employ all of the various types of installation workers themselves, but have arrangements with subcontractors from the local community. It is good for home improvement stores to communicate customer requirements to installation subcontractors, *and* to communicate installation subcontractor requirements to customers. For example, customers should be informed if there are certain types of materials that installers are unable to install effectively, such as odd-thickness drywall, so that the customers will not purchase them and then be disappointed with the installation results.

Architectural firms often call on engineering firms to supply the engineering process of building design. The architectural firm may become aware of client requirement information that will help the engineering firm more fully provide a quality service. In addition, the architectural firm may become aware of engineering firm requirement information that would help the customer more fully contribute to the quality of engineering. For example, engineers may require a certain type of geological report regarding the building site (called a geotechnical or soils report) in order to minimize the likelihood of structural damage due to soil shifts. Architectural firms need to manage product flows and requirements communications in both directions of the supply chain.

My airline application... Who supplies the so-called "food" to airlines? How is it that a passenger can order the beef on one flight and the chicken on the next, and find it hard to tell the difference? Some airlines may produce the food in their own kitchens, while others may subcontract it to outside suppliers. In either case, there is a need to communicate customer reactions back to food suppliers.

Airlines often employ service-suppliers. For example, major airlines often do not service small towns, but have commuter airline partners that feed into the major airline routes. When I call a major airline to request a flight from Appleton, Wisconsin to Charlottesville, Virginia, they will likely book me on a commuter airline flight at each end connected by a major airline flight in the middle. Those commuter airline partners are process suppliers who act on the major airlines customer input, the physical passenger and baggage. Good supply chain management dictates that we communicate to our suppliers what our customers' requirements are. Obviously, this includes communicating to the commuter airline partners what our passengers need, such as flights at certain times of the day. Less obvious is the need for communicating to the *passengers* what the commuter airline partners' requirements are, so that those partners can then more effectively serve the customer.

For example, some commuter airlines have planes that are so small that it is impossible to hang garment bags or have more than one tiny carry-on bag in the plane. (On one commuter flight I flew on, the passengers had to bend over to make their way to their seats–and *every* passenger got a window and an aisle seat at the same time.) Think how upset passengers would be if their baggage inputs were not well-received by a commuter airline partner–if their soft-sided garment bag could not be hung up but had to be stuffed in a tiny compartment. Further, think of the awkward position that the commuter airline partner would be in when the booking airline fails to inform customers of the restriction, and the passenger shows up with baggage problems.

Supply chain management for airlines includes assuring that relevant requirement and process restriction information are communicated across the supply chain.

How manufacturing differs from services...

With manufacturing, the supply chain management trend is to increase responsiveness to customer needs by closer coordination throughout the supply chain. Since this usually implies that suppliers act on customer information, we might say that the trend is for manufacturing supply chains to behave more like services in some respects.

Quantitative analysis... (covered at the discretion of the instructor)

A logistic problem that occurs in product supply chains is known as the "transportation problem," in which a number of supply locations need to be linked up with a number of demand locations. The question of the transportation problem is how to most efficiently meet the demand with the available supply. The problem is often formulated as a linear program. Fitzsimmons2 page 563 discusses this problem.

SBP 4a: Supply Chain Linkages   Name (if turned in):_____

Analysis questions...   To help apply this Service Business Principle, consider and answer the following questions about your specific service business process. (❑Check here if you are going outside of your target service business.)

Service company/business:_____

The service process:_____
① Besides customers, who are the major suppliers to your service process? Who supplies equipment? materials and supplies? energy? knowledge and technology?
② Who are the major suppliers to those suppliers from question ①?
③ In what ways does your service business rely on the supplier's suppliers? What happens if a supplier's supplier fails to perform as required?
④ Does your service business employ external service-suppliers as part of the service process? Who?
⑤ What communication and/or partnering does or should occur with these various suppliers?

Unit 4

①_____

_____

_____

_____

_____

_____

_____

_____

_____

_____

_____

_____

_____

_____

_____

_____

SBP 4a: Supply Chain Linkages   Name (if turned in):_____

Application exercise...

Also to help you apply this Service Business Principle, complete the following analysis with regard to your specific service business process, or another service process in your business. (☐Check here if you are going outside of your target service business, which was _____.)

Service company/business:_____

The service process:_____

Identify a major non-customer input to your service process and diagram the supply chain for that process: List the type of company that supplies that input, and what type of company supplies to that supplier. Proceed backward to the "raw materials." For each step in the supply chain, identify a potential process problem that impacts the end customer, such as poor quality or delayed production, and list how that failure would impact the end service process. Identify what information might be shared up the supply chain to help prevent that problem from repeating.

If submitting this Application Exercise electronically, you may choose to use the FlowViewer language. The following is an example using that language:

```
#imply eol
#begin flowchart
#heading Steps of the Airline Meal Supply Chain
[cattle ranchers];problem if supply is well below demand.
      !cows
[meat packing plant];problem if excessive use of fillers.
      !packaged meat
[meat distributor];problem if meat spends too long in inventory.
      !delivered meat
[food preparation kitchen];problem if ignores passenger dietary restrictions.
      !packaged meals
[meal preparation on plane];problem if food not heated properly.
      !prepared meals
[delivery of food to passenger]
#end flowchart
Information that airlines can share upstream in this process includes...
```

Preparation for the next Service Business Principle (4b)

To consider... Before proceeding, consider the following and write thoughts and ideas below:

The Unified Services Theory states that the fundamental difference between manufacturing processes and service processes is the absence or presence of customer-provided inputs. What about manufacturing in which the customer specifies how they want the product to be?—could not those specifications be considered to be customer-information inputs into the manufacturing process? How would customer manufacturing fit in to the Unified Services Theory? Should custom manufacturing be managed differently than non-custom manufacturing? (Consider the importance of employees' communications skills, quality management techniques, efficiency and effectiveness objectives, etc.)

_____

_____

_____

_____

_____

_____

_____

_____

Service Business Principle 4b:

THE CUSTOM MANUFACTURING OXYMORON

Service Business Principle	*"With manufacturing, the introduction of custom processes represents customer-information input, therefore causes the process to behave like a service. The paradigms and systems for successfully managing custom manufacturing are dramatically different from those warranted for non-custom manufacturing."*

Why it occurs...   THE CUSTOM MANUFACTURING OXYMORON occurs because the advantages of manufacturing come from the lack of customer inputs. When customers provide information as an input to the production process, the particular challenges found in managing services begin to emerge.

Closely related to...   SBP: *Potential Operating Objectives*

Details...   (An oxymoron is a phrase that appears to contradict itself, such as "jumbo shrimp.")

A business case about a company[6] that produces reverse vending machines (automatic container recycle machines) asks the question "is [the company] selling machines or solutions?" The question was one of a potential need to either standardize or customize production. Is there a difference between selling machines and selling (custom) solutions? This Service Business Principle acknowledges that there is a very real difference.

Recall from the *Weighting the Mixture* Service Business Principle that the degree of service intensity in a production process is related to the significance of customer inputs and the value-added which is ascribed to those inputs. If a manufacturing process has customer-information inputs that lead to customization, then that process is to some degree a service process, and service management issues apply. In some cases, the product is highly customized, where the customer provides extensive information towards specifying the product. An example might be custom home building, where the customer may specify minute details. Another example would be custom computer chip manufacturing, where the customer specifies details about chip functions and perhaps even the exact schematics (detailed diagrams) of the product.

Other custom-manufacturing is only custom in a superficial sense, meaning that the customer only provides minor amounts of information about the overall product. One example is when a customer places a special order for an automobile. The special order may indicate the color of the paint and the type of upholstery. However these specifications are generally from a list of very specific options. The special order will say nothing about how to design the automobile nor about how to apply even the specified product features. Thus, the customer-information inputs are so minute and minor, relative to the non-customer information inputs, that the overall production process is hardly affected. As a result, such superficially-custom manufacturing can be managed as practically pure manufacturing without too adverse of consequences.

In fact, most of the actual customization of automobiles takes place at the dealership. Features such as stereo system, exterior trim, and presence of reading lamps are dealer-installed options that the customer selects before taking delivery. Postponing these custom features to the dealership makes good sense, since the dealer is equipped and skilled at dealing with customer-information inputs, whereas the factory is not.

---

[6] Halton System Group, Brigham Young University: Provo, Utah.

There are a few automobile companies that allow customers to give more detailed product specifications, such as the exact wood to use to make the dashboard. That is a very different situation than the mass-production example described in the past few paragraph. Nevertheless, many so-called "custom-manufacturers" in fact provide dramatically limited options for customization so as to not forfeit the ease and advantages of non-service production.

A topic which has been discussed in management literature recently is *mass customization*, which attempts to blend the benefits of manufacturing with the challenges and opportunities of managing services. Manufacturers implement mass customization by producing introducing customer inputs (order specifications) just prior to final assembly. Up until that point, the manufacturer obtains or produces a relatively finite number of product components. When they receive the customer order, they quickly assemble the final product from the selected components. (This approach has been called a "T" production process. The letter "T" is narrow at the bottom but wide at the top, which symbolizes a narrow number of component parts throughout much of the process, but a great variety that is possible at final assembly.)

Unit 4

With current manufacturing technologies, mass customization will generally not work if customization permeates the entire production process, due to the loss of efficiencies and economies of scale. The fact is, the per-item cost of an item produced in a custom process is much greater than for the same item produced in a mass-production process. Almost every manufactured good is an example. For example, you can purchase a nice alarm clock for perhaps US$20, but having someone make a completely custom-designed alarm clock would cost thousands of dollars. (Only the government is allowed to pay prices like that–see the NASA example below.)

Manufacturing companies typically have the "mass" portion, but not the "customization" portion. With service companies it is just the opposite. Service companies tend to have a degree of customization based on customer inputs. Service companies implement mass customization by introducing mass-production techniques, which are procedures and technologies that introduce high efficiency and allow many customers to be served as required. An example of a technology approach is World Wide Web-based retail, where customer browse product descriptions and place orders on-line. A characteristic of this example that also assists service mass customization is the greater involvement of customer labor. When each customer provides their own service labor, the service provider is typically able to meet surges in demand without straining employee resources.

One other way to implement service mass customization is to standardize the service offerings and simply let customers choose the combination they want. This is like college education, which offers a standard offering of courses that students can choose from to gain a customized education.

How it impacts decisions... Custom manufacturing should not be managed the same as standardized manufacturing. Custom manufacturing requires managers that have service skills commensurate with the extent of customization.

What to do about it... If a manufacturing process involves some degree of customization, by postponing customization some advantages of mass production can be recaptured.

For example... There has been a recent and highly successful trend on the part of computer manufacturers to not assemble the customer's computer system until *after* they have ordered it and indicated the desired options. Thus, they allow some degree of customization. Yet, these companies are still able to maintain many of the advantages of mass-production manufacturing. How do they do it? In fact, the customization only takes place *at final assembly*. All of the assembled components such as disk drives, memory chips, video cards, etc. are kept in inventory waiting for a customer order (or manufactured by suppliers just in time for use). Thus, perhaps 99 percent of the process to make a computer has been completed, and all that is left is final assembly and final testing. When the customer indicates her selections (provides her information input), the company simply assembles the final product from the various components, and ships it. That final assembly is one of the most difficult to manage of the entire production process. Why? Because it behaves more like a service than other process segments (due to the customer-information inputs). For example, if there is an October lull in demand for disk drives with an expected large increase in demand in November, the disk drive facility can simply inventory the drives produced in October. However, if there is an October lull in demand for custom-assembled computer systems before the anticipated Christmas rush, it is not possible or practical to custom-assemble systems to inventory—the customers' wants could differ from the inventory configurations. (The company may produce some standard-configuration models for inventory to help with that problem.)

Why do people place special orders at fast food restaurants like McDonald's? It is often because they want to undermine the mass-production food manufacturing process (cooking food in anticipation of demand and inventorying it under heat lamps) and forcing the restaurant to make a product based on customer inputs. In fact, some people make a special request they don't even care about—such as to hold the catchup even though they like catchup—so that the cook will have to use that customer-input in the process. (Then the customer might put catchup on the food anyway.) You can be assured that if every lunch-time customer at a busy restaurant demanded customized production, the ability to process customers in a timely manner would be seriously hindered. So, companies who proclaim "Have it your way" have to rely on relatively few customers actually making dramatic customization requests.

To illustrate how much less-efficient custom manufacturing is from mass-production manufacturing, consider the efforts of NASA (the National Aeronautical and Space Administration) to procure tools like screwdrivers and hammers. A good hammer costs US$20 or US$30 at a hardware store, and costs much less than that to manufacture. However, when NASA has engineers design a hammer to meet certain specifications, then creates custom dies and molds to create the hammer, it is no surprise that the resulting hammer costs US$1000 or more. It may or may not be practical to just use a hardware store hammer instead. If it must be a custom hammer, then the high price is not as unreasonable as the media makes it out to be.

My airline application... Boeing has been called a manufacturer of jet airplanes. However, anyone who has studied their manufacturing process will see that it is replete with service elements and issues. Why is this the case? It is because of the extensive amount of customization (customer-information input) involved in making an airplane. By and large, every jumbo jet off of the assembly line is potentially unique. It would be a dramatic exaggeration to say that these commercial jumbo jets are mass produced. However, during times of war, we would imagine that productivity would need to be much greater in making military jets. The way to free the process from the management challenges of services management is to eliminate the individual customer-information inputs. In other words, during such times the military would request numerous jets with exactly the same configuration, regardless of the division or branch of the military they would ultimately be used by.

How manufacturing differs from services...

With manufacturing, that is with non-custom manufacturing, there are no direct customer inputs into the production process, decreasing the likelihood that the challenges of services management will occur.

SBP 4b: The Custom Manufacturing Oxymoron   Name (if turned in):_____

Analysis questions...   To help apply this Service Business Principle. consider and answer the following questions about your specific service business process. (❑Check here if you are going outside of your target service business.)

Service company/business:_____

The service process:_____
   (These questions should be asked about a manufacturing process, perhaps one that provides facilitating goods or supporting facilities for your service process.)
   ① In what ways are the manufactured products customized?
   ② In the manufacturing process, how much of production takes place before customizing stages?
   ③ Can the point of customization be shifted to later in the process? What would be the effects?

①_____

_____

_____

_____

_____

_____

_____

_____

_____

_____

_____

_____

_____

_____

_____

_____

_____

SBP 4b: The Custom Manufacturing Oxymoron   Name (if turned in):_____

Application exercise...

Also to help you apply this Service Business Principle, complete the following analysis with regard to your specific service business process, or another service process in your business. (❑Check here if you are going outside of your target service business, which was _____.)

Service company/business:_____

The service process:_____

Identify a manufactured input to your service process that is mass produced. Your example might be anything from a pencil to a copy machine. List the item and how much you typically would pay for one. Next, create a list of half-a-dozen specifications for a version of the item which would be custom manufactured. Your specifications should describe the item as unique, different from anything currently available on the market (such as a pencil with two leads). List the extra steps a manufacturer would have to go through to make one of the items to meet your custom specifications. How much do you think the custom-manufactured item would cost?

Preparation for the next Service Business Principle (4c)

To consider... Before proceeding, consider the following and write thoughts and ideas below:

Previously, a plunger that a customer would use to unclog a drain was compared to a plumber that would be hired to unclog a drain. The plunger is considered a manufactured good, and the plumber is considered a service provider. However, either can be employed to accomplish the same task. What would you consider to be the fundamental difference(s) between the plunger and the plumber? Can any of the differences you are thinking of be generalized to distinguish between manufactured goods and substitute services?

Unit 4

_____

_____

_____

_____

_____

_____

_____

_____

Service Business Principle 4c:

THE SERVER-OWNERSHIP PERSPECTIVE

Service Business Principle	*"With manufactured goods, the customer takes ownership (or extended possession) of the service provider. Therefore, manufacturers are typically service-provider providers."*

Why it occurs... THE SERVER-OWNERSHIP PERSPECTIVE occurs because all production occurs to meet the needs of the customer. Customers only purchase based on needs. (Avoid trivializing that important truism.)

Details... This principle states that manufactured goods are simply service providers that the customer takes ownership of. The manufacturing process is not said to be a service process. However, when the customer uses the manufactured good to meet a need, that is a self-service process! (What might be considered a "post-production process" as defined in the *Defining the Process* Service Business Principle.) Therefore, manufacturers do not *serve* the customers directly, but serve them through their products. Manufacturers are wise to assure that customers will be able to use the product to serve themselves and fill their specific need(s).

Here is a useful approach to understanding the commonalty between many manufactured goods and substitute services. For any good or service, ask the question "Why is it necessary?" You may have to ask the question a few different times before you arrive at the root reason why the good or service is necessary. This root reason why a good or service exists is what some call the "core benefit." You will see that the core benefit of goods and substitute services is the same.

With the plunger versus plumber example, we observe the same core benefit. Why is a plunger necessary? Because we have a plugged drain? Lets say it is a sink drain. Why does it need to be unplugged? Because we want to use the drain again? Why do we want to use it again? Because eventually we will have a physical need, such as washing our hands, that the drain will facilitate. Why do we need to wash our hands? Because we believe we will be ill or disgusted if we do not wash our hands? Why don't we want to be ill or disgusted? Because we think that will prevent us from being happy (or from feeling good, or whatever you call it).

Now we really did not need to go through that many "Whys" to get to a root reason for the plunger that is in common with the plumber. In fact, right off of the bat we would see a commonality in why we would employ one or another. So, why do some people choose one over the other? This Service Business Principle indicates that much of the decision comes down to advantages and disadvantages of ownership.

There are a number of reasons in favor of employing the plunger (that we would own). The plunger typically costs a lot less than the plumber, even if you only use it once. The plunger is self-serve drain unclogging, and thus is available twenty-four hours a day, seven days a week. Plumbers may also be available over such a time span, but the cost differential is dramatically increased. Since you own the plunger, you know where it has been used in the past, which may bring peace of mind. Perhaps best of all, the plunger is available on a second's notice, whereas even the speediest plumber will take perhaps thirty minutes to get to your house.

In defense of plumbers, there are a number of advantages to not taking ownership of the service provider (the plumber). For one, the plumber is free to serve the needs of many different people, thus experience economies of scale to study and learn much more about plumbing. One would expect that employing a plumber would require much less effort on the part of the customer than employing the self-serve plunger. (Which is what you hopefully are paying for.) Some plumbers guarantee the result, but plungers don't come with such a guarantee. Finally, the plumber is equipped to serve a greater variety of needs than a plunger. (The plumber may find and fix a plug caused by a bent pipe, which the plunger will not fix.)

In some cases, a product with a common core benefit is not a obvious. For example, we may hire a lawyer to write us a real estate contract. Why? Because we want security in knowing that an agreement is enforceable. Why? Because agreements that are not enforceable can lead to foreclosed property. Why is this bad? Because if we did not have the property, we would be unhappy (or something like that). Well, ultimately we are seeking a benefit of not just a legal document (the contract) but of *security* by hiring a lawyer. We could get the same security if we knew everything about real estate law ourselves. And for that, we could purchase books and get our own security by doing it ourselves and becoming a legal expert. But perhaps that would be a bit costly in time and effort. (I don't think lawyers feel too threatened by books, but perhaps they do by the recent "do-it-yourself" legal software.)

Unit 4

How it impacts decisions...   Capital expenditures (ownership) often trade off against hiring (employing service); the decision to make a capital expenditure should consider the benefits and costs of ownership. Managers need to know what ownership implies.

For example...   The following example was brought up by the North American Industrial Classification System committee in a document defining service businesses[7]: In what sense is a painter different from a paint manufacturer? (or a painting equipment manufacturer) A person can hire a painter to paint a house, or can purchase the equipment and paint and do it himself. They both can meet the same core need. The primary difference is in ownership and implications thereof.

Buying a music CD and going to a concert both fill the need for music entertainment. The music CD is a manufactured good that the customer uses. The concert is a service that requires customer-self inputs in order to produce. (It would be pointless to have a concert without any listeners present.) With a CD, the customer takes ownership of the service provider. With the concert, the customer does not take ownership of the service provider—the music group. There are certainly advantages and disadvantages to each, and each can meet slightly different needs.

What about a CD that a person would rent from a music store and return a few days later? Who owns that service provider? In that case, the customer of the CD manufacturer is the music store. The music store takes ownership of the CD to use it to provide a service of attracting customers. The music store provides a service to the customer by making the CD available. Music stores cannot rent out CDs unless customers arrive and present their tastes. Finally, the customer uses the rented CD to serve their own need until the rental period is over.

Note that the Service Business Principle includes the phrase "or extended possession." This is because some manufacturers, such as automobile manufacturers, have disguised the sale of their goods into long-term leases. There are tax and cash flow advantages to leases. Since the leases are long-term, the company does not have to be too involved in the service process of managing the day-to-day use of the vehicle. (Not nearly as much as a car rental company, with short-term rentals).

My airline application...   An airline provides passenger transportation, but is there a reasonable substitute product that the customer could take ownership of? Is it reasonable for the typical

---

[7] Committee, E. C. P. (1994). Service Classifications. Document #6, Economic Classification Policy Committee, Bureau of Economic Analysis, U.S. Department of Commerce, Washington, D.C.

airline customer to instead purchase an airplane and learn to fly to meet his or her air transportation needs? Probably not. However, there are substitute manufactured products that compete with air service. An executive from a very successful discount airline told a group of my students that they considered their primary competitor to be the family car! What he was observing was that a family may choose to drive to a National Park or other recreation to "get away," or they may fly to a city of interest. So, their objective would be to make air transportation as convenient and cost effective as making payments on, say, a Sport Utility Vehicle. (Or even just driving the station wagon already owned.) The there are common core benefits between air transportation and taking a driving vacation in a vehicle one owns.

We could also look at the options for goods or services to the airline itself. An airline founded in Salt Lake City, Utah, Morris Air, began doing business by offering flights to various locations. The airline owned none of the jets, but chartered them from other (service) companies and sold the seats to their customers. Eventually the company was bought out and shifted to jets which were owned by the company (purchased from manufacturers or purchased used). As you might imagine, there are dramatic advantages and disadvantages of either approach.

Quantitative analysis... (covered at the discretion of the instructor)

Breakeven Analysis (applied to customer's hire versus buy-and-do-it-myself tradeoff decision)
Conjoint Analysis (a customer survey method which can be used to estimating monetary values for non-monetary costs associated with hire versus buy-and-do-it-myself tradeoff decisions)

SBP 4c: The Server-Ownership Perspective   Name (if turned in):_____

Analysis questions...   To help apply this Service Business Principle, consider and answer the following questions about your specific service business process. (❑Check here if you are going outside of your target service business.)

Service company/business:_____

The service process:_____
   (These questions should be asked about a manufacturing process, perhaps one that provides facilitating goods for your service process.)
   ① Is there a substitute service for that good?
   ② Why would one purchase the good instead of using the service provider? What are the advantages of ownership? Cost? Convenience? Control?

① _____

_____

_____

_____

_____

_____

_____

_____

_____

_____

_____

_____

_____

_____

_____

_____

SBP 4c: The Server-Ownership Perspective   Name (if turned in):_____

Application exercise...   Also to help you apply this Service Business Principle, complete the following analysis with regard to your specific service business process, or another service process in your business. (☐Check here if you are going outside of your target service business, which was _____.)

Service company/business:_____

The service process:_____

    Is it possible for customers to buy a manufactured good or goods as a substitute for the service process? What would those goods be? What are some of the costs to the customer of that self-serve approach? Consider costs of the goods, costs of inconvenience, costs of skill acquisition, costs of quality control, etc. Attempt to quantify those costs by estimating what a customer would be willing to pay to avoid each. (For example, how much would a customer be willing to pay to avoid the inconvenience of doing it herself?) Compare that cost with the cost of having you provide the service. What costs of ownership and self-service are most likely to keep customers coming to you for the service?

Preparation for the next Service Business Principle (4d)

To consider... Before proceeding, consider the following and write thoughts and ideas below:

If a production process does not involve customer inputs but still exhibits a "Symptom of Service" outlined in the previous unit, does that mean it is a service? No. The symptoms of services (discussed in Units 2 and 3) are caused by customer inputs, but in some instances can be caused by other reasons. (Just because a process has a service symptom does not assure it is a service process.) Consider the following examples. Is electric power generation a service process or a manufacturing process? Do any symptoms of service apply? Why? Is movie production a service process or a manufacturing process? Why?

_____

_____

_____

_____

_____

_____

_____

_____

_____

Service Business Principle 4d:

MANUFACTURING IN SHEEP'S CLOTHING

Service Business Principle	*"All manufacturing is not alike. Manufacturing where most of the value is added in product development is often mistaken for services. Other manufacturing is mistaken for services because of service symptoms not caused by the Unified Services Theory."*

Why it occurs...   MANUFACTURING IN SHEEP'S CLOTHING occurs because the symptoms of service, although caused by the UST, can also be caused by other factors. Also, manufacturers serve customers indirectly through their goods. (As discussed under *The Server-Ownership Perspective* Service Business Principle)

Details...   Units 2 and 3 introduced some fundamental characteristics of service businesses. Those characteristics are "symptoms" of a service business–they occur as a result of a business being a service, but they do not conclusively define a service as a service. (A service is a service by the Unified Services Theory.)

First, an analogy. The symptoms of influenza include muscle soreness, nasal congestion, fever, and so forth. If a person has influenza, they are likely to experience those symptoms. However, if they have those symptoms, it does not necessarily mean they have the flu. Muscle soreness can be caused by strain, nasal congestion by allergies, fever by other viruses. Influenza is caused by the presence of the influenza virus, not by the symptoms. Just as symptoms of influenza can be attributed to other causes, the symptoms of services can sometimes be caused by things other than the Unified Services Theory. The presence of service symptoms does not make a process a service.

For example, what input does an electric power generation company receive from customers in the production process? None. They can produce power to their heart's content without any inputs from customers. Therefore, the Unified Services Theory prescribes that electric power generation is a manufacturing process, not a service process. Then why is it that power is produced just as customers demand it (simultaneous production and consumption), and not inventoried? The answer is because of technical and cost limitations. Where would power companies inventory electricity? In huge batteries. However, it would be so costly (if not impossible) to construct batteries capable of storing much demand for power, that the companies resort instead to demand-driven (just-in-time) production.

Do movie studios require customer inputs in the process of making movies? If we consider the customers to be theaters or the movie viewers, the answer again is no. The studios may gain a survey of viewer preferences, but still do not require any inputs from individual customers in order to make movies. Even though movie production is not a service process, some of the symptoms of services still occur. Movie production tends to be very labor-intensive. Why? Probably because of the large creative element involved. The actual process of copying the finished film for distribution to theaters is probably not very labor-intensive. With movies it is difficult to measure output and quality, and there is certainly heterogeneous production. A 120 minute movie is not 20 percent better than a 100 minute movie. Again, these symptoms are probably caused by the large creative element involved in movie making.

The movie production example is one where most of the value of the finished product is generated in product devolvement (as per wording of the Service Business Principle). If one were to consider an actual roll of film, the film material itself is of very little value. It is the ideas and creative development recorded on the film that give the film value.

How it impacts decisions... It is important to understand the Unified Services Theory. Service symptoms not caused by the Unified Services Theory should be addressed, but the overall process may still be managed as a manufacturing process.

For example... Let us consider software publishers. Are companies that write and mass-market computer software service providers? Surely the technical support process is a service process—dependant on the input of customer questions and problems. But what about the process of writing and producing the software? Again, there are no individual customer inputs involved (although most software publishers survey customers to identify bugs and get ideas for new product features). Software does involve a sense of intangibility—computer code may be represented in magnetic form, but the ideas it represents are quite intangible. The software writing process is somewhat labor-intensive, which keeps many computer programmers employed. However, the process of copying the finished product onto disks for distribution is probably not labor-intensive. Software is quite variable and heterogeneous, and it is difficult to measure output. These symptoms are likely to occur due to the creative nature of the software development process.

Is a cable-TV company a service company? What is the primary production process of a cable-TV company? Recalling the *Identifying the Customer* Service Business Principle, who is the customer? The cable-TV viewer seems to be the customer. What is the cable-TV company's production process. It is likely receiving satellite signals which are amplified and channeled to customers' homes. What customer inputs are there into that process? Probably none. The customer just selects and views the output. The signals are not inventoried by the company, although they could be inventoried on videotape. For legal reasons, cable companies are prohibited from recording signals and later distributing them for profit. Despite the presence of some symptoms of services, (non-interactive) cable-TV companies are assemblers of electronic signals which they procure from suppliers and thus fit the manufacturing model.

What about airwave broadcast television? Are they a service provider, or a manufacturer? Do airwave broadcasters require customer inputs in the production process? Are the customers the viewers? Well, they are not direct customers, but are the critical audience. Viewers do not compensate the airwave broadcaster, but advertisers do. The broadcasters receive advertisement inputs from customers, package them with programming, and thus try to get the critical audience (viewers) to watch the result. (This is different from cable-TV, which often has no advertising that is paid to the cable company.) Thus, the reason we would expect the symptoms of services to occur for airwave television broadcasting is because it *is* a service process, as defined by the Unified Services Theory.

My airline application... We previously established that as a highly custom jumbo jet manufacturer, Boeing in fact acts as a service provider. Another part of the company makes helicopters. For the sake of discussion, lets suppose that the helicopters are manufactured as a standardized product. Therefore, the process would be a manufacturing process. Even if they were standardized, they are probably still only produced as customers order them. Why? Not because the company is waiting for customer inputs. Instead it is likely because each helicopter may sell for the better part of a million dollars, and the costs of keeping finished helicopters in inventory would be too expensive. Therefore a symptom of service—*Impracticability to Inventory*—occurs for a reason other than customer inputs.

Unit 4

SBP 4d: Manufacturing in Sheep's Clothing   Name (if turned in):_____

Analysis questions... To help apply this Service Business Principle, consider and answer the following questions about your specific service business process. (❏Check here if you are going outside of your target service business.)

Service company/business:_____

The service process:_____
   (These questions should be asked about a manufacturing process, perhaps one that provides facilitating goods for your service process.)
   ① Does the production process require customer inputs besides selection of output?
   ② What symptoms of services exist in the manufacturing process? Why? Are they caused by customer inputs, or other practicalities?

①_____

_____

_____

_____

_____

_____

_____

_____

_____

_____

_____

_____

_____

_____

_____

_____

_____

_____

SBP 4d: Manufacturing in Sheep's Clothing   Name (if turned in):_____

Application exercise...
Also to help you apply this Service Business Principle, complete the following analysis with regard to your specific service business process, or another service process in your business. (❑Check here if you are going outside of your target service business, which was _____.)

Service company/business:_____

The service process:_____
   Think of a manufacturing process that could either substitute for your service process or provide facilitating goods for your service process. Write what that substitute is. Which of the ideas covered in the Fundamentals units seem to apply for that process? Why do they occur? (If it is actually a manufacturing process, then the reason for the symptoms will be other than "customer inputs.")

Part II - Service Business Strategy
Unit 5:
IDENTIFYING STRATEGIC OPPORTUNITIES

In this unit, we will consider strategic issues which follow from the Unified Services Theory and which give companies strategic advantage. There are two ways to view strategic advantages. The traditional perspective is to gain "competitive advantage"—or the ability to excel above the other companies who serve the same customer needs. A new perspective is to gain "contributive advantage"—which is an ability to contribute in a way that you were not able to previously. These two perspectives are related, but different. For example, the "competitive advantage" paradigm requires the presence of competition, and breaks down in monopolistic situations such as governments. This is because competitive advantage focuses on besting the competitor—and no impending competitor means no need for advantage. The "contributive advantage" focuses on increasing one's ability to serve, recognizing that both the service provider and the customer benefit from better serviceability. (For example, employees are generally happier and more conscientious when they feel they are contributing more.)

The Service Business Principles outlined in this unit have application under either a contributive advantage or a contributive advantage objective, and thus are not limited to competitive situations.

Unit reading... The following reading pertains to Service Business Principles included in this unit. The instructor will let you know which of the readings you are responsible for studying.

Fitzsimmons2 chapter 3 on Service Strategy

Preparation for the next Service Business Principle (5a)

To consider... Before proceeding, consider the following and write thoughts and ideas below:

Despite the inherently dynamic nature of service businesses, surprisingly few service companies are truly innovative. Even fewer companies use innovation for sustainable competitive advantage. Think of some service companies that are known for their innovation? What types of innovations have they employed? Where do you suppose they got the ideas for those innovations? Where might companies look for innovation ideas for future competitive advantage?

_____

_____

_____

_____

_____

_____

_____

_____

Service Business Principle 5a:

LIKENING A SERVICE

Service Business Principle	*"With services, significant strategic insights come from defining the process and identifying services with similar processes."*

Why it occurs...   LIKENING A SERVICE occurs because the Unified Services Theory and its symptoms reveal commonalities between what otherwise might seem like disparate businesses. In other words, as we come to understand the Unified Services Theory, we will see that strategic innovations in one service industry can be applicable in different but related industries.

Details...   The way we "liken" a service process is to explore what other service processes it is like. To do this, we begin by identifying key process features. Christopher Lovelock discussed a good way to do this in his article "Classifying Services to Gain Strategic Marketing Insights" [Journal of Marketing, Vol. 47, Summer 1983, p. 12]. (Our purpose in classifying services is to gain more than just marketing insights—we will also seek to gain strategic operational insights, strategic human resource management insights, etc.)

An examples of Lovelock's analysis looks at services on a 2x2 matrix. On one dimension he identifies whether the service is directed at "people" (i.e. customers) or "things" (customer's belongings). On the other dimension he identifies if the nature of the service act is "tangible actions" (i.e. physically manipulate the customer or their belongings) or "intangible actions" (not manipulating things physically, but perhaps manipulating information). Lovelock then places various service industries in each of the four boxes of the resulting 2x2 matrix. For example, in the box for the direct recipient of the service being people and the nature of the service act being "tangible actions," Lovelock places: health care, passenger transportation, beauty salons, exercise clinics, restaurants, and hair cutting. The implication is that these six industries share process elements in common. Is that true??? For example, is health care in fact similar to passenger transportation??? Let's explore this further...

Both health care and passenger transportation manipulate customers' selves: health care changes the customer to promote improved health and passenger transportation changes the customers to a new (and improved) location. We might observe that in both cases the process of being changed is less than enjoyable to the customer—something customers feel that have to do—but the final result (or "output") is often much more desirable than the process. So, imagine that you are a health care provider with the problem that customers perceive the health care service delivery as generally cold and not very personable (which is a fair assessment of much of health care). Well, in fact, we may observe that passenger transportation is also generally cold and not too personable. So, how can we as a health care provider possibly gain strategic insights by studying passenger transportation. Well, we might observe that some passenger transportation companies, such as Southwest Airlines, are able to provide service that is known to be extremely personable—passengers are amazed that flight employees will break into conversation about the passengers' jobs, their families, etc., and that the employees are known to "break through the ice" by having fun with the passengers. (like trivia contests or sing-alongs during the flight) Granted, some air travelers do not care for "fun" or personable service, which fact probably does not cause Southwest too much distress—in some recent years Southwest has had enough passengers to make them the only profitable major U.S. air carrier.

So, perhaps if we are a health care provider, such as a hospital, in a competitive environment, one way we might gain a strategics opportunity is to use Southwest Airline's procedures to provide "fun" and personable health care. We might instruct our employees to get to know patients on a more personable level ("tell me about your job or your family"). Or what about that idea of having a trivia contest in multi-patient rooms? If employees are not busy at the time (which, we have learned, often happens in service situations due to the challenge of matching capacity with demand), why not employ them in improving the personableness of service?

Even if there are reasons why that particular strategic insight might not work, there are surely dozes of other strategic insights we might discover by comparing health care with passenger transportation.

Thus we see one technique for gaining strategic insights by process element comparison: Borrow strategic insights from related industries. (It goes without saying that we can borrow strategic insights from excellent companies in the same industry.)

A second way to gain strategic insights by likening a service is to identify companies that have shifted from one process category to another to gain competitive advantage. Then we can explore how they did it and investigate whether we could gain a strategic advantage by making a similar shift. For example, one disadvantage of health care being a tangible action on customers' selves is that the customer needs to be present at the health care location to receive the service. Customers at remote locations may have to travel a great distance to the health care provider. The same is true for exercise clinics in non-urban settings. One way that exercise clinics have been able to reach people at remote locations is to broadcast exercise programs over public television systems. (Many cities have public access channels that can be used for this service. Also, some cable-TV broadcasters such as ESPN provide this service.)

Unit 5

How could a health care organization provide a service that could be broadcast to remote locations? Health care is much more heterogeneous than exercise programs. What if a health care provider sold remote patients a kit that would allow them to take their own temperature, blood pressure, heart rate, etc. Then, if the patient felt an ailment coming on, they could call in and speak with a nurse who could evaluate the measurements and other symptoms and determine if the patient needs to come in or if they can begin treatment on their own (for example, with over-the-counter drugs). Probably a lot of things people go in for could be handled in that manner. Some health care providers may already be employing such strategic initiatives, but that would just serve to confirm the value of the insight.

Thus, the second method for gaining strategic insights by classifying service processes is to identify advantages and means for shifting some of the production process from one classification to another.

Another way to view this service principle is as a means of effectively "*benchmarking*," which is identifying standards of performance excellence and gaining strategic insights as to how our company might achieve such superior performance. In particular, the principle helps us identify companies in *different* industries that we might use as benchmarks.

Here are a few other comments about Lovelock's matrices. First, he chooses to compare services on two dimensions at a time. Certainly we could compare service on one dimension at a time (identifying more services sharing less commonality) or more than two dimensions at a time (identifying fewer service but with more commonality). Second, Lovelock describes some very useful dimensions for comparing service processes, but many other useful dimensions are sure to exist. One way to identify useful dimensions for classification is to ask: "What is it about this service process that is interesting or is presenting a challenge? How does that categorize this service? What other services fit in this category?"

Third, Lovelock describes mostly two-category dimensions, although some dimensions will have more than two categories. One that Lovelock lists is "Nature of the Interaction between Customer and Service Organization," which includes as categories: (1) customer goes to the service organization, (2) service organization comes to customer, and (3) customer and service organization transact at arm's length (mail or electronic communication).

How it impacts decisions...   Very often the problem in service companies is not so much deciding between alternatives for process improvement, but *coming up* with the alternative to begin with. *Likening a Service* can be a powerful technique for discovering strategic alternatives.

For example...   One major problem in the restaurant industry is that demand tends to be high as a restaurant first opens up—customers are interested in trying it out—but it is increasingly difficult to maintain that customer interest over time. A related classification dimension is whether the company has a formal "membership" relationship with the customer or not. Most restaurants have individual transactions with the customers, with no tie from one visit to the next. Airlines used to be like that, until they introduced frequent flier programs. Discount retailers generally have that same problem, except for companies like Sam's Club, which charges an annual membership fee. Egghead software has a membership that does not require an annual fee, but provides discounts to members who care a "Cue" card. Might restaurants employ frequent visit clubs? Might they charge a nominal fee for a "membership," providing discounts for future business? These ideas would shift the restaurant from the "no formal relationship" category to the "membership relationship" category, thus addressing the "shop around" problem inherent in having no formal relationship. (Again, some restaurants are probably already doing some of these things, which would only verify the value of the insight.)

Along that line, it always amazes me how little effort auto service companies put into developing an ongoing relationship with customers and their cars. We would be quite put off if our physician treated every medical visit as though it was the first. We do not expect physicians to remember everything about patients, but we do expect them to keep good records. Could we not expect that of our auto repair service providers as well? Would it not be helpful if they were able to follow-up on prior repairs? The auto service industry could learn a lot from the best practices of health care, who also "repairs" things.

My airline application...   We previously gave an example of health care learning from an airline. Are there strategic insights that an airline can gain from other industries with process similarities? The following is an example.

One problem that airlines have is that demand fluctuates dramatically over time. What are other industries that are plagued with dramatic demand fluctuations over time? One is certainly tax preparation, with extremely high demand during "tax season" and very little demand during the other times of the year. How do tax accounting firms deal with that problem? They might put their accountants to work during the slow times of the year doing other accounting type of work. (Would it be possible to put airline employees to work during the slow season doing this such as conducting market research or improving communication with corporate customers?) Tax accounting firms also require their employees to work extra time during tax season, but have extended vacations during the slow time. (Could an airline require non-pilot employees to work extra time during the busy times, to earn extra time off during slow times.) Again, some airlines may be employing these strategic insights already, which simply verifies the value of the insight. And how many more insights might we gain through such analysis?

Supplemental reading...   Fitzsimmons2 chapter 3 pages 46-51 on Classifying Services for Strategic Insights.

How manufacturing differs from services...

With manufacturing, commonalities also exist, but manufacturing processes are much more homogeneous, making them easier to compare with one another. Manufacturing process innovations, such as just-in-time production techniques, are often handily applied across a wide variety of manufacturing industries.

SBP 5a: Likening a Service   Name (if turned in):_____

Analysis questions...

To help apply this Service Business Principle, consider and answer the following questions about your specific service business process. (❑Check here if you are going outside of your target service business.)

Service company/business:_____

The service process:_____

① For some service process classification methods such as the following, ask "How does this apply to my service business?": Serving people vs. serving things, tangible actions vs. intangible actions; membership relationship vs. no formal relationship, continuous delivery of service vs. discrete transactions, etc.

② For each categorization, what other industries share that process characteristic?

③ What companies in those industries are effective at addressing that issue, and what do they do?

④ Would that apply to your industry?

⑤ Have related companies moved to a more desirable process positioning? How?

①_____

_____

_____

_____

_____

_____

_____

_____

_____

_____

_____

_____

_____

_____

_____

_____

_____

SBP 5a: Likening a Service   Name (if turned in):_____

Application exercise...   Also to help you apply this Service Business Principle, complete the following analysis with regard to your specific service business process, or another service process in your business. (❑Check here if you are going outside of your target service business, which was _____.)

Service company/business:_____

The service process:_____

Choose two significant dimensions of process classification, such as the ones Lovelock provided or others. Create a 2x2 matrix with one dimension on the horizontal and one on the vertical. Split each dimension into two or three general categories. Identify where your service business process occurs on this matrix. Identify three or four other service industries for each box, possibly using the ideas from Lovelock. Show an example of borrowing strategic insights from a different industry that is in the same box. Show an example of learning from a company that shifted to a different box to gain strategic advantage.

Preparation for the next Service Business Principle (5b)

To consider... Before proceeding, consider the following and write thoughts and ideas below:

The last Service Business Principle discussed a "differentiation" strategy. An important element of that strategy is identifying the most appropriate ways of differentiating. How can we know if a particular means of differentiation will give us any strategic advantage? For example, an automotive service company may consider differentiating by providing a more pleasant waiting room. Is that a good way to differentiate? What is it about potential service features that makes them good ways to differentiate?

_____

_____

_____

_____

_____

_____

_____

_____

Unit 5

Service Business Principle 5b:

IDENTIFYING KEY PRODUCTION ELEMENTS

Service Business Principle	*"With services, the key production process elements are often identified by understanding (a) how their presence or absence motivates the customer, and (b) how we are performing on each of those elements."*

Why it occurs...   IDENTIFYING KEY PRODUCTION ELEMENTS occurs because of the involvement of the customer in the production process. The customer cares not only what is produced, but how it is produced, since he or she has provided inputs to that process.

Closely related to...   Service Business Principles in the units "Defining Service Quality and Value" and "Measuring Service Quality and Productivity," which will be covered later.

Details...   When a company's service excels in a particular way, there are a number of ways this might affect the customer:
(1) it may be of no interest to the customer,
(2) it may satisfy the customer, or
(3) it may delight the customer, producing strong feelings for the company.

The distinction between "satisfying" the customer and "delighting" the customer is one of emotional degree, with "delight" being a much stronger emotional reaction. For example, when your dentist remodels the waiting room to offer *the most comfortable* waiting room chairs of any dentist around, you may be satisfied with the improvement, but not delighted. As such, the excellent chairs will be a factor in choosing a dentist, but not a driving factor. However, if the dentist offered a free foot massage for customers in the waiting room, the result might delight customers and increased loyalty.

So also, if a company does a particularly terrible job at a component of service delivery, the customer may react in different ways such as:
(1) it may be of no interest to the customer,
(2) it may cause the customer to be dissatisfied,
(3) it may cause the customer to be enraged, producing strong negative feelings for the company.

In the case of (2), dissatisfaction, the customer may simply choose to not patronize that service provider at that time, but would happily reconsider the next time (especially if circumstances or needs changed). In the case of (3), enragement, the customer is likely to vow to never do business with that service provider again, and to encourage others to avoid the company.

A few authors, including Terry Hill, have proposed the following terms that describe various characteristics of manufactured products: order-winning criteria (product features that motivate customers to buy our products), qualifiers (product features that qualify our products for the marketplace), and order-losing sensitive (qualifiers that customers tend to be particularly sensitive to).[8] Other authors have adapted that nomenclature somewhat to describe how characteristics of services affect customers.[9] The following is my translation of those adaptations.

---

[8] Terry Hill, Manufacturing Strategy, Irwin, Homewood, Ill. 1989, p. 36-46.
[9] Fitzsimmons2 chapter 2 pages 55-57 on Winning Customers in the Marketplace.
    also e.g. Heineke, J., and Davis, M. M. The Service Quality Priority Model. *Decision Sciences Institute Annual Meeting*, Honolulu, Hawaii, 1886-1888.

- Service **winners** are those characteristics that a company might excel at and thus gain a strong positive affective response from the customer.

- **Losing-sensitive** service characteristics are those that, when done <u>poorly</u>, causes the customer to have strong negative feelings against the service provider. These strong negative feelings often drive a customer's *overall* negative perceptions of the company.

- Service **qualifiers** are those characteristics that, if met to an adequate degree, result in the customer being just satisfied, and if not met to an adequate degree, causes the customer to temporarily not select that service provider. Meeting these characteristics to a more-than-adequate degree has little additional affect on the customer. Also, if the characteristic is not adequately met one time, but is adequately met the next time, the customer will be more than happy to give the service provider her business that next time.

Herein we are making a significant distinction between a qualifier and a losing-sensitive characteristic—losing-sensitive characteristics impact the emotional memory of customers. Qualifiers inspire a cognitive response, but little or no emotional response.

Unit 5

Important note: For clarity, winners, qualifiers, and losing-sensitive characteristics are positively scaled, meaning more is better. When a service provider does a good job at providing a service losing-sensitive characteristic they *avoid* any negative impact on the customer. Service providers only experience the negative impact of service losing-sensitive characteristics when they fail to adequately prove that characteristic of the service. The Quick Oil Change examples listed below should clarify this.

How do we know how a service characteristic will impact the customers? Certainly focus groups and other customer research techniques are helpful. Specific techniques will be discussed later in the "Measuring Service Quality and Productivity" unit.

Once we know how the presence or absence of a characteristic will impact the customer, we can use the following table to identify each of the characteristic types:

IF performance was...	...and customers tend to react as follows...		
terrible	enraged ☹☹☹, motivated to never return	not satisfied, not consider purchase that time	-
exceptional	-	satisfied, consider purchase that time	delighted ☺☺☺, motivated to patronize
...then we would call it a...	**"losing-sensitive characteristic"**	**"qualifier"**	**"winner"**

And as seen in the examples below, some service characteristics fit into more than one category.

How it impacts decisions... Understanding the nature of service characteristics helps us know which to focus on for improvement.

What to do about it... When trying to determine what to focus on for service differentiation or simply service improvement, we need to consider (a) whether specific attributes are service winners, qualifiers, and/or losing-sensitive characteristics, (b) how our service is presently performing on those attributes, and (c) how much it will cost to improve.

What should a company focus improvement efforts on first? There is strong argument for initially focusing on service losing-sensitive characteristics that the company is doing a terrible job providing—since that is surely causing many enemies. A second area of focus should be things keeping the service provider from qualifying in the marketplace, or qualifiers that we are doing an inadequate job at meeting. Yet it is not often that either of these two actions will give a strategic differentiating advantage. The way to gain advantage is to focus on service winners that we are not currently excelling at. At this point we can consider the cost of excelling at various service winners, and choose the ones that will allow us to gain the most with customers for the lowest cost.

Where should a company **not** focus improvement efforts? For one, companies should not focus efforts on *adequately* achieved service characteristics which are **not** at all service winners. For example, if an auto service shop's waiting room decor is adequate, and if the waiting room decor characteristic is not a service winners, then little is to be gained by improving the waiting room decor to a level of excellence.

For example... The following are examples of various characteristics of a Quick Oil Change service. The classifications are my opinions and that of students from my class. Attributes marked "loser" are order-losing sensitive. Reactions to each attribute level is recorded as follows: ☺☺☺=delighted, ☺=just satisfied, ☹=dissatisfied, ☹☹☹=enraged. (Some attribute levels inspire somewhat neutral reactions, but could be satisfaction or dissatisfaction depending on the situation. For example, "open doctors hours" could be fine if that is when I want to take my car in, or not if not.)

| | Service Attribute | Customer reaction given the service attribute at a... | | | classified as a... |
		poor (terrible) level	expected level	realistically exceptional level	
1	availability	open doctors hours ☹	open 9 to 6 Mon-Sat ☺	open 24 hours a day ☺	qualifier
2	convenience	far from target market (just go somewhere else) ☹	near target market ☺	pick up car at your house ☺☺☺	qualifier / winner
3	free services	no free services, charge for every nitpicking item ☹☹	check wiper fluid, reminder of next service ☺	free re-checks, tire rotation, vacuum/wash ☺☺☺	winner / loser
4	personalization	calls you "customer with (such-and-such car)" ☹	calls you by name after you tell your name ☺	resumes conversation from last visit, ☺☺☺ remembers car	winner
5	price	$40 ☹	$20 ☺	$12 ☺	qualifier
6	car smell	reeks ☹☹☹	same as car smelled	smells like a new car	loser
7	courtesy	pushy as Sergeant Carter ("move-it move-it") ☹☹☹	nice as Andy Griffith in Mayberry ☺	overbearing as Gomer Pile ("su-prise su-prise") ☺	loser
8	clean work	grease marks everywhere ☹☹☹	no apparent grease marks ☺	plastic bags over seat, steering, floor, etc.☺	loser

Note that the order-losing sensitive attributes have a negative emotional effect on the customer when performance is at a poor level.

My airline application... The following are examples of characteristics of airline service (in my opinion):

- winner - flight times - how well does the flight fit with my time requirements. (I prefer quick flights that get me there with just a little bit of buffer time. I am thrilled with airlines that can get me perfect connections.)
- qualifier - flight routes - do they fly to a certain location. (If I need to fly to San Diego, I will only consider airlines that have flights to San Diego. However, there are no hard feelings against the airlines that do not fly to San Diego—I will consider flying with those airlines when I need to go to other places.)
- losing-sensitive characteristic - rude treatment by employees. (A Delta Airlines manager called a colleague of mine a "liar," even though the colleague was ultimately proven to have been telling the truth.)

Supplemental reading...   Fitzsimmons2 chapter 3 pages 55-56 on Winning Customers in the Marketplace

Unit 5

How manufacturing differs from services...

With manufacturing, the customer is insulated from the production process. Either the customer likes and purchases the output, or does not purchase the output.

SBP 5b: Identifying Key Production Elements   Name (if turned in):_____

Analysis questions...   To help apply this Service Business Principle, consider and answer the following questions about your specific service business process. (❏Check here if you are going outside of your target service business.)

Service company/business:_____

The service process:_____
   ① What elements, when present, *motivate* customers to select your company over alternatives (service winners)?
   ② What elements allow your company to enter the market when present, or disqualify when not present (service qualifiers)?
   ③ What elements, when not present, *anger* the customers and thus cause them to be lost forever (service losing-sensitive characteristics)?
   ④ How might this information help us design our service?

Unit 5

①_____

_____

_____

_____

_____

_____

_____

_____

_____

_____

_____

_____

_____

_____

_____

_____

_____

_____

SBP 5b: Identifying Key Production Elements   Name (if turned in):_____

Application exercise...   Also to help you apply this Service Business Principle, complete the following analysis with regard to your specific service business process, or another service process in your business. (❏Check here if you are going outside of your target service business, which was _____.)

Service company/business:_____

The service process:_____

> Create a table for your service business process like the auto service example table given as an example in the workbook. You may choose to use the same or different characteristics. For each characteristic, <u>identify how the customer would react</u> under poor or excellent performance. (You might use ☺ and ☹ symbols, or words like "delighted," "satisfied," "dissatisfied," and "enraged.") Categorize each characteristic as a winner, qualifier, or losing-sensitive characteristic.

Preparation for the next Service Business Principle (5c)

To consider... Before proceeding, consider the following and write thoughts and ideas below:

Strategic "positioning" is determining the significant ways our company's "product" is similar or different from what our competitors do. In some ways, customers require that our products be similar to the competitors' products. But by appropriate positioning, we can make our products different from competing product in ways that customers will value, thus helping the customers in their desire to choose our products. Three generic positioning strategies are (1) overall cost leadership, which is to make our products for less cost than competing products, (2) focus, which is to provide a product that meets the needs of specific customers, and (3) differentiation, which is to emphasize specific ways our products are different from competing products. In what ways might customer inputs limit our ability to execute each of the three generic positioning strategies?

Unit 5

Service Business Principle 5c:

POSITIONING AMID CUSTOMERS AND COMPETITORS

Service Business Principle	*"With services, the service provider can attain competitive positioning by defining the relationship with the customer relative to competitors."*

Why it occurs...   POSITIONING AMID CUSTOMERS AND COMPETITORS occurs because customer involvement allows for differing types of relationships between the customer and the company. Customer involvement is a natural consequence of the Unified Services Theory.

Closely related to...   SBP: *Lowered Entry Barriers*, which will be covered later.

Details...   It is important to note that there are a myriad of positioning strategies a service provider might take. Herein, we only consider three very generic strategies: cost leadership, focus, and differentiation. Let's consider each, particularly looking at the way customer inputs impacts our ability to position in that way.

(1) Cost leadership

There can be clear advantages in many service industries to being the low-cost producer. An assumption in this positioning strategy is that the internal efficiencies of the company's production process results in lower costs of service production, which allows the company to charge the customer less for the service.

What is the *relationship* between the customer and the company which is assuming an overall cost leadership strategy? The relationship is often something like: "We (the service provider) will work hard to be efficient and keep costs down for us and you (the customer), and in return, you (the customer) will conform to our efficient procedures."

What limits the ability to establish such a relationship in service businesses? What limits the ability of a service provider to operate efficiently? Two thing that go hand in hand: customer inputs and variability. Variability is the enemy of efficiency. Variability in a production process diminishes the learning advantages of repetition, of simple (non-divergent) procedures, and of economies of scale. (As will be revisited in the *Lowered Entry Barriers* Service Business Principle)

In manufacturing processes the way we improve our efficiency is to drive out variability. Can we not drive out variability in service processes? Where does variability largely come from in service processes? *From customer inputs.* Therefore, if we wanted to *flagrantly* drive variability out of service processes then we would need to *eliminate* customer inputs, which will drive us out of the service business. (The Unified Services Theory reminds us that those customer inputs are essential to the service process.)

Besides causing variability, customer inputs cause further challenges in our ability to attain production efficiency and cost leadership by allowing for unreasonable expectations from the customer. Customers may claim they want low-cost service, but they may simultaneously expect to have *customized* service— service that conforms to the specific production requirements of their customer inputs. With very few exceptions, the customer can't have it both ways. Therefore, as much as customers may claim to like a low-cost service, if they are not willing to allow their customer inputs to conform to standardized production, the low-cost strategy will generally not work.

That's the bad news. The good news is that *if* a company *can* attain efficiency and low cost in a way customers don't mind, then cost leadership can be an extremely successful strategy that will be hard to duplicate by other companies. And how might a company attain efficiency and low cost? Perhaps the best way is to reduce the *extent* of customer inputs allowed into the production process. Here are a few examples:

A number of years ago, Taco Bell introduced the "value meal" strategy, which was for the most part a cost leadership strategy. With competitors (other fast food restaurants), the customer inputs entered the process quite early, even before the food was actually produced. Competitors were thus able to customize the food production to some degree. Taco Bell, on the other hand, produced all of the food item components at a more centralized location apart from the restaurant. Since the food was centrally manufactured (i.e. without customer inputs), Taco Bell experienced tremendous efficiencies and cost savings. The customer inputs (i.e. the customer's specifications of an order) trigger nothing more than the *final assembly* of the food items. (Food items are all inventoried in bags, including the pre-cooked meat that is reheated before being sold.) This, however, limits the ability to conform to various customer inputs (or order specifications). The fact is, you can "have it your way" in extremely few ways. (Try this, for example—visit a Taco Bell restaurant and request, "Instead of having diced tomatoes on my taco, could I please have a whole tomato slice?" It is unlikely they have ever had a whole tomato slice anywhere in the restaurant. Slicing tomatoes for customer is inefficient.)

Taco Bell's strategy was successful because customers *did not mind* (or did not perceive) that the company did most of the food production prior to their arrival (with customer inputs) at the restaurant. And many competitors have had a hard time providing low costs as well as Taco Bell.

Another cost leadership example is Southwest Airlines. They also have successfully minimized the adverse inefficiency affects of customer inputs in their air transportation production process. Here are a few examples for you to try... Next time you are making a flight reservation with Southwest Airlines, give them an additional customer-information input: tell them you really would like a window seat. What will they do with that gem of information? Nothing! They will likely tell you that if you really want a window seat then you should arrive at the airport early so that you can be a first passenger on the plane. Or, tell them you would really like some low-salt food to eat on the plane (they will probably suggest a location where you can buy it before you board). Finally, if your "self input" is a little late to catch a Southwest connecting flight, observe how long Southwest is willing to delay the connection for you to board. In my experience, other airlines tend delay connecting flights quite frequently (when it is required). But Southwest will just put you on the next flight. Southwest's efficient strategy has no room for variability in the arrival times of customer-self inputs. (But I like they way they get you to your destination on time, and I love their low fares!)

As we would see in both of these examples, another key to success in implementing a cost leadership strategy is being able to communicate to customers exactly what the service provider intends to provide. That way customers can be prepared to conform, or choose to go elsewhere.

(2) Focus

The focus strategy is to meet the exclusive needs of a (perhaps narrowly defined) target customer group.

What is the *relationship* between the customer and the company that is taking a focus strategy? The relationship is something like: "You (the customer) will allow yourself to be identified with a particular customer group that has particular needs, and we (the service provider) will try to meet the specific needs of that customer group."

Unit 5

One way to look at focus is as a narrow intensity. We don't try to do everything. In fact, the phrase "focus on everything" is an oxymoron. Instead, the focus strategy is to just provide that service which would appeal to a specific customer group. If that group has somewhat unique needs, then the expectation is that they will be more likely to patronize a service provider that focuses on those needs (than on one that doesn't quite meet the needs).

What limits the ability to establish such a relationship with customers in service businesses? A significant potential problem occurs if the customer group being focused on is *not* in fact a group with unique homogenous needs. Why is that a problem? Because the limited scope of production of a focus strategy causes inefficiencies that cause cost problems. (Increases costs to the producer, such as by lower economies of scale, and costs to the customer, such as less convenient locations.) And, if the needs are *not* in fact somewhat unique, then *any general service provider* can provide the service! (nullifying the competitive advantage)

The real challenge in pursuing the focus positioning strategy is that customer inputs tend to be heterogeneous (all a little bit different), not homogenous (all mostly the same). Thus, the key to effectively implementing a focus strategy in a service environment is being able to qualify the homogeneity of customer inputs.

Here are a few examples...

Shouldice Hospital is a hospital in Canada that operates (literally) *only* on a particular type of hernia. They are extremely focuses, not providing any other surgical procedure except for this particular hernia operation. The great thing is that if you need that operation, there is probably no hospital more able to meet your needs than Shouldice. A key to Shouldice's success in their focus strategy is the ability to qualify customer inputs. One way they do this is by sending the potential patient a questionnaire to describe the condition. If it does not appear to fit the focused procedures of Shouldice, such as a patient with corresponding obesity problems, then the customer will be turned away and will have to go to a less-focused hospital for the procedure.

Another example of a focus strategy is the adult education chain known as the University of Phoenix. Even though many educational institutions provide adult education to employed persons, few have near the focus on that customer group as the University of Phoenix does. As a result, they cater to the specific needs of that group, including "one night a week" education and a complete curriculum geared specifically for students with already stressful full-time jobs. Their entire operation system is designed for that type of student, and even their instructors are mostly individuals with full-time jobs in the community. (And not like university faculty who mix a lot of theory in with even applied instruction.) The University of Phoenix qualifies the somewhat heterogeneous needs of their target customers—people expecting the breadth and depth of curriculum of other educational institutions would not likely be satisfied with the University of Phoenix offerings—but it is just right for the target market.

(3) Differentiation

The differentiation strategy is to provide a unique service—or to provide a service in a way that is different from the way competitors provide the service. With manufactured goods, differentiation is simply to make a relatively unique product, or to deliver it in a different way. With services, a common way that we might differentiate is in the handling of customer inputs. We may handle customer inputs in a way that is different from the way our competitors do. Examples will be given below.

What is the *relationship* between the customer and the company that is taking a differentiation strategy? The relationship is often something like: "You (the customer) can provide your inputs for service from us (the service provider) or *any* of our competitors; however, none of them will handle your inputs the way we will."

Implicit in the appropriateness of a differentiation strategy is the idea that customers will *value* the ways in which service production is different for the differentiator. If the service is perceived by customers to be a "commodity," such as the way camera film processing or long-distance telephone service often is viewed, then the low-cost provider will have a dramatic advantage over a higher cost differentiator. Nevertheless, there are dramatically fewer service commodities than goods commodities, for reasons explained by the Unified Services Theory. (see, for example, SBP: *Heterogeneous Production*)

What else limits the ability to establish such a relationship in service businesses? We have explored the implication of *customization* in services. If our competitors customize, then it would be quite difficult to say that we provide a *unique* service, since customizing competitors could simply customize the service to do exactly what we do. The advantage we may gain over the customizing competitors is that we are *better* at the way we are different. In fact, uniquely heightened customization is an example of differentiation.

Some wonder how differentiation strategy differs from the focus strategy. Consider the difference in the relationships with the customer: With differentiation we are not focusing on a specific group of customers, but on a *general* way we can be better than our competitors. With differentiation, we do not require our customers to have somewhat homogeneous needs, but treat all potential customers in a way that is different and potentially valued. Despite this dramatic oversimplification of a complex issue, in some instances differentiation and focus strategies are intertwined. (In fact, to differentiate by being lower cost is the essence of the cost leadership strategy. Yet "cost leadership" is the preferred and more precise name for that generic strategy.)

Unit 5

Disney is an example of a differentiator. Lots of companies have theme parks, resorts, water parks, etc. But Disney (the parks division) is different in their attempt to provide what they call the "magic" of Disney. They extensively leverage their fictional characters, particularly Mickey Mouse. Whereas potential competitors offer "rides" or "attractions," Disney provides a fantasy experience. (And they are clearly not taking a focus or a cost leadership strategy!)

The Ritz-Carlton luxury hotel chain attempted to differentiate on the basis of customization. They had a computer system which tracked a dramatic variety of customer preferences (which are customer-information inputs describing ways the customer-self input wants to be processed). Ritz-Carlton was successful at differentiating, with very few competing hotels that would be considered peers. Unfortunately, many potential Ritz-Carlton customers viewed a hotel stay as a little more of a commodity than Ritz-Carlton required payment for, and thus the high costs of customization led to serious financial problems. Marriott Corporation, the purchaser of Ritz-Carlton, has a big task of keeping the high-quality image of Ritz-Carlton while reducing the inefficiency caused by the hyper-customized service system.

For example... (examples were given above)

My airline application... We previously described Southwest Airlines cost leadership strategy. An example of airlines with a focus strategy are those that only fly gamblers to Las Vegas. A differentiating airline would be the Concorde portion of British Airways—no one gets you there faster and in more style.

Supplemental reading... Fitzsimmons2 chapter 3 pages 52-55 on Competitive Service Strategies.
Case: Taco Bell 1994. (HBS)
Case: Southwest Airlines 1993 (A). (HBS)
Case: Shouldice Hospital. (HBS)
Case: Ritz-Carlton. (HBS)
Case: Disney (HBS)

How manufacturing differs from services...

With manufacturing, the relationship between the customer and the company is that the customer selects and consumes the output, and on occasion provides general feedback.

SBP 5c: Positioning Amid Customers and Competitors   Name (if turned in):_____

Analysis questions...   To help apply this Service Business Principle, consider and answer the following questions about your specific service business process. (❑Check here if you are going outside of your target service business.)

Service company/business:_____

The service process:_____

   ① Are we focused on meeting specific needs at a price that attracts customers to us (cost leadership)?

   ② Are we focused on meeting the needs of a specific customer group (focus)?

   ③ Are we focused on meeting needs in a way that is different from the way our competitors meet those needs (differentiation)?

   ④ What operational actions are appropriate for that generic strategy? In other words, how do we implement the chosen strategy?

Unit 5

① _____

_____

_____

_____

_____

_____

_____

_____

_____

_____

_____

_____

_____

_____

_____

_____

SBP 5c: Positioning Amid Customers and Competitors   Name (if turned in):_____

Application exercise...

Also to help you apply this Service Business Principle, complete the following analysis with regard to your specific service business process, or another service process in your business. (❑Check here if you are going outside of your target service business, which was _____.)

Service company/business:_____

The service process:_____

Construct a strategic positioning map. Pick two of the three generic strategies for axes, and put "yes" and "no" at each end of the axis. "Yes" is for companies that absolutely follow that strategy, "no" is for those that do not, and degrees of "somewhat" are in between. For focus and differentiation strategies, identify exactly what the focus is or what the differentiation is. Plot a point that shows where your company exists relative to the general industry. Plot points for a few other companies in the industry. (All plots are your estimates.) Comment on what ways your company is well positioned and what ways it is not. Here is a simple example: (S=Southwest Airlines, C=the Concorde, D1=Delta Airlines on routes that Southwest also serves, D2=Delta Airlines on all other routes, M=my airline that only flies business travelers to Japan)

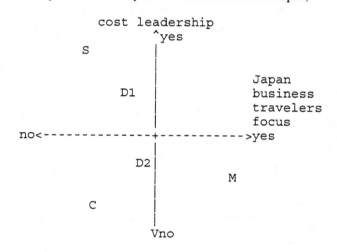

I observe that my ("M") company's nearest competitor is Delta Airlines. Successful positioning will require establishing a close need-filling relationship with my specific target customer group—business travelers to Japan.

Preparation for the next Service Business Principle (5d)

To consider... Before proceeding, consider the following and write thoughts and ideas below:

The manufacturing concept of "batch processing" seeks to determine an appropriate amount of inputs (the batch size) to process at any given time. Big batches can be efficient, but result in a lot of product tied up in the process. The just-in-time (JIT) production philosophy includes an attempt to decrease the batch size to be more responsive with less product sitting around. Some companies process information in large batches. Usually it does not cost the company very much to store information. However, there may be dramatic costs to the customer in having to wait for a batch of information to become available, some of which might by then be obsolete. Can you think of some examples of companies that collect information over time, and then make it available to customers in a "batch"? Is there some way the company might make the information available to customers soon after the company receives it? Would this provide any advantage for the customers?

Unit 5

Service Business Principle 5d:

JIT INFORMATION

Service Business Principle	*"With services that process information, strategic advantages can be gained by using technology to switch from batch processing to delivery on demand (JIT - or "Just In Time"). JIT information is a "pull" system, meaning that information is processed as the customer requests it. This switch to JIT information can in fact convert an information manufacturing process into an information service process."*

Why it occurs... JIT INFORMATION occurs because when the customer dictates what information they want, that is a form of customization, which changes the procedures of the information provider. (Customized information providers operate differently than mass-produced information providers.)

Details... Up until recently, information was provided to customers in many industries in physical form. Telephone companies produced phone books, retailers produced catalogs, textbook publishers produced textbooks, news agencies produced newspapers, and banks produced bank statements. In each of these cases, the company collects information over time, compiles it into an overall document, then sells or gives the entire document to the customer. There can be problems with this approach:

- What if the customer is only interested in a small portion of the information? Why should we waste all of that glossy paper on a fancy catalog when all I care about is the small sporting goods section? Why do students have to pay for an entire text, when in a normal semester there is only time to cover a third of the chapters?
- What if the customer needed the information before the company was ready to distribute it? What if I need a phone number of a new person before the next edition of the phone book arrives? What if there is a problem with my bank account before the bank statement arrives?
- Is there some chance that the big batches of information companies send might contribute to "information overload"? Wouldn't it be better if they just sent the information that we need when we need it? Why do I have to dig through all of the garbage and gore that is described in newspaper headlines in order to find those stories that are worth reading? Can't they just give me the type of stories I want to read?

Up until recently, the answer to all of these questions would have been "it is not practical to deliver information JIT." However, with recent advances in information technology, particularly Internet technologies, it has become very practical to provide JIT information production and delivery. It is important to note that since JIT information is a "pull" system (the customer pulls or requests the specific information), an additional service element (i.e. customer input) is introduced into the information delivery process.

For example... An easy way to find telephone number information today is via information services on the Internet. The customer types in the name, the city, or other identifying information, and the computer looks up that the phone number.

The World Wide Web is particularly suited to provide product catalog information just as the customer requests it. If a company decides to add or change sale information, they can do it instantaneously.

Textbook publishers will now allow instructors to select chapters and writings from various authors, and publish them in one volume just-in-time for the new semester.

Many major newspapers have put their news stories on-line, allowing customers to request just the stories and information of interest to them. Further, a technology called "agents" will select a combination of stories based on a profile of the customer's interests.

Many bank statements have gone on-line, allowing customers to view or download up-to-the-hour account information. Customers who do not track their check register as closely as they should can view their balances and spot if they need to transfer funds earlier than they would if they had to wait for the next mailed statement.

My airline application... Up until quite recently, if people wanted to compare the flight schedules of various airlines, they would either call a travel agent or purchase a flight guide. This latter method is an example of batch delivery of information. Now customers can enter their departure and arrival preferences into an on-line system, and the computer will list possible flights, including fares and restrictions.

Unit 5

Supplemental reading... Fitzsimmons2 chapter 4 pages 68-74 on The Competitive Role of Information in Services

---

How manufacturing differs from services...

With manufacturing, specifically manufacturing of information, the information product is assembled from raw-material information, and delivered as a final package to the customer. JIT information involves delaying final processing of the information until after the customer requests it.

SBP 5d: JIT Information   Name (if turned in):_____

Analysis questions...   To help apply this Service Business Principle. consider and answer the following questions about your specific service business process. (❏Check here if you are going outside of your target service business.)

Service company/business:_____

The service process:_____
    ① What information is delivered in batch?
    ② What advantages are there to batch delivery?
    ③ What disadvantages are there to batch delivery?
    ④ In what ways could the information be delivered just when needed, and only what is needed?

①_____

_____

_____

_____

_____

_____

_____

_____

_____

_____

_____

_____

_____

_____

_____

_____

Unit 5

SBP 5d: JIT Information   Name (if turned in):_____

Application exercise... Also to help you apply this Service Business Principle, complete the following analysis with regard to your specific service business process, or another service process in your business. (❏Check here if you are going outside of your target service business, which was _____.)

Service company/business:_____

The service process:_____

Identify a type of non-customer information that is necessary to complete your service process, such as weather reports, supply information, regulation information, etc. List the information and where it comes from. Describe the form that the information arrives in. Does the information arrive just as needed, or a batch at a time? How much of the information does the service process need at a given time? Describe how the information could arrive a batch at a time, and how the information could arrive JIT. List advantages of the JIT approach, such as having more up-to-date information. What technologies would be involved in the JIT delivery of the information? Is JIT information delivery practical in this situation? Describe why or why not.

Preparation for the next Service Business Principle (5e)

To consider... Before proceeding, consider the following and write thoughts and ideas below:

A great strategic opportunity for manufacturing companies is expanding product distribution globally. One thing that makes global distribution appealing is that when the domestic market for a product is matured (implying little or no growth potential), foreign markets can be developing with tremendous growth opportunity. Exporting physical goods is often just a matter of arranging distribution channels in the country receiving the exports. Exporting services is not so easy. How does one go about exporting a service? Consider a few services that are purchased by foreign customers—What is the process of "delivering" a service to a foreign customer?

_____

_____

_____

_____

_____

_____

_____

_____

Service Business Principle 5e:
SERVICE EXPORTING

Service Business Principle	*"With services, exporting sometimes involves importing customers, their belongings, or their information. Another form of service exporting is to export the production process, which can limit the amount of operating profits that can be returned to the home country. Companies who export a production process need to carefully consider the cultural specificity of customer inputs."*

Why it occurs...   SERVICE EXPORTING occurs because production cannot begin without customer inputs, as per the Unified Services Theory. The customer inputs either need to be delivered to the process, or the process needs to be delivered to the location of the inputs. Customer inputs to a production process in one culture may be fundamentally different from customer inputs to an identical process in a different culture.

Details...   In some situations, foreign customers are happy to send their inputs and be served in a different country. For example, the hospitality industry (hotels, resorts, restaurants, etc.) cater to many foreign guests. Is having foreign guests *exporting*? It is in a big way, as reported by James Everett:[10]

> "Spending by international visitors reached a record level of $90 billion in 1996. With just under $21 billion for passenger fare receipts, almost $70 billion was injected directly in the U.S. economy, demonstrating that *international travel to the United States is an export*, just like the sale of agriculture products, automobiles or consumer goods."

Serving foreign guests who deliver their inputs (their selves, in this case) is a form of exporting the service. I call this "Exporting by Importing," since the foreign customers "import" their inputs. A New York City hotel that is full of European visitors is as valuable to the company as having a hotel in Europe full of the same people, and even more valuable to the New York economy.

Another example of Exporting by Importing is medical facilities that attract patients from neighboring countries. Some countries restrict experimental medical treatments or have insurance systems that ration some major procedures. Patients may choose to take their self-inputs to other countries where the treatments and procedures are offered. By serving foreign patients, the medical facilities that attract those patients are in a sense exporting their medical services to other countries.

In other cases, exporting a service involves *exporting the service process*, so that the process will be near the location of customer inputs. This often means setting up an office or production facility in the foreign country. The reason exporting the production process can limit the amount of operating profits is that the foreign countries may not recognize that anything was actually "exported" to their country (since production, labor, the production facility, etc., are all located on their ground, and taxed accordingly). This contrasts with the "importing customers" approach, in which it is quite easy to keep all operating profits in the service provider's home country.

When exporting a service process, the issue of *"cultural specificity"* needs to be considered. Cultural specificity is a fundamental characteristic of many service businesses. Cultural specificity is the idea that a given service process may need to be adjusted from one culture to the next. Because the customers can vary dramatically across cultures, the inputs they provide and the expectations for the

---

[10] Everette, J. (1998). Services--U.S. Firms are Leaders in the Global Economy. *Business America*, 119(4), 5-7. Italics added.

service can also vary. Customer inputs means that customers can influence the production process, forcing the process to comply with local cultural norms.

For example, in the United States there tends to be an expectation that the customer being served not be rushed, and that time is taken to meet the customer's needs. When discussing waiting lines in class one year, a student from Europe (or Australia, I cannot remember exactly) made a comment to the effect of, "What is it with you Americans, who are always standing in line!" The point was that in his country they do not put up with commonly waiting in lines, and that service providers are under obligation to eliminate lines. What was implied was that if necessary, service providers should hurry the customer being served to keep waiting customers from waiting longer than necessary. North Americans might perceive this as impolite, just as people from that student's country might perceive not rushing customers as inappropriate. Multinational service companies need to have policies and training in place to meet the expectations of local cultures.

Related to cultural specificity is language issues. The presence of customer inputs causes the service exporter to consider language proficiency. With manufactured exports, product information and instructions merely need to be translated (a process which is called "localization" in some industries). For many exported services, either the service process needs to be adapted to customer language, or the customer needs to adapt to the service provider language[11]. An example of the former is resorts which attract many foreign tourists who can be served in various languages. An example of the latter is education, where foreign students are usually required to learn the language of instruction.

Unit 5

How it impacts decisions... Service providers who decide to export the production process must determine if there are ways the process should differ based on cultural differences.

What to do about it... Service providers who expand to international markets need to understand the differences in culture of expansion regions. One way to gain this information is employ citizens of that culture in the design and management of the service process. Service providers may choose to partner with a firm that is from that country and is familiar with local customer expectations.

For example... Universities can "export" by two primary means: First, they often "import" students from other countries, thus exporting by importing. Second, they may send faculty to other countries to offer courses, which is to export the production process. So-called "distance learning" uses communication technology to do both—faculty lectures are transmitted to the foreign location, and student questions and assignments (their inputs) are transmitted to the faculty location. Although distance learning is in its infancy, education exporting is a major economic activity, particularly in the U.S. In 1996, U.S. exports of training and education reached $8.2 billion![12]

Consulting firms export by opening foreign offices or taking production employees to the foreign client's site. It is less likely that a consulting firm would require customer inputs to be delivered across borders to the consulting firm's home country, although with communication technologies this is becoming more and more practical.

Disney® learned the lesson of cultural specificity the hard way. Their theme parks have been extremely successful in Anaheim, California, and in Orlando, Florida. Even the park in Tokyo, Japan has been very popular. They clearly had a formula for success. When Disney opened Euro-Disney near Paris they found their formula for success was taking them down the path to failure. The park experienced huge financial losses and required major financial infusions to keep operating. What went wrong? For one thing, customer inputs in Europe were quite

---

[11] see Michael Porter's book "The Competitive Advantage of Nations," 1990, New York: The Free Press, page 257.
[12] *ibid.*

different from what they were at the other Disney parks. Disney makes much of their profits from food sales within the park, but Europeans were more likely to bring food or eat outside of the park. Also, customer expectations for the park experience differed. Europeans visiting Disney World in Florida view that as an American vacation, and thus expect an American experience. Europeans visiting a park in Europe may expect an American experience, since it is an American company, or may expect a European experience, since the park is in Europe. This makes it very difficult to meet customers expectations and avoid customer disappointment.

My airline application... Airlines "export" by taking the production process and facilities (airplanes) to the foreign location. Then they may bring customers to the airline's home country, which is sort of importing customers. International airlines are an interesting example of exporting, since their facilities continually move from country to country.

Supplemental reading... Fitzsimmons2 chapter 15 pages 467-470 on Multinational Development.
Fitzsimmons2 chapter 15 pages 470-475 on Global Service Strategies.
Michael Porter's book "The Competitive Advantage of Nations" contains an interesting section on "National Competitive Advantages in Services." This Service Business Principle particularly relates to his pages 448-450 on "Types of International Service Competition."

How manufacturing differs from services...

With manufacturing, exporting can be accomplished by simply setting up distribution channels in foreign countries. The production process can be located at any remote location deemed appropriate.

SBP 5e: Service Exporting   Name (if turned in):_____

Analysis questions...

To help apply this Service Business Principle, consider and answer the following questions about your specific service business process. (☐Check here if you are going outside of your target service business.)

Service company/business:_____

The service process:_____
　① How might a customer in a foreign market purchase our service product?
　② Could domestic production facilities meet the needs of foreign customers?
　③ Is it more practical to export production facilities? What are some cultural specificity issues? In other words, how might foreign cultures expect the service be different from that which is provided in the company's home country?

① _____

_____

_____

_____

_____

_____

_____

_____

_____

_____

_____

_____

_____

_____

_____

Unit 5

SBP 5e: Service Exporting   Name (if turned in):_____

Application exercise...

Also to help you apply this Service Business Principle, complete the following analysis with regard to your specific service business process, or another service process in your business. (❑Check here if you are going outside of your target service business, which was _____.)

Service company/business:_____

The service process:_____

Imagine that your service company was going to expand into a country which has a very different culture from the company's home country. Try to choose a country in which you know something about the cultural differences. List that country and a few of the significant cultural differences. For each of the differences listed, indicate how the service process may differ from the home country to the foreign country. You might list a procedural difference or a policy that would be different.

Part II - Service Business Strategy
Unit 6:
IDENTIFYING STRATEGIC THREATS

In the last unit, we considered potential strategic opportunities for service firms. This unit continues by looking at sources of potential strategic threats that are drawn from the Unified Services Theory. One good thing about the many strategic threats to service firms is that if they are overcome by effective management, the threats can be turned into great opportunities that cannot easily be replicated. This is to say that while establishing and implementing an effective services strategy can be very difficult, those who effectively meet the challenge will have extraordinary opportunity to contribute.

Unit 6

Unit reading... The following reading pertains to Service Business Principles included in this unit. The instructor will let you know which of the readings you are responsible for studying.

Fitzsimmons2 chapter 3 on Service Strategy

Preparation for the next Service Business Principle (6a)

To consider... Before proceeding, consider the following and write thoughts and ideas below:

Manufacturing firms would like customers to be loyal to their products. The makers of toothpaste would like customers to choose their brand of toothpaste every time. Auto manufacturers would like customers to purchase their make of automobile whenever they need a new car. Service providers would also like customers to be loyal to their services. Considering what we have learned thus far from the Unified Services Theory, would you expect service providers *in general* to have an easier or more difficult time attaining customer loyalty? Why?

_____

_____

_____

_____

_____

_____

_____

_____

_____

Service Business Principle 6a:

SWAYING DIVIDED LOYALTIES

Service Business Principle	*"With services, customers often have a greater opportunity to be disloyal when each opportunity for service is a separate transaction. However, producers often have a greater opportunity to build loyalty by personalization."*

Why it occurs... SWAYING DIVIDED LOYALTIES occurs because the service customer does not own the service provider as do goods customers (see SBP: *Server-Ownership Perspective*). Thus, service customers are less likely to have any long-term commitment to that particular service provider.

Details... Think back to the *Server-Ownership Perspective* Service Business Principle. There was an example given comparing a manufactured plunger to a service-providing plumber. Even though they both can be employed to unstop a clogged sink, a major difference is that the customer takes ownership of the plunger, but not the plumber. The fact that the customer has expended a fixed cost (although small) in procuring the plunger makes the customer more likely to employ *that plunger* whenever a drain is clogged. The customer is "loyal" to the plunger *he owns*, and is unlikely to purchase a new and different plunger every time he needs to plunge a drain.

On the other hand, the customer may *potentially employ* a completely different plumber each time a plumber is needed. Even if he tries to call the plumber he used last time, it would generally not take much to get him to try another plumber. For example, if he calls the plumber he used last time and the line is busy, that may be enough to push him to instead try the next plumber in the phone book. That is not loyalty.

In summary, the reason customers tend to be disloyal to service providers is that, since they do not take ownership of the service provider, every occasion to seek that service is a separate transaction. A major problem with this phenomena is that loyal customers have been shown to be much more profitable to a company than shop-around customers.[13] Some have estimated that it costs five times as much to gain new customers as it does to retain old customers.

How it impacts decisions... Service providers must determine the costs of non-loyalty, such as costs of customer turnover (recruiting new customers instead of keeping the ones you have). From that, decisions regarding appropriate efforts to increase customer loyalty should be made.

What to do about it... There are a couple of things a service provider might do to counter the non-loyalty propensity of his service business. For both, the idea is to increase the affiliation that the customer feels with the service provider.

The first is not unique to services: It is to establish a membership, or frequent user relationship, with customers. Customers might pay a fixed cost for a membership, and receive subsequent discounts (e.g. Sam's Club). Or, they might establish a service

---

[13] "Zero Defections: Quality Comes to Services" by Fredrick F. Reichheld and W. Earl Sasser Jr., *Harvard Business Review* September/October 1990.

contract to receive service over an extended time at a specific price. Or, customers might receive a reward for repeat patronage of the service provider (such as frequent flier clubs).

The second way of countering the non-loyalty propensity of service customers is unique to services. It is to increase the personalization of the service to give the customers the sense of belonging with that service provider. A "personalized" service is one that treats each customer as a unique individual, rather than just another "consumer." ("Personalization" is often confused with "personable," which is friendly and warm interactions. A service can be personalized with or without also being personable.)

A technique for personalizing a service is to track information about each customer, so that on subsequent visits you already know about the customer and her needs. An example of this is some Pizza Hut delivery locations, who keep data on the last pizza order for each customer. That way, when a customer calls in to order pizza, the Caller ID triggers the store's computer to display the last order. Then, the employee simply asks if the customer would like the same pizza as they ordered previously. The point is to simplify the process of placing an order by personalized suggestions.

It seems that most automobile owners would like to identify an auto repair shop which knew the needs of their particular car. However, auto repair shops generally treat each visit as unique, even if the same care had been in for a related problem a few weeks prior. (Why else would we keep needing to explain the situation to the mechanic?) Customers may or may not want person*able* service from mechanics, but we all want service that meets the specific needs of our individual vehicle.

In order to personalize service, the company needs to (a) determine relevant things about the customers or their inputs, (b) store that information so that it can be later used, and (c) use the information in guiding service delivery. The information may be stored in a card file or computer file. In some cases, the information is stored in the minds of employees who work with particular customers. That way, when a customer returns, the employee can recall the situation and needs of that particular customer and personalize the service accordingly. The problem with this latter approach is that the customers are likely to be loyal to that *employee*, not to the service organization. Loss of the employee may mean loss of those customers.

For example... Automobile owners tend to be very loyal to cars they own—whenever they need local transportation, they are much more likely to take their own car than one they do not yet own. (Except for in some places of high crime.) However, customers that use taxi services are likely to consider using a different taxi company every time they need local transportation. How might a taxi company improve customer loyalty? Well, certainly they can provide a better service, just as auto manufacturers can provide a better product. Further, they can provide a membership relationship, such as a "frequent rider" program. With services, a primary way to promote increased customer loyalty is to act upon the *uniqueness* of customer inputs and needs. Taxi companies could store information about locations, route preferences, and receipt requirements of customers, increasing the ability to give those customers exactly what they need on subsequent trips.

My airline application... Airlines certainly recognize the propensity customers have for shopping around whenever they need air transportation service—thus the prevalence of frequent flier programs.

Supplemental reading... Fitzsimmons2 chapter 3 page 48 on Relationship with Customers.

Unit 6

Fitzsimmons2 chapter 3 page 51 on Customer Loyalty.
mini-case: Village Volvo (found in Fitzsimmons2 chapter 2 page 38)
case: Ritz-Carlton (HBS)
article: "Zero Defections: Quality Comes to Services" by Fredrick F. Reichheld and W.
Earl Sasser Jr., *Harvard Business Review* September/October 1990. (This is
an excellent article on the cost of disloyal customers.)
Harvard Business Review article: "Managing to Keep the Customer."

How manufacturing differs from services...

With manufacturing, the customer owns the service provider, and often uses it repeatedly to recover the fixed procurement cost.

Quantitative analysis... (covered at the discretion of the instructor)

One reason service providers often under-invest in building customer loyalty is that they under-estimate the costs of acquiring new customers and the profit advantages of loyal customers. The costs of acquiring new customers include advertising, promotion, and the inefficiencies of customers who are not familiar with service procedures. The profit advantages of loyal customers include greater frequency of purchase and possibly greater revenues per purchase. If a service provider could estimate those costs and profits, then some basic calculations could be used to determine the value of customer loyalty.

For example, a particular dry cleaning company might desire to serve a thousand customers per month. A certain percent of customers will be loyal, and will give repeat business from month to month. Since some customers are not loyal, the company will continually advertise to gain enough new customers to maintain the one thousand customer per month level. For simplicity, imagine that the company charged $4 to clean a garment with $1 in variable costs. Some of the $3 of gross profit would go towards overhead expenses of $3000 per month. Imagine that the company estimates that each $1 of advertising will bring one new customer into the store. If the company had zero percent loyalty, and every customer was a new customer, then the company would spend $1000 per month for advertising.

An important question is how much more profitable the company would be if customers were loyal. If no customers were loyal, then the company would pay $1000 a month to attract 1000 new customers. If each customer had 2 garments cleaned then revenues would be $8000. Subtracting $1000 advertising expense, $2000 variable cost, and $3000 overhead cost leaves $2000 profit. We might think that each loyal customer would simply lower the advertising expense required by $1. However, the fact is that loyal customers are likely to give more business per visit than disloyal customers. If half of the customers were loyal and had 4 garments cleaned per month then revenues would be (500x4 + 500x2) x 4 = $12000. Subtracting $500 advertising expense, $3000 variable cost, and $3000 overhead leaves $5500 in profit! Even if the company spent $1 per customer per month to maintain that loyalty level, the profit would still be more than double what it would be if none of the customers were loyal. This illustrates how companies can sometimes get a better return on money invested in customer retention than in customer recruitment.

This example is simply an illustration. The fact is, it can be difficult to accurately estimate the costs and effects of customer retention efforts. However, such analysis can show the wide range of assumptions over which customer retention investments are easily justified.

SBP 6a: Swaying Divided Loyalties   Name (if turned in):_____

Analysis questions...   To help apply this Service Business Principle, consider and answer the following questions about your specific service business process. (❑Check here if you are going outside of your target service business.)

Service company/business:_____

The service process:_____
   ① Do customers choose a potentially different service provider each time they need the service?
   ② Are there means and advantages to allowing the customer to purchase the service by some type of membership or contract?
   ③ Can the relationship/service with each individual be enhanced by providing more personalization? At what cost?

①_____

_____

_____

_____

_____

_____

_____

_____

_____

_____

_____

_____

_____

_____

_____

_____

_____

Unit 6

SBP 6a: Swaying Divided Loyalties   Name (if turned in):_____

Application exercise...

Also to help you apply this Service Business Principle, complete the following analysis with regard to your specific service business process, or another service process in your business. (☐Check here if you are going outside of your target service business, which was _____.)

Service company/business:_____

The service process:_____

Design a plan for customer retention at your target service business. List three or more major reasons why customers would <u>not</u> be loyal, but would continually shop around for that service. List three or more advantages to the <u>company</u> from customers being loyal. List three or more advantages that could be presented to <u>customers</u> to them to encourage them to be loyal and give repeat business. How might an effective customer retention program be built around those advantages? (One that would promote good customer loyalty at a reasonable cost.)

Preparation for the next Service Business Principle (6b)

To consider...   Before proceeding, consider the following and write thoughts and ideas below:

Instead of hiring a company to provide a service, customers often have the alternative of doing it themselves. What general types of advantages do customers gain by doing it themselves? What disadvantages? How can this knowledge be used to make it more attractive for customers to hire the service provider instead of doing it themselves?

_____

_____

_____

_____

_____

_____

_____

_____

Unit 6

Service Business Principle 6b:

COMPETING WITH CUSTOMERS

Service Business Principle	*"With services, often the chief competitor is the customers who can provide the service themselves. Customers' typically have competitive advantage in controlling their inputs and providing maximum personalization (they get it exactly how they want it). Self-serving customers have fixed cost disadvantages due to low economies of scale, and quality disadvantages due to lack of specialization. They can have a variable cost advantage or disadvantages depending largely on the value of their time."*

Why it occurs... COMPETING WITH CUSTOMERS occurs because the customers have absolute access and control of the primary process inputs—their selves, their belongings, and their information (as per the Unified Services Theory). Customers can thus decide to retain the inputs instead of turning them over to the service provider.

Closely related to... SBP: *Swaying Divided Loyalties*

Details... Another way to look at this Service Business Principle is from the perspective of "make versus buy decisions." The traditional make versus buy decision in manufacturing is to decide whether a manufacturing company should make the components itself, or buy the components from outside suppliers. For example, a computer keyboard manufacturer would need to decide whether to obtain the ability to make plastic key caps in-house, or whether to hire an injection molded plastic company to make them. The in-house (make) decision would represent higher fixed costs but lower variable (per-item) costs than they buy-from-a-supplier decision.

With service companies who lack manufacturing expertise, the decision to make or buy facilitating goods or other physical items is a moot point—they could probably not make them even if they wanted to. For example, how many dental clinics make their own dental equipment? How many law firms make their own bonded paper? How many trash collectors make their own trucks? In most cases the answer is probably none. The reason is that service providers typically lack the skills and specific resources needed to manufacture the various process inputs. (There are some exceptions to this, such as AT&T, who supposedly manufactures its own telephone switching equipment. However, in this day and age it is rare for even telecommunications companies to manufacture their own equipment.)

Therefore, with services we are generally *not* laden with a supplier make versus buy decision—the decision is "buy." The make versus buy decision that challenges service providers pertains not to suppliers, but to *customers*. The customers have to decide whether to hire the service or provide the service *for themselves*. By serving themselves, potential customers are in effect eliminating the service-provider "middle-man." A common way that these customers accomplish this is to go directly to manufacturers for the equipment and supplies needed to meet the particular need. Here are a few examples: a customer may buy a car from an auto manufacturer instead of hiring a taxi, or buy clothes washing equipment from an appliance manufacturer instead of hiring a laundry, or buy yard tools and machines from manufacturers instead of hiring a landscaping company. So, in some sense, when a service provider is competing with customers, they are in fact competing with manufacturer-suppliers as well, who may sell the tools of the trade directly to customers. (It sounds almost like the customers and manufacturers being in collusion to eliminate the service-provider in the middle!)

Customers gain certain advantages by serving themselves, as described in this Service Business Principle. They have extreme personalization, or the ability to treat themselves as an individual and not like everyone else. There can also be convenience advantages–since the customer is typically always available to serve himself should the need arise. This is a reason why people buy cars when they could take taxis everywhere–a car is there waiting in the driveway to fill the transportation need on a second's notice. (Of course, there are other advantages of owning a car.)

However, service providers have certain advantages over self-serving customers. Service providers specialize, which promotes expertise. Also, service providers can have greater utilization of service capacity, since they are using their fixed-cost equipment to serve a number of different customers. Thus, service providers can have some advantages in economies of scale. Also, customers are generally not required to make the large fixed-cost investment themselves, since the service provider simply amortizes (or spreads out) its fixed-cost investments over all of the customers. Perhaps the biggest advantage service providers can have over self-serving customers occurs when the customer considers their own time to be extremely valuable. Service providers can be real time savers due to their expertise and efficiencies (such as by employing low-cost labor, if possible).

The following table summarizes some of the costs of customer "make versus buy" decisions:

	Typical cost to the customer when the customer chooses to...	
Type of Cost	**"make"** the service: customer serves himself or herself	**"buy"** the service: customer hires the service provider
fixed time cost	high: cost of learning how to provide the service	low: cost of searching for an acceptable service provider
fixed $ cost	high: buying tools and equipment to provide the service	low: service provider owns the needed equipment
variable time cost	high: few "learning curve" benefits	low: "professionals" usually complete service faster
variable $ cost	low. This is the primary advantage of self-service!	high: part of service price goes to cover service provider's fixed costs
quality cost	low if customer can learn how to provide good service. high if service is more technical than customer can reasonably master.	depends on the nature of the service provider

Examples of these various costs will be listed below.

How it impacts decisions... The service provider needs to decide how to position itself relative to this chief competitor: the customer.

What to do about it... If customer-competitors do appear to be a real threat, the service provider should consider its positioning relative to self-serve customers. This includes considering the costs to customers of either "make" (doing it themselves) or "buy" (hiring the service provider). An important cost to consider is the cost of the customer's time, and any time savings the service provider might offer. (Time itself is becoming more of a strategic issue as time goes on.)

For example... Even something as complex as legal or personal tax accounting services can find that potential customers are primary competitors. These days there is computer software available that will guide an individual through all of the legal mumbo-jumbo of completing basic legal documents or tax forms. If those software developers can enable customers to have equally high-quality legal or tax service with little time expenditure, they can pose a great strategic threat to legal and tax service providers.

Indeed, one of the biggest threats to knowledge-intensive services is technology that enables customers to serve themselves. The following is a summary of costs to a customer of having income taxes done.

Taxes	Cost to the customer when the customer chooses to...	
Type of Cost	"**make**" the service: customer does own taxes	"**buy**" the service: customer hires a tax accountant
fixed time cost	high: cost of time studying tax complex codes	low: cost of locating a tax accountant to hire
fixed $ cost	medium or low: possible cost of purchasing software	low to none
variable time cost	high: changes in tax codes make it time consuming year after year	low: tax accountants use their expertise to complete taxes in a fraction of the time
variable $ cost	low. Not much more than the cost of a postage stamp.	high: Good tax accountants are not cheap.
quality cost	low if customer has taxes which are simple to understand. high if the customer has complex taxes.	low if a competent tax accountant is employed.

So, how might customers be convinced to hire a tax accountant rather than do their own taxes. The advantages to customers of hiring the tax accountant include low fixed $ and time costs, low variable time costs, and high quality. The only disadvantage of hiring the accountant is the variable $ cost, which is the fee to complete the tax filing.

Successful restaurants are able to effectively deal with this issue of competing with customers, who can prepare their own meals. They typically do this by leveraging the quality and/or time advantages—the restaurant provides a quality of food that the non-expert customer is unable to match, and/or provides the food with much less time investment than the customer would spend on his or her own.

Food service	Cost to the customer when the customer chooses to...	
Type of Cost	"**make**" the service: customer does the cooking and serving	"**buy**" the service: customer goes to restaurant
fixed time cost	high: cost of acquiring good recipes and cooking skills	low: cost of searching for a good restaurant
fixed $ cost	high: buying the right cooking equipment. (may already have.)	low: restaurants have all of the needed equipment
variable time cost	high: it takes a lot of time to prepare a fancy meal	low: customer can spend cooking time socializing
variable $ cost	low. food is cheaper from a grocery store than from a restaurant.	high: cost of meal includes servers, building, equipment, advertising, etc.

Food service	Cost to the customer when the customer chooses to...	
Type of Cost	**"make"** the service: customer does the cooking and serving	**"buy"** the service: customer goes to restaurant
quality cost	low if customer has developed expertise. high if customer is unfamiliar with that type of cooking.	low to medium: most restaurants specialize in a particular food type, developing expertise.

Restaurants can emphasize the high costs of customers cooking at home. In particular, many restaurants focus customers' attention on the high time costs of cooking their own meals, emphasizing the speed and convenience of letting the restaurant do the cooking.

My airline application... The Vice President of Operations for a discount air carrier that was acquired by Southwest Airlines said that their chief competitor is the family station wagon. What he meant by this is that the airline assisted families in taking trips and vacations, and passengers' primary alternative was taking a driving trip or vacation. Driving the car on vacation can save monetary costs for the trip (the variable cost), although some recreational vehicles can be quite expensive (a fixed cost). Flying to a vacation destination will usually have a much lower time cost to customers than driving. For many trips, the "quality" of a flight can be much higher than the "quality" of riding in a car for hours or days, but that depends on the traveler's perspective.

Unit 6

How manufacturing differs from services...

With manufacturing, we would seldom find consumer goods producers competing with individual customers— it is generally not practical for a customer to make their own goods. (How much would it cost for an individual to make his own car? his own washing machine? his own tube of toothpaste? his own pencil? — having those items manufactured saves many times their costs.) Industrial suppliers may compete with customers who decide to vertically integrate (or make their component parts themselves). Nevertheless, forces such as economies of scale often provide a strong advantage to letting the supplier produce.

SBP 6b: Competing With Customers   Name (if turned in):_____

Analysis questions...   To help apply this Service Business Principle, consider and answer the following questions about your specific service business process. (❑Check here if you are going outside of your target service business.)

Service company/business:_____

The service process:_____
   ① Are we worried about customers providing the service for themselves? How likely is it to happen? How would it happen?
   ② What advantages do we have as a service provider over customers serving themselves?
   ③ What disadvantages?

① _____

_____

_____

_____

_____

_____

_____

_____

_____

_____

_____

_____

_____

_____

_____

_____

_____

_____

Unit 6

SBP 6b: Competing With Customers   Name (if turned in):_____

Application exercise...   Also to help you apply this Service Business Principle, complete the following analysis with regard to your specific service business process, or another service process in your business. (❑Check here if you are going outside of your target service business, which was _____.)

Service company/business:_____

The service process:_____

Do a make (i.e. self-serve) versus buy (i.e. hire service provider) analysis from the perspective of your potential customer. Describe what would be involved in a customer serving herself without hiring the service provider. What are the costs in time, money, quality, risk, etc. of the customer performing the service herself? What are the corresponding costs of the customer hiring your company to provide the service? List specific costs. (You may decide to construct a table as with the examples listed in this Service Business Principle.) Which of these costs would tend to dominate? Why? How can the company use this knowledge to have contributive advantage relative to the self-serving customer? (i.e. how the company can contribute in a way that the customer cannot)

Preparation for the next Service Business Principle (6c)

To consider... Before proceeding, consider the following and write thoughts and ideas below:

In the last Service Business Principle (*Competing with Customers*), it was mentioned that in some instances technology presents a strategic threat to knowledge-intensive services by allowing customers to serve themselves. What about technologies employed by the service provider? In what ways can server-based technologies provide the service provider with strategic advantage? In what ways might server-based technologies present problems? (This latter question is an important one to consider, since these days many people take the technocratic view that as a general rule, more technology is better.)

_____

_____

_____

_____

_____

_____

_____

_____

Unit 6

TECHNOLOGICAL DEPERSONALIZATION

Service Business Principle	*"With services, customers will often react negatively to technologies which depersonalize (or standardize) the service. The exception is when "customer cost" savings are valued. (Generally, customers will react positively to technologies which increase the level of personalization.)"*

Why it occurs... TECHNOLOGICAL DEPERSONALIZATION occurs because depersonalizing technologies fail to acknowledge the uniqueness of customer inputs, which are the core of the Unified Services Theory.

Closely related to... SBP: *Capricious Labor*, which will be covered later.

Details... (Recall that "personalize" means treat each customer as an individual, which is different from "personable" which has to do with server friendliness.)

Why does any company want to introduce process technologies? There may be any number of reasons, but generally it is to produce more with higher quality at lower cost. These cost savings often come by allowing technology or empowered customers to substitute for expensive labor. A disadvantage of using technology to eliminate labor is that there is no production resource more adaptable to various customer inputs than labor. Despite labor's sometimes stubborn temperament, there will never be a machine created that is as versatile and adaptable as a human being. Thus, by removing labor we risk losing the ability to adapt to various customer inputs.

In the early 1980s, home banking was introduced as a revolutionary technology to advance the banking process. Bank customers could use their home computers to access account information, make transfers, and perhaps even pay bills. Ultimately, that introduction of home banking was a failure in the marketplace. The fact is, even without home banking, customers could call up the bank to access account information and make transfers. And, they could write checks to pay bills. Home banking decreased the personalization of the service with little to no cost savings to the customer.

On the other hand, the early 1980s also marked the first widespread introduction of Automatic Teller Machine (ATM) technologies. ATMs are common now, but when they were first made widely available in the early 1980s, it was not at all clear if they would be adopted. The concern in the banking industry was whether customers would put up with an impersonal machine to conduct transactions that otherwise are conducted with a teller. What was different about ATMs that would make them successful when home banking was not? Both ATMs and home banking serve to depersonalize the service. However, ATMs do something that a customer cannot do through home banking: deposit checks and get cash. In fact, ATMs have been come to be known as "cash machines." (Money may not grow on trees, but it does come out of a machine!) And what is the alternative to getting cash out of an ATM? It is waiting in longer lines to get money from personalizing tellers! The great advantage of ATMs is that they are impersonal, and thus get people through the line more quickly! This time savings (coupled with the convenience of more ATM locations than branch offices) is ultimately what made ATMs a successful service-process technology.

In some cases, process technologies can in fact increase personalization of the service. A number of years ago Mrs. Field's Cookies, a fresh-baked cookie chain, introduced process technologies that directed the efforts of the store manager. This technology assisted a variety of management responsibilities, from employee hiring to production scheduling. The way this technology increased the personalization of the service is that it allowed the store manager to spend more time up-front at the counter interacting with customers. The store managers were no longer primarily administrators, but were able to focus attention on identifying specific customer needs and desires.

So, to summarize, service process technologies often depersonalize service delivery. Service providers often want to introduce process technologies for cost savings. However, if customers perceives that the depersonalization does not provide *the customers* with any cost savings, it is likely they will reject the technologies. Those technologies which increase the personalization generally stand on their own merits.

How it impacts decisions...   The service provider must decide whether to introduce new production technologies or to stay with current production methods.

What to do about it...   Consider the costs production technologies bring to the customer, including loss of personalization. Weigh that against the cost savings to the customer in terms of time, money, etc.

Unit 6

One strategy for reducing the risks of technological depersonalization is to give customers service alternatives involving various degrees of technology. (This idea will be revisited in the *Capricious Labor* Service Business Principle.) For example, Lovelock identifies the many alternatives customers have for conducting retail banking:[14]
- visit the bank in person and transact with a live teller,
- conduct transaction over the phone with a customer service rep,
- use at automated teller machine (ATM),
- use the telephone keypad to enter commands to an automated system,
- conduct home banking with proprietary banking software,
- execute banking transactions over the World Wide Web.

I listed Lovelock's banking alternatives with the most personal, but least automated, at the top. Some customers are going to be comfortable with one alternative but not with another. Technophobes who demand personalized attention are more likely to visit the bank and talk with a teller, which is the least efficient alternative from the bank's and the customer's perspective. Other customers will be happier with other alternatives. Of course, the cost of providing many alternatives must be weighed against the value of the various alternatives to the customers and the company.

For example...   Years ago when I was in graduate school my wife worked for an office that decided to "upgrade" its telephone system. They purchased a telephone system called Star Talk, which had a computerized receptionist that allowed callers to select a department from a menu of choices or type in an extension number. They only had the system for a short time when the organization president had Star Talk disabled. Apparently, some of the most important callers were put off by having to listen to a computer, even though one menu option was to talk to a human receptionist. At the time, I was amazed at the president's decision. I am amazed no more, having come to understand *Technological Depersonalization*.

Recently I attempted to modify my health insurance coverage, which I was told I could do over the phone. I called the company's number, and found I was connected with an automated response system. The first request was for me to type in my social security number, which I

---

[14] Lovelock, Christopher, *Services Marketing*, Third Edition, Prentice Hall: Upper Saddle River, New Jersey, 1996. p. 54.

could handle. Next, I was asked for an "access number" of some type, which I had no idea about. So, I just tried hitting "0" to talk with a real person, but was given an "Invalid code" type of message. I finally was able to talk with a human operator, and I explained my difficulty with the computer system. She did not know what the access number was, claiming to be unfamiliar with the automated response system. So she put me on hold while she checked it out. When she returned, she said (she believed) the access number was in some document I was supposed to have gotten in the mail. Since I did not have that document, she offered to send me a form to make the coverage change by mail. (And, if I did not have the whole thing completed by the end of the impending open-enrollment deadline, I could not make the change for another year.) I am sure the health insurance benefits company is thrilled with how efficient their automated telephone response system is, and how much money it saves them in reduced labor costs. But I doubt they have any idea how much it is costing them in good-will by the way it depersonalizes interactions with customers.

Many have wondered if Internet and video technologies will replace the classroom as the primary means education is delivered. Those technologies tend to depersonalize the education delivery process—it is difficult to ask an arbitrary question to the computer or video machine. As a result, those education technologies will likely gain widespread acceptance only if they result in sufficient cost savings to the student.

An example where the customer cost savings of technologies is dramatic is in stock broker services. It is much more impersonal to conduct stock trades on-line, but the transaction commissions are minute when compared with calling a human stock broker. As a result, the adoption of on-line trading has been phenomenal.

One reason that on-line services will ultimately be more successful than traditional cable television in providing entertainment is that the Internet technologies will allow dramatically increased personalization of the information received. For example, a news customer will be able to select exactly the types of stories and reports he wants to view on his screen, as compared with just watching the standard news feeds on a cable news channel.

A process technology that I despise is the "fax back" technical support service provided by computer software and hardware companies. The customer chooses her question from a list of pre-recorded options. I generally consider it more worthwhile to spend a half-hour on hold waiting to talk with a technical support employee.

The following are a couple of examples of technologies that increase the level of personalization for customers. A few years ago Federal Express introduced their package tracking system, which kept track of every package as it passed from one part of the delivery process to another. A customer with a package tracking number could call Federal Express or query a Federal Express computer (over the Internet) and identify when and where the package was last recorded and, if delivered, who signed for it. This is much more personalized service than telling customers that the daily shipment from point A to point B has occurred without identifying if the customers' specific packages made it with the shipment. Personalized means individualized, and the Federal Express package trackage system views every package as an individual shipment.

Previously, I criticized automated telephone receptionists for being impersonal. Pizza Hut Delivery has installed a computer system at some locations which *increases* the level of personalization. Most pizza delivery stores have telephone order-taking procedures which do not vary much from customer to customer. The Pizza Hut computer system uses Caller ID to help identify customers who give repeat business. If the computer detects a call coming from a repeat customer, it tells the employee what the customer at that number ordered last time. The employee can ask if the customer would like the same order, which is a highly personalized request.

A few years ago, a sister-company to Pizza Hut considered introducing order-taking technology. That company was Taco Bell. Taco Bell considered installing computer terminals that would allow customers to place orders in the restaurant without talking to a person.[15] Perhaps the thinking was that order-taking employees are largely programmed in their interactions with customers, so why not let a computer do the job? Do you think computer order-taking would have been a good thing to implement? What might be the potential cost savings which could be passed on to the customer? What might be potential costs in terms of depersonalization?

My airline application... A technology that is probably not going to be successful is the airline ticket kiosks located at some airports. The advantage of those kiosks is that there will rarely be any line—who would want to use a computer that can only ask a very structured set of flight information requests. So, unless the airlines provide a ticket cost savings to customers, the kiosks are unlikely to win out over just talking to a ticket agent.

However, on-line airline ticketing seems more likely to gain widespread acceptance by passengers, since it avoids the costs of being on hold with the airline, it saves money by facilitating shopping for low fares, and it is easy to abandon and simply call the airline if necessary.

Unit 6

Supplemental reading... mini-case: The Best Little Cookie House Around (found in Fitzsimmons2 chapter 4 pages 80-81).
case: Mrs. Field's Cookies. (HBS)

How manufacturing differs from services...

With manufacturing, production is more standardized, lending itself to efficient technologies. In addition, inanimate manufactured products typically do not care if they are produced by high-tech or low-tech production processes.

---

[15] see Harvard Business School case: Taco Bell 1994

SBP 6c: Technological Depersonalization   Name (if turned in):_____

Analysis questions... To help apply this Service Business Principle, consider and answer the following questions about your specific service business process. (❑Check here if you are going outside of your target service business.)

Service company/business:_____

The service process:_____
   ① What technologies have or might be employed in the production of the service?
   ② Which of these increases or decreases personalization?
   ③ Which of these results in customer cost savings, such as increased convenience, reduced transaction costs, etc.?

①_____

_____

_____

_____

_____

_____

_____

_____

_____

_____

_____

_____

_____

_____

_____

_____

Unit 6

SBP 6c: Technological Depersonalization   Name (if turned in):_____

Application exercise... Also to help you apply this Service Business Principle, complete the following analysis with regard to your specific service business process, or another service process in your business. (❑Check here if you are going outside of your target service business, which was _____.)

Service company/business:_____

The service process:_____
   Conduct a cost/benefit analysis of introducing a particular process technology *from the perspective of the customer*. Describe costs, including impact on personalization of the service and how peculiar customer concerns would be handled. Describe benefits, including cost and convenience savings. Comment on the likelihood of general acceptance of the process technology by customers.

Preparation for the next Service Business Principle (6d)

To consider... Before proceeding, consider the following and write thoughts and ideas below:

One strategic trend in manufacturing, associated with the "just-in-time" production philosophy, is to establish strategic alliances with suppliers. With these alliances, information is shared and production is coordinated to the mutual benefit of the company and its suppliers. A key step that precedes establishing these alliances is *supply base reduction*, which is to reduce the number of suppliers of component parts dramatically. Whereas a manufacturer would have had perhaps three or four suppliers of a given part (for safety and price competition reasons), supplier reduction would mean cutting it down to one supplier of that part, then establishing a mutually beneficial alliance with that one supplier (including just-in-time delivery of components). Sounds like a great idea. Will it also work for service businesses? Why or why not? (Don't forget the Unified Services Theory.)

Unit 6

Service Business Principle 6d:
MASS ALLIANCES

Service Business Principle	*"With consumer services and some industrial services, the number of customers (i.e. customer-suppliers) is so great that it is impractical to establish close alliances with each. However, other means can be employed to create a perceived relationship with the customer."*

Why it occurs... MASS ALLIANCES occurs because the production for individual customers is for their own consumption, not for the consumption of others. This is because each customer needs to provide their own inputs (according to the Unified Services Theory). Many customers each purchasing a small amount spreads the potential for alliances very thin.

Closely related to... the *Swaying Divided Loyalties* Service Business Principle, which looks at customer relationships. (*Mass Alliances* looks at these as supplier relationships.)

Details... The idea of "supply base reduction" does not make sense with services where customers are the chief suppliers: Reducing customer-suppliers means reducing the number of customers! So, in fact, the service provider's objective is to *increase* the number of customer-suppliers. (A "customer-supplier" is a customer that supplies inputs to the production process.)

The inability, or unwillingness, to reduce the supply base makes it prohibitively costly to establish personalized alliances. Therefore, service providers may seek to establish mass alliances.

This Service Business Principle alludes to the fact that some industrial services are exceptions to the mass-alliance requirement. In fact, some industrial services have relatively few customers, allowing the close, personalized alliance relationships sought in manufacturing. For example, some consulting firms have only a small number of clients for a given office. Also, corporate accounting firms often assign accountant employees to only a few major customers. On a different scale, a custom home builder may only have a few customers at any given time, allowing a personalized "alliance" with those customers.

How it impacts decisions... Given that it is impractical to form close working alliances with the large number of customer-suppliers, the service provider might need to decide on an alternate strategy: mass alliances.

What to do about it... A mass alliance is a more cost-effective surrogate for supplier alliances. Such an alliance requires establishing a relationship with the customer-supplier that provides mutual benefit for the supplier and the customer. An example is a membership relationship in which the supplier-customer assists the service provider in the service delivery process, and in return receives a benefit. An example is the Savings Club cards that are offered by some grocery stores. The customer is given a card that is scanned at the register at each purchase. This helps the grocery store by providing an accurate profile of specific customer purchases over time. (That data is useful in planning promotions and product offerings.) In return, the customer is given a special price on selected items—customers who do not use the card pay the regular price.

In prior Service Business Principles we discussed membership relationships, such as frequent purchase clubs. The membership relationships described in this Service Business Principle are of a particular type: the relationship requires that the customer *do something* to assist the service delivery process, in exchange for a benefit from the service provider.

Such membership relationships can be considered "alliances" that require less personalization and fewer resources to maintain than traditional alliances, thus being more cost-effective.

Sometimes it may still be impractical to have mass alliances with *all* of the customers who are supplying their inputs. In such cases, "ABC analysis" can be used to select those customers who provide the largest volume of demand for the service. The "A" customers might be the small group (perhaps 20 percent) who supply much (perhaps 80 percent) of the business. (The "Pareto Principle" indicates that 20 percent of a firm's customers will typically drive 80 percent of its sales.) The "C" customers are those individuals who provide very little business each. And the "B" customers are somewhere in between. In some cases, personalized alliances can be maintained with the "A" group, and mass alliances with the other customers. In other cases, mass alliances are set up with the "A" group, with no alliance with the others.

Unit 6

For example...   A medical office has many customers. The primary supplier is patients who supply their illnesses and injuries. "Alliances" come in the form of membership relationships such as Health Maintenance Organizations (HMOs) or Preferred Provider Organizations (PPOs). With HMOs and PPOs, the customer-supplier agrees to only see certain physicians and never see a specialist without first consulting a less-expensive primary care physician. In return, the HMO or PPO provides health care "insurance" to the patient (or to the patient's employer) at a lower cost.

My airline application...   An airline has many customers, who supply themselves and their baggage. One form of membership relationship is frequent flier clubs. However, these are not really "alliances," since the customer doesn't agree to do anything different to assist the airline in the transportation production process.

One alliance strategy some airlines use is to form relationships with corporate clients who have large travel requirements (the "A" clients). The airline helps the client in planning her travel needs, avoiding last-minute booking of flights where possible. The airline might also help the client identify typically underutilized flights, to take advantage of potential discounts. This helps the airline in planning and capacity management, and helps the customer control her travel expenses.

How manufacturing differs from services...

With manufacturing, there are often relatively few supplied parts that represent a large portion of cost of goods sold. Manufactures may implement "supply base reduction" programs to narrow the number of suppliers, making it reasonable to maintain personalized alliances with each one. For example, Xerox was able to reduce suppliers in its worldwide copier division from over 5,000 to about 450. [16] By reducing the number of suppliers, manufacturers are able to devote the resources to maintain more intimate alliances with each supplier, including shared quality initiatives and certification.

With consumer goods, the direct customers are often a distributers, of which there are relatively few. Manufacturers typically maintain a close relationship with these direct customers, but simply mass-market to end customers.

---

[16] see McGrath, M. E. and R. W. Hoole, "Manufacturing's New Economies of Scale." *Harvard Business Review*, 70/3 (1992), 94-102.

SBP 6d: Mass Alliances   Name (if turned in):_____

Analysis questions...

To help apply this Service Business Principle, consider and answer the following questions about your specific service business process. (❑Check here if you are going outside of your target service business.)

Service company/business:_____

The service process:_____

① How many suppliers are there to the service production process over the course of a year, including customers who supply their inputs? Is it practical to establish a close "alliance" with each one? If not, why not?

② What types of membership relationships are there between customers and the company?

③ Are there customer-company relationships that require the customer to do something to help the company deliver the service? What benefit is there to the customer? What benefit is there to the service provider?

①_____

_____

_____

_____

_____

_____

_____

_____

_____

_____

_____

_____

_____

_____

_____

_____

Unit 6

SBP 6d: Mass Alliances   Name (if turned in):_____

Application exercise... Also to help you apply this Service Business Principle, complete the following analysis with regard to your specific service business process, or another service process in your business. (❑Check here if you are going outside of your target service business, which was _____.)

Service company/business:_____

The service process:_____

Consider where your company fits on the following continuum.

Number of Suppliers and Customer-Suppliers			
few (10s)	100s	1000s	many (10,000s)
(typical relationship with customer-suppliers)			
partnerships	<----------------------->		everyone for himself
(possible type of alliances)			
personalized alliances	<----------------------->		mass alliances (membership)

If you have more than a few customer-suppliers, how might ABC analysis be used to target alliances? Devise a strategy for identifying "A" customers. Is there something that the "A" customers could do that would help your company in the service delivery process? Is there a way that you could modify the service process for the "A" customers for mutual benefit? How would an "alliance" be established with these customers? Would it be practical to establish mass alliances with *all* of the company's customers?

Preparation for the next Service Business Principle (6e)

To consider... Before proceeding, consider the following and write thoughts and ideas below:

Some manufacturers maintain strategic advantage through propriety product or process technologies. For example, pharmaceutical manufacturers always patent their new drugs to give them an opportunity (for 17 or 27 years) to produce them without competition. Without patents, competitors could purchase the product and "reverse engineer" (take it apart) to discover the product composition—allowing them to duplicate it. Production process technologies, such as the way to make a new high-density microchip, might also be patented. Some manufacturers avoid patenting their production process innovations because filing a patent reveals the secret, and competitors may find a way to vary the innovation enough to overcome the patent protection and overcome the advantage of the innovation. Instead of patenting, these manufacturers attempt to keep their production process a secret, and require production employees, suppliers, and visitors to sign "non-disclosure agreements" promising to not reveal the process innovation. Can service providers likewise maintain the advantages of service-product and process innovations? What is there about services that helps or hinders the ability to keep innovation secrets? (hint: recall the Unified Services Theory)

Unit 6

_____

_____

_____

_____

_____

_____

_____

_____

THE EPHEMERAL SECRET SERVICE

Service Business Principle	*"With services, competitors posing as customers can study not only the service product, but often also the production process. Since most service processes cannot be patented, it can be difficult to keep the secrets of competitive advantage."*

Why it occurs... THE EPHEMERAL SECRET SERVICE occurs because customers, be they competitors or others, are involved in the production process by virtue of the fact that they provide inputs to the process.

Closely related to... the *Lowered Entry Barriers* SBP, which will be covered next. Also relates to the *Likening a Service* SBP, which shows new entrants how to borrow innovation ideas from other service providers. (*The Ephemeral Secret Service* is about attempting to keep others from borrowing innovation ideas.)

Details... How does a competitor posing as a customer study the service innovation? In services that involve customer-self inputs, such as hotels, theme parks, and retailers, the competitors are free to spend as much time as they care to at the service facility observing exactly how things are done. With other services, the customer does not physically go to the service facility, but sends their belongings or information. In those cases, competitors can experiment by sending various belongings or information through the service process and observing how each is handled. The result can be a good idea how the service innovation is accomplished. (Isn't that sneaky.)

As mentioned previously, some manufacturers require employees and suppliers to sign non-disclosure agreements upon accepting employment. Such a contract is enforceable should an employee or supplier later choose to go into competition with the company. With service organizations, it would generally be unreasonable to ask every customer-suppliers to sign a non-disclosure agreement. Not only are customers suppliers of inputs, but in some cases the customer supplies her own efforts as labor (such as self-service gasoline). (This issue will be revisited later in SBP: *Capricious Labor*) As such, the customer-labor gets to know the service process well, and is not likely to be bound by non-disclosure agreements.

An extension of this service principle involves how an innovator makes the innovation available to others. With manufactured products, which are patented, the patent holder can *license* the product to others, allowing them to produce the product. The patent holder typically gets a fee for each patented product so produced.

With service innovations that cannot be patented, the innovator might employ a different strategy to allow others to use the innovation. That strategy is *franchising*, which is to "package" the service process and make it available to others for a franchise fee. A franchise is basically a do-it-yourself "kit" for duplicating a service (concept) innovation. What is to stop a competitor from duplicating the innovation without purchasing the franchise "kit?" Not a lot. However, they cannot copy the franchise brand name, which is usually trademarked. And with that brand name typically comes national advertising and an established reputation. Nevertheless, there are particular advantages to franchising companies to expand rapidly before competitors are able to establish competing brand names and reputations.

How it impacts decisions... The service provider must decide if and how to protect service product and process innovations.

What to do about it... Time is generally of the essence when it comes to capitalizing on service innovations. This is why franchising is so popular among many innovative service businesses—franchising allows for rapid expansion.

Some service process innovations can be understood but not easily duplicated. An example is innovations based on corporate culture. Corporate culture is like a 40-ton ship—once it is moving a particular direction it is not easily turned. An example of service advantage through culture is the approach Disney takes to human resources at their theme parks and resorts. Every employee is a "cast member" that is well trained in the Disney traditions. There is a significant expectation for interaction with "guests," and even the trash collectors are expected to personify the Disney experience. Despite a competitors' understanding and belief in the value of the Disney way, this information would be difficult to implement in an organization that has been doing things a different way.

For example... The idea of a quick-change oil, lube, and filter, was and is a great innovation. Vehicle owners know that the oil needs to be changed regularly, but were put off by the awful waits to have the vehicle serviced at traditional auto-mechanic shops. A gentleman whom I heard speak some years ago claims to be the originator of that innovation. Recognizing the value of his innovation, he immediately set out on a dramatic expansion campaign. (In fact, he expanded so rapidly that he ran into serious financial trouble—new stores were in progressively less desirable locations, meaning less profit.) Today there are all types of quick-change auto service companies around—you can bet the managers take their cars to competing shops to learn of any new innovations.

Banks and other financial services companies are constantly innovating. For example, American Express claims that they provide an advantage of a consolidated, itemized year-end statement. Well, if that is something that is *indeed* of value to customers, then what is to stop a competitor from being an American Express customer, getting the statement, and instructing the computer programmers to duplicate it.

My airline application... Perhaps the most innovative of the major airlines is Southwest, who has defined an entirely new segment of low-cost air travel. One of their innovations is the twenty-minute turn around of a plane, meaning that from the time a plane lands until it takes off again is twenty minutes or less. This advantage gives Southwest tremendous cost advantages, since their airplanes are in the air generating revenue much more than planes of competing airlines. Southwest achieves twenty-minute turnarounds by getting everyone, including passengers, ready to go prior to the time the plane lands. With everyone ready and waiting, the process of changing baggage, fuel, and passengers is done quickly and efficiently. No food is loaded onto the planes except for nuts and soft drinks. And all employees do what it is takes to keep things moving, even if that means the pilot has to help load baggage. Employees and passengers feel this sense of urgency, which is the driving force of the airline's efficiency and cost savings. And it is a great dishonor to employees if their flight is delayed. (If such was the case for some other airlines, the employees would be constantly living in dishonor.)

Unit 6

Since the production efficiency of Southwest Airlines is based on procedures *and* on culture, it is not easily duplicated. Although major competitors can and have attempted to duplicate the efficient procedures, cultural inefficiency has prevented any from matching the Southwest cost structure (which in the early 1990's was about 7 cents per passenger mile, compared with 8-11 cents for competitors[17]).

Supplemental reading...   Fitzsimmons2 chapter 3 page 51 on Understanding the Competitive Environment of Services.
Fitzsimmons2 chapter 15 pages 464-467 on Franchising.
case: Southwest Airlines 1993 (A) (HBS)

How manufacturing differs from services...

With manufacturing, products can be patented, and/or customers, competitors, and suppliers can be kept from production facilities.

---

[17] *Southwest Airlines: 1993 (A)* Harvard Business School case, page 6 and exhibit 8.

SBP 6e: The Ephemeral Secret Service   Name (if turned in):_____

Analysis questions...

To help apply this Service Business Principle, consider and answer the following questions about your specific service business process. (❑Check here if you are going outside of your target service business.)

Service company/business:_____

The service process:_____

① What have been innovations in our service product or process?
② How did competitors respond?
③ How sustainable was the advantage of that innovation? Why?

① _____

_____

_____

_____

_____

_____

_____

_____

_____

_____

_____

_____

_____

_____

_____

_____

_____

Unit 6

SBP 6e: The Ephemeral Secret Service   Name (if turned in):_____

Application exercise...   Also to help you apply this Service Business Principle, complete the following analysis with regard to your specific service business process, or another service process in your business. (☐Check here if you are going outside of your target service business, which was _____.)

Service company/business:_____

The service process:_____

Describe a successful process innovation that occurred in your service business in recent memory. How do you suppose the innovation originated? Which do you think was the first company to adopt the innovation? Describe how you suppose competitors responded to the innovation. What attempts might the original innovator have made to keep the innovation a secret? Describe how competitors might have "discovered" the secret. How long do you suppose the innovation was truly a "secret?"

Preparation for the next Service Business Principle (6f)

To consider... Before proceeding, consider the following and write thoughts and ideas below:

A basic concept of business strategy is barriers to market entry. Companies presently serving a market desire to fortify their position, and prevent new entrants from encroaching on their market. When markets are lucrative, other companies may desire to overcome market entry barriers and enter as competition. Some of the barriers to market entry are grounded in market realities or other environmental factors, such as government regulation. Many of the barriers are grounded in operational principles, such as economies of scale. Can you think of some examples of barriers that make it difficult for start-up manufacturers to compete with long-established manufacturers of specific products? (such as economies of scale or government regulation) Do those barriers seem to be more or less significant in service organizations? In other words, does it seem more or less difficult for new service providers to compete with long-established service providers?

Unit 6

Service Business Principle 6f:
LOWERED ENTRY BARRIERS

Service Business Principle	*"With services, the relevance of various barriers to entry is generally lower than corresponding barriers in manufacturing situations. However, in most cases the lower barriers can be fortified."*

Why it occurs... LOWERED ENTRY BARRIERS occurs because of various symptoms and implications coming from the Unified Services Theory, as will be discussed below.

Details... Perhaps the most commonly referred to list of barriers to market entry are those published some years ago by Michael Porter. His general list (not exclusive of manufacturing or service organizations) includes the following:[18]

- **economies of scale** (It is not worth it to enter a market in a small way.),
- **product differentiation** (It can be hard to overcome brand loyalty for current producers.),
- **capital requirements** (Start-up often involves significant capital investment: plant, equipment, working capital, etc.),
- **access to distribution channels** (It may be difficult to compete in wholesale or retail channels that already carry competing products.),
- **government policy** (It may be difficult to comply with government regulations, especially for a new market entry.), and
- **cost advantages independent of size** (e.g. experience curves, proprietary technology, access to the best sources of inputs, assets purchased at pre-inflation prices, government subsidies, favorable locations).

For each of the barriers described by Porter, we will consider how (a) the Unified Services Theory impacts the barrier's manifestation in services industries, (b) whether the barrier is generally higher or lower for services, and (c) how current service providers might fortify that barrier. As with all Service Business Principles in this workbook, this evaluation of barriers is founded in the Unified Services Theory. We will consider the first five barriers listed above, followed by a number of barriers pertaining to "cost advantages independent of size."

Economies of Scale.

As mentioned in the *Heterogeneous Production* Service Business Principle, the individual units of output of many service processes are unique. Since customers provide inputs, the inputs are unique. This implies that the entire production process may need to be tailored to each individual customer. As such, economies of scale are much less likely to occur in services.

If economies of scale is a much lower barrier to entry for services, how might current service providers fortify the barrier? For most service companies, some parts of the process *do not* have customer inputs and thus can be treated the same as they would in manufacturing. For example, at a restaurant, the process of taking orders, preparing food to order, and serving the food for consumption in a pleasant atmosphere involves customer inputs, which hinders economies of scale. However, the procurement of food (raw materials) and other supplies can happen independent of the customer. Therefore, the procurement processes can enjoy the benefits of economies of scale. An example of this is large

---
[18] Porter, M. E. (1979). How Competitive Forces Shape Strategy. *Harvard Business Review*, Vol. 57.

restaurant chains which have centralized purchasing functions. This gives large chains an advantage over new market entries who likely purchase in smaller amounts.

Another area where the economies of scale barrier can be fortified is in mass marketing, which again can be accomplished without customer input (customers just consume the output of mass marketing). Again, large producers can have their mass marketing efforts work for multiple locations. Consortiums of auto dealers (e.g. the metropolitan area Ford dealers) have an advantage of pooling their advertising dollars to increase the breadth of exposure.

Product Differentiation.

Services production is often nonstandard for reasons described previously. Therefore, every unit of production can practically be differentiated from every other unit. The production of current producers may be different over time depending on customer inputs. So then, why would it not be easy for new competitors to likewise differentiate?

In addition, "quality" is often hard to define for services. This is because much of quality depends on customer inputs. What is quality of education? An important part of quality of output is quality of input. Is ability part of quality? What about adaptability? If quality is indeed hard to define for services, then it would be easy for a new market entry to claim higher quality without easily accomplished verification.

Also, services tend to be high in "credence" properties, which are those properties that cannot be easily evaluated even after purchase and consumption.[19] How does one student know if he received a better education than another? How does a patient know if she got better surgery from one hospital than she would have received from another hospital? With credence properties, the customer has to take the word of some expert—often the service provider (doctor, professor)—that the product is better. New entries can (and often do) claim to be different and better than current providers, which can be hard to either prove or disprove.

So, product differentiation is also tends to be a lower barrier for services. How might present providers fortify this barrier? One way is to emphasize personalization, which is to customize production to the individual characteristics and needs of individual customers. If we are meeting specific needs of individual customers, any attempts to "differentiate" by competitors may be considered of little value to the customer. In other words, if we are already hitting the target, differentiating from where we are hitting means missing the target.

Capital Requirements.

One of the major capital requirements of manufacturing organizations is working capital to pay for inventories of raw materials and purchased parts to use for production. With many services, customers provide most of the inputs, and the company does not have to pay the customer for these inputs, leading to a lower working capital requirement. For example, the primary input in auto repair is automobiles with problems. Auto shops do not have to pay for that input, which is good, since it represents what would otherwise be the most expensive input.

Another demand on working capital is financing inventories. Since service customers often resist extended inventories, this is also less of a cost.

Therefore, as far as working capital goes, there are reasons that the barrier to entry for service industries might be lower than for manufacturing industries. However, the capital requirements barrier can be fortified by concentrating on other types of capital requirements such as plant and equipment. A hotel could provide nicer facilities. A shipping company could provide more advanced computer technology

Unit 6

---

[19] Heskett, J. L., Sasser, W. E., Jr., and Hart, C. W. L. (1990). *Service Breakthroughs: Changing the Rules of the Game*, The Free Press, New York, page 37.
   "Credence" properties will also be discussed later in *The Marketing of Properties* Service Business Principle.

for tracking packages. An Internet Service Provider could provide faster modems, which would be more expensive. In these ways, current providers can raise customer expectations for service and make it more expensive for new market entries to compete.

Access to Distribution Channels.

In manufacturing, the distribution channels are the means of getting the production output from the factory to the customer. Companies like Frito Lay or Coca-Cola have access (or own) distribution channels and command premium shelf space at supermarkets. A real challenge for a new auto manufacturer would be finding out where to sell the product.

With many services, production takes place *when the customer is present* as an input, or is providing inputs. Therefore, every customer represents a unique distribution channel. New competitors who have access to customers simultaneously have access to the distribution channels.

As a lower barrier, access to distribution channels can be fortified for services by making exclusive distribution arrangements with customers. The retailer Sam's Club does this by charging an annual membership fee. Airlines have a membership arrangement in the form of frequent flier programs. Other companies make ties to customers by providing distribution technology on-site. The drug distributor McKesson installs computer terminals for placing orders in hospitals and pharmacies. The Internet Service Provider WebTV (or Microsoft) controls the distribution channel into customers' homes by selling customers the TV-top box that controls the access.

Government Policy.

Complying with government policies and regulations can be a challenge, particularly for new market entries. The question is, do service businesses tend to be more or less regulated by governments? To answer this we might ask why governments regulate businesses. Very often, the answer is to protect consumers (i.e. voters and taxpayers). In this regard, how do services differ from manufacturing organizations? Again, by the UST we see that customers are providing inputs to service production processes, and are very often *the inputs themselves*. As such, we might suppose that governments are *more* likely to regulate service businesses.

In manufacturing, if there is a product defect, the company simply issues a product recall. Examples in recent memory are lawn darts and exploding gas tanks. Tens of thousands of vehicles were produced with faulty gas tanks, yet only a handful of people were harmed as a result.

On the other hand, consider the effect of a problem with a service process with its customer-provided inputs. Banks act on peoples' money. Dentists act on peoples' teeth. Airlines act on customers' selves. Think how highly regulated these industries are. Why? If a certain dental procedure produces defects in ten thousand units of production, every one of those customers is affected by that defect, even if a recall is initiated.

We thus have reason to believe that the government policy barrier would be generally higher for service companies than for manufacturing companies. Nevertheless, current producers may still want to fortify that barrier, or at least get as much "milage" as possible out of the existing barrier. The barrier can be fortified by seeking more government regulation (heaven forbid), such as by hiring lobbyists. An example of this can be seen in the banking industry. Credit unions, who enjoyed the benefits of fewer regulations and taxes than traditional banks, desired to offer many of the investment services provided by banks. The traditional banks desired to protect their market positions by encouraging more government regulation of credit union activities.

One way for current producers to get milage out of government regulation barriers is to publicize their compliance with the regulations. In this way, potential new competitors will see this as a barrier, with compliance coming at a cost. A manufacturing example is automakers who publicize that they comply with safety regulations, such as air bags, prior to the time they are required by law. Service companies such as airlines could likewise publicize superior compliance with government-imposed safety regulations.

Cost Advantages Independent of Size.

Porter lists six of these other cost advantages in his original article.[20] The application of the Unified Services Theory makes each of them quite interesting. Therefore, this section will look at these other cost advantages in detail. Since they were listed but not described in the prior section, their manufacturing application is included here for reference. As with the prior six barriers, I will describe the implications of the Unified Services Theory for each of these cost advantages, and how current service providers might fortify the barrier to entry.

Experience Curves.

With manufacturing, current producers have a cost advantage because they have moved down the experience curve—or have learned how to produce more efficiently and effectively. With service companies, it is hard to gain experience when every customer presents unique inputs and every unit of production is potentially unique. Experience is more likely to be gained by production components that tend to be common across the various units of production. However, generally the cost advantage do to experience curves will be lower for service providers than for manufacturers. Current service providers can fortify this cost advantage barrier by decreasing employee turnover and standardizing procedures where appropriate.

Proprietary Technology.

Manufacturers with proprietary technologies often require employees and plant visitors to sign non-disclosure agreements. This protects the advantage brought of those technologies. With many services, customers have free access to production facilities and technologies, since they are providing inputs. (see SBP: *The Ephemeral Secret Service*) Potential *competitors* posing as customers can study the production technologies, allowing competing companies to more easily duplicate those technologies. For example, when Federal Express came out with their on-line tracking of packages, we can be sure that competitors posing as customers studied the technology to see how it interacted with customers. This would greatly simplify the process of developing similar technologies. These technology imitating companies have the advantage of not having to design the technology purely from a blank drawing board.

In addition, many service process *technologies* are very intangible (even though the service overall service has many tangible elements) and not patentable, which limits the legal protection of proprietary technologies. (also see SBP: *The Ephemeral Secret Service*)

Current producers can fortify the technology cost advantage by investing in Research and Development to develop production technologies that continually offer new features. Thus, they become a moving target with technologies that are difficult to keep up with.

Access to the Best Sources of Inputs.

Manufacturers may own the input source or have some exclusive agreement for obtaining raw materials or component parts. The fact that IBM makes computer memory chips certainly helped their ability to compete when the memory shortage occurred a few years ago. With service processes, primary inputs come from customers, who are not owned by the service producer, and who are less likely to make an exclusive agreement. Therefore, by gaining access to customers, new competitors have access to these key sources of inputs.

---

[20] Porter, M. E. (1979). How Competitive Forces Shape Strategy. *Harvard Business Review*, Vol. 57.

As with "access to distribution channels" discussed previously, this cost advantage may be fortified by establishing membership or other relationships with customers. For example, a dry cleaning service may establish contracts with customers to pick up soiled clothing, which is a major input in the dry cleaning process.

Assets Purchased at Pre-inflation Prices.

Current producers of manufactured goods can have a cost advantage over new entries because of lower book values of assets, implying not only lower purchase price but also lower depreciation expense. It can certainly be an advantage for a manufacturer to have an older facility that is paid for. Further, the customer does not care (or is not aware) that the goods are being produced in an older facility.

With services, the customer often sees the service provider's facilities when she is providing inputs. Do service customers prefer new production assets to older assets? Do customers prefer new hotels to older hotels? New hospitals to older hospitals? New retail facilities to older facilities? Generally, yes. Therefore, it can, in fact, be a *disadvantage* for a service provider to have older facilities. Further, changes in architectural styles or construction coding may make it very expensive to upgrade old facilities. New competitors may very well have an advantage. When assets represent changing technologies, such as the modems used by Internet Service Providers, the old technologies may not even be paid for when new technologies need to be purchased.

The cost advantage for older producers can be somewhat reclaimed by conscientiously planning expenditures to keep assets in new condition. In this way, the costs of providing updated assets and facilities can be planned and controlled.

Government Subsidies.

Very often, the government subsidizes current producers of goods to protect the existence of those current producers. Common examples are farming and aerospace, where the government protects industries for national security reasons. How does the government determine where to provide subsidies? Very often the subsidies are given based on the producers' prior production. For example, farmers involved with protected crops will typically receive a subsidy based on the average production over the last five or so years. (Sometimes this subsidy is payment to produce less grain in the future in order to keep prices up.) New competitors have less prior production, and thus have less access to government subsidies.

Government subsidies provide less cost advantage to current service providers. One reason for this is that with manufacturing, the subsidies are generally to protect the *producers*, whereas with services, the subsidies are often to protect the *consumers* (i.e. voters and taxpayers), who are providing inputs into the production process. Health care is subsidized not so much to protect the doctors and hospitals, but to protect the patients. Education is subsidized more to protect the interests of needy students than to protect the educational institutions. Therefore, new competitors who have access to subsidized customers have access to the subsidies.

Current producers might fortify this cost advantage somewhat by specifically catering to the needs of customers with subsidies, thus improving the access to those subsides. For example, medical clinics might hire employee with particular skill in processing government subsidized medical claims.

Favorable Locations.

Some manufacturers have cost advantage by being located near a key resource. One computer peripheral manufacturer moved its production facility to Malaysia, which was nearer to parts suppliers. This would supposedly give that company advantage by shorter distances from suppliers and thus greater responsiveness. A steel manufacturer might be located near a major source of ore or near a centralized railroad hub for inexpensively shipping the product.

Service businesses often have to be located near the customers, so that customer can easily provide their inputs (see SBP: *Customer Proximity*). This means that many services need to have decentralized production facilities. (You cannot locate a copy center or dry cleaners in Kansas City and serve the entire Midwest.) Being decentralized, the production facilities are often small and dispersed. New market entries can thus position their service facilities in between competitors facilities. In fact, often the best place for a new market entry to locate their facilities is *right next door* to competing facilities. The best place to locate a new restaurant is often near a current restaurant that is doing well. (Burger King does this all the time with McDonald's.) There is an advantage for retail companies to locate near competing retail companies, such as in a mall or shopping center. Auto sales and service companies tend to locate near one another for similar reasons.

Thus we conclude that the cost advantage of favorable locations is often a weak barrier to new service companies. Current service providers can attempt to fortify this cost advantage by making arrangements with complementary service providers to share locations. For example, a restaurant chain might make an exclusive agreement to locate a facility within a hospital or an educational institution.

How it impacts decisions... Current service providers must decide how to prepare for the threat of new entrants. New entrants need to decide if any barriers are a threat to success in a service industry.

What to do about it... Examples of how to fortify various barriers were described above.

For example... (General examples were given in the details section above.)

My airline application... **Economies of scale** might be a barrier for transoceanic airlines, which need sufficient numbers of passengers to justify flying large long-range planes (like 747s). But for shorter-range routes, small airlines can compete by flying smaller planes and feeding passengers into other airlines' hub airports.

Product differentiation is generally not a major barrier, since many passengers view air travel as a commodity and are thus not very loyal to current providers. (In the *Positioning Amid Customers and Competitors* Service Business Principle, I described the Concorde jet as effectively differentiating. Yet there are not a lot of customers willing to pay for such non-commodity travel.)

Capital requirements might be a significant barrier, given the high cost of aircraft. However, startup companies can lease jets, requiring much less up-front capital.

Access to distribution channels can be a barrier when there are a limited number of gates at certain airports. (Air travel is "distributed" at airport gates.) Airlines can get around the gate availability barrier by sharing gates or leasing them from other carriers.

Government policy might be a barrier for highly regulated regions. For example, an absurd legislative agreement in the state of Texas restricts Southwest airlines from having flights out of Dallas's Love Field to any state that does not border Texas. (What ever happened to deregulation?)

(Cost advantages independent of size...)

Experience curves might bring an airline cost advantages if they have skills at efficient operations. However, as discussed in other Service Business Principles, the inefficient traditions of most airlines makes this a weak barrier to new entrants.

Proprietary technology there was a time when some airlines thought reservations systems like Saber provided advantage to the airlines who owned them. However, with the Internet, any airline can provide automated reservation systems at relatively low cost.

Access to the best sources of inputs is a weak barrier since the inputs to the airline process are available to anyone who seeks them. Some airlines may have preferred provider agreements with large companies, but the commodity nature of air travel makes these agreements subject to competitive bidding each time the agreement is renewed.

Assets purchased at pre-inflation prices can be an advantage when the price of aircraft is going up. However, the cost goes up when those older aircraft need to be retired. The vice president of one startup airline said that his company gained a great advantage by purchasing used 737 jets at dramatically discounted prices.

Government subsidies are certainly a barrier which gives advantages to aircraft manufacturers like Airbus Industries. One regional discount airline was supposedly subsidized by its home state in the Southeast—probably to provide inexpensive service where it was not otherwise available. But generally, the multi-regional and international nature of air travel can make it unnecessary for governments to subsidize what foreign air travelers can easily provide.

Favorable locations might mean favorable locations in airports, which was discussed above. The location of airplanes in the air is subject to national airspace approval, but is otherwise open to anyone who wants to fly.

The conclusion is that the barriers to entry in the airline industry are relatively low, or can be easily overcome by new entrants into the industry. This probably explains why so many airlines have sprung up over the past few decades. And many of these airlines startups have gone bankrupt—since it is easier to enter the airline business than it is to operate in it profitably. (They needed to take my Services Management course.)

Supplemental reading...

Fitzsimmons2 chapter 1 pages 15-18 on Management Challenges (Economies of Scale, etc.).

Porter, M. E. (1979). How Competitive Forces Shape Strategy. *Harvard Business Review*, Volume 57.

Thomas, D. R. E. (1978). Strategy is Different in Service Businesses. *Harvard Business Review*, July-August.

How manufacturing differs from services...

With manufacturing, a number of significant entry barriers exist, as discussed under this Service Business Principle.

SBP 6f: Lowered Entry Barriers   Name (if turned in):_____

Analysis questions... To help apply this Service Business Principle, consider and answer the following questions about your specific service business process. (❏Check here if you are going outside of your target service business.)

Service company/business:_____

The service process:_____

Consider the traditional entry barriers: economies of scale, product differentiation, capital requirements, cost advantages, access to distribution channels, and government policy. Also, consider other cost advantages for current producers such as experience curves, proprietary technology, access to the best sources of inputs, assets purchased at pre-inflation prices, government subsidies, and favorable locations.

① What traditional barriers to entry are significant in this industry (preventing new entrants from easily competing)?

② In what ways can weak barriers to entry be fortified? Or, how can current producers increase their competitive (or contributive) advantage of being current producers?

① _____

_____

_____

_____

_____

_____

_____

_____

_____

_____

_____

_____

_____

_____

_____

_____

_____

Unit 6

SBP 6f: Lowered Entry Barriers   Name (if turned in):_____

Application exercise...   Also to help you apply this Service Business Principle, complete the following analysis with regard to your specific service business process, or another service process in your business. (❑Check here if you are going outside of your target service business, which was _____.)

Service company/business:_____

The service process:_____
Identify which two or three of the barriers to entry give the greatest advantage to current service providers. In other words, what barriers make it most difficult for new service providers to enter as competition? Describe why they are so significant in your industry. Next, identify which of the barriers are of little concern to potential new competitors—or which of Porter's barriers give relatively little advantage to current service providers. Describe how two or three of them could be fortified to give current service providers additional advantage. (Porter's barriers include
- economies of scale
- product differentiation
- capital requirements
- access to distribution channels
- government policy

cost advantages independent of size, which includes
- experience curves
- proprietary technology
- access to the best sources of inputs
- assets purchased at pre-inflation prices
- government subsidies
- favorable locations)

Part III - Managing Service Processes
Unit 7:
COST ISSUES

In this unit, we will consider cost issues that are important to consider in managing service processes, all of which are an outcropping of the Unified Services Theory.

Unit reading... The following reading pertains to Service Business Principles included in this unit. The instructor will let you know which of the readings you are responsible for studying.

Fitzsimmons2 chapter 5 on The Service Delivery System.
Fitzsimmons2 chapter 13 on Managing Capacity and Demand.

Unit 7

Preparation for the next Service Business Principle (7a)

To consider... Before proceeding, consider the following and write thoughts and ideas below:

"Utilization" is the portion of production capacity which is actually used, and not idle. Production capacity often involves large fixed costs. Therefore, increasing utilization will allow the fixed costs to be allocated (or amortized) over more product, meaning lower fixed-cost overhead tacked on to each item. The cost advantages of higher utilization are more significant when the ratio of fixed costs to variable product costs are higher. (A variable cost is one that goes up in direct proportion to the number of items produced.) What tends to be the nature of the cost structure of services—do fixed costs or variable costs tend to dominate? What does this imply about utilization? In what sense can the service provider control or not control utilization?

_____

_____

_____

_____

_____

_____

_____

_____

_____

Service Business Principle 7a:

THE COSTS OF UTILIZATION

Service Business Principle	*"With many services, the variable costs of production are minute. Simultaneous production and consumption implies that even "direct" labor is often a fixed cost. Thus, cost advantage can also be realized through increased volume and utilization. However, the variable cost to the customer is typically higher than for a substitute goods product, which inhibits utilization of the service provider."*

Why it occurs... THE COSTS OF UTILIZATION occurs because many of the variable inputs are provided by customers, who do not charge the service provider for those inputs (keeping variable costs down). Simultaneous production and consumption implies that we need to plan labor staffing for *forecasted* demand, and time-perishable capacity implies that we need to pay scheduled workers even when there are no customers to motivate production. Thus, service labor costs tend to be largely fixed.

Details... This Service Business Principle implies that service providers will generally be more cost-competitive if they have higher utilization. Unfortunately, having high utilization is not so simple. For one thing, the higher our utilization, the more likely a "blip" in demand will disrupt our ability to serve. Simultaneous production and consumption coupled with uncertain demand implies that we need to have a certain amount of "safety capacity" just in case demand is larger than expected.

Also, many researchers have observed that in manufacturing environments, when utilization approaches 100 percent of capacity, quality problems grow exponentially. This phenomena also occurs in service situation. For example, if a cashier can serve ten customers per hour, and an average of ten customers per hour arrive at independently random intervals, then the science of queuing theory reveals that the waiting line length will grow to unwieldy proportions! (Queuing theory is discussed in Appendix C.)

Further, there are customer forces that hinder higher utilization. For example, customers who need the service frequently are the ones who are most likely to do it themselves! (see SBP: *Competing with Customers*). Why is this the case? Because from the customer's perspective, allowing the service provider to fill the need represents a greater variable cost but a lower fixed cost than buying the equipment and serving herself (time cost notwithstanding). (see SBP: *Servier-Ownership Perspective*) For example, imagine that homeowner A has her carpet steam cleaned once every couple of years, and homeowner B has her carpet cleaned once each month. Which of the two is most likely to hire a carpet cleaning service, and which is most likely to purchase a carpet cleaning machine? We would have to agree that, notwithstanding time costs, homeowner B would find purchasing her own carpet cleaning machine to be more cost effective than A would—making B less likely to be a customer. Unfortunately, it is people like homeowner B that carpet cleaning companies would love to serve!

Some service industries such as retail and custom home building have high variable costs. In such situations, utilization is significant but does not have as dramatic effect on profitability as when variable costs are low.

How it impacts decisions... Service providers need to decide on how to manage capacity and the utilization of capacity, given the nature of the cost structure. High fixed costs and tiny variable costs means that unutilized capacity is costly, and insufficient capacity is costly.

What to do about it... There are a number of strategies for managing capacity and demand in service settings. Capacity can be controlled through utilizing customer labor in the production process, subcontracting capacity (such as through outsourcing), or developing flexible capacity (such as by cross-training employees). These and other examples are discussed in Fitzsimmons2 chapter 13 on Strategies for Managing Capacity.)

With some services, demand can be *scheduled* to smooth demand out so that it is more in line with capacity. For example, doctors offices will schedule patient appointments in accordance with expected capacity, which may mean patients during times of high demand may have to wait quite some time to receive service.

In other cases, demand cannot be scheduled but it can still be influenced. For example, by promoting off-peak demand or offering price incentives (discussed in Fitzsimmons2 chapter 13 on Strategies for Managing Demand).

In some situations it is desirable to simultaneously control demand and capacity in order to maximize overall revenues. A technique for accomplishing this is known as "yield management." Yield management uses information about the probability of specific types of demand occurring over a specific time periods to calculate the price to offer different classes of service to certain customers at certain times. Sound complicated? Well it is. Yield management is why on some airlines, every passenger on a given flight may have paid a different amount from every other passenger.

Unit 7

For example... Why does it cost so much more for an emergency room visit than for a visit to a regular medical clinic? Is it because emergency rooms expend more supplies for an typical visit? Probably not. By and large, the difference comes down to utilization. At medical clinics that accept patient appointments, patient demand can be scheduled to match the capacity of the clinic (including number of physicians, number of rooms, etc.). On the other hands, emergency rooms need to staff for highly uncertain and uncontrolled patient demand. As a result, emergency room capacity is generally utilized to a low degree. In a sense, when you see an emergency room physician you are paying not only for the physician's time at your attention, but for his or her time waiting for you to show up.

Believe it or not, the variable costs of service at even the most expensive hotels are almost nothing. Even if the room-cleaning labor is paid by the hour, the wages are not very high and most housekeepers are quite efficient (due to tremendous repetition). The other variable costs include laundering of towels and linens, a little electricity for the climate control and vacuum, and a few small soaps, etc. for the bathroom. But the fixed costs of a hotel can be tremendous. In fact, it is the cost of the supporting facility (the building) that drives the price of the hotel. It was reported that one hotel magnate said that the average rate for night's stay in a room should be roughly $1 for every $1,000 of building construction costs (probably based on breakeven and investment payback analysis). The point was that construction costs drive the pricing of rooms. Further, utilization of the hotel property will be key to financial profitability (since low utilization provides little variable cost savings, but the fixed costs remain).

My airline application... As alluded to previously, airlines are often the most flagrant appliers of yield management. Why? Because in 1997 a new jet cost $30 million or more, but the variable cost of production was and is pretty much "peanuts" (plus a little fuel and a soft drink or juice). The name of the game for airlines is covering the fixed costs, which is most often attempted through yield management.

Southwest Airlines takes a slightly different strategy than other carriers. Instead of adjusting fares to squeeze every penny out of particular flights, they offer a handful of basic fares. Then, they focus on cost savings by increasing utilization of their fixed assets. The airline example given in SBP: *The Ephemeral Secret Service* alluded to Southwest's operating strategy for quick turnaround of jets at airport gates. Southwest's turnarounds typically take less than half the time than those of other carriers. Further, airlines like Southwest tend to start flights earlier in the morning and finish later in the evening. It may seem like an inconvenience to offer flights at those odd hours, but it allows the fixed cost of the jet to be allocated over more flights. The result is having planes "in the air," producing air transportation and revenues perhaps twice as great as competitors. Even with the same percentage of seats filled, the result is a greater utilization of each jet, enabling significant cost savings.

Supplemental reading...   Fitzsimmons2 chapter 13 on Managing Capacity and Demand

How manufacturing differs from services...

With manufacturing, major inputs include raw materials, parts, and direct labor, which are quite variable. Since production is *scheduled*, labor is often a variable cost—if there is no production scheduled for a particular hour, the hourly wage employees are not required to report.

Quantitative analysis... (covered at the discretion of the instructor)

Breakeven analysis is a simple way of looking at the impact of volume on profitability. The following is a brief description.

If FC is the fixed cost of production (the cost incurred each time period regardless of volume), and VC is the variable cost of one unit of production, and VR is the revenue for each item produced, then:

$$\text{BEV} = \text{Breakeven Volume} = FC / (VR - VC)$$

The breakeven volume is the number of units that must be produced and sold in a given period to achieve zero gross profits. Note that BEV goes up when FC goes up. Thus, we might think that services with high fixed costs would have a high breakeven volumes. However, those service companies likely also have low variable costs. Since BEV goes down as VC goes down, the overall BEV is reduced.

When we have low variable costs relative to variable revenues, then we have a high degree of "leverage." This means that every unit of sales below the BEV has a great impact on our losses, and every unit of sales above the BEV has a great impact on profits. That is why utilization is key. (Breakeven utilization is calculated as BEV divided by the overall production capacity for the same period of time.)

A more complex form of analysis pertaining to capacity utilization is Yield Management. With Yield Management, we attempt to adjust VR, which changes the BEV. If VR is decreased then customer may be more motivated to purchase the service, increasing the sales volume. Since BEV is also increased by increasing VR, the increase in sales volume needs to be above a certain amount.

Yield Management has been used in airline and hotel industries, which have extremely high fixed costs and extremely low variable costs.

For more information about Yield Management, see Fitzsimmons2 chapter 4 pages 70-71 on Yield Management and Fitzsimmons2 chapter 13 pages 402-412 on Yield Management.

SBP 7a: The Costs of Utilization   Name (if turned in):_____

Analysis questions...   To help apply this Service Business Principle, consider and answer the following questions about your specific service business process. (❑Check here if you are going outside of your target service business.)

Service company/business:_____

The service process:_____

    ① What are the variable costs of production?
    ② What are the fixed costs of production?
    ③ What is the cost impact of increased production? How would profitability be impacted by increased utilization of capacity?
    ④ Are there disincentives for high utilization by individual customers?

① _____

_____

_____

_____

_____

_____

_____

_____

_____

_____

_____

_____

_____

_____

_____

Unit 7

SBP 7a: The Costs of Utilization   Name (if turned in):_____

Application exercise... Also to help you apply this Service Business Principle, complete the following analysis with regard to your specific service business process, or another service process in your business. (❑Check here if you are going outside of your target service business, which was _____.)

Service company/business:_____

The service process:_____

Construct a breakeven analysis for your company. (See the "Quantitative Analysis" section of this Service Business Principle for a discussion of breakeven analysis.) What are the variable costs of production? (List cost names and estimated per-unit amounts.) What are the fixed costs? How much of the fixed cost is allocated to a given year? What is the average expected revenue per customer? How many customers need to be served over a given year in order to cover the fixed costs? What capacity utilization does this imply? (i.e. what percent of overall capacity needs to be spent in actual production in order to cover fixed costs and make a profit?)

Preparation for the next Service Business Principle (7b)

To consider... Before proceeding, consider the following and write thoughts and ideas below:

Most manufacturing organizations would like to be more efficient, implying that they get more output for the same or fewer inputs. One way to increase efficiency is to drive inefficiencies out of the production process. An inefficiency may be improper production planning, such that the machines produce sequences of dissimilar items, requiring substantial reconfiguration of the machines between each item. Greater efficiency might be gained by scheduling similar items adjacent in time, to minimize the need for dramatic reconfiguration between items.

Service organizations might also have the objective of increasing efficiency. What is it about service production processes that is likely to limit the potential for achieving an efficiency objective?

Unit 7

_____

_____

_____

_____

_____

_____

_____

_____

_____

Service Business Principle 7b:

POTENTIAL OPERATING OBJECTIVES

Service Business Principle	*"With services, the potential objectives of the production process is limited by the types and amounts of customer content. The potential operating efficiency will be inversely related to the amount and variety of customer-self content."*

Why it occurs... POTENTIAL OPERATING OBJECTIVES occurs because customers consider themselves as unique individuals (and rightly so), and are resistant to the impersonalization that generally comes with high efficiency. This is an issue for service organizations because customers are providing themselves (or their belongings or information) as inputs to the production process.

Closely related to... SBP: *Positioning Amid Customers and Competitors*
SBP: *The Custom Manufacturing Oxymoron*

Details... The idea behind this Service Business Principle came from Richard Chase, who wrote an article titled "The Customer Contact Approach to Services." In his article[21] he presented the following equation:

$$\text{potential facility efficiency} = f(1 - [\text{customer contact time} \div \text{service creation time}])$$

This equation means that services involving more contact with customer will have less potential for operating efficiently. Customer contact breeds inefficiency. In the words of Dr. Chase: "Service facilities characterized by high customer contact are perceived as being inherently limited in their production efficiency because of the uncertainty that people introduce into the service creation process."

I have found that the more I study Chase's supposition, the more it makes sense. One modification I would make to his perspective is to change from calling it characterizing by "customer contact" to characterizing by "customer *content*," which is semantically more aligned with the Unified Services Theory.

How it impacts decisions... The service organization needs to decide whether to allow for large amounts of "customer content" or for increased efficiency (or an optimal balance between the two).

What to do about it... If a service that involves substantial customer inputs wants to increase operating efficiency, then probably the amount and types of customer inputs need to be controlled or reduced. One way to do this is to delay the introduction of customer inputs until later stages of the production process, which will be discussed in the next Service Business Principle (*Cost Savings by Service-Manufacturing*).

Another way to control the customer inputs into the production process is to provide structure in the receipt of inputs. Shouldice Hospital, mentioned under the *Positioning Amid Customers and Competitors* Service Business Principle, is one of

---

[21] "The Customer Contact Approach to Services: Theoretical Bases and Practical Extensions," by Richard B. Chase, *Operations Research*, Volume 29, Issue 4, 1981.

the most efficient hospitals in existence. A key way they do this is by limiting the variety of customer-self inputs into the process. Customers have to conform to a certain profile to be considered. For one thing, Shouldice only treats a certain type of hernia. Customers with other problems, including more complex hernias, will be rejected. Also, people with health problems such as high blood pressure are also generally filtered out. The result is tightly controlled customer inputs, allowing for high "operating" efficiencies.

For example... Federal Express has a need to operate efficiently, despite the necessity of processing customer-belonging inputs (i.e. the packages and documents to ship). One way the company reduces the variety of inputs is by providing standardized packaging. There are FedEx envelopes for documents, FedEx boxes for items of small or medium size, and FedEx tubes for large documents. Even though it costs the company money to produce those forms of packaging, one would expect the benefits of increased efficiency to outweigh the costs. This increased efficiency comes as a result of controlling the variability in the way many items are shipped.

Two types of popular fast food restaurants are hamburger places like Wendy's and McDonald's, and sandwich places like Subway and Hogi Yogi. One main difference is that customers of the hamburger places order items directly from the menu with only occasional modification, whereas at the sandwich shops, customers specify which of perhaps ten optional ingredients (pickles, oil, peppers, etc.) to include, and in what amounts. This increased intensity of customer preference inputs makes the sandwich shops much less efficient than the hamburger shops. If I go to Wendy's and see that there are twenty customers in line in front of me I will probably wait, since the line moves quite fast. However if there were twenty customers in line at Hogi Yogi, the twentieth will be waiting a long time before getting to the front of the line.

Some custom home builders want to appeal to entry-level home buyers who require affordable housing. The problem with custom home building is that it can be extremely inefficient. This inefficiency is largely caused by preferences and change orders of customers. Customers who insist on this feature and that feature, and who change the specifications during construction make it difficult to achieve any close approximation to mass production efficiencies. There are two ways home builders get around this. One is to give the home purchaser a set of pre-drawn plans from which to choose, allowing only minor modifications (without a lot of additional expense). In this manner, the need for customer interaction and information exchange is kept under control, allowing the builder to schedule subcontractors in a more efficient manner.

The second way to reduce home-building inefficiencies caused by customer inputs will be described in the next Service Business Principle.

My airline application... A manifestation of this Service Business Principle in the airline industry is in the typical "passenger load factor," which is the percent of available flight-seats which are occupied. (Load factor is a measure of utilization.) A normal load factor might be around perhaps 65-70 percent. Wouldn't it be better to have 80 or 90 percent utilization? Wouldn't that result in more production output with roughly the same resource inputs—thus increasing efficiency? Well, a big reason why a higher passenger load factor is not attainable is because *customers are involved in the production process*! And, those customers just refuse to cooperate fully. For example, if the desired 8:00 a.m. flight is full, and the closest available flight is the evening before, many passengers will try another air carrier rather than improve the utilization of the prior evening's flight. Of course, the reason for this is that passengers want what they want, which may or may not be exactly what the airline planned to offer. Without more "cooperation" from customers, 65-70 percent passenger load factors is probably the limit of what can be generally achieved.

Unit 7

Supplemental reading... Fitzsimmons2 chapter 5 pages 97-101 on the Customer Contact Approach.

article: "The Customer Contact Approach to Services: Theoretical Bases and Practical Extensions," by Richard B. Chase, *Operations Research*, Volume 29, Issue 4, 1981.

article: "Where Does the Customer Fit in the Service Operation?" by Richard B. Chase, in *Harvard Business Review*, November-December 1978, pages 137-142.

How manufacturing differs from services...

With manufacturing, the manufactured goods do not mind being treated impersonally. Inanimate objects are not affected if they are mass produced in an impersonal manner.

SBP 7b: Potential Operating Objectives   Name (if turned in):_____

Analysis questions...   To help apply this Service Business Principle, consider and answer the following questions about your specific service business process. (❑Check here if you are going outside of your target service business.)

Service company/business:_____

The service process:_____
    ① What are evidences of efficiency in this industry?
    ② What are evidences of inefficiency in this industry?
    ③ How do customers react to increases in efficiency?

①_____

_____

_____

_____

_____

_____

_____

_____

_____

_____

_____

_____

_____

_____

Unit 7

SBP 7b: Potential Operating Objectives   Name (if turned in):_____

Application exercise... Also to help you apply this Service Business Principle, complete the following analysis with regard to your specific service business process, or another service process in your business. (❑Check here if you are going outside of your target service business, which was _____.)

Service company/business:_____

The service process:_____

Revisit your service process flowchart constructed in the first unit. Where do the most intense customer inputs occur? <u>Redraw</u> the flowchart, indicating procedures that could be put in place to control the types, intensities (amounts), or varieties of customer inputs accepted. How does that affect the potential for operating efficiently? Why? What are disadvantages of such a manipulation of the process, such as how it affects the customer?

Preparation for the next Service Business Principle (7c)

To consider... Before proceeding, consider the following and write thoughts and ideas below:

Manufacturing organizations may not be the masters of efficiency, but they certainly have an efficiency advantage over service organizations. Can you think of any way service providers could borrow some of the efficiency potential of manufacturing? What would service organizations need to do in order to behave more like manufacturers? Could this be done at minimal cost to effectiveness at serving customers?

_____

_____

_____

_____

_____

_____

_____

_____

_____

Unit 7

Service Business Principle 7c:

COST SAVINGS BY SERVICE-MANUFACTURING

Service Business Principle	*"With services, companies can gain cost advantage by converting portions of the process to manufacturing by eliminating customer inputs or shifting the customer input point to later in the process."*

Why it occurs...   COST SAVINGS BY SERVICE-MANUFACTURING occurs because, as discussed in the prior Service Business Principle (*Potential Operating Objectives*), customer inputs are a major factor limiting the potential efficiency of service organizations.

Closely related to...   SBP: *Potential Operating Objectives*

Details...   If we eliminate all customer inputs from a service process, by the Unified Services Theory that process ceases to be a service process. In most cases, customers will have a problem with that. An alternative is to eliminate customer inputs from *just a portion* of the process. In this manner, cost efficiencies can be gained in an area that will not adversely affect the ability to serve the customer.

Another way to look at this Service Business Principle is from the perspective of "service blueprints," which are process flowcharts that distinguish between the "front office" and the "back office." The front office is that portion of the process that occurs within the customer's view, and the back office is that which takes place behind the scenes. One way to implement a degree of service-manufacturing is to push a portion of the process from the front office to the back office. However, if the process steps which are shifted to the back office still involve customer belongings or information inputs, efficiency gains can still be quite limited. (The limited efficiency is due to "divergence" requirements, which will be discussed later under *The Choice of Employees* Service Business Principle.)

In the case of "custom-manufacturing" services (see SBP: *The Custom-Manufacturing Oxymoron*), a way to implement this Service Business Principle is to postpone customization until final assembly. One bicycle manufacturer, National Bicycle, does this and sells 11,231,862 possible combinations of bicycles by assembling them from component parts.[22] Dell Computer uses this technique to "custom manufacture" personal computer systems. Dell keeps component parts in inventory, and a customer order triggers the final assembly and overall testing. In this manner, Dell is able to sell custom computer systems at manufactured system prices. Such an approach is a form of "*mass customization*," or the ability to provide custom production while maintaining near-manufacturing efficiencies.

In some cases it is not appropriate to implement service-manufacturing: I clipped an article about a consulting firm that was giving the same consulting analysis report to various clients as though the report was custom-prepared for each client. The firm was being extremely efficient, but charging for consulting that one would expect to be custom work.

How it impacts decisions...   The service provider that aspires to further cost saving needs to decide if and where it is appropriate to eliminate or shift some of the customer inputs to later stages of the production process.

---

[22] National Bicycle Industrial Company is a subsidiary of Matsushita. Information about their mass customization is found on page 91 of Marilyn M. Parkers excellent book: Strategic Transformation and Information Technology, 1996, Prentice-Hall: Upper Saddle River, New Jersey.

What to do about it... When considering the service process, focus on the various points in which customer inputs enter the production process. At each of those points, ascertain the impact of shifting or eliminating the inputs (on effectiveness and efficiency). The costs of reduced effectiveness are traded off against the cost savings of increased efficiency in order to make the process adjustment decision.

For example... Let's return to the custom home building example given in the prior Service Business Principle. The home builder desires to have cost savings, to compete in the entry-level home buyer market. One way to achieve that is to provide a structured set of home specifications to limit the variety of customer requests (without substantial cost increases).

The other way to provide cost savings in "custom" home construction is by "Service-Manufacturing." This is to manufacture *most* of the home before putting it up for sale, and then sell it just in time for the customer to select paint colors, floor coverings, and light fixtures. In that manner, the customer perceives getting some customization, but at manufacturing efficiencies! This latter technique is similar to the delayed final-assembly approach taken by Taco Bell...

This Taco Bell example was previously described in the cost leadership section of the *Positioning Amid Customers and Competitors* Service Business Principle. Taco Bell completes all of the food preparation except for final assembly prior to the time the customer presents her order inputs. In that manner, the food preparation can be accomplished in the most efficient manner possible. Restaurants who accept customer-order inputs early in the food preparation process will find that the preferences and peculiarities of individual customers will limit the ability to produce food at maximum efficiency.

Unit 7

My airline application... Where is the most inefficient part of an airlines operations, causing avoidable time costs? In baggage handling? Probably not, although passengers expect some degree of careful handling even of poorly constructed luggage. The preparation of planes for takeoff is not too inefficient. Arguably, the most inefficient part of an airline—where the greatest amount of stalled production seems to be found—is in the lines of customers waiting to check in. Passengers like lines to move rapidly, but when they are at the front of the line being served, they are much more concerned about having their specific needs met. (Of course, this varies culturally.)

Southwest Airlines addressed this issue of check-in inefficiency by eliminating a customer input—the customer's request for a particular seat assignment. Instead of spending a lot of time confirming or changing seat assignments, or trying to determine if a flight has any available seats, Southwest gives every passenger who checks in at the gate a colored card with a number on it. Since there are the same number of cards as there are seats on the flight, the gate agent knows exactly how many passengers there are, and if seats are available for standby passengers. This elimination of customer-seat-request inputs has a significant affect on the operating efficiency at the gate.

Supplemental reading... Fitzsimmons2 chapter 5 pages 87-89 on Service Blueprinting.
Fitzsimmons2 chapter 5 pages 94-96 on Production-Line Approach.
case: Taco Bell 1994 (HBS)

How manufacturing differs from services...

With manufacturing, there are already no customer inputs, thus no customer-input-caused limits to efficiency.

SBP 7c: Cost Savings by Service-Manufacturing   Name (if turned in):_____

Analysis questions...   To help apply this Service Business Principle, consider and answer the following questions about your specific service business process. (❏Check here if you are going outside of your target service business.)

Service company/business:_____

The service process:_____
    ① At what point do customer inputs enter the process?
    ② Can customer inputs be shifted to later in the process?
    ③ What implications will this have for efficiencies?
    ④ What implications will this have for effectiveness at serving the customer?

① _____

_____

_____

_____

_____

_____

_____

_____

_____

_____

_____

_____

_____

_____

_____

_____

_____

_____

Unit 7

SBP 7c: Cost Savings by Service-Manufacturing   Name (if turned in):_____

Application exercise...   Also to help you apply this Service Business Principle, complete the following analysis with regard to your specific service business process, or another service process in your business. (❏Check here if you are going outside of your target service business, which was _____.)

Service company/business:_____

The service process:_____
    Redraw the service process flowchart from the last Service Business Principle. Identify where the various customer inputs occur. Chose a customer input into the process that could be moved forward in the process or eliminated, with the least adverse effect on the customer. Redraw or modify the flowchart with that customer input modification. How does that affect the potential for operating efficiently? What are the expected cost savings? Why? What impacts might the change have on the customer?

Part III - Managing Service Processes
Unit 8:
HUMAN RESOURCES MANAGEMENT

The Unified Services Theory has major implications for the Human Resource functions of organizations. In this unit some of these implications will be explored.

Unit reading... The following reading pertains to Service Business Principles included in this unit. The instructor will let you know which of the readings you are responsible for studying.

Fitzsimmons2 chapter 5 on The Service Delivery System.
Fitzsimmons2 chapter 9 on The Service Encounter.

Preparation for the next Service Business Principle (8a)

To consider... Before proceeding, consider the following and write thoughts and ideas below:

For decades, futurists have talked about the day when workers would be replaced by machines. Has it happened? In some instances, the answer is definitely yes. Much of the tremendous productivity gains in manufacturing can be attributed to replacing labor with highly consistent machines such as robots. Manufacturing output continues to grow, even though the labor requirements continue to decline. Are machines a substitute for services workers also? What types of service employees are most at risk of being replaced by machines? What types of service employees are at little risk of being replaced by machines? What is the difference between the two types?

_____

_____

_____

_____

_____

_____

_____

_____

Service Business Principle 8a:
THE CHOICE OF EMPLOYEES

Service Business Principle	*"With services, a critical employee skill is the ability to exercise judgment in divergent processes. When the consequences of poor judgment are great, judgment ability often requires years of training and experience and the employees tend to be very costly. However, even complex rule-governed systems can be trained or automated. Good employee selection is much more important for divergent processes than for complex processes."*

Why it occurs... THE CHOICE OF EMPLOYEES occurs because nonstandard customer inputs can lead to nonstandard production. With some services, no two units of production are handled exactly alike, preventing the establishment of highly standard operating procedures.

Details... Two definitions are in order: complexity and divergence.

- **Complexity** is the number and intricacy of the steps in a process. Complex procedures have a lot of steps, and may include a lot of process branches. A process branch is a rule that changes the procedure based on a condition. For example, a dry cleaner may say that anything made of synthetic materials goes in one machine, and anything made of organic materials goes in the other.

- **Divergence** is the requirement for exercising judgment, or discretion, in a process. Divergent processes can go any number of ways, and there are no small set of rules that can make the decision. In divergent processes, the service employee is expected to figure out the best thing to do at the time of the decision.

The way to spot complexity in a process flowchart is to count the number of steps: complex procedures have many steps (or the steps have many substeps). Divergence is seen in the nature of the steps: divergent procedures have steps that can be handled any number of ways depending on the circumstances of production.

Substituting Complexity for Divergence

Complexity and divergence are not opposites on a continuum. In fact, they can exist independently of one another. A process can be complex and divergent, or neither complex nor divergent. However, in some situations divergence can be replaced with complexity to some degree. This is done by replacing a divergent step with a set of rules (if possible). In many cases, the number of rules necessary to replace a divergent step would be enormous. A software company that creates rule-based software to help managers in retail environments estimates that a typical rule-based system for a company will contain perhaps 100,000 rules! These highly complex systems are called "expert systems," because they mimic the judgment of an expert.

The reason to substitute complexity for divergence is that an amount of divergence tends to be much more costly than an amount of complexity. One source of divergence's high cost is the more expensive labor it typically requires. Further, divergence drives out efficiencies of task specialization. For example, Ritz-Carlton Hotels designed the job descriptions for various hotel employees to include "breaking away" from the employee's task whenever it appeared a customer needed anything. This meant that the employees needed to expend quite a bit of judgment about when to break away and what to do to resolve the customer problems. The result of such a job description approach is much higher labor costs. (One industry executive reported that Ritz-Carlton had twice the number of employees per room as other hotels, which was not confirmed, but would make sense.)

Divergence differs from mere *customization* in a process. Customization can be accomplished by a set of low-divergence process steps (if customers ask for A, give them A; B, give them B, etc.) *Mass customization* can be accomplished by providing a high degree of customization with little divergence. This customization is accomplished by *complexity* instead of divergence, often using computer technology. The on-line service Yahoo! is able to provide highly customized Internet services with little divergence requirements–the customization is all handled by their software. In the *Cost Savings by Service-Manufacturing* Service Business Principle, Dell Computer was described as employing mass customization–computer systems undergo final assembly based on customer orders (the company does not exercise divergence in this process, nor do they make a computer from scratch for every customer).

In many cases it may not be *practical* to substitute complexity for divergence. This is because a lot of complexity is typically required to replace a little divergence. For example, how complex would it be to substitute a standard telephone operator with a computer who understands when customers mis-pronounce common names? (like saying "seen" instead of "shawn" for the name "Sean") It is easier to just hire an employee that can handle enough divergence to understand people's peculiar accents. However, something simple such as having customers say "yes" or "no" to the computer's question "Will you accept a collect call from ___?" may be quite practical.[23]

Even when it is practical to substitute complexity for divergence, sometimes it may not be a good idea. Service providers should be careful about eliminating divergence arbitrarily, since often the greatest value of a service is added at the divergence step. For example, the greatest value in a physician's service is the highly-divergent step of identifying a diagnosis and prescribed treatment.

Unit 8

The most expensive labor is that for divergence processes with critical outcomes for poor judgment. Physicians come to mind, as do corporate attorneys, investment bankers, and CEOs. Despite the numerous books describing the seven easy steps to making it big as a investment banker, CEO, etc., the fact is that such positions require a *great deal* of judgment, and poor judgment can be extremely costly.

How it impacts decisions...

Decisions must be made about where judgment should be allowed in the service process, and where it is more appropriate to establish standard operating procedures. Sometimes we may desire to eliminate process complexity by trusting employees to exercise their judgment. In other cases, we may not want to hire employees with judgment skills (which can be costly); therefore we may need to replace the divergence with structured decision steps.

When employee judgment is required, management needs to decide on effective means of selecting and developing employees.

What to do about it...

The service provider should match "judgment capacity" with "judgment requirements." Judgment capacity is the ability of a service employee to exercise good judgment. Judgment capacity is managed largely by the selection procedures described above. Nevertheless, it is possible, over a course of years, to give employees experiences that will help them develop their judgment capacity.

The judgment requirement is defined by the divergence in the service process. The judgment requirement can be manipulated by exchanging decision rule complexity for judgment, if possible. Remember that the exchange is not simple—it usually takes a lot of decision rule complexity to substitute for a small amount of divergence.

---

[23] see February 18, 1998 Business Week.

Selecting Employees for Divergent Processes

How does one select employee to work in divergent processes? Since divergence is difficult to train, it is often necessary to evaluate the prospective employee's potential for exercising good judgment prior to making a hiring decision. Evaluating a person's judgment can be difficult, but not impossible. The following are a few techniques:

- Case interviews, which is to give the job candidate a business decision scenario and ask her to what she would do. Although the interviewer is concerned with the decision that would be made by the candidate, she is perhaps even more concerned about the thought process the candidate goes through to reach that decision. The case-interview technique is particularly popular with consulting firms, which require that employees deal with a great deal of consulting-process divergence (and pay them accordingly).

- Experience questioning, where the job candidate is asked of an instance where they had to make a difficult decision, and what they did. Decisions are difficult when they involve divergence. The candidate is likely to describe an instance where the result of the decision was positive. Nevertheless, experience questioning can reveal much about the process of exercising judgment.

- Reference questioning, in which people who have supervised the candidate's references are questioned about the candidates ability to exercise judgment. Often, this is accomplished by simply reading letters of recommendation. More specific information can be gained by contacting references.

Other useful techniques include abstract questioning, situational vignettes (similar to case interview), and role playing. (These techniques are discussed on Fitzsimmons2 pages 243-244.)

It should be obvious that selecting employees for judgment positions can be much more time-consuming and costly than traditional hiring methods. The amount of effort should be commensurate with the position requirements as defined by the divergence of the process.

For example... What is the difference between a midwife and an obstetrician? About $2,000. What else? Midwives are trained in the many steps to deliver a baby. In fact, many midwives give more superior bedside manner than most obstetricians. The difference, as explained by an obstetric friend, is that obstetricians have training and experience for the highly divergent process of handling abnormal situations. How many abnormal situations might occur? The list is probably endless. As a result, it is not practical to train a midwife in millions of step of procedures for handing abnormalities. The extensive training and experience of obstetricians is intended to prepare them to make judgements in situations with circumstances which may be completely unique. (In fact, the whole concept of medical "residencies"—three years of on-the-job experience as part of medical training—captures the idea that you cannot train divergence by classroom study alone.)

Investment banking has been a very divergent process—and investment bankers with good judgment are very expensive. Some investment banking firms have reduced the need for divergence by developing complex computer algorithms that make securities (stocks, bonds, etc.) trading decisions. This is called "programmed trading," and it can fill the process needs of a large portion of the day-to-day work of investment banking firms.

My airline application... Perhaps the most divergent component of an airline process is the work of pilots. A pilot must be able to handle an extreme variety of operational conditions. Nevertheless, most of what pilots do in the course of a flight does not require great deals of judgment. I observed this one time when I rode in the cockpit of a jumbo jet. Surprisingly, once the jet had ascended to the desired altitude, the work of the pilot and co-pilot was mostly just chatting about unrelated topics. Occasionally one would check the map book to assure they were flying in the right direction. Also, on air traffic controller suggestion, they would flip the knob on a little dial that would cause the jet to slowly change altitude or bearing. But, all of the control of the direction and altitude was implemented by the "autopilot"—a sophisticated computer program that knew how to fly the plane and adjust for atmospheric conditions (wind and turbulence). As we approached the San Francisco airport, the co-pilot finally disengaged the auto-pilot and manually landed the jet. The pilot told me that pilots are paid as much as they are primarily to takeoff and land planes, which is the part of the air transportation process where most of the risk and judgment steps occur.

Supplemental reading... Fitzsimmons2 chapter 5 pages 89-90 on Strategic Positioning Through Process Structure.
Fitzsimmons2 chapter 5 pages 90-93 on Taxonomy for Service Process Design.
Fitzsimmons2 chapter 9 pages 243-246 on Contact Personnel.
article: "Breaking the Cycle of Failure in Services," by Schlesinger, L. A., and Heskett, J. L. (1991). *Sloan Management Review*, 32(3), 17-28.
article: "Putting the Service-Profit Chain to Work," by Heskett, J. L., Jones, T. O., Loveman, G. W., Sasser, W. E. J., and Schlesinger, L. A. (1994). *Harvard Business Review*, 72(2), pp. 164-174.

Unit 8

How manufacturing differs from services...

With manufacturing, the production processes are often complex, but seldom divergent.

SBP 8a: The Choice of Employees   Name (if turned in):_____

Analysis questions... To help apply this Service Business Principle, consider and answer the following questions about your specific service business process. (❏Check here if you are going outside of your target service business.)

Service company/business:_____

The service process:_____
    ① What parts of the process have high divergence?
    ② What parts of the process have low divergence?
    ③ How do the employees and labor costs differ between the two areas?
    ④ Can divergence be decreased by developing standardized procedures? (substituting complexity for divergence)

① _____

_____

_____

_____

_____

_____

_____

_____

_____

_____

_____

_____

_____

_____

_____

_____

_____

Unit 8

SBP 8a: The Choice of Employees   Name (if turned in):_____

Application exercise...
Also to help you apply this Service Business Principle, complete the following analysis with regard to your specific service business process, or another service process in your business. (❑Check here if you are going outside of your target service business, which was _____.)

Service company/business:_____

The service process:_____

In your service business process, identify a step that contains a degree of divergence—a step where the service employee is required to exercise judgment. (If you are unable to locate such a step, then think of a divergent part of a related process.) Describe this step, and how judgment influences the outcome. What happens if the employee exercises poor judgment? Design a simple technique for selecting new employees with sufficient judgment capacity to handle that process step. (For example, describe a simple case interview question or situational vignette.) Attempt to describe what would be involved in breaking that divergent step down into a series of rule steps ("if this, do this" "if that, do that" etc.). Comment on how much more complex the process would be if the need for employee judgment was diminished and that divergent step were replaced with standard operating procedures.

Preparation for the next Service Business Principle (8b)

To consider... Before proceeding, consider the following and write thoughts and ideas below:

Why do employees choose to work for one company instead of another? Depending on the job market, the answer can be "because they were hiring." However, even in a tight job market, some companies are more successful at hiring and retaining the best employees than other companies. What makes the difference? Is it that they pay more? Within a given industry and job type it is rare that one company pays significantly more than other companies. Are there ways other than higher wages and salaries that companies can use to attract and motivate the best employees? What are some of the nonmonetary forms of compensations that companies can offer employees to differentiate them as employers of choice?

_____

_____

_____

_____

_____

_____

_____

_____

Unit 8

Service Business Principle 8b:
CULTURE COMPENSATION

Service Business Principle	*"With services, a significant part of employee compensation can be the organization's culture."*

Why it occurs... CULTURE COMPENSATION occurs because employees often interact with a large number of people in the course of their work. Labor intensity implies that employees are likely to interact with other employees, not just machines, and customer input implies that employees are likely to interact with customers. (see *Labor Intensity* and *The Unified Services Theory* SBPs) Nonstandard production and process divergence implies that the interactions can take many forms. (see *Heterogeneous Production* and *The Choice of Employees* SBPs) The interactions can be pleasant or unpleasant, largely depending on the culture of the organization.

Details... What is culture? Culture is the values (noun) of the organization, or things the organization values (verb). Organizations are composed of people, therefore culture is the general belief about what the organization considers to be important.

How Culture is Perpetuated

Sometimes cultures evolve of their own accord. Culture is influenced by internal factors, such as the combination of dominant personalities in the organization, and by external factors, such as industry practices and the state of the economy.

The best cultures are perpetuated by the actions of upper management. Management sends signals about what is valued in the organization, both in words and in policies. Policies dictate such things as measurement, programs, and reward systems.

If management's words about what is valued are inconsistent with policies, the words will be of little effect. For example, if a management says "quality is our most important priority" then bases the reward system purely on number of units produced, then employees will believe that "quantity is the most important priority."

Cultures Which Are Attractive to Employees

Cultures which can contribute to the compensation of employees are those which the employees also value, independent of the organization. It is a great thing when the organization values the same things the employee values. The following are some of the things that often fit in that category:

• **Employee security.** Some companies have a no-layoff policy, which promotes this culture. For example, the difficulty of losing a government job is one attractive feature of working for the government. However, the value of employee security can be demonstrated by other means as well, such as benefits packages that include good life, health, and disability insurance.

• **Employee development.** Some companies have a culture of building the skills and opportunities of employees. A former executive of a large hotel company said that it is easy to maintain a good culture when the company is growing at 20 to 30 percent a year, since there are opportunities for advancement. Even companies that are not growing can have a culture of advancement, by encouraging employees to develop skills. The company might offer training or it might assist employees with tuition expenses for continuing education.

- **Employee ideas.** Some organizations encourage employees to share ideas of how to advance the company. One way to do this is to actually let employees implement their own ideas (subject to supervisor approval). This will only work if it is recognized that with new ideas comes risk which implies the possibility of failure. If the reprimand for failure is great, employees will be discouraged from taking risk by presenting new ideas.

- **Excellence.** Employees generally prefer to be part of an organization they can be proud of. Companies with a reputation for being "best in class" usually have the best chance of recruiting graduates who are "best in class." However, companies should have the same excellence on the inside (how they are run) as they have on the outside (their reputation) or the best employees will soon leave for other opportunities.

Now, of course, such culture advantages are not free, nor will they continue without ongoing management attention. The cost of maintaining a particular culture by a particular means should be considered carefully. There is a tendency to underestimate the profit potential of an attractive culture.

Command and Control

What if the decision makers of a company make no attempt to promote a culture that would be attractive to employees? Such companies still compensate employees by monetary means. Organizations that *only* compensate employees by monetary means often have a culture known as "command and control."

Unit 8

Command and control is a system in which the prosperity of the owners and leaders of the organization is valued at the expense of "labor." Labor is considered a machine by which work is accomplished. Labor is retained simply because there is no less-expensive technology which could adequately be substituted.

Companies employing a command and control culture often make superficial attempts to convince employees that they are valued, such as through financial rewards for productivity. However, such programs have short-term effect; if the rewards are discontinued the effect is lost. Another problem is that if the monetary rewards are given too frequently they may be considered part of "base pay," causing them to lose motivational value.

This Service Business Principle states that culture can be a significant source of compensation in service organizations. If the culture is not attractive to employees, or is unattractive, then the compensation becomes purely monetary. Such companies can retain employees by providing sufficient salaries relative to job opportunities elsewhere.

Changing a Company's Culture

It is not an easy thing to change a company's culture, since it requires convincing everyone that things are valued that were previously perceived as not valued. Culture possesses a lot of inertia, or resistance to change in speed and direction. For large organizations, changing culture is like trying to turn a seventy-five-ton ship, a slow process which consumes a lot of energy.

An ineffective way to change culture is to implement an internal P.R. (public relations) campaign. The nice thing about this is talk is cheap, at least relative to action.

A more effective way to change culture is to replace policies that signal one set of values with policies that signal the desired set of values. This is a difficult process.

How it impacts decisions...   The labor intensity of service businesses implies that companies need to pay careful attention to recruiting and motivating employees. Experts have established that external service value–the value of the service seen by customers–is primarily a function of employee retention and employee productivity.[24] Further, those experts indicate that employee retention and productivity are driven by employee satisfaction, which is driven by so-called "internal quality." This "internal quality" is the environment in which the employees work.

We can extend this logic by observing that the work environment is largely a function of the shared values, or culture, of the organization. Therefore, if a company has a culture that leads to employee satisfaction, then employee retention and productivity will be high and the company will be able to provide good service value to customers.

Hence, a critical decision leaders must make is what culture to perpetuate within their organizations. They must decide how to signal the culture (value system) to employees, such as through appropriate policies. Organizations that do not pay any attention to culture are by default deciding to be subject to cultural drift–a tendency to go wherever things happen to go.

What to do about it...   Cultures drift so gradually that it is often difficult to see the change until problems occur. This is particularly a problem when organizations are growing rapidly. When a company is small it is quite easy to maintain a positive culture. When a company becomes or is large, it can be quite difficult to communicate the shared values throughout the organization. The numerous policies that often come with being a large organization can be seen by employees as existing for the sole purpose of controlling employees and limiting their discretion.

What should organization leaders do to assure a positive culture? First, pay close attention to culture. There are fewer more important internal functions of managers and leaders than perpetuating a positive culture.

Second, seek to understand the importance of employee satisfaction, retention, and productivity to the organization's success. It will be much easier to invest in culturally compensating employees if you understand the potentially high returns on that compensation.

Third, choose company policies carefully. Policies can both build a positive culture or can destroy it. Remember that company policies are signals to employees that speak much louder than mere words.

For example...   Companies who are known for their culture have opportunities to hire the best employees, even though they pay nothing more than the going wage. One example is Marriott Hotels and Resorts. The founder of the company, J. Willard Marriott, continually espoused the idea that if you take good care of your employees, they will take good care of your guests. Throughout the years, Marriott has built a culture which values the development of employees.[25] Company policy provides for training and development seminars and career progression. The company also values employee opinions and ideas, and has administered annual opinion surveys of employees. They also value the fair treatment of employees, and have had an ombudsperson to

---

[24] see Heskett, J. L., Jones, T. O., Loveman, G. W., Sasser, W. E. J., and Schlesinger, L. A. (1994). "Putting the Service-Profit Chain to Work." *Harvard Business Review*, 72(2), pp. 164-174.

[25] see, e.g., Hostage, G. M., "Quality Control in a Service Business," *Harvard Business Review*, Vol. 53, No. 4, July-August 1975, pp. 98-106.

assure employees' complaints will be heard. These policies, programs, and values have formed a culture that gives Marriott an advantage in the labor market while paying wages that are not unusual.

The service divisions of IBM have had a major change in culture in recent years. For many years IBM had a culture of professionalism, which was perpetuated by a dress policy of white shirts and ties. This culture was likely valued by employees who wanted to work for a world-class company. In the 1980s the computer industry turned upside down. The prevailing culture in the new industry was one of hardworking, creative mavericks, not stodgy white-shirt professionals. IBM went from being an employer of choice to being a company that provided little in the way of cultural compensation. The company's leaders made a major decision to change the culture in order to remain competitive in the labor market and attract the best employees. Part of this was eliminating the strict dress policy. There was also a big shift to allowing employees to work out of their homes, which emphasized employee independence and empowerment. The ability to change policies in order to update the culture has allowed IBM to survive in what is an increasingly competitive industry.

My airline application... Southwest Airlines is known for a "fun" culture. Their employee dress code is fun: casual attire, often including shorts, for many employees. Their boarding process is relatively low-pressure, allowing for pleasant customer interaction. Their cabin service is simple, and sometime comical. Stewards hide in overhead bins to surprise passengers. On-board activities like passenger games or sing-alongs can keep things light. Employees seem to value that culture, since Southwest is known as a preferred employer, despite quite ordinary wages. Who could not value having fun at work?

Unit 8

Supplemental reading... article: "Putting the Service-Profit Chain to Work," by Heskett, J. L., Jones, T. O., Loveman, G. W., Sasser, W. E. J., and Schlesinger, L. A. (1994). *Harvard Business Review*, 72(2), pp. 164-174.

case: Southwest Airlines: 1993 (A) (HBS 9-694-023)

How manufacturing differs from services...

With manufacturing, most employees deal with a finite (and small) number of individuals on a regular basis. Manufacturing organizations' culture is important, but less influential than in service organizations, due to the differences in day-to-day interactions.

SBP 8b: Culture Compensation   Name (if turned in):_____

Analysis questions...   To help apply this Service Business Principle, consider and answer the following questions about your specific service business process. (❑Check here if you are going outside of your target service business.)

Service company/business:_____

The service process:_____

   ① What things are valued by the organization that are also particularly valued by the individual employees within the organization? Employee security? development? ideas? service excellence? others?

   ② How are those values communicated to employees? What policies demonstrate the values?

   ③ To what degree do those values compensate employees for their work? Are they a factor in people wanting to work for the company or being motivated to be more productive?

① _____

_____

_____

_____

_____

_____

_____

_____

_____

_____

_____

_____

_____

_____

_____

_____

_____

Unit 8

SBP 8b: Culture Compensation   Name (if turned in):_____

Application exercise...

Also to help you apply this Service Business Principle, complete the following analysis with regard to your specific service business process, or another service process in your business. (☐Check here if you are going outside of your target service business, which was _____.)

Service company/business:_____

The service process:_____

What company is the preferred employer in your target service industry? In other words, of all the companies in the industry, which is most likely to hire the best employees? Identify what you would imagine the top three characteristics of that company are which makes them a premier employer? Note which of the three, if any, represent superior monetary compensation (i.e. the company pays more than other companies). For each of the three, write down what values the company portrays which are valued by employees. Examples might include employee security, development, ideas, service excellence, or other things. Write down a fourth company value that would be appealing to employees, and a policy that would promote that value in the organization.

Preparation for the next Service Business Principle (8c)

To consider...   Before proceeding, consider the following and write thoughts and ideas below:

When manufacturers have products to produce, they typically have engineers design the product and the production procedures. These specifications are then given to production employees, whose job it is to follow the procedures and meet the specifications. Some manufacturing companies welcome production procedure suggestions from production workers, however the adoption of a suggestion is generally preceded by engineering and management approval. It would be inappropriate for a production worker to arbitrarily change the product or the process. It would also be generally inappropriate for a customer to walk into the factory and change the product or the production process. As a general rule, product and process changes must be approved by engineering and by management. Is this true also for services? Can you think of examples of service businesses in which the production employee is free to modify the service process at will? (hint: think of the concept of divergence) Also, can you think of examples of service businesses in which the *customer* can change the course of the production process at will?

_____

_____

_____

_____

_____

_____

_____

_____

_____

Unit 8

Service Business Principle 8c:

WHO IS IN CONTROL

Service Business Principle	*"With services, the production process can be controlled by the organization, the employees, or the customers, depending on who is qualified to meet the company objectives. Nevertheless, the customers and employees need to buy into this."*

Why it occurs... WHO IS IN CONTROL occurs because the presence of varying customer inputs and nonstandard production sometimes necessitates divergence (see SBP: *The Choice of Employees*), which is the need for employees to modify the process as conditions require. In some cases, it is the customer who handles the divergence and specifies adjustments to the service process, which is justified by the significant presence of customer inputs.

Details... John Bateson described a "service encounter triad" which depicts the relationships between the service organization, the service employees, and the customers. [Bateson, John E. G., "Perceived Control and the Service Encounter," in J. A. Czepiel, M. R. Solomon, and C. F. Suprenant (eds.), *The Service Encounter*, Lexington Books: Lexington, Mass., 1985, p. 76.] Any of the three can control the course of the service process, depending on the particular service situation. Bateson points out that the three may have potentially conflicting objectives: The **service organizations** generally want *efficiency*, which is the ability to produce at a reasonable cost. The **service employees** often want *autonomy*, or a liberty to exercise some degree of discretion. The **customers** want *satisfaction*, which is that their needs and expectations for the service be fulfilled. Conflicts can occur when these objectives clash:

- Efficiency versus autonomy. As was discussed in SBP: *The Choice of Employees*, divergence in processes can be very costly and limit efficiency. Employees may be frustrated in their ability to provide the appropriate service under constraints of company policy. For example, Health Maintenance Organizations (HMOs) want doctors to follow certain patient treatment procedures which control costs, which often does not bode well with the doctors who prefer to "call the shots." The HMO will refuse to process payment for procedures which do not meet company guidelines (such as exploratory or experimental procedures).

- Efficiency versus satisfaction. Customers often want to be satisfied regardless of the cost to the company. This means being able to meet needs of specific customers as a result of specific customer-inputs. The company also wants the customer to be satisfied, but under the constraints of reasonable expenditures of time and other resources. For example, a business case describes an overnight delivery company which misrouted a customer's package that contained materials for an important presentation. When the package did not arrive the morning of the presentation (as expected and needed), the customer demanded that the company hire a helicopter to fly the package from the misrouted location to the correct location. The justification was that the company's failure to satisfy the need would result in an important audience staring at a blank screen. (And, what do people pay the high prices for overnight delivery for anyway?)

- Autonomy versus satisfaction. When the service organization controls the service process, service employees presented with potentially unreasonable customer demands have an "easy out"—to defer to company policy. That way the customer just leaves mad, but only blames the employee for not making an exception to policy. However, when the employee is given autonomy to make such decisions, customer demands can cause much anxiety for service employees. You just have to work as a waiter or waitress in a restaurant to realize this! In many restaurants, the waiters are given the autonomy to do what is appropriate to provide good service. However, some customer want the restaurant process to be a bit more complex than the employee thinks it should be. For example, the customer might demand the disproportionate attention of the waiter, causing the waiter to neglect his other customers.

Whether the company, the service employee, or the customer should direct the service process is very situational. Nevertheless, if the arrangement is not acceptable to customers, then problems and complaints are sure to occur, since customer do not want to be directed unless they believe it is necessary or in their best interest. The arrangement should also be acceptable to employees, to avoid frustration and deteriorating attitudes.

How it impacts decisions... The company must decide the degree to which the organization (i.e. policy), the service employee, and the customer is allowed to control the service process.

What to do about it... In each situation there will be an appropriate balance between the three. Rather than expound on determining the appropriate balance, we will focus on how to effectively implement a balance:

If it is decided that the **service organization** should dominate, then employees and customers need to be selected accordingly. Selecting customers? How could that be? Don't we want everyone to be a customer? The answer is, companies cannot *afford* some types of customers. For example if a Motel-6 customer demands the service of a Ritz-Carlton—rejecting assigned rooms because of stains on the carpet, expecting delivery of extra pillows and tissue boxes, demanding extra room cleaning throughout the day, check-out at 3:00 p.m., etc.—the Motel-6 manager will probably feel a little put out.

How does a company select customers? The wrong way is to select them after they are already customers. This means telling the demanding customer "Sorry, but we cannot serve your needs and expectations." Thus the customer departs angry. *The better way is to adequately communicate the service process limits to the customer.* Discount motels do this by posting signs by the check-in desk describing company policies. Retail stores do this by putting "receipt required for return or exchange" signs by cash registers. Fast food chains do this by providing consistent service at all locations. This communicates to potential customers what to expect from the service provider, and that they must go elsewhere if the needs are beyond the scope of the service that is offered.

Also, if the service organization is chosen to dominate the service process, employees who buy into this should be chosen. Prospective employees should be given a realistic picture of the extent of company policies and procedures prior to their joining the company. Mrs. Field's Cookies was previously cited as an example (under SBP: *Technological Depersonalization*) of technology that controlled the day-to-day functions of the store manager. When business management students are asked if they would like to work as a Mrs. Field's Cookies store manager, they generally say "no"—the company controls all of the usual management functions. The appropriate instructor response is "good, since Mrs. Field's would not want to hire you as a store manager—you demand too much autonomy!" Mrs. Field's wants store managers who would rather chat with customers than fill out work schedules, and their hiring process looks for such propensities.

Successful hotel companies also implement selection techniques for the low-autonomy position of housekeeping staff member. Most hotels prefer employees who (a) like

Unit 8

housekeeping, and (b) are capable of doing it according to company procedures. Direct questioning such as "Do you like to clean your own house?" and "Do you clean your house according to a regular procedure?" can do much to communicate the expectations and abilities for the position.

If it is decided that the **service employee** should dominate in the control of the service process, then employees need to be instructed in the appropriate way to exercise their autonomy and judgment in denying unreasonable customer requests. It is not ethical to "defer to policy" when in fact no policy exists. Instead, the employee might be trained to "bail out" and refund the customer's money at appropriate times and ways (attempting to minimize the overall damage). Also, the adverse affect of demanding customers on employee autonomy can be mitigated by allowing employees to turn difficult cases over to a manager or designated employee who is trained in tact and discretion. (Ways for handling when things go wrong with the service process will be covered later in the *Service Recovery* unit.)

If it is determined that the **customer** should be allowed to dominate the control of the service process, then employees should be given incentive to heed customer requirements. If it is a self-serve process, then the customer is acting as the "production employee," so this is not a problem. However, if company employees need to continually deal with demanding customers, they need to be encouraged to "buy in" to this arrangement. For example, a major purpose of the large tips paid in fancy restaurants is to motivate the waiters and waitresses to heed a wide range of customer demands. In some situations, employees can be compensated by the company according to their ability to satisfy a wide range of customer demands. For example, a major automotive service chain paid its manager and employee bonuses partially based on various customer satisfaction measures.

For example... Examples of companies in which the *service organization* dominates control of the process is McDonald's, Jiffy Lube (quick oil change), and H&R Block (standard tax preparation). These companies are very efficient, having well-defined standard operating procedures.

The *service employees* tend to dominate technical, highly-divergent services such as medicine, law, and education. In each case, the course of the service process is dictated by the judgment of the trained service employee.

Customers are often in control of loosely defined self-service processes such as retail. A customer entering a department store can view products in most any way she cares to and can ask questions and compare options as she desires. In many such cases, the only policies to restrict customers control are those to prevent customers from damaging products which they do not purchase. It is assumed that most customers will exercise good judgment in executing their shopping process.

My airline application... With an airline, we can consider who dominates control at various process segments.

The process of checking baggage is primarily controlled by the airline. Policy prevents the customer or the employee from checking things that are improperly packaged, baggage that is unacceptable proportioned, or items that are potentially unsafe. Airlines have instructions on ticket jackets and signs near the baggage check-in to communicate baggage policies to customers.

The process of flying the aircraft is clearly dominated by the pilots. Nevertheless, the customer needs to buy in to this. In particular, if the pilot is taking action to avoid turbulence or other weather patterns, it is a good idea to communicate the actions and intentions to the customers over the aircraft speaker system.

What process segment of the airline process might the customer dominate? Probably the process of reading, sleeping, etc. on the plane. This is a "self-serve" process that the customer is left to control (unless it interferes with other passengers or with flight safety).

Supplemental reading...   Fitzsimmons2 chapter 9 pages 239-242 on The Service Encounter Triad.
Fitzsimmons2 chapter 9 pages 245 on Unrealistic Customer Expectations.
mini-case: The Best Little Cookie House Around. (in Fitzsimmons2)
case: Mrs. Field's Cookies. (HBS)
case: Federal Express: The Money Back Guarantee. (HBS)

How manufacturing differs from services...

With manufacturing, engineers are hired to determine product and process specifications, and general customer involvement is restricted to selecting and consuming the output ("Custom manufacturing" was described as an exception in SBP: *The Custom-Manufacturing Oxymoron*.)

Unit 8

SBP 8c: Who is in Control   Name (if turned in):_____

Analysis questions...   To help apply this Service Business Principle. consider and answer the following questions about your specific service business process. (❑Check here if you are going outside of your target service business.)

Service company/business:_____

The service process:_____

　　① What are the objectives of (the organization, the employees, and the customers) in the service process?
　　② Who thinks they control the service encounter process?
　　③ Who actually controls the service encounter process?
　　④ If a shift in control is desired, how might customer and employee buy-in be established?

①_____

_____

_____

_____

_____

_____

_____

_____

_____

_____

_____

_____

_____

_____

_____

_____

_____

Unit 8

SBP 8c: Who is in Control   Name (if turned in):_____

Application exercise...

Also to help you apply this Service Business Principle, complete the following analysis with regard to your specific service business process, or another service process in your business. (❑Check here if you are going outside of your target service business, which was _____.)

Service company/business:_____

The service process:_____

For your service business process, identify whether the organization, the service employee, or the customer should dominate the control of the progression of the service process. Develop a plan for *employee* "buy-in." How can expectations be communicated to prospective employees during the hiring process? What employee incentives are necessary to encourage employees to allow the process to be controlled as decided upon? Indicate how you would promote *customer* "buy-in." When and where should information be communicated to customers about the limits of the service process? (You might redraw your service process flowchart, and note the types of information that would be presented to customers at various points in the process.) For example, would it be appropriate to place a sign at the service location for customers to see? If so, draw such a sign.

Part III - Managing Service Processes
Unit 9:
MARKETING IN SERVICES

In some ways the marketing of services is similar to the marketing of manufactured goods, but in some ways different. The Unified Services Theory reveals some of those differences, as discussed in this unit.

Preparation for the next Service Business Principle (9a)

To consider... Before proceeding, consider the following and write thoughts and ideas below:

When manufacturers market their products, how do they attempt to convince potential customers that their products are superior to competing products? For example, in what ways do auto manufacturers describe their vehicles as being superior to competing products? What information do customers typically use to compare products in order to make a selection? For example, how do you select which computer to purchase, given a wide variety at about the same price? Do these marketing and selection approaches also work with service businesses. How does the process of marketing a service differ from marketing manufactured goods? How does the type of information customers use to select services differ from the type of information used to select manufactured goods?

Unit 9

_____

_____

_____

_____

_____

_____

_____

_____

THE MARKETING OF PROPERTIES

Service Business Principle	*"With services, the products tend to be high in experience properties and low in search properties. Highly divergent services are often high in credence properties."*

Why it occurs... THE MARKETING OF PROPERTIES occurs because customers recognize that customer inputs results in the need for nonstandard production. In other words, they are concerned about the *process* experienced in service delivery, and they do not expect (nor often want) the *outcome* to be exactly the same as other customers experienced.

Closely related to... SBP: *The Who's Who of Marketing*, which will follow.

Details... Marketing scientists refer to three general types of product features, or properties: search properties, experience properties, and credence properties. (In this discussion a "product" might be a manufactured goods product or a service product.) These property types are distinguished as follows:

- **Search properties** are product characteristics that customers can easily evaluate and compare prior to purchasing the product. Search properties help the customer search for the best product to purchase. They are often objective measures of product performance, such as speed, capacity, or energy requirements. Automobiles can be evaluated for their acceleration, cubic feet of inside space, and miles per gallon of fuel. Refrigerators can be compared based on their holding space and energy efficiency. Prepackaged food items are advertised for their nutritional components and speed of preparation. For each of these items, customers can gather information and make comparisons prior to the time they make a purchase.

- **Experience properties** are product characteristics that cannot be evaluated prior to purchase, but must be experienced by the customer in order to be evaluated. Marketers may attempt to describe these properties in advertising, but ultimately customers realize that evaluating them requires experiencing the product. Disney may say their theme parks are among the most delightful vacations, but the customer really needs to visit the park to know. So also for architects, barber shops, banks, home builders, hotels, Internet Service Providers, real estate agencies, retail stores, and zoos—it is difficult for a customer to do a comparative evaluation of "product" characteristics without actually experiencing what is offered.

- **Credence properties** are product characteristics which *cannot* be easily evaluated *even after* the customer has experienced the product—instead the customer has to rely on the evaluation given by a credible source. The reason they cannot be evaluated is that the typical customer does not have enough knowledge or expertise to make an accurate evaluation. As a result, customers wind up relying on the opinion of supposed "experts," who give an evaluation and make comparisons. For example, how does a college graduate know he or she received a good education? How do a law firm's clients know they received the best legal advise? How does the client of a consulting firm know the consultant's recommendations are the best? In each of these cases, the customer largely has to take the company's word for it, or the word of others esteemed to know.

This service principle indicates that a fundamental difference between the properties of manufactured goods and the properties of services is that manufactured goods tend to be rich in search properties, whereas services are predominantly latent with experience properties.[26] An exception is that some services rely so much on the expert opinions of the service provider (i.e. they are highly divergent processes) that the evaluation itself has to rely on expert opinion—in other words these services are high in credence properties.

This is not to say that services do not contain some search properties, nor that manufactured goods do not contain some experience or credence properties. Indeed, different goods or services contain different combinations of the three. Yet we should expect the dominant characteristics of goods or services to tend to fit in the categories as described above.

How it impacts decisions... Companies need to decide the most appropriate way to market their goods or services. The most appropriate way to market something will depend on the types of properties it possesses.

What to do about it... For companies who produce superior manufactured goods, heavy in *search* properties, the product characteristics can be easily described to customers in advertising. Further, customers can seek out (search) for product information without actually having to make a purchase and without having to rely on the opinions of others. Customers can use that product information to compare competing products, and pick whichever product is deemed to be the superior one to fill the need.

For services which predominantly possess *experience* properties, a way to effectively market a superior service is to give customers the opportunity to experience it on some type of a trial basis (such as a reduced-cost initial visit). Another way is to encourage those who have experienced it to relate the observations to other prospective customers. The service itself is marketed *in-process*, or during actual service delivery (which concept will be discussed further in the next Service Business Principle).

For highly-divergent services where *credence* properties dominate, it is not enough to get customers to experience the service—customers need credible opinions of others to tell them that the service is superior. This credible opinion might come from prior customers, from independent service critics, or from credible friends and associates of prospective customers.

For example... These days there are many companies attempting to market various types of credit cards. A primary *property* of credit cards used as a selling point is their *convenience* relative to other forms of payment or credit. (Which is in fact the major ethical problem with many credit cards—providing such convenient "easy credit" that it tempts many people to go into unnecessary debt.) To a minor degree, "convenience" is a search property, in that it can be somewhat described to prospective customers in terms of the number of businesses that accept a particular credit card. One particular credit card company touts that their card is "Accepted in more locations..." including some where "...they don't take American Express" (the competing card). The reason convenience is limited as a search property is because the significance of scope of acceptance of a card is only defined by the actual businesses each customer ever patronizes. (Customers probably do not care whether a card is accepted at businesses they never patronize.) So, in a large sense, "convenience" is an experience property. Card issuers believe that if customers try their credit card, they will come to see how

Unit 9

---

[26] Heskett, J. L., Sasser, W. E., Jr., and Hart, C. W. L. (1990). *Service Breakthroughs: Changing the Rules of the Game*, The Free Press, New York, page 37.

convenient it is and want to continue to use it. One way issuers lure customers into trying their card is to offer sign-up bonuses such as frequent flier miles or other gifts. Another way to lure customers is to charge "introductory" interest rates for a period such as the first six months. These introductory rates are *significantly* lower than the subsequent rate—and customers who intend to cancel the credit card after the introductory rate period are likely to forget. (Which is why it is generally a good idea for customers to evaluate the card based on the subsequent rate.)

Consulting firms largely provide an advice service—taking the client company's business situation as an input, processing with analysis and expertise, and giving recommendations as the service "product." The process characteristic of being "expert" (or "well-informed") is not much of a search property—it would be difficult to describe objective measures of expertise that could be compared across consulting firms. In some sense, "expertise" is an experience property—once a client experiences the good work of the consulting firm, they might see how expert the advice really is (or appears to be). As an experience property, consulting firms might offer free initial consultation, or might rely heavily on referrals from clients who have already experienced the expertise. However, the highly divergent (i.e. judgment-based) nature of the consulting process is such that even when clients experience the service they may still find it difficult to judge the expertise—the hallmark of a credence property. Therefore, the consulting firm may attempt to promote their services by relying on evaluations from sources that clients would deem credible. For example, some consulting firms have promotional material which describes the successful "Fortune 500" companies that they have had as clients. The idea might be that large, successful, companies like that *would know* expert consulting when they saw it. (Which may or may not be a valid assumption, depending on the case.)

My airline application...

Air transportation is a generic enough process that it can be extremely difficult to describe significant objective ways in which one airline is better than another. As a result, we would conclude that airlines are not intense in substantial search properties. Yet an example of an airline search property would be "where they fly," which can be evaluated prior to purchase by checking the flight schedule. This, however, is simply a service qualifier—a passenger would consider any airline that flies to where they want to go.

In perhaps a larger sense, airlines have major properties that are experience properties. Customers will only learn the difference in service by actually taking a flight. Some airlines offer promotional fares, which can encourage having the experience, or companion-fares which encourage passengers to bring someone else along. Nevertheless, it is often hard to judge even from taking a flight if there is any difference between that airline and competing airlines. Each flight experience may be different from each other flight, and each interaction with an airline employee may be completely different from each other interaction.

In fact, there is quite a bit of divergence that can be experienced in the air travel process, such as in the interactions with airline employees. (Certainly not as much as the surgery or the legal council process, but still some.) How could a customer evaluate an airline based on the few interactions they experience? Not easily. So, airlines might tout the information of experts who are supposedly able to evaluate issues like customer service. For example, a recent Southwest Airlines advertisement described the airline as winning a supposedly prestigious customer service award three years in a row. The customers could then rely on the evaluative ability of the group producing the award to evaluate the service.

Supplemental reading...

Heskett, J. L., Sasser, W. E., Jr., and Hart, C. W. L. (1990). *Service Breakthroughs: Changing the Rules of the Game*, The Free Press, New York, page 37.

How manufacturing differs from services...

With manufacturing, all customers are generally concerned about is the outcome of the production process, which is the finished-goods product. Finished-goods products are often consistent. Also, they can usually can be measured in quantitative ways which are easily advertised and compared between competing products.

Unit 9

SBP 9a: The Marketing of Properties   Name (if turned in):_____

Analysis questions... To help apply this Service Business Principle, consider and answer the following questions about your specific service business process. (❑Check here if you are going outside of your target service business.)

Service company/business:_____

The service process:_____
  ① Can the service "product" be easily evaluated by the customer prior to purchase? If so, what are these "search" properties and how might they be described?
  ② What is the relative influence of advertising, word-of-mouth recommendations, and actual experience? How might we get prospective customers to initially experience the service?
  ③ If the service is highly divergent and driven by credence properties, what types of credible opinions would help in promoting the service?
  ④ What does all of this say about the appropriate marketing strategy for this service?

①_____

_____

_____

_____

_____

_____

_____

_____

_____

_____

_____

_____

_____

_____

_____

_____

_____

Unit 9

SBP 9a: The Marketing of Properties   Name (if turned in):_____

Application exercise... Also to help you apply this Service Business Principle, complete the following analysis with regard to your specific service business process, or another service process in your business. (❑Check here if you are going outside of your target service business, which was _____).

Service company/business:_____

The service process:_____

List five or more characteristics of your company's service that are potentially its biggest selling points—and tell whether each is a search, experience, or credence property. Create a flier that would be used to promote service based on a few of the major characteristics. For search properties, you will probably describe objective information about the characteristic. For experience properties, you will likely want to encourage or draw on the experience of the service. For credence properties, you will probably need to refer to a credible source of characteristic evaluation. Comment on some strengths and some weaknesses of your flier.

Preparation for the next Service Business Principle (9b)

To consider... Before proceeding, consider the following and write thoughts and ideas below:

In nearly all manufacturing companies, there is one part of the organization dedicated to producing the product, and a separate part of the organization dedicated to marketing the product—promoting it and selling it to customers. It is not within the production employees' scope of responsibility to market the product (although they do need to be somewhat responsive to the needs of the marketing department). Further, it would be rare for the marketing employees to spend extended time in the factory assisting with the production of the product. Would such a distinction normally be found in service businesses as well? Why or why not? In what ways might marketing employees have production responsibilities, and do production employees have marketing responsibilities?

_____

_____

_____

_____

_____

_____

_____

_____

Unit 9

Service Business Principle 9b:
THE WHO'S WHO OF MARKETING

Service Business Principle	*"With services, the most influential marketing employees are production employees. The focus of marketing departments is to attract new customers, but production employees often have the primary responsibility of retaining current customers."*

Why it occurs... THE WHO'S WHO OF MARKETING occurs because the major selling points of services are usually experience properties (see SBP: *The Marketing of Properties*) and experience properties are portrayed to customers by service production employees.

Closely related to... SBP: *The Marketing of Properties*.

Details... This Service Business Principle can be the source of significant "turf battles" in companies and in academics, but it need not be so. These turf battles originate from the traditional contentious relationship between marketing and production departments seen in many manufacturing organizations. In manufacturing organizations these two departments are distinct, and often assume conflicting objectives. Marketing is viewed as a *profit center*, implying that the goal is to boost profits. Profits are boosted by filling demand for products in the way that will be appealing to the customer—in the volumes and at the time the customer wants. As a result, marketing tends to promise delivery that the production department may or may not be able to fulfill. Production, on the other hand, is generally viewed as a *cost center*, implying that their objective is to produce what is needed (at acceptable quality levels) at the minimum cost. Minimum cost requires well-planned and executed production scheduling, which is at odds with the marketing department's efforts to make what the customer needs exactly when the customer wants it. If marketing gets its way, production costs will go up. If the production department gets its way, the ability to respond to every customer request will suffer. This is the perpetual conflict in such manufacturing companies.

Some service companies insist on a similar conflicting relationship between marketing and production functions, but it should not be so. Usually, customers get their most significant service product information from the production process—and thus are targeted by marketers based on their experience with the service provider. Marketing department employees generally have the charge of getting the customers "in the door" the first time. But, once a customer is in the door, it is the production employees who are most likely to influence the customer to give repeat business or not. As a result, production should also be viewed as a profit center, not merely a cost center. This is especially justified given that it is generally much more expensive to gain new customers than to retain current customers, and the profitability of individual customers tends to increase the longer they have been customers.[27]

Further, production employees should be *trained* in their marketing and customer retention responsibilities. The interaction employees have with customers is often a "losing-sensitive characteristic" (see SBP: *Unlocking Key Elements*), meaning that poor interactions can lead to disgruntled customers who will never return. Richard Norman called these key interactions "moments of truth," implying the instance when the true quality of the service is revealed.[28]

---

[27] "Zero Defections: Quality Comes to Services" by Fredrick F. Reichheld and W. Earl Sasser Jr., *Harvard Business Review* September/October 1990.

[28] Norman, Richard, *Service Management*, John Wiley & Sons: New York, 1984, p. 89. (Cited on Fitzsimmons2 chapter 9 page 239.) One text claims that the term "moment of truth" was coined by Jan Carlzon, former president of Scandinavian Airlines. (see Chase, Richard B., and Aquilano, Nicholas J., *Production and Operations Management: Manufacturing and Services*, Seventh Edition, 1995, Irwin:

Nevertheless, not all service processes contain the same marketing opportunities. "Front office" service production employees have much greater marketing opportunities than "back office" employees (see Appendix B and Fitzsimmons2 chapter 5 pages 87-89 on Service Blueprinting). Also, some types of service delivery lend themselves to more marketing opportunities (often at the expense of efficiency). (See Fitzsimmons2 chapter 5 pages 100-101 on Sales Opportunity and Service Delivery Options, noting Figure 5.3.)

How it impacts decisions... Companies need to decide how to manage the relationship between marketing departments and production employees, and how to assure that the marketing responsibilities of production employees are being met.

What to do about it... Employee training is an important activity in service organizations, particularly for customer-contact employees. Employees need to be trained in standard operating procedures, as well as exceptions. (see Fitzsimmons2 chapter 9 pages 244-246 on Training.)

For example... Disney is a company that trains every theme park production employee to be a marketing employee. In fact, the company recognizes that even the trash collection employees play a key roll in portraying the Disney image. This is because these employees roam the park throughout the day collecting trash, making them common targets of customer questions. A customer who simply wants to know the location of the nearest restroom or to know the park hours will likely judge the entire park based on the quality of interaction with the employee questioned.

Unit 9

My airline application... Telephone reservation employees are key players in the ability to attract repeat business from airline customers. If the employees are helpful and courteous, the customer is much more likely to call the airline again. However, if the employees are terse, that may be sufficient reason to call the competing airline first in the future. Therefore, the selection and training of reservation agents needs to cover more than just the standard operating procedures—it needs to emphasize the important marketing role accomplished by the various interactions with customers. (Some, in fact, may consider reservation agents to fall under the company's marketing function, which is debatable since it can also be viewed as gathering inputs for the air-travel production process.)

The marketing efforts of air travel production employees is particularly key when problems occur in a procedure. For example, when a flight is delayed, it is the airline personnel who can make all the difference in the reaction of customers—effective employees will be skilled in the "damage control" of recovering customer good will. Ineffective employees will simply give the customers more justification of their negative attitude towards the airline.

Even employees who do not have direct interaction with customers can influence the probability of customer repurchase. Few things will anger an airline passenger more than seeing his luggage come up the ramp at the destination airport with a tear in the side and the contents hanging out. It may be impossible to avoid ever damaging luggage, but when damage does occur, baggage handling employees can have great marketing ability by conscientiously handling the situation. For example, it can actually have a positive affect on the customer if the company, not the customer, first identifies the damage and initiates the solution.

Chicago, page 104 footnote.)

Supplemental reading...
Fitzsimmons2 chapter 5 pages 100-101 on Sales Opportunity and Service Delivery Options, noting Figure 5.3).
Fitzsimmons2 chapter 9 pages 244-246 on Training.
Fitzsimmons2 chapter 2 pages 32-33 on Labor-Intensiveness.
article: "Zero Defections: Quality Comes to Services" by Fredrick F. Reichheld and W. Earl Sasser Jr., *Harvard Business Review* September/October 1990. (This is an excellent article on the cost of turning over customers, and the value of retaining customers.)
article: "Managing to Keep the Customer." (Harvard Business Review)
case: Shouldice Hospital (HBS)

How manufacturing differs from services...

With manufacturing, the production employees usually have no interaction with customers, except for through the finished product. When a product is finished, it is left to the non-production marketing employees to portray product information to customers.

Quantitative analysis... (covered at the discretion of the instructor)

Net Present Value (NPV) analysis can be applied to calculating the lifetime value of a retained customer versus costs of high customer turnover. (see SBP: *Divided Loyalties*)

SBP 9b: The Who's Who of Marketing   Name (if turned in):_____

Analysis questions... To help apply this Service Business Principle, consider and answer the following questions about your specific service business process. (❑Check here if you are going outside of your target service business.)

Service company/business:_____

The service process:_____
    ① What marketing roles do or can production employees play?
    ② Are production employees aware of that role?
    ③ How might that role be developed?

① _____

_____

_____

_____

_____

_____

_____

_____

_____

_____

_____

_____

_____

_____

_____

_____

_____

Unit 9

SBP 9b: The Who's Who of Marketing   Name (if turned in):_____

Application exercise... Also to help you apply this Service Business Principle, complete the following analysis with regard to your specific service business process, or another service process in your business. (❏Check here if you are going outside of your target service business, which was _____.)

Service company/business:_____

The service process:_____

In the last Service Business Principle, *The Marketing of Properties*, we discussed ways of attracting new customers to service businesses. For this exercise, consider the methods for involving production employees in customer retention efforts. Redraw your service process flowchart, identifying the process location of a couple of "moments of truth" or other points where customers can make positive impressions on customers. In what ways can service employees at those points increase the likelihood of customer repurchase? Are there opportunities in the production process for employees to invite customers to purchase additional services? Where and how?

Preparation for the next Service Business Principle (9c)

To consider... Before proceeding, consider the following and write thoughts and ideas below:

An important marketing decision to be made by manufacturers and service providers is how much to charge for a given product or service. Manufacturers take into consideration information such as the cost to produce the product, what competitors are charging for similar products, and product availability. The goal is typically to price the product high enough to make an acceptable profit, but low enough to attract customers. (Although other goals exist, such as to gain market share at the expense of profit–a *loss leader* strategy.)

What information do service providers use to make pricing decisions? How does the cost of producing a service influence its price? Think of banks and amusement parks–what does it truly cost to serve *one more* customer? What about the price competitors are charging: Do service providers typically charge what competitors are charging, or does everyone charge different amounts? Think of attorneys and consulting firms–are they sometimes more attractive to customers if they charge more than competitors charge? Further, are different customers charged a different amount for the same service? Think of airlines and hotels–if customers are receiving the exact same service, why are they paying different amounts?

_____

_____

_____

_____

_____

_____

_____

_____

_____

_____

Service Business Principle 9c:
PRICE GUESSING

Service Business Principle	*"With services, pricing can be a bewildering process. Traditional cost-based, market-based, and value-base pricing strategies often fall apart with services, requiring pricing decisions to be made by less certain means."*

Why it occurs... PRICE GUESSING occurs because services have peculiar cost structures (see SBP: *The Costs of Utilization*), are variable and nonstandard (see SBP: *Heterogeneous Production*), and are of uncertain value prior to purchase (see SBP: *The Marketing of Properties*).

Details... How much should customers be charged for a particular service? The answer may not be obvious. For example, how much should a customer pay for a nights' stay at a hotel? Imagine that the owner of a new hotel hires a consultant to advise him on how much to charge customers. The conversation goes something like the following:

Owner: *So, how much should we charge customers for a night's stay at our hotel?*

Consultant: That depends.

Owner: *On what?*

Consultant: How much does it cost to serve each customer? If you tell me your cost per customer and your desired gross profit margin, I can calculate the price.

Owner: *Well, there is the cost of housekeeping, the cost of soap bars, the cost of heating and cooling, the cost of laundering towels and bedding, and the cost of check-in and check-out. It comes to about $8 per customer. I would like to generate a 20 percent profit margin.*

Consultant: No problem. That would be $8/(1− 0.20)=$10. Therefore, you should charge each customer $10 for a 20 percent profit margin.

Owner: *What about my mortgage and insurance on the property? That is about $10,000 per month.*

Consultant: How much per customer?

Owner: *Depends on our occupancy rate.*

Consultant: Well, since the occupancy rate depends on how much you charge, it might be difficult to determine cost based on your costs. How about if you tell me what your competitors are charging.

Owner: *The nearest hotel to the south charges $39.95 per night. The one to the north charges $139 per night. Of course the one to the north is nicer than the one to the south.*

Consultant: Which is most like your hotel?

Owner: *Well, we don't have as many features as the $139 hotel, but we are newer and cleaner than they are. We have pretty much the same features as the $39.95 hotel. In fact, from the outside our hotel looks similar to that hotel.*

Consultant: So you probably should charge more than $39.95, but not a lot more, unless customers think newness and cleanliness is more important than other features, in which case you can charge closer to $139. By charging more you might give customers the idea that you are in the same class as the $139 hotel, but they may be disappointed with your lack of amenities.

Owner: *That is kind of a broad range–from $39.95 to $139.*

Consultant: Yes, perhaps we should look at what customers are willing to pay. How valuable is a hotel room to a customer?

Owner: *Which customer?*

Consultant: A typical customer.

Owner: *Some customers stay on business and others on leisure travel. Some are paying out of their own pockets, and others are paying from an expense account. Some business travelers have fixed per diem amounts, and others have any expenses reimbursed. Sometimes customers stay here because there are no other vacancies in town, and other times almost all hotel rooms in town are vacant. Some customer shop around for the lowest price, and others want to stay here because we are near the convention center. I am not sure which of these we would call the "typical customer," since our customers and their circumstances vary quite widely.*

Consultant: I see what you mean. You may need to charge every customer a different amount, based on what you think each is willing to pay.

Owner: *That sounds like a great idea, but I don't think I am willing to pay you much for that advice.*

This imaginary dialogue illustrates some of the difficulty in determining the price of services. The consultant haphazardly tried three popular approaches to product pricing:

- **Cost-based pricing.** With this approach, companies determine what their per-item costs are, tack on a desired gross profit margin, and the result is the price to the customer. It can be extremely difficult to estimate the per-item cost of services since variable costs are often insignificant (see SBP: *The Costs of Utilization*).

- **Market-based pricing.** One form of market-based pricing is competitor-based, which is to base price on what competitors are charging. Services are often heterogeneous, making it difficult to compare one service provider to another. A hotel is not the same as another hotel. A four hundred-mile flight to New York is not the same as a four hundred-mile flight to Peoria. Dinner at McDonald's is not the same as dinner at the Deluxe hamburger shop. Service companies can have a hard time assessing who the true competitors are. In fact, the true competitors may not even appear to be in the same industry. Do television, the opera, amusement parks, and sporting events compete with one another? If they are all competing for the customers' entertainment dollars, should the opera be priced to compete with the professional sports team?

- **Value-based pricing.** Under this approach, companies attempt to set the price commensurate with the value received by the customer. Again, heterogeneous production implies that the value different customers receive from the service can vary *dramatically*. For a given price, some customers will get much more value than they pay for while other customers will pay too much. In some cases, service companies attempt to estimate how much value is received by various customers, as manifested by a willingness to pay. Such companies wind up charging different amounts to different customers for similar services.

To compound things even more, often customers do not even know the value of the service prior to purchase (see SBP: *The Marketing of Properties*). Pricing can thus be used as a *signal* to customers about how much value to expect. This is particularly applicable when the value is still not fully known even after the service has been received ("credence properties"). For example, one part-time counselor reported charging about $50 per hour for counseling initially. He was busy enough that he raised his rate to something like $100 per hour, and became even busier. At something like $150 his reputation seemed to do even better. The customers were apparently perceiving that they were getting better counseling from the $150 counselor than from the $50 counselor, even though it was the same counselor.

How it impacts decisions... Obviously, pricing is an important decision for any company. Theory would seem to indicate that there is an optimal pricing level for any given product or service, but things are usually more complicated than that. If a company prices too high, they lose customers and if they price too low, they will lose potential revenues. What is "too high" and "too low" can change from day to day and even from customer to customer. Therefore, pricing decisions in service can often be an ongoing concern.

What to do about it... The following are a few examples of pricing approaches which are used by service businesses. Which combination is most appropriate depends on the nature of the particular service industry, environment, and business.

Standardized pricing

Some service industries have a tradition of a particular type of pricing. For example, real estate agents in the U.S. typically charge a 6% commission on the sale of residential property. It is not exactly clear how that tradition came to be, whether by vote of some real estate organization or by happenstance. The advantage of such standardized pricing is that it removes the need for constant negotiation with the customer. It also simplifies the process for deciding which real estate agent to use. Further, it limits the likelihood of competitors starting a price war. Price wars are great for customers but harmful to service providers.

Competitive (market-based) pricing

In some service industries, customers are price-sensitive and typically know what prices are before they select a service provider. This allows customers to shop around before making a decision, and forces companies to watch competitors' prices.

Signal pricing

With some services, particularly those high in credence properties (see SBP: *The Marketing of Properties*), there is a feeling that the more it costs, the better the service. The customer's concern may be that if he or she is not paying enough, the service might not be too valuable. Other than price, it may be difficult to identify obvious criteria by which to judge the quality of a service. For example, my wife sometimes has gotten her hair cut at a place that charges $45 (ugh!), even though she does not seem to like the result any more than when she has gone to the places that charge $6.50. It is difficult to say exactly what a "good" haircut is (but easier to tell what a bad haircut is). But, there is just a feeling that you are going to get a better haircut from a $45 stylist than from a $6.50 stylist.

Variable pricing (often value-based)

If the value that customers attribute to the service varies significantly from one customer to another, then the company may want to charge each customer according to what he or she is willing to pay. The key is estimating how much each customer is willing to pay and legally setting the price according to that discrimination, then having pricing policies which set a price according to that discrimination. For example, an airline customer who has to take an emergency trip to Chicago to transact some important business is willing to pay a lot more for an airline ticket than a person who wants to fly to Chicago to visit Aunt Edna. The way airlines legally discriminate among customers is according to the amount of lead time the ticket is purchased prior to the flight. A ticket bought less than seven days before a flight will usually cost a lot more than one bought many weeks ahead. Also, airlines discriminate according to how long the stay over is for round-trip flights. Business people often do not want to stay over weekends, so tickets without a Saturday night stay are more expensive. Aunt Edna's visitors are more flexible, and usually more price-sensitive since their willingness to pay is much lower.

Yield management involves a form of variable pricing in which the price is determined not only by customer willingness to pay (a demand factor) but also by the amount of capacity which is available at any given time (a supply factor). Yield management works in situations where customers typically purchase the service some time before receiving it, such as through reservation systems. The service provider desires to get as much revenue ("yield") out of the available capacity as possible. They forecast demand for the service and make overall capacity planning decisions. Then, as time passes, they adjust the price to customers according to demand that has occurred up to that point. If sales (reservations) are higher than what was forecasted, the price is typically raised. If sales/reservations are lower than the forecast, the price may be dropped. Also, there can be specific classifications of service that can reserved or unreserved for potential higher-paying customers (such as last-minute reservations that will cost a lot of money). Complex computer algorithms are employed to manage the ongoing price adjustments.

It is common for service providers to employ some combination of the above strategies. Services pricing can be a complex process, and pricing practice within an industry can change over time.

Unit 9

For example... One example of *standardized pricing* is residential property appraisal services. In this area appraisers charge $300 for a standard interior appraisal. It is not because of a law or some other mandate. It is just what is charged.

Sometime standardized pricing is regulated, such as what people pay for local telephone service. If companies priced telephone service according to cost, they would charge rural customers a lot more than urban customers. Since local telephone service has traditionally been a monopoly (in the U.S.), it is highly regulated by public utilities commissions. Businesses can be charged more than residential customers, but local telephone companies usually are not allowed to discriminate among residential customers according to willingness to pay.

An example of *competitive pricing* is long-distance telephone service (since deregulation). Long-distance companies are continually dropping per-minute prices a fraction of a cent to beat competitors. Price is a major theme of long-distance service advertising. One company even called itself the "Dime Line," even though they seem to have now dropped their prices below a dime in response to competitive pressures.

Most examples of *signal pricing* are with services high in credence properties–where judging the quality of the service relies on the judgment of experts or others. Examples are:
- Education. Parents might be concerned about sending their children to a new private school that is inexpensive for no apparent reason.
- Consulting. Firms might be hesitant about hiring a consultant that charges lower than expected fees.
- Health care. Many customers will avoid going to a dentist that advertises discount prices.

Variable pricing occurs in situations where companies are able to estimate the value of the service to each individual customer. I have taken a few vacation cruises, and always on the super-saver discounts. On one cruise I was standing in line for some reason when fellow passengers broke into discussion about how much they paid for the cruise. Oh no! Trouble was brewing! I paid about half of what was paid by those who paid the brochure price for my cabin category. (I was smart enough to not participate in the conversation.) I had paid in giving up my convenience–traveling at a time I would not have otherwise, handling my own transportation to the ship port, etc.–because I was not willing to pay as much in cruise fare. Other passengers were willing (or unknowing) to pay more to cruise at their convenience.

Another example of variable pricing is auto inspection stations in the state of Utah. Each car must be registered during a given month, which requires an annual emissions and safety inspection. Inspection stations charge more at the end and the beginning of each month, when procrastinators get their cars inspected, since procrastinators are willing to pay more to avoid expensive tickets for not being registered.

My airline application... Since the time of U.S. airline deregulation, air travel pricing has become a bizarre and often confusing process. Prior to deregulation, pricing was *standardized* with a flight from one point to another being fixed by the government.

Customers benefitted greatly by deregulation, largely because of *competitive pricing*. Occasional fare wars have made air travel extremely affordable and attractive. (A few years ago my family and I flew from Salt Lake City to Seattle and back for $150 total!) When one airline drops prices, the other airlines are usually forced to follow.

Airlines are probably the most prevalent users of variable pricing and yield management. It is not uncommon for price shoppers to call an airline for three or four days in a row to see if the price of a future flight is going up or going down. It would not be surprising to find a flight of one hundred passengers paying fifty different prices for identical seats.

One "innovation" Southwest Airlines has espoused is simplified pricing, with only a few standard fares for each flight. One purpose is to simplify the decision for passengers. This system has a chance of working because Southwest's fares are generally twenty percent or more below competing airline fares.

Supplemental reading... Fitzsimmons2 page 403-409 on Yield Management.
article: "Yield Management: A Tool for Capacity-Constrained Service Firms," by Sheryl E. Kimes, in *Journal of Operations Management*, October 1989, Vol. 8, No. 4, pp. 348-364.

How manufacturing differs from services...

With manufacturing, variable costs often dominate, thereby allowing cost-based pricing; products can be objectively compared to facilitate market-based pricing; and market surveys can be conducted to allow value-based pricing. Therefore, pricing decisions for manufactured goods tend to be much more certain than for services.

SBP 9c: Price Guessing   Name (if turned in):_____

Analysis questions... To help apply this Service Business Principle, consider and answer the following questions about your specific service business process. (❑Check here if you are going outside of your target service business.)

Service company/business:_____

The service process:_____
① What tends to be the basis for pricing decisions in this industry? Costs? Competitors prices? Availability? Demand? Inflation? Others? How frequently do prices change?
② Is pricing relatively standardized in this service industry? What is the standard pricing method? What would happen if a company priced significantly above or below that standardized pricing?
③ Is pricing a significant competitive dimension? Is pricing a common theme in advertising and promotion? How do customers typically gather price information for comparison?
④ Is pricing a signal about the quality of the service? Would customers prefer to pay more if they thought that as a result they would receive better service? What are other ways customers can pre-judge quality more accurately than by price?
⑤ Is each customer typically charged a different pricing rate for this service? How does the service provider estimate "willingness to pay?" What are some company policies about pricing that discriminate according to customer willingness to pay?

①_____

_____

_____

_____

_____

_____

_____

_____

_____

_____

_____

_____

_____

_____

_____

_____

Unit 9

SBP 9c: Price Guessing   Name (if turned in):_____

Application exercise...

Also to help you apply this Service Business Principle, complete the following analysis with regard to your specific service business process, or another service process in your business. (☐Check here if you are going outside of your target service business, which was _____.)

Service company/business:_____

The service process:_____

First, identify which of the four pricing strategies listed in this Service Business Principle is most prevalent in your target service business (standardized pricing, competitive pricing, signaling pricing, variable pricing). Comment on the why that pricing strategy occurs in that industry.

Second, diagram (flowchart) the process of determining the price to charge for the particular service process listed above. As part of your diagram, indicate what information is gathered from customers or competitors in making the pricing decision. Describe when and how that information is gathered. Include some decision rules for making pricing decisions. (Examples of decision rules might be "If the airline passenger stays over a Saturday night, reduce the round trip fare by some percent," or "If a competing airline offers a lower price on that route, match it.")

What are problems with this pricing process which might cause the service provider to make pricing decisions with bad outcomes? (An example would be charging the standard $300 to appraise a home which is so large that it takes twice as long to complete. Another example is pricing wars with competitors. Another example is incorrectly estimating willingness to pay and therefore pricing your service out of the market.)

Preparation for the next Service Business Principle (9d)

To consider... Before proceeding, consider the following and write thoughts and ideas below:

When customers purchase manufactured goods, they are usually certain they got *something* for their money—they have ownership of the product which was purchased. This is not easy to say for many services. What do you have when you are done attending the movie theater? Done having your car's oil changed? Done with college? What do you say when a well-meaning friend asks, "So, what do you have to show for all the money you spent on that service?" The reality with many services is that the customer does not own anything after the service that they did not already own before. (You owned yourself and your car before going to the movie, the auto shop, or college.) As a result, many services are perceived to have an ephemeral (short-lived) nature, even though they may provide lasting value. How can this ephemeral nature of services be overcome? In other words, how can the value of services be portrayed to customers in lasting, tangible terms?

_____

_____

_____

_____

_____

_____

_____

_____

Unit 9

Service Business Principle 9d:

GIVE THEM SOMETHING NEW

Service Business Principle	*"With services, perceived value and marketing opportunities can sometimes be enhanced by giving customers something tangible that they did not already own."*

Why it occurs... GIVE THEM SOMETHING NEW occurs because the tangible outputs which are given to customers are often nothing more than the modified inputs the customers had in the first place!

Closely related to... SBP: *Intangibility Myth*
SBP: *The Server Ownership Perspective*
SBP: *The Marketing of Properties*

Details... Some authors have called this "Making the Intangible Tangible," (e.g. Fitzsimmons2 chapter 3 page 54) although I disagree with the general idea that services are intangible. (see SBP: *Intangibility Myth*) Granted, some services are indeed intangible, such as... well... lets see... telephone service. No, the phone is tangible and the signal vibrates my ear drum in a tangible way. Auto repair. No, the car is tangible as are the tools used to work on the car. Psychiatry. No, there is the funny shaped couch and the pages of ink blots. I am sure there are examples of truly intangible services, but I am having a hard time thinking of them right now.

The reason many services appear to be intangible is that the customer is not allowed to keep tangible portions of the service *other than those which the customer provided*. The telephone customer probably owns the telephone and the eardrum. The auto repair customer owns the car, but is not allowed to keep the tools used to work on it. The psychiatric patient is allowed to keep their brain, but not the funny-shaped couch. The customer may come away from services happy that a need was met, but with nothing tangible that they did not already own.

So, why should service companies give customers something tangible they do not *already* own? The answer is in perceived value. In the words of Dorthy Riddle, "...one of the key marketing challenges for services is to provide a tangible representation of the service in order to ensure the customer's sense of having made a worthwhile purchase."[29]

The gist of this Service Business Principle is that customers' perceptions of value received can be enhanced by giving them something tangible that they did *not* already own. For example, the telephone company could provide a mini-directory which summarizes frequently called telephone numbers (delivery restaurants, movie theaters, etc.); the auto repair company could give the customer a free tire gauge with an alignment or tire service; the psychiatrist could give the patient a booklet of helpful suggestions for dealing with stress, or a poster of positive sayings. In each case, it is particularly good that the thing given to the customer relate to the service, helping the customer realize the value given.

The marketing potential of such tangible service "takeaways" can be significant. The telephone mini-directory might include a list of other company services, such as call waiting. The tire gauge could be inscribed with the name and phone number of the auto shop (with instructions for tire gauge use, lest

---

[29] Riddle, D. (1985). *Service-Lead Growth*, Praeger Publishing, New York, p. 10.

customers think they have faulty tires). The psychologist's "gifts" could have a sticker "From Dr. so-and-so." These can remind the customer about the service provider at times of future service needs.

For example... Have you ever been to a half-day or one-day seminar that you or your employer paid substantial money for. Seminars are often dominated by credence properties, implying that even when you are done with the seminar you may not be able to evaluate if it was worth the money. (recall SBP: *The Marketing of Properties*) A way some seminar companies increase the perception of value added is to give the participants a workbook based on the materials of the seminar. The workbook is a tangible evidence and reminder of the service.

Likewise, consider the service of this Services Management course. There are many tangible elements, but I am afraid you cannot take the chairs or the chalkboard or the building with you when the semester is finished. You may even sell your text back—which I would not recommend—but you will certainly not sell this workbook back. (They would not take it anyway, since it is designed to be a "consumable.") This workbook will serve to remind you about all of the important concepts covered in the course. In some sense, the workbook extends the value of this course by making the principles more accessible years after the course is completed.

Some restaurants give away non-laminated versions of their menus to customers. The menus may facilitate a delivery service, or simply remind the customer about favorite dishes offered by the restaurant.

One store where I shop gives away refrigerator magnet shopping list note pads. The note pad is inscribed with the store name and "Don't forget to bring your film!" (They must have good profit margins on their one-hour photo processing.)

A company that cleaned our carpets sold us a small container of carpet stain remover. However, they would have been much wiser to give it away to *every* customer. Why? For one thing it will remind customers how clean their carpets were after the service. Also the container is inscribed with the name of the company—and what better time to remind customers about the name of the company than when they are thinking about carpet stains! For simple or small stains, the customer would probably not hire the carpet cleaning company anyway. But, when the stain is more major or the clean-carpet look is gone, the customer is reminded who to hire to fix things.

My bank gives away calendars every year. I also got a calendar from the shoe repair shop I patronize. Calendars are not specifically a banking or a shoe repair thing. Yet they can serve to remind me of the service providers (if I can remember where I put them).

My airline application... There is very little of value which the airline lets the customer keep that was not previously provided by the customer. The airline primarily modifies the location of passengers and their luggage. One thing that may serve as a tangible reminder of the service is the in-flight magazine. Often, such magazines are marked as "complimentary copies," although it is unlikely that a large percentage of customers take them. I would advise airlines to take greater effort to get customers to take a copy, such as pointing it out just prior to landing. If the articles and photography are of high quality, then many customers will read them or place them where others might read them. The magazine can remind people about the fun of traveling, and might even describe locations worth considering for a trip.

Unit 9

How manufacturing differs from services...

With manufacturing, customers receive tangible outputs which they never had before.

SBP 9d: Give Them Something New   Name (if turned in):_____

Analysis questions...   To help apply this Service Business Principle, consider and answer the following questions about your specific service business process. (❑Check here if you are going outside of your target service business.)

Service company/business:_____

The service process:_____
    ① What are the tangible elements of the service? Which do the customers take with them after the service is complete? Of those, which are simply modifications of what the customer already owned? Which are not?
    ② What could the customer be given as a tangible token of the service received?
    ③ How can these tangible tokens be prepared to enhance the chances of gaining future business?

①_____

_____

_____

_____

_____

_____

_____

_____

_____

_____

_____

_____

_____

_____

_____

Unit 9

SBP 9d: Give Them Something New   Name (if turned in):_____

Application exercise...
Also to help you apply this Service Business Principle, complete the following analysis with regard to your specific service business process, or another service process in your business. (❏Check here if you are going outside of your target service business, which was _____.)

Service company/business:_____

The service process:_____

Describe a tangible "takeaway" that can be given to the customer as part of service delivery. If possible, draw an example of the takeaway. Estimate the unit cost of such an item. How would the item serve to enhance the perceived value of the service? How would it serve as a reminder to the customer in instances of future service need?

Part III - Managing Service Processes
Unit 10:
PRODUCTION AND INVENTORY CONTROL

Unit reading... The following reading pertains to Service Business Principles included in this unit. The instructor will let you know which of the readings you are responsible for studying.
Fitzsimmons2 chapter 11 on Managing Queues.

Preparation for the next Service Business Principle (10a)

To consider... Before proceeding, consider the following and write thoughts and ideas below:
In manufacturing environments we inventory raw materials, partially-finished goods, and finished goods. As discussed previously (under SBP: *Simultaneous Production and Consumption*), inventory allows goods or materials to be produced at one time and consumed at another. In some cases, these manufacturing inventories can contain many months worth of production or production inputs. Some manufacturers, however, have implemented just-in-time (JIT) production systems in which items are procured and produced as closely to when they are needed as possible—thus eliminating the need for large inventories. How appropriate would a JIT system be for services production? What factors would influence an implementation of JIT production in service processes?

Unit 10

_____

_____

_____

_____

_____

_____

_____

_____

Service Business Principle 10a:
INADVERTENT JIT

Service Business Principle	*"With services, the primary inventory system is often called a queue. Time in such inventories is measured in minutes, not months. The production process lends itself to just-in-time (JIT) inventory."*

Why it occurs... INADVERTENT JIT occurs because customers are aware of how long their inputs have been in the production process, have expectations for how long production should take, and are intolerant of avoidable delays.

Closely related to... SBP: *Customers in Inventory*

Details... We usually think of inventory as stored goods. Why do we keep inventories? There are a number of reasons, including
- production smoothing (meeting varying demand with stable production, which is helpful even if the demand can be perfectly predicted or scheduled),
- process decoupling (creating an inventory buffer between stages of a production process),
- realizing economies of scale (such as order quantity or production batch size advantages),
- maintaining buffer stocks (extra product to be used in the case of higher than normal demand), and,
- simplifying material handling (it might be very difficult to move production in quantities of one).

All of these reasons are included in the idea that inventories are used move items forward in time from the point at which they are available until the point at which they are needed. Inventory is a *temporal transformation* process, or in other words, inventory moves things forward through time. Why do we need to move things forward in time? Because we are unable or unwilling to properly match production with demand.

Manufacturing companies that are willing and able to match production with demand do so by implementing just-in-time (JIT) production systems. With JIT systems, production is scheduled and controlled so that it occurs just prior to the time it is needed. Manufacturers often implement JIT systems by utilizing a signaling device known as a *kanban* or card. The "downstream" portion of the process sends a kanban card to the "upstream" supplier requesting more production. The upstream process produces the amount requested on the card, sends the card and the product to the requester, then *waits* for the next card (or does something else for the time being). The kanban card is therefore a signal for a production station to produce. The result is *dramatically* reduced inventories, since the upstream supplier only produces what is needed. In other words, effective JIT systems avoid the need for the temporal transformation that comes from production which is not in sync with demand.

Warehousing and storage services exist to temporally transform customers' belongings–making them available at a later date. Also, a primary reason retailers and wholesalers exist is to stock manufactured goods until the customer wants them. A retailer might have an item in inventory for months before it is sold. However, when a customer visits the retailer and selects the item, that customer does <u>not</u> want to be delayed in a queue for an extended period of time. This disdain of delays tends to be true of all services in which customer inputs enter a queue.

When, then, is a queue? A queue is a waiting line. It can be a waiting line of people, such as the line waiting to buy tickets at the movie theater; it can be a waiting line of things, such as the rolls of film waiting to be processed at the photo processing lab; or, it can be a waiting line of information, such as the line stack of loan applications waiting to be processed or the buffer of Internet queries waiting to be transferred (which is why the Internet can be slow during some times of the day.) In all of these cases, queues exist because demand has temporarily exceeded the rate of production. Sound familiar? A *queue* is in fact *a short-term inventory system*! (This is why the *Customers in Inventory* Service Business Principle indicated that services *can* be inventoried—the inventories are manifest as queues!)

There are, in fact, some fundamental differences between queues and traditional conceptualizations of inventories. In the business sense queues are typically described as waiting which belongs to a customer, whereas inventories simply belong to the company (until sold). This we see in the example above, with queues of customer-self inputs, of customer-belonging inputs, and customer-information inputs.

An implication of customer ownership of queue items is the customer concern about waiting times. For manufacturing, inventories are evaluated in terms of "inventory turnover," which is the number of times that inventory is replace in a given period. This is a function of the amount of time items spend in inventory. It is not unreasonable for an average manufactured item to spend weeks or months in inventory. Not so for customer-input inventories. Customers are often enraged if we make them or their belongings wait weeks or months in a queue! (Imagine spending a week waiting to be served at the bank or a month waiting to have your home's air conditioner repaired!)

The result of customer impatience is that we often measure queue performance in terms of *seconds* or *minutes* waiting. (Although sometimes hours or days.) In other words, we require the production system to be no more than a small amount of time out of sync with demand—which is the essence of a JIT system! This JIT system comes not as a result of management initiative, but rather is motivated by market necessities (customers would depart if they had to wait more than a short time for service). Therefore the JIT approach taken by service companies is to a large extent *inadvertent*!

Unit 10

How it impacts decisions... Most services do not have the option of avoiding a JIT or near-JIT system—either they achieve a JIT production system or they lose customers. This is because customers will not wait more than a short amount of time to be served. Service providers must determine what wait is acceptable, and plan capacity accordingly.

What to do about it... A useful way to plan capacity to manage queues is through "queuing theory." With queuing theory we make simplifying assumptions about service process flows, which allows us to calculate the impact on capacity (service rate) decisions on waiting. The cost of increasing the service rate needs to be traded off against the cost of customers having a long wait in line. Queuing theory helps us estimate those costs.

(Queuing theory was introduced with the *Customers in Inventory* SBP, and is further discussed in Appendix C. A brief mention of queuing theory is included in the Quantitative Analysis section of this SBP.)

For even more complex queuing situations, we might employ computer *simulation* to determine the effect of capacity changes on queue performance. With simulation we have a computer model, or representation, of the service process. The model can be "run" to show how the service system will behave given different conditions, such as changes in the number of servers.

My airline application... What are the major "inventories" in the airline service process? Passengers are inventoried in airport terminals waiting for scheduled capacity (i.e. the airplane). These passenger inventories can be used to handle the delays between various phases of the process: With the hub system, various flights land in a central "hub" airport, where the passengers wait for their connecting flights. The fact that some layovers can be quite long illustrates that this is not an exact JIT system. A exact JIT system (of which few likely exist even in manufacturing) would have arriving flights landing mere minutes before connecting flights. However, the problems of delayed incoming flights would be very costly, hence the need for airlines to inventory passengers for an amount of time in hub airports. But, too much waiting will cause costs for customers.

Another place we see inventories in the airline process is in the queue of luggage going up ramp. Because personnel cannot load and unload luggage until the plane lands, they wind up inventorying the luggage at the gate in a near-JIT manner.

It sometimes seems peculiar that airlines will allow extremely long lines of customers checking in at the gate. Since most passengers have advance reservations, it would seem that airlines should be able to forecast demand for check-ins at the gate quite accurately. Then, queuing theory could be used to estimate how much capacity is needed at specific flight times in order to keep lines small.

Supplemental reading... Fitzsimmons2 chapter 14 pages 436-437 on Inventory and Waiting Line Analogy.
Fitzsimmons2 chapter 17 on Queuing Models and Capacity Planning. (Don't get hung up on the detailed calculations unless the instructor tell you to.)

How manufacturing differs from services...

With manufacturing, the customers have no idea how long a product or the components of the product were in inventory, nor do they usually care.

Quantitative analysis... (covered at the discretion of the instructor)

Queuing theory is covered in Fitzsimmons2 chapter 17 (on Queuing Models and Capacity Planning). The following is an example of a simple queuing model (called the standard M/M/1 model). We start by making certain simplifying assumptions about the random nature in which customers arrive, the random nature of the time it takes to serve each customer, an effectively unlimited number of customers, ordering to the queue, *et cetera*. If we also assume that we have only one server, we can use the following equations.
Determine:
- λ (called lambda) as the average rate customers arrive (e.g. customers/minute), and
- μ (called mu) as the average rate each customer is served (e.g. customers/minute).
Then:
- The "traffic intensity" of the server (ρ or rho) is λ/μ.
- Since there is just one server, this traffic intensity is equal to the average utilization (percentage of time busy) of that server.
- The average number of customers in the queue (L_q) is $\rho\lambda/(\mu-\lambda)$.
- The average amount of time a customer waits before being served (W_q) is $\rho/(\mu-\lambda)$.

We can then use these equations, for example, to calculate the average service rate (μ) that would be required to reduce the average wait time (W_q) by a certain amount.

Instead of speeding up the single server from the model above, we may instead desire to add additional servers. In that case (give all the other assumptions the same) we would have a standard M/M/c model. If the total number of servers is denoted c, then we have:

- The traffic intensity (ρ) is still λ/μ.
- (The utilization factor is now $\lambda/(c\mu)$ since there are c servers.)
- The probability that all servers are idle (P_0) is
- $1/[\Sigma(\rho^i/i!) + \rho^c/(c!(1-\rho/c))]$, with Σ going from i=0 to i=c-1.
- The average number of customers in the queue (L_q) is $(P_0)\rho^{(c+1)}/[(c-1)!(c-\rho)^2]$.
- The average amount of time a customer waits before being served (W_q) is L_q/λ.

As you can see, by adding one level of assumption complexity—that there is more than one server—the complexity of the equations grew tremendously. Tables and computer programs are available to simplify the process of estimating queuing theory equation values.

An additional description of queuing theory is found in Appendix C.

Unit 10

SBP 10a: Inadvertent JIT   Name (if turned in):_____

Analysis questions...   To help apply this Service Business Principle, consider and answer the following questions about your specific service business process. (❑Check here if you are going outside of your target service business.)

Service company/business:_____

The service process:_____
   ① Where are customer-inputs delayed in the system?
   ② How long are they delayed?
   ③ Why are they delayed?
   ④ What is the result when delays occur?

①_____

_____

_____

_____

_____

_____

_____

_____

_____

_____

_____

_____

_____

_____

_____

_____

Unit 10

SBP 10a: Inadvertent JIT   Name (if turned in):_____

Application exercise...

Also to help you apply this Service Business Principle, complete the following analysis with regard to your specific service business process, or another service process in your business. (❑Check here if you are going outside of your target service business, which was _____.)

Service company/business:_____

The service process:_____

The details of this Service Business Principle indicated that queues exist because of a temporary mismatch between capacity and demand. If capacity and demand were better matched then the service could operate with minimal waiting. Describe a place in your service process where customers or their inputs wait to be served. Are there ways that demand and capacity could be kept more in line with one another? List a few ways that capacity could be temporarily increased for those times that demand is high. Also list a few ways the excess demand at high customer-waiting times could be shifted to times when customers would not have to wait. Would a "kanban" system be appropriate, in which the service provider signals to customers when it is a good time to present their inputs for wait-free service?

Preparation for the next Service Business Principle (10b)

To consider... Before proceeding, consider the following and write thoughts and ideas below:

In the last Service Business Principle, a comparison was made between manufacturing inventories and service queues. One difference between the two is in terms of costs. With manufacturing, the inventory holding costs from producing too much of an item are traded off against the setup costs of making or purchasing the item too frequently. Are these the same costs to trade off in service queue situations? If not, what are the costs to trade off in queue management situations? (Hint: some costs might be monetary, and others might be psychological.)

_____

_____

_____

_____

_____

_____

_____

_____

Unit 10

Service Business Principle 10b:

CUSTOMER INVENTORY COSTS

Service Business Principle	*"With services, the primary inventory costs are costs to the customer, including psychological costs of being inventoried in a queue and good will costs of being unable to receive appropriate service."*

Why it occurs... CUSTOMER INVENTORY COSTS occurs because customers expect to be served shortly after they demand service (near JIT) and have presented their inputs. Also, waiting can wear down customer-self inputs.

Closely related to... SBP: *Inadvertent JIT*

Details... Our approach to managing queuing systems is similar to the way we manage inventories in that we attempt to plan the system so as to minimize total costs. The main difference is which costs dominate. With some manufacturing inventory systems, if we make or purchase too much of an item at one time, we have high costs of holding the items in inventory until we need them, but at least we do not have to set up to make the item for a longer time. Therefore, we trade off inventory holding costs against procurement costs. In other manufacturing systems we trade off the holding costs against the costs of not having enough of an item when it is needed. (Examples are the "perishable inventory model" or the "safety stock" calculation.) In either case, if we run out of the item, we incur back-order costs or a lost sale.

With services, we cannot complete production in advance of demand because we do not yet have the customer inputs (from the Unified Services Theory). Therefore, the queue management issue is how much we should be *prepared* to produce at the time demand occurs (and customer inputs are received). If the service provider has too little capacity, there will be potentially great costs to the customer (such as inconvenience, lost time, and lost good will with the service provider). You should note that the most significant customer costs are psychological, which can dramatically influence the potential for repurchase and loyalty. Too much capacity lowers the potential costs to the customer, but results in higher costs in terms of idle capacity. Which is preferable? It depends on the estimates of the costs. The fact is, the magnitude of psychological costs of delay to customers are generally *much* higher than the corresponding monetary costs of delay to manufacturing inventories—which accounts for the significant differences in the acceptable times in inventory between the two systems. Nevertheless, too much service capacity may be good for the customers, but someone has to pay for all of that idle capacity.

How it impacts decisions... Service providers must consider the time costs of customer waiting, and the accompanying psychological costs to the customer. These costs are balanced against the cost of capacity and the costs of reducing negative psychological effects.

What to do about it... When customer waiting costs are lowered by increasing the service capacity, a capacity cost is incurred. The amount of capacity necessary for a corresponding benefit to the customer can be estimated using "Queuing Theory" as was discussed in the *Inadvertent JIT* Service Business Principle.

Another way to decrease the customer-waiting costs *without increasing capacity (the service rate)* is through understanding and using the "psychology of queuing." This psychology captures the idea that costs to customers are not realized according to the actual amount of waiting, but rather according to the amount of waiting *perceived* by the customer! Therefore, if the perceived wait can be decreased, the waiting cost decreases, even if the actual wait is the same. An oft quoted pioneer of queuing psychology is David Maister. He made the following observations:[30]

• Unoccupied waits seem longer than occupied waits.
• Pre-process waits seem longer than in-process waits.
• Anxiety makes waits seem longer.
• Uncertain waits seem longer than waits of a known duration.
• Unexplained waits seem longer than explained waits.
• Unfair waits seem longer than equitable waits.
• The more valuable the service, the longer people will be willing to wait.
• Waiting alone seems longer than waiting with a group.

Maister's points could stand some scientific study, and should be taken with careful thought. (In fact, I am in the middle of a multi-year study of explained waits involving experiments we have conducted around the globe.) Nevertheless, there is great merit in considering the psychological implications of customer inventories.

For example... Post offices are notorious for extended waits at times when it is convenient to visit the post office but not convenient to wait. One day I left my family in the car while I ran into the local post office. To the side of the long line was a screen playing my favorite scene from the Lion King (Akuna Matada). The problem was that the line seemed to move so rapidly that I was unable to see the rest of the scene by the time I was at the front of the line. Had not my family been waiting in the car, I could have gone through the line again to catch the rest of the scene. (Occupied waits seem shorter than unoccupied waits.)

Some amusement parks place signs a ways back in a line telling waiters how many minutes to the front of the line. (Waits of a known duration should seem shorter than uncertain waits.) One time at Universal Studios Florida, my wife and I were waiting in the popular "Back to the Future" ride. The sign said something like "forty five minutes wait from here." The line sure did not seem like it could be that long of a wait. After waiting perhaps twenty minutes we were already at the front of the line! Although it was only the line *we could see from the beginning*! There was another line of equal duration on the other side of a partition. After another 20 minutes or so, we started on a line up a ramp to the ride. Sure enough, it was about forty five minutes. It *seemed* like forty five minutes. Without the sign at the beginning, it might have seemed like more than forty five minutes. The park failed in an opportunity to ease the burden of the line. They had television monitors hanging from the ceiling throughout the line. Every so often, a short segment featuring "Back to the Future" star Christopher Lloyd would come on, which dramatically improved the wait situation. But, most of the time the monitors were blank, which left us to spend our time conversing about the questioned legitimacy of the forecasted forty five minute wait.

My airline application... Let's come back to the problem of extremely long lines of customers checking in at the gate. I often wonder: "Is such a wait necessary?" "What if I just boarded directly at the gate without checking in?" "What is this so-called boarding pass I got

[30] Maister, David H., "The Psychology of Waiting Lines" in *The Service Encounter*, edited by Czepiel, J. A., Solomon, M. R., and Surprenant, C. F., Lexington Books / D.C. Heath: Lexington, Mass, 1985.
  This Maister article reference is from Lovelock, Christopher H., *Services Marketing*, Third Edition, Prentice Hall: Upper Saddle River, New Jersey, pages 219-220.

from my travel agent, anyway?" So, I wind up standing in line to prevent a major incident at boarding time because I don't have the right kind of boarding pass. If the airline either (a) put up a sign, or (b) had an employee walk down the line identifying people who do not need to stand in line, the queue would probably be much smaller. In addition, the people who remain in the line would then know it is all for a purpose.

Supplemental reading...   Fitzsimmons2 chapter 11 on Managing Queues.
mini case: Christmas at UPS. (in Appendix D of this workbook)
article: "Prescription for the Waiting Line Blues: Entertain, Enlighten, and Engage," by Katz, Karen L., Larson, Blaire M., and Larson, Richard C., *Sloan Management Review*, Winter 1991, pages 44-55.

How manufacturing differs from services...

With manufacturing, the customers are not directly involved with inventory costs, but the inventory costs are holding costs incurred to the company.

Quantitative analysis... (covered at the discretion of the instructor)

Queuing Theory was introduced in the *Inadvertent JIT* and *Customers in Inventory* SBPs, and is described in Fitzsimmons2 chapter 17 (on Queuing Models and Capacity Planning).

SBP 10b: Customer Inventory Costs   Name (if turned in):_____

Analysis questions... To help apply this Service Business Principle, consider and answer the following questions about your specific service business process. (❑Check here if you are going outside of your target service business.)

Service company/business:_____

The service process:_____
　　① What are the costs to customers in terms of waiting in queues (themselves, their belongings, or their information)? Which of these costs are psychological? Can these costs be estimated in monetary terms?
　　② What are the costs of additional capacity?
　　③ In what ways do some of these costs tend to dominate service process planning decisions? In other words, which costs tend to (or should) drive planning decisions?
　　④ How might psychological costs of customer waiting be reduced without adding additional capacity?

① _____

_____

_____

_____

_____

_____

_____

_____

_____

_____

_____

_____

_____

_____

_____

_____

_____

Unit 10

SBP 10b: Customer Inventory Costs   Name (if turned in):_____

Application exercise...   Also to help you apply this Service Business Principle, complete the following analysis with regard to your specific service business process, or another service process in your business. (❑Check here if you are going outside of your target service business, which was _____.)

Service company/business:_____

The service process:_____

Develop a plan for managing the psychology of queues. Describe a major customer queue in your service business process (or in an alternate process if necessary). Explain how some of Maister's principles might be applied to decrease the psychological costs of the queue without increasing server capacity. (Or, suppose your own reasonable principles of queuing psychology.) For example, describe an effective way customers could be occupied in a meaningful activity while they are waiting. Or, how could a pre-process wait be turned into an in-process wait by starting customers with the production process while they are waiting? Be creative.

(Maister's principles were:
- Unoccupied waits seem longer than occupied waits.
- Pre-process waits seem longer than in-process waits.
- Anxiety makes waits seem longer.
- Uncertain waits seem longer than waits of a known duration.
- Unexplained waits seem longer than explained waits.
- Unfair waits seem longer than equitable waits.
- The more valuable the service, the longer people will be willing to wait.
- Waiting alone seems longer than waiting with a group.)

Preparation for the next Service Business Principle (10c)

To consider... Before proceeding, consider the following and write thoughts and ideas below:

Manufacturing organizations may be interested in knowing what was produced during each time period. That information can be helpful in evaluating productivity and effective capacity utilization. If a major defect was found to have occurred in a batch of production, it may be necessary to issue a recall of that batch. Such a recall would require knowing which were produced were produced during which times. The faulty products would be identified by a serial number or manufacturing date stamp. Service organizations may also have reasons for tracking production. Can you think of some examples? What would be involved in tracking services production? (For example, would a serial number of production date stamp method be adequate?)

_____

_____

_____

_____

_____

_____

_____

_____

Unit 10

Service Business Principle 10c:

DETAILED PRODUCTION TRACKING

Service Business Principle	*"With services, keeping track of production and inventory can mean tracking details about every customer. This often requires highly complex information systems."*

Why it occurs... DETAILED PRODUCTION TRACKING occurs because production is nonstandard, and one unit of production (a customer) may be relevant to a future unit of production (that customer returning). For example, if a customer provides peculiar inputs, the service provider may need to know that each time they are presented.

Details... Manufacturers tend to track production in aggregate. Instead of logging every widget produced, the company counts how many widgets were produced during a specific time period. If the widgets have serial numbers, the range of serial number values produced during a particular day might be recorded. How do manufacturers use the production information? The serial number might help identify products that were produced with a quality defect, in case a produce recall is warranted. Otherwise, production tracking data can be useful in identifying how much was produced and how productivity has changed over time.

The production of service companies tends to be nonstandard. It may be of interest to know how many customers were processed over a given period of time. However, in many instances, it is important to know what *specific processing* took place with each individual customer. This is considerably more difficult than simply counting the number of customers. It involves gathering data about when and what took place with a particular customer. Often, the system must be able to identify return customers so that their new service encounters can be appended to the records of their prior encounters. In some cases this is accomplished by assigning a customer number. In other cases, it can be quite difficult to know when a customer has returned.

How it impacts decisions... Service providers need to decide at what level of detail they should track production, and whether it would be cost-justified to track specific encounters with each customer.

For example... Banks need to track every transaction that takes place on each customer's account. It is not enough to simply report "We had 432 customers visit the bank today." What did they do? Did they deposit or withdraw money? Involving which accounts? A great deal of what banks do is to track the production data the describes every transaction and allows complete accounting of funds.

(The most notorious transaction trackers are credit card companies. I have heard that they exploit purchase information by unabashedly selling to anyone and everyone who is interested in paying for it.)

Universities track every time a student takes and/or completes a course. If the registrar's office only recorded the number of student each semester, the departments would have a hard time knowing if a student qualifies to graduate. Therefore, complex computer systems which keep track of all course completion (i.e. education production) data are in place at most universities.

Dental offices, as with all medical clinics, keep detailed records of every patient visit and every type of production (i.e. treatment). That information is used to assure that the dentist is aware of particular patient conditions on subsequent visits.

In each of these examples there is a clear need and often even a legal requirement for keeping detailed customer records. Some other services don't have such stringent requirements, but nonetheless reap benefits of detailed production tracking.

Some retailers, such as Radio Shack and Toys 'R Us, ask each customer to for their phone number at the time they make a purchase. In that manner, they are able to track customers who make repeat purchases. The data can be used to more precisely target advertising mailings.

Some Pizza Hut delivery locations have computers that are equipped with Caller ID. Whenever a customer places an order, the order is recorded in the computer. When another order is placed from that same telephone number, the computer displays the prior order. The Pizza Hut employee can then ask the caller if they would like the same thing they ordered last time, which can simplify the ordering process. The system also has the potential for assisting the process of locating customers—since detailed directions to obscure addresses only need to be gathered once.

Hotels typically track the occupancy for each day. The Ritz-Carlton implemented an information system that also tracked the individual customer preferences. That way, if a prior customer visits the Ritz-Carlton again, the computer system tells the employees about the specific preference so they can be ready. An example would be a customer who prefers extra blankets on the bed or an extra ice bucket.

My airline application... Airlines track not only the number of customers, but who each customer on a flight is (the flight manifest). Prior to the flight, they track individual reservations and amounts paid, data which is used to guide yield management systems (enabling them to adjust fares depending on projected demand and capacity utilization).

In addition, airlines track the travel of specific customers through frequent flier programs. Frequent flier programs inherently encourage loyalty, but have other benefits as well. For example, they can help the airline identify certain types of customers to target for special offers or promotions. Many frequent flier clubs have Premier or Medallion types of memberships exclusively for the most frequent fliers. The airlines reserve certain perks, such as special check-in lines and free access to airline lounges.

Supplemental reading... Fitzsimmons2 chapter 4 (particularly on data base asset)
case: Ritz-Carlton (HBS)

How manufacturing differs from services...

With manufacturing, production is relatively standard, allowing the tracking of production via aggregate measures. Also, manufacturers often do not know who end customers are, especially given low returns on warranty or product registration.

SBP 10c: Detailed Production Tracking   Name (if turned in):_____

Analysis questions... To help apply this Service Business Principle, consider and answer the following questions about your specific service business process. (❑Check here if you are going outside of your target service business.)

Service company/business:_____

The service process:_____
   ① Does the company have the need to track what was produced over time? Why/how might the data be used?
   ② Is each "product" unique? In what ways?
   ③ Can the uniqueness allow us to personalize future production by tracking current production?

① _____

_____

_____

_____

_____

_____

_____

_____

_____

_____

_____

_____

_____

_____

_____

_____

_____

_____

Unit 10

SBP 10c: Detailed Production Tracking   Name (if turned in):_____

Application exercise...

Also to help you apply this Service Business Principle, complete the following analysis with regard to your specific service business process, or another service process in your business. (❑Check here if you are going outside of your target service business, which was _____.)

Service company/business:_____

The service process:_____

Make a list of items of information your service business should track about each customer. For example, you might track the customer's name, his or her customer number, the type of service the customer requested, any peculiar requests, and the service outcome (was it successfully completed?). After you have created your list of information items, address the following questions: Where and when in the production process is that customer information collected and recorded (in a database)? and where and when might the information be used by the service provider to enhance the ability to provide or market the service? For these two questions, you might redraw a process flowchart, with arrows indicating the flow of data to and from the customer-information database.

Part IV - Service Quality and Value
Unit 11:
DEFINING SERVICE QUALITY

Unit reading... The following reading pertains to Service Business Principles included in this unit. The instructor will let you know which of the readings you are responsible for studying.
Fitzsimmons2 chapter 10 on Service Quality.

Preparation for the next Service Business Principle (11a)

To consider... Before proceeding, consider the following and write thoughts and ideas below:
Manufacturers have various ways of defining quality—identifying when quality exists and when defects occur. One common definition is "conformance to specifications," which is that the product has features (or "qualities") and performance that are sufficiently in accordance with the product's design. Others define quality as "doing it right the first time," which is simply a process view of conformance to specifications. Another common view is "meeting or exceeding customer expectations"—which for manufactured products is largely a product design issue. If a manufactured product is not designed to meet customers' expectations, it us unlikely anyone in production can or will do anything to rectify the problem. These three perspectives on goods quality are each based on an evaluation of what was produced relative to design specifications, and a "defect" is defined as an instance where the product does not meet specifications. Specifications typically come from product engineers, who may be designing the product based on market research data or other communication with customer groups.

What role do specifications play in defining service quality? Who is to say what the appropriate service features should be, and when the service is being produced improperly?

SWAYING THE CUSTOMER-JUDGE

Service Business Principle	*"With services, quality "specifications" come from multiple simultaneous sources, including the company and the individual customers. The company presents specifications as standard operating procedures. The customer presents specifications based on their need-driven expectations for changes to their process-inputs. Misalignment between company- and customer-specifications for the service process leads to dissatisfaction, even when the process goes exactly as it was designed. The misalignment of specifications can be avoided through communication. However, if the service performance does not address individual customer needs, the customer will not require the service."*

Why it occurs... SWAYING THE CUSTOMER-JUDGE occurs because each customer has unique specifications for the service process. Customer-specifications are based on (a) customer experience with similar service processes, and (b) the needs of their individual inputs into the process (by the Unified Services Theory). Therefore, each customer's expectation for the service process can be unique.

Closely related to...   SBP: *The Marketing of Properties*
SBP: *Measuring Customers*

Details... Understanding this Service Business Principle requires understanding the difference between quality and value. **"Quality"** comes from the satisfaction of *expectations*, which are cognitive or formal descriptions of the service process and outcome. On the other hand, **"value"** comes from the satisfaction of *needs*, which are changes that customers perceive will increase their happiness (or whatever you choose to call "feeling good"–consider your favorite "happy" term in this discussion) or decrease their unhappiness. Needs come from customers' beliefs about what will increase their happiness. Service expectations come from customers' beliefs about what a service provider is willing and able to do for the customer. When expectations for a service provider appear to fill customer needs, the customer will consider purchasing the service, otherwise they will not. For example, a customer might expect that a particular well-known flower shop will produce *exactly* what is ordered, will deliver it *precisely* where and when requested, will only use the highest quality, long-lasting flowers, and all this for a low, low price—the customer will *not* patronize such a high-quality flow shop unless the service fills a need.

(Think about how many high-quality services there are that you do not patronize because they do not fill a need. Stroll through the yellow pages of the phone book. Surely there are some high-quality air-conditioner repair shops, beauticians, car painters, ditch diggers, etc. in your community. Even if they were high-quality at a low price, you still would not patronize them unless they filled a need. Or, look at a recent issue of *Consumer Reports*, which rates the quality of various goods and services. Do you patronize all of the "high-quality" companies, even the ones at a low price? No, because many of the goods and services do not fill your particular needs.)

Often, customers mistakenly assume quality is value, or that value defines quality. Much of this is a semantic confusion based on the inadequacy of the English language. Further, customers assume that companies define quality based on customer needs (which should be the case, but often is not). This is captured in the *Provident Provider Hypothesis*, which might be stated: "service providers are in business to fill customer needs, which implies that they will want to attend to needs that are common, and since my needs appear to be common, service providers should attempt to fill my needs." Many customers believe the Provident Provider Hypothesis, yet find that some companies who do exactly what they intend to do still fail to meet customer needs. This is because the Provident Provider Hypothesis is not always true.

- Some companies are not in the business to fill needs, although successful companies generally are.
- Some companies are not aware of common needs of customers, although market research can help identify those needs.
- A customer may think their needs are common, when in fact they are not (and may be beyond the scope of the service process).
- For economic and practical reasons, there is a limit to the scope of needs filled by service providers, meaning that some customer needs will be out of the scope of service.

The adverse effects of a misapplied Provident Provider Hypothesis can be mitigated by improved communication between the company and the customer. Companies who strive to fill a range of customer needs can gather information from customers about their needs and adjust the service process accordingly, and can communicate limits to the need-filling ability early to avoid investment resulting in dissatisfaction.

One last comment about "value." As discussed above, value comes from the satisfaction of needs. By acquiring value, the customer usually has to give up the opportunity to satisfy other needs. For example, by spending money to have a service provider paint your house, you are sacrificing the opportunity to use that money to fulfill another need, such as going on a vacation. Therefore, the filling of needs usually involves some degree of *sacrifice*, which is the giving up of something good for something better. So, as a broader concept, value of a service is the need filling potential of the service *minus* the sacrificed need-filling opportunity (of time and money expenditures).

How it impacts decisions... The company must decide what the service specifications will be, where they will come from, and how they will be achieved.

Unit 11

What to do about it... This Service Business Principle indicates that one reason communication with customers is important in service processes is to avoid misaligned specifications of quality. Customers communicate their expectations, and service providers communicate the service features that customers might expect. If customer expectations are not within the realm of the service being provided, the customer can usually opt out before committing to the service. For this to work, the communication needs to be earlier in the service process rather than later, since late communication implies that the customer has probably already committed himself or herself to the process.

An additional advantage of early and frequent communication with customers can be realized when the service fails to meet agreed-upon expectations. If such service failures are detected early, the opportunity for effective recovery is much greater. (This topic will be revisited in SBP: *Early Communication/Early Recovery*.)

Issues pertaining to sources of service-process specifications were discussed in detail under the *Who is in Control* Service Business Principle. Even when the service organization or the service employee is responsible for defining the service process, care must be taken to assure that it adequately addresses customer needs and expectations. Techniques such as customer focus groups or customer surveys can help determine this *ex post facto*. Another method is to conduct a *walk-through audit*, which is a study of the service process from the customer's point of view. The studier creates a list of scales for measuring various aspects of the service process. Customers or company employees can walk-through the service process and record measurements. This data can help identify components of the service process where customer needs are not being met, or where customers may have different expectations than what is designed into the service process.

The following table shows some walk-through audit questions that might be used for a doctor's office. (Another example is shown in Fitzsimmons2 chapter 6.)

Sample Questions from a Doctor's Office Walk-through Audit
1. How clear is it where patients should park? obvious 5 - 4 - 3 - 2 - 1 unclear
2. How available is parking? plenty 5 - 4 - 3 - 2 - 1 none
3. How easy is it for people with physical disabilities to access the office? easy 5 - 4 - 3 - 2 - 1 difficult
4. Is it clear how and where patients should check-in when then arrive? clear 5 - 4 - 3 - 2 - 1 unclear
5. How comfortable is the waiting area? (temperature? seating?) comfort-able 5 - 4 - 3 - 2 - 1 uncomfortable
6. Will patients likely be interested in the reading material in the waiting area? (current? variety?) likely 5 - 4 - 3 - 2 - 1 unlikely
etc...

A general method for evaluating the alignment between customer expectations and the service that is delivered is the SERVQUAL survey instrument.[31] (cited in Fitzsimmons2 chapter 10 pages 274). SERVQUAL contains forty four general questions about a service, half of which are about customer expectations, and half of which are about the specific company's performance. Differences between responses on the two survey halves identifies possible areas of service specification misalignment.

For example...   One illustration of the importance of early and frequent communication with customers occurred when my wife requested kitchen designs from cabinet retailers. One cabinet retailer put together a kitchen design based on detailed communication about her preferences and the company's style options. She considered the design to be high-quality, since it reflected both her interests and what the company was capable of installing. A different cabinet retailer put together a kitchen design based on what they could provide, but with little communication with my wife. My wife considered the result to be low-quality, since it did not meet *her* definition of a excellent kitchen design. As a result, this second company did not have a chance to make the sale, regardless of the "quality" of the cabinets themselves.

My airline application...   An airline might define quality in terms of on-time departures and arrivals, low amounts of misrouted baggage, or the food and beverages served on board the aircraft. These service features may fill customers' needs for meeting schedules, having their belongings, and not being hungry. The idea is that customers will be happier if they are on time for their meetings, have their belongings, and are not hungry. However, customers may have other needs that motivate expectations for reasonable service (by a Provident Provider Hypothesis). Customers have social interaction needs, and are happier if gate personnel treat them with respect (not as a nuisance). They have comfort needs, and are happier if they are not required to sit

[31] Parasuraman, A., Zeithaml, V. A., and Berry, L. L., "SERVQUAL: A Multiple-Item Scale for Measuring Consumer Perceptions of Service Quality," *Journal of Retailing*, Vol. 64, No. 1, Spring 1988, pages 12-40.

in a stuffy cabin prior to departure. They have planning needs, and are less upset if they know a flight is going to be delayed before spending a great deal of time waiting in a plane that is delayed. Should passengers expect gate personnel to treat them with respect, stuffy cabins to be aired out, and delays to be announced when the airline is aware of them? If initial expectations are superseded by experience to the contrary, customers conclude that the airline is not interested in satisfying customer needs.

Supplemental reading...   Fitzsimmons2 chapter 10 pages 270-273 on Defining Service Quality. Fitzsimmons2 chapter 6 pages 139-149 on Walk-Through Audits.

How manufacturing differs from services...

With manufacturing, product quality is more standardized, as specified by product engineers. Customers judge a product by its ability to fill needs, which customers attempt to determine *before* the product is purchased (through "search" properties—see SBP: *The Marketing of Properties*). If customer requirements are different from engineering specifications, the customer may motivate the product engineer to change the specifications, but otherwise individual customers have little impact on the product specifications.

Quantitative analysis... (covered at the discretion of the instructor)

Statistical Process Control (SPC)

   (Fitzsimmons2 chapter 10 pages 289-296 on Statistical Process Control)

SBP 11a: Swaying the Customer-Judge   Name (if turned in):_____

Analysis questions...   To help apply this Service Business Principle, consider and answer the following questions about your specific service business process. (❑Check here if you are going outside of your target service business.)

Service company/business:_____

The service process:_____
   ① What is "quality" in this industry? How do "high-quality" service providers differ from "low-quality" service providers?
   ② In what way is quality determined? Where and by whom is it specified?
   ③ Where do customers get their expectations for service?
   ④ In what ways do customers "value" the service? What needs does the service fulfill? How do those needs relate to customer happiness?

① _____

_____

_____

_____

_____

_____

_____

_____

_____

_____

_____

_____

_____

_____

_____

Unit 11

SBP 11a: Swaying the Customer-Judge   Name (if turned in):_____

Application exercise...   Also to help you apply this Service Business Principle, complete the following analysis with regard to your specific service business process, or another service process in your business. (☐Check here if you are going outside of your target service business, which was _____.)

Service company/business:_____

The service process:_____
    Create a walk-through audit for your service business process, considering a part of the process that has perhaps a half-dozen steps. For each step of that process, identify a question or two that measures service performance on a 5-point scale. List the meaning of each point on the scale, or the meaning of just the end points. Estimate the performance specification (the acceptable point on the scale) for each measure. If possible, visit the service facility and complete the audit. Make some observations about the appropriateness of service performance specifications and actual performance relative to probable customer requirements.

Preparation for the next Service Business Principle (11b)

To consider...   Before proceeding, consider the following and write thoughts and ideas below:

The last Service Business Principle discussed customer expectations, which are often based on their needs. In many cases, companyies can influence customer expectation prior to the time the customer provides his or her inputs to the service. If quality is defined as "meeting or exceeding customer expectations," then it is clear that companies should try to *lower* customers' expectations so that it will be easier to exceed them. Unfortunately, the advertising efforts often try to *raise* expectations in an attempt to make the service more attractive to new customers. Which is a better strategy: to lower customer's expectations or to raise them? For example, if the hostess at a restaurant knows that the wait to be seated for the next customer is somewhere between twenty and forty minutes, how long should she tell the customer the wait estimate is? (Assume the customer would not be satisfied with "somewhere between twenty and forty minutes") Would the best strategy depend on the circumstances? In what way?

_____

_____

_____

_____

_____

_____

_____

_____

Unit 11

Service Business Principle 11b:
UNCERTAIN EXPECTATIONS

Service Business Principle	*"With services, expectations are often subjectively acquired and subjectively defined. Therefore service providers need to be careful when attempting to define expectations for customers. Too low expectations can lead to lost sales. Too high expectations can lead to disappointment and lost future sales."*

Why it occurs... UNCERTAIN EXPECTATIONS occurs because expectations for services tend to be experiential or credence based (see SBP: *The Marketing of Properties*).

Closely related to... SBP: *Swaying the Customer Judge*

Details... If it were possible to precisely know customer expectations, the willing service provider could provide service that would meet those specifications. Even if the service provider is willing, this can be an extremely difficult objective. Two problems occur. First, usually even the customers do not precisely know what they expect! Expectations tend to occur in a range. A customer might know what is clearly unacceptable service (such as waiting an hour for an order at a restaurant) and what is clearly acceptable service (waiting five minutes for the order), but have a difficult time drawing a line between the two. In fact, such a line may vary according to the circumstances or the customer's mood or hunger level on a given day.

Even if the service provider could precisely know the customer's expectations, the variable nature of service delivery would make it nearly impossible to consistently hit the target. (The difficulty in providing consistent service will be expounded in later Service Business Principles.)

How it impacts decisions... Companies need to decide on how to depict the service to prospective customers. As stated above, it is nearly impossible to precisely know what the expectation target is in service situations, and even if it were, it is nearly impossible to consistently hit the target! Given this uncertainty, which is preferable: To attempt to raise customer expectations prior to purchase, or to attempt to lower customer expectations prior to purchase? (read on...)

What to do about it... Raising expectations increases the probability of purchase, but also increases the probability of disappointment. Lowering expectations decreases both. Perhaps a better strategy is the following: *With differentiating service features that are valued by customers, maintain expectations at a level which exceeds what customers would expect of your competitors.* This strategy comes from the idea that, ultimately, customers form their expectations about a service by the way it performs, not the way it is portrayed (experience properties versus search properties). So, the best of all worlds is to depict service performance which is *truly* superior at meeting customer needs (at an acceptable price)—customers will select the service provider and subsequently will have expectation met.

This Service Business Principle further emphasizes the need for close coordination between production and marketing in service businesses. The best marketing efforts are based on service delivery that is truly superior. "Hype," which depicts a service as being better than what is actually delivered, will have a short-lived effect. Such unsubstantiated hype only serves to build customer distrust for the service provider.

For example... Federal Express built its overnight delivery business on a slogan that was something like "When it absolutely, positively, has to be there overnight." They recognize that their delivery timing is not perfect, and that even if only 99.9 percent of the packages were delivered on time, there would still be thousands that were late. Federal Express has since discontinued that slogan, but their performance level is so much superior than most of their competitors, that customer still flock to Federal Express for overnight delivery—expectations for Federal Express are often superior to expectations for competitors.

The U.S. Postal Service does not attempt to compete with Federal Express on the reliability dimension. Instead they claim to deliver "Priority" letters usually within a couple of business days, but for a lot less money than the competitors. This is a wise strategy, since to raise customer expectations by guaranteeing two-day delivery, and then frequently not to achieve it, would result in thousands of angry customers.

My airline application... What do customers expect from airline food? Every customer has expectations for food quality in general, largely based on their tastes and prior experience. Nevertheless, for many passengers, the gap between food performance and expectations is large enough to clearly define quality. Some people may actually think that airline food exceeds their expectations! Airlines are wise to not build customers' expectations for food, which would lead many to be disappointed. (However, some airlines advertise the high quality of their first-class cabin meals—which is what one might expect for paying double the cost for a ticket.)

Supplemental reading... Fitzsimmons2 chapter 10 pages 271-273 on Gaps in Service Quality.

How manufacturing differs from services...

With manufacturing, expectations can be defined by objective product specifications.

Unit 11

SBP 11b: Uncertain Expectations   Name (if turned in):_____

Analysis questions...   To help apply this Service Business Principle, consider and answer the following questions about your specific service business process. (❑Check here if you are going outside of your target service business.)

Service company/business:_____

The service process:_____
    ① How do customers know what to expect from the service provider?
    ② How can the service provider influence customer expectations prior to purchase?
    ③ Once the customer has experienced the service, what is the ability of the service provider to influence customer expectations for subsequent service?

①_____

_____

_____

_____

_____

_____

_____

_____

_____

_____

_____

_____

_____

_____

_____

_____

_____

Unit 11

SBP 11b: Uncertain Expectations   Name (if turned in):_____

Application exercise...   Also to help you apply this Service Business Principle, complete the following analysis with regard to your specific service business process, or another service process in your business. (❑Check here if you are going outside of your target service business, which was _____.)

Service company/business:_____

The service process:_____
Identify a service winner from the application exercise of the *Identifying Key Production Elements* Service Business Principle. How might your service business provide superior performance on that dimension? In what ways would it be appropriate to influence customer expectations for that performance? Compose an advertising slogan that describes the level of performance that customers can expect for that service dimension. Comment on the impact of that slogan on the ability to satisfy customer expectations. Comment on the likelihood and potential impact of not meeting the expectation.

Preparation for the next Service Business Principle (11c)

To consider...   Before proceeding, consider the following and write thoughts and ideas below:

We purchase manufactured goods not only to fill our present needs, but also to fill our anticipated future needs. In fact, there are often significant cost advantages to purchasing goods well in advance of the time they are needed. Sometimes we purchase things on sale because we think we will eventually need them. Other times we realize savings by purchasing items in bulk. Economizing customers are happy to "inventory" such items until they are needed. How do these economizing customers deal with services? Do they purchase services in advance of the time they need them, or wait until the need is present? How can customers realize purchase economies of scale with services?

_____

_____

_____

_____

_____

_____

_____

_____

Unit 11

Service Business Principle 11c:

WHAT WE VALUE TODAY

Service Business Principle	*"With services, customers usually purchase based on present needs, unless given the opportunity to defer delivery."*

Why it occurs...   WHAT WE VALUE TODAY occurs because *customers* do not inventory services (although they may inventory the result of the service). For repeat purchase services, customers usually present their inputs each time they need the service.

Details...   Recall from the *Swaying the Customer-Judge* Service Business Principle that need-filling and sacrifice define value, which forms the basis for customer purchases. Customers would prefer to have their needs filled with lower sacrifice, such as by quantity discounts. However, many services can only fill the need that occurs at the time of service delivery. This makes it difficult or impossible to take delivery of the service for future needs. Service providers who desire to attract customers based on their anticipated future needs should provide the opportunity for customers to purchase the service now and take delivery later when the need is present. One way to do this is through a service contract.

For example...   Copy machines is a great business to be in. Manufacturing copy machines may or may not be highly profitably, but *fixing* copy machines has got to be extremely lucrative. This is because of the way people often treat copy machines, and how the machine complexity brings a high probability of breakdown. Companies who own copy machines can count on needing periodic repairs in the future. How can copy machine repair companies get their customers to purchase repair service in advance. The common way they do this is by establishing service contracts. A service contract may cover all copier repairs over a certain number of months or for a certain number of copies. The companies can potentially save money when disaster strikes, and the copier repair companies can enjoy a lasting relationship of customer service.

My airline application...   Airlines realize that passengers typically do not take a flight until they have the need to fly. This allows them to offer price promotions during the slow times of year without significantly cannibalizing the sales during the busy times of the year. (Although some passengers who are flexible when they travel might shift the day of their flight somewhat to take advantage of a promotion.)

Some airlines sell coupon books for first-class upgrades. These upgrades are intended to be used over time, and are effectively an opportunity to defer delivery of the first-class flight.

How manufacturing differs from services...

With manufacturing, customers purchase and store the goods so they can be used to meet both present and future needs.

SBP 11c: What We Value Today   Name (if turned in):_____

Analysis questions... To help apply this Service Business Principle, consider and answer the following questions about your specific service business process. (❑Check here if you are going outside of your target service business.)

Service company/business:_____

The service process:_____
① How does the customer know when he or she needs the service?
② How difficult is it for the customer to anticipate future needs for the service?
② Is there any advantage to having customers purchase the service for future needs?
③ What sacrifice does the customer make to have his or her needs filled?

①_____

_____

_____

_____

_____

_____

_____

_____

_____

_____

_____

_____

_____

_____

_____

Unit 11

SBP 11c: What We Value Today   Name (if turned in):_____

Application exercise...   Also to help you apply this Service Business Principle, complete the following analysis with regard to your specific service business process, or another service process in your business. (❏Check here if you are going outside of your target service business, which was _____.)

Service company/business:_____

The service process:_____
    Design a mechanism for allowing customers to purchase a service in anticipation of future needs. How would it be executed (such as with a service contract or a coupon book)? Would such an arrangement bring advantages to the service provider? What advantages would there be to the customer?

Part IV - Service Quality and Value
Unit 12:
CHALLENGES IN DELIVERING SERVICE QUALITY

Preparation for the next Service Business Principle (12a)

To consider...   Before proceeding, consider the following and write thoughts and ideas below:

Manufacturers may desire to hear customer suggestions for quality improvement. One thing that limits the extent of customer suggestions is that customers do not know enough about product development to give very sophisticated suggestions. As a result, customer suggestions tend to be quite superficial, without regard for how the improvements would actually be implemented. For example, an auto owner might complain about how difficult it is to install a child safety seat when there are automatic seatbelts, but an improvement might be technically impossible. Rare is the customer that would have suggestions for improving the manufacturing process itself.

Why is it that service businesses inspire so many critics? Service customers tend to be quite free with their suggestions, either given to the service provider, or more often spoken to friends and co-workers. What is it about services that inspires so many people to offer ideas for quality improvement?

_____

_____

_____

_____

_____

_____

_____

_____

Unit 12

Service Business Principle 12a:

EVERYONE THINKS THEY'RE AN EXPERT

Service Business Principle	*"With services, the customer often provides product specifications (what to make) and process design (how to make it), often without the invitation of the service provider."*

Why it occurs... EVERYONE THINKS THEY'RE AN EXPERT occurs because the necessity for customer-inputs in service processes means that most customers have extensive experience with the service process. This experience breeds process knowledge and ideas for improvement.

Closely related to... SBP: *Swaying the Customer-Judge*
SBP: *Who is in Control*

Details... The words of Richard Chase capture this Service Business Principle well[32]: "Everyone is an expert on services. We all think we know what we want from a service organization and, by the very process of living, we have a good deal of experience with the service creation process."

This Service Business Principle can both be a blessing and a curse to the service provider. On one hand, it can be a great thing to have customers participate in the quality improvement efforts by offering improvement suggestions. (Unless, of course, the company is not willing to act on the suggestions.)

On the other hand, even though customers *think* they are experts, they may not understand the complexities of implementing a given quality improvement suggestion. The suggestion may not affect a sufficient number of customers to warrant the high cost. This brings to mind the Service Encounter Triad discussion from the *Who is in Control* Service Business Principle: If the customer thinks he or she should be in control, but the service organization or the service employee insists on being in control, conflict will occur.

However, an extremely common problem in service businesses is to underrate the potential benefit of customer suggestions. In fact, in many cases customers *do* know the best way to do things, and ways to improve quality at low cost. Service providers need to be very careful about the often-fatal "Not Invented Here" syndrome, which is that "if the company is not already doing it, it must not be a good idea." Wise service providers will not let the valuable customer-feedback resource go to waste.

How it impacts decisions... Service providers need to decide how to handle quality improvement suggestions from customers.

What to do about it... Every suggestion from a customer, either solicited or unsolicited, should be acknowledged to the customer. If it is sincere, the service provider should tell the customer that suggestions are appreciated. This does not mean that every suggestion should be implemented, but that there is great potential from listening to customer suggestions.

---

[32] Chase, Richard B., and Aquilano, Nicholas J., *Production and Operations Management: Manufacturing and Services*, Seventh Edition, 1995, Irwin: Chicago, page 104.

My airline application... It is likely that most airline passengers think they know some way the air travel process could be improved. With such a huge suggestion resource, why is it that there are not more perfect airlines? The answer may lie somewhat in the ability of the airline to maintain control of the process. There is not much in the process of air travel that is not subject to various forms of regulation or risk control. As a result, airlines tend to operate "by the book," with a policy for just about everything. Such inflexibility is not conducive to quality improvement suggestions. Many improvement suggestions may be beyond the limits of regulation, or may not be cost effective. Yet others may be perfectly doable.

Supplemental reading... article: "An Empirically Derived Framework for Designing Customer Feedback Systems," found in Appendix D.

How manufacturing differs from services...

With manufacturing, customers usually have no experience in the product design or product manufacturing processes. Most customers have very little idea of how a given product is made, and as a result have little knowledge that would lead to improvement suggestions. (Consider a manufactured item as simple as a pencil. Most customers do not have a clue how a pencil is made, much less how a microchip is manufactured.)

Unit 12

SBP 12a: Everyone Thinks They're an Expert   Name (if turned in):_____

Analysis questions...
To help apply this Service Business Principle, consider and answer the following questions about your specific service business process. (❏Check here if you are going outside of your target service business.)

Service company/business:_____

The service process:_____
    ① In what ways can customers tell the service provider what to provide?
    ② In what ways can customers tell the service provider how to provide it?
    ③ Where do customers get this knowledge?
    ④ How should the company respond to this customer expertise?

① _____

_____

_____

_____

_____

_____

_____

_____

_____

_____

_____

_____

_____

_____

_____

_____

_____

Unit 12

SBP 12a: Everyone Thinks They're an Expert   Name (if turned in):_____

Application exercise...   Also to help you apply this Service Business Principle, complete the following analysis with regard to your specific service business process, or another service process in your business. (❏Check here if you are going outside of your target service business, which was _____.)

Service company/business:_____

The service process:_____
   Design a customer-suggestion system. What is an appropriate procedure for handling unsolicited suggestions for quality improvement? Should suggestions be solicited? In what manner? (such as on customer comment cards?) What is an effective procedure for handling solicited suggestions? (draw a flowchart) What types of "customer-expertise" would be particularly helpful in a company's quality improvement efforts?

Preparation for the next Service Business Principle (12b)

To consider...   Before proceeding, consider the following and write thoughts and ideas below:

There is an old saying, "garbage in-garbage out," which means you cannot make good outputs from bad inputs. For manufacturers, this means that you cannot make high-quality products from low-quality raw materials and component parts. The implication is that quality-conscious manufacturers need to assure that their suppliers are supplying quality inputs to the production process. If a particular supplier is unable or unwilling to provide inputs of acceptable quality, the manufacturer should turn to other suppliers so that the unreliable supplier can be dropped. The situation with service suppliers is not quite as easily managed. Many suppliers to a service provider provide inputs of unreliable quality, yet the service provider finds it extremely difficult to eliminate them as suppliers. How can this be?

_____

_____

_____

_____

_____

_____

_____

_____

_____

Unit 12

Service Business Principle 12b:
THE UNRELIABLE SUPPLIER DILEMMA

Service Business Principle	*"With services, the customer-suppliers often provide unreliable inputs."*

Why it occurs... THE UNRELIABLE SUPPLIER DILEMMA occurs because customers provide themselves, their belongings, and/or their information as process inputs. This simultaneous relationship as supplier and customer makes it difficult for the service provider to control the supplied inputs.

Details... Why is it so difficult to eliminate unreliable suppliers to service businesses? The answer is because most of the suppliers are also customers! That is the dilemma!

The implications of the *Unreliable Supplier Dilemma* on quality management are far reaching. The following are some examples:

Implications for process efficiency

To some degree, every service process has to be efficient to maintain acceptable cost levels. Consistency breeds efficiency. Divergence breeds inefficiency. Unexpected divergence breeds inefficiency in a big way. A given service process may be robust, in that it works well given a wide range of customer inputs. However, if a customer input is presented which is clearly out of the acceptable range, the process can become somewhat arbitrary. For example, a dentist office needs a certain degree of efficiency in order to keep the patient flow moving. Dental service can usually handle a wide variety of patients and patient needs. It just takes one screaming four-year-old to throw the process out of kilter. What is the standard operating procedure for a child who attempts to bite the hygenist? or insists on playing with the dental instruments? or runs away and hides somewhere in the dental office?

Implications for job design

Imagine that you worked for a manufacturer and that your job was to bolt a display assembly into a housing. Imagine that the supplier of the bolts and nuts was unreliable—sometimes the bolts were too large for the nuts, and sometimes they were too small. Therefore, you found that you spent much of your working day trying to match up bolts with corresponding-sized nuts. Then, imagine that you were paid by your "productivity," which was measured by the number of pieces you assembled in a day. What would be your reaction? Frustration!

In a similar manner, service employees who deal with unreliable customer inputs can be frustrated. Think of the employees that work at a computer company's installation help hotline. Many customers who call in may have actually followed the installation instructions, but many others are unwilling to do so when a person at the help hotline number will walk them through the process. This may be fine if no one cares whether the installation help hot-line employees are productive or not, but can be extremely frustrating if the employees are under call quotas.

Implications for customer satisfaction

Customers who supply low-quality inputs into the production process should not be surprised to find low-quality outputs. Yet sometimes they are. It is surprising to find that a car that has been long denied preventative maintenance such as oil changes is in need of major repairs at the auto shop. It is surprising to learn that the stain in the clothing that was run through the drier cannot be removed by the dry cleaner. (Never dry a stained cloth in the drier, unless you want the stain to be permanent!) Students who cram for exams and assignments are often surprised to see how hard it is to use their education to get ahead in their careers. (Not you, of course, but other students.) Customer-satisfaction problems arise when the customers expects a degree of input-transformation that the service provider is unable or unwilling to provide.

How it impacts decisions... Service providers need to decide how to deal with unreliable suppliers and how to reduce the occurrence of unreliability.

What to do about it... One way to reduce the incidence of customer-inputs of inadequate quality is to train the customers. Ski resorts put signs at the top of the ski lift that says "Keep your ski tips up as you disembark." Failure to keep ski tips up results in a face full of snow and the need to stop the lift to remove the skier from the side of the hill. Retailers train customers in their return/exchange process by saying "Help keep costs down, save your receipt." The process of handling returns is likely to be more difficult without the receipt. Trash collectors have an effective way of training customer about when and where to place their trash receptacles for pick-up: They simply bypass customers when they do not comply, and find that customers tend to learn the appropriate procedures quickly!

Another way to reduce the incidence of problematic customer-inputs is to implement *poka yoke* methods, which are foolproofing devices. Poka yokes have been used in manufacturing settings for years to prevent the occurrence of certain types of quality defects. For example, the story goes that a Japanese auto assembler was responsible for attaching the fender of the car. If the fender was not attached just right, a quality problem would occur when the door was later attached. (The gap between the door and the fender needed to be just right.) So, this enterprising employee found a broom stick and cut it off to exactly the size of the door. That way, when he attached a fender he could insert the broom stick in the space and determine if the fender was acceptably attached. That broomstick was a poka yoke, or foolproofing device.

Service poka yokes may include checking systems as with the broomstick example, or might include a checklist or other type of reminder. Some service poka yoke examples are listed below.

Nevertheless, every service process that is standard operating procedure needs to have a corresponding "exception handling procedure." This is a procedure for dealing with unreliable customer inputs so as not to disrupt the standard operating procedure. If the exception handling procedure is created "on the fly," without prior forethought, it is likely going to be inadequate and will leave the service employees and the customers upset.

For example... The following are some service poka yoke examples:
- Mail-order companies often take credit card numbers for purchases. A customer-input problem occurs when a customer uses an expired credit card. To prevent telephone personnel from taking any orders with expired credit cards, there can be a poka yoke in the computer system: The order screen will not let the order be processed unless a

Unit 12

valid expiration date is entered. This prevents the employee from accidentally overlooking the expiration date.

- A primary input to the amusement park process is the customer's self. Some rides are not safe for people with health problems or who are shorter than a certain height. The park includes signs at the entrance to all such rides listing types of customers who should not ride, and height markers that say "You must be this tall to ride this ride."
- Banks accept customer-money and check inputs into the deposit process. If customers forget to endorse their checks or complete their deposit slip at an automatic teller machine (ATM), the process of posting the deposit is much more difficult (and may include having to have the customer come all the way down to the bank to rectify the problem). As a result, banks put a reminder checklist on the ATM deposit envelopes.
- Doctors offices expect new patients to supply accurate insurance information. When new patients show up unprepared with this information, it wreaks havoc on the billing process. Therefore, some medical offices (such as my eye doctor), send out insurance and medical history information sheets to be completed and brought on the first visit.

You will see that not only do these types of poka yokes drastically reduce the chance of customer input problems, they also assist in training customers in their part of the production process.

My airline application... One customer input into the airline process is carry-on baggage. Space restrictions and airline regulations limit the size and amount of baggage carried on by each passenger. Airlines recognize that this is a potential source of unreliable and unacceptable customer inputs. Therefore, many airlines attempt to train the customers in acceptable sizes of their baggage inputs. They do this by placing "size wise" or other named displays in the terminal which show exactly the maximum size of carry-on baggage. In fact, the signs invite passengers to insert their bags into the display to see if they comply, which I have *never* seen anyone else do. Why not? Because, frankly, passenger do not want to learn that they are in violation! Yet the displays are still serving a useful purpose by warning passengers how big their carry-ons need to be on their next trip. The displays serve to train the customer.

What about the passenger who shows up with some oversized baggage that he claims is priceless art that cannot be checked? That situation is not quite so simple. Perhaps airlines have a "priceless art that is oversized" policy, but perhaps they do not. This might be a situation for an exception handling procedure—to get the customer out of the regular line so as to not hold up other passengers, and have a manager deal with the problem situation. (The same approach could also be used for passengers who show up with their pet pigs or iguanas.)

Another input to the airline process are the passengers themselves. Sometimes, they arrive unreliably, being late for whatever reason. Airline gate employees are put in a precarious situation when the ramp door is closed and a passenger shows up with still five minutes until departure. To the passenger, five minutes is plenty of time to get on the plane, but the airline may require a larger margin of time. An approach some airlines take is to require passengers to be at the gate twenty minutes prior to departure. That way, even if they are ten minutes late, it is no problem.

Southwest Airlines addresses the concern about passengers checking-in on time by issuing every passenger a colored plastic card at the time of check-in. The card is presented to the agent upon boarding. This assures that the passengers ticket has been checked, and speeds up the boarding process. That plastic card method is an excellent example of a poka yoke.

Supplemental reading... Fitzsimmons2 chapter 9 page 245 on Unrealistic Customer Expectations.

How manufacturing differs from services...

With manufacturing, suppliers work for the manufacturer, and must provide inputs that meet manufacturers' specifications, or be eliminated as suppliers.

Unit 12

SBP 12b: The Unreliable Supplier Dilemma   Name (if turned in):_____

Analysis questions...   To help apply this Service Business Principle, consider and answer the following questions about your specific service business process. (❑Check here if you are going outside of your target service business.)

Service company/business:_____

The service process:_____
    ① In what ways might customers provide inadequate inputs?
    ② What happens when customers provide inadequate inputs?
    ③ How might the company assure that customer-provided inputs are appropriate?

① _____

_____

_____

_____

_____

_____

_____

_____

_____

_____

_____

_____

_____

_____

_____

_____

_____

Unit 12

SBP 12b: The Unreliable Supplier Dilemma   Name (if turned in):_____

Application exercise... Also to help you apply this Service Business Principle, complete the following analysis with regard to your specific service business process, or another service process in your business. (☐Check here if you are going outside of your target service business, which was _____.)

Service company/business:_____

The service process:_____
   Redraw your service process to anticipate potential problems with customer inputs. Identify likely sources of problems with customer inputs with a circled "F," for fail-point. Design a poka yoke to help reduce the probability of problems. At what degree would problems with customer inputs be severe enough to warrant an exception handling procedure. Design a simple exception handling procedure, including identifying who is responsible for handling such problems.

Preparation for the next Service Business Principle (12c)

To consider... Before proceeding, consider the following and write thoughts and ideas below:

Total quality management (TQM) is an approach to quality that spans the organization and the entire production process (as compared with the traditional approach where quality was relegated to a quality assurance department who, among other things, inspected the final product). In order to implement a TQM system, every employee needs to be involved in the process and product improvement efforts. Labor needs to be adaptable in the way things are done, and willing to adopt process improvements which are set forth.

Imagine a portion of labor that sometimes refuses to accept process improvement plans. Imagine that the company has acquired new technology that will make the production process more productive and will assure higher quality—but some of the labor force refuses to use it. The reason given? "Because we are use to doing it the old way." What would your reaction be? What if you could not fire that rebellious labor?

_____

_____

_____

_____

_____

_____

_____

_____

Unit 12

Service Business Principle 12c:

CAPRICIOUS LABOR

Service Business Principle	*"With services, customer-labor may ignore, avoid, or reject technologies or process improvements which are intended to increase quality and productivity. As a result, customer buy-in to process changes must be carefully addressed."*

Why it occurs... CAPRICIOUS LABOR occurs because with many services, customers provide themselves as labor inputs into the production process.

Closely related to... SBP: *Technological Depersonalization*

Details... In the prior Service Business Principle (*The Unreliable Supplier Dilemma*) we discussed training customers to provide better-quality customer inputs. In this Service Business Principle, we focus specifically on customer-labor inputs—those portions of the service process which are executed by the customer.

One would think that customers would be happy to adopt technologies and process improvements that improve quality and productivity. Far-sighted customers should realize that ultimately, the improvements are in their best interest. Of course, this is a dramatic oversimplification of a very complex problem, for customers (and employees) usually find that change is difficult. Customers will be particularly resistant to technologies which depersonalize the service (see SBP: *Technological Depersonalization*). Further, it *may not be obvious* how the change will benefit customers—who might assume that the changes are simply for the convenience of the service provider. The bottom line is that there are many factors which influence customer adoption of improvements and technologies. Whether a particular improvement will be adopted is often anybody's guess, which is why customer-labor is described as capricious.

Here is one example (other examples will be given below): In 1980, two major process improvements were introduced in the banking industry: home banking and Automatic Teller Machines (ATMs). (They were actually introduced prior to that time, but widespread introduction occurred around 1980.) The purpose of each was to improve the quality and productivity of banking transactions and information exchange. Regardless of the virtues of the technologies, it was still very uncertain whether either would gain widespread acceptance by customers. As discussed in the *Technological Depersonalization* Service Business Principle, it turned out that ATMs were adopted and home banking was rejected by the marketplace. With 20/20 hindsight it is easy to see why that occurred, but at the time of introduction, it was hard to predict.

Even today, banks are attempting to promote home banking and other forms of electronic banking to realize process cost savings—but it has not been as well-received as bankers would have liked. As stated by Jim Jordan in a recent newspaper article[33]: "Checks are expensive to print, to write, to mail and to process, bankers say over and over, but customers aren't listening." In his article he quotes banking professor Donald J. Mullineaux who said "People are very comfortable with using checks, and to switch to some other form of banking makes them uncomfortable." Even though most customers could understand how electronic banking improves the overall transaction process, they will need a little more convincing that it is worth changing what they do. Customer-labor can be quite capricious.

---

[33] Jordan, Jim, "Paper checks are giving electronic bankers a run for customers' money," Knight-Ridder Newspapers, printed in the Provo, Utah Daily Herald, 11/18/97, page B5.

How it impacts decisions... Service providers need to evaluate process improvements not only by the potential contribution to quality and productivity, but on the potential for buy-in from the customer. Companies need to decide on ways to improve the likelihood of customer buy-in.

What to do about it... An important aspect of total quality management (TQM) is employee involvement. With service businesses, this should be expanded to "*customer involvement*." Customers should be involved in the exploration of new technologies, such as in focus groups. Early-adopting customers might be involved in promoting the change to other customers. (Such as through advertising campaigns with actual customers describing the virtues of the process advancements.) And generally, customers should be involved in reaping the benefits of the process changes. Passing some of the cost savings on to customers can go a long way towards increasing customer buy-in.

Further, service providers can take action to smooth the transition to the new processes. One way is to have improvement technologies somewhat mimic the old way of doing things. The familiarity will help customers be more comfortable with the technologies. Another way is to provide parallel operating systems—allowing customers the option of choosing the method they are most comfortable with at the time. For example, CompUSA computer stores have implemented technologies to improve the process for purchasing computer equipment. Customers could use the "old-fashioned" method of walking into the CompUSA computer store. Or, they can use a telephone ordering system. Or, they can use the CompUSA on-line ordering system located on the World Wide Web. Each customer can use what they are most comfortable with at the time. The on-line ordering system is much more cost-effective (and automated) than the other two methods, and allows CompUSA to compete in the price-sensitive market segment that requires low personal interaction.

(See also Lovelock's banking example described in SBP: *Technological Depersonalization.*)

Unit 12

For example... Previously we discussed a "club card" that was offered by a number of grocery store chains. The customer had the card scanned each time he or she went through the checkout line, which provided the store with valuable purchase pattern data and provided the customer with special "club" discounts. For some reason, there does not appear to be as many grocery stores using those club cards as there used to be. It seemed like a great idea, but some customers "reject" this improvement by failing to bring their card each time they visit the store. (The cards that are part of a key-chain seem to be more popular.)

Also, in grocery retail, there seemed to have been a time when grocers encouraged customers to bag their own groceries to help save costs. There even were some grocers who would pay customers to bring bags from home (some may still do this). Again, it seems like this cost-saving innovation does not occur as much any more, and maybe grocers discovered that bagging is better left to the professionals.

Ever since the deregulation of long-distance telephone in about 1981, scores of companies have emerged to compete for customers' attention. In order to realize cost savings, some companies require the customer to enter a long-distance access code prior to dialing the number. Yet many customers forego the savings because they are unwilling to dial extra numbers, or are just forgetful.

Often, health care services require the customer to follow specific procedures in order to improve the quality of health. For example, dentists request that patients floss their teeth regularly, and physicians request that patients take their prescribed medications until they are gone. What percent of dental patients actually floss as instructed? It is likely that many patients neglect this activity, despite the reported benefits for dental hygiene. (Teeth flossing might not be considered an "innovation" since it has been around—and neglected—for decades.)

The U.S. Postal Service introduced a method for purchasing postage stamps through the local mail carrier by accompanying a form with payment in the mail box. Some customers take advantage of this cost-saving innovation, but it has certainly not eliminated the lines of people waiting to buy stamps at the post office. Some customers may not be aware of the service, and others are probably just in the habit of going to the post office for stamps.

My airline application... Airline ticket kiosks are a great example of a productivity enhancing innovation that does not appear to have caught on with customers. The kiosks allow customers to purchase tickets without the need to talk to an agent, thus reducing labor requirements. Perhaps the kiosks will be popular with customers at some point in the future, but currently customers who desire to use them need not worry about waiting in line.

Supplemental reading... Fitzsimmons2 chapter 9 page 248 on The Customer as Coproducer.

How manufacturing differs from services...

With manufacturing, all labor is employed by the organization in most cases (or hired through staffing agencies). Notwithstanding union restrictions, labor is generally required to conform to improvement initiatives.

SBP 12c: Capricious Labor   Name (if turned in):_____

Analysis questions...   To help apply this Service Business Principle, consider and answer the following questions about your specific service business process. (❏Check here if you are going outside of your target service business.)

Service company/business:_____

The service process:_____
    ① What technologies might customers use to improve quality and productivity?
    ② What are the customers' incentives for adopting such process technologies and improvements?
    ③ How might the company further motivate customers to adopt such process technologies and improvements?

①_____

_____

_____

_____

_____

_____

_____

_____

_____

_____

_____

_____

_____

_____

_____

_____

Unit 12

SBP 12c: Capricious Labor   Name (if turned in):_____

Application exercise...   Also to help you apply this Service Business Principle, complete the following analysis with regard to your specific service business process, or another service process in your business. (❏Check here if you are going outside of your target service business, which was _____.)

Service company/business:_____

The service process:_____

What is a part of your service business process that could be made more productive or producing higher quality by requiring the customer to do something different? If you decided to implement that change, how would you increase the likelihood that customers would accept it and do their part? Describe a plan for communicating the change to customers. In what ways could the new system be made similar to the old system, to increase customers' comfort with the new system. Would it be appropriate to allow customers the opportunity to choose between the old or the new system?

Part IV - Service Quality and Value
Unit 13:
SERVICE RECOVERY

Ambitious manufacturers strive for a quality goal known as "zero defects," which is an effort to eliminate *all* defects. Implied in the zero-defects philosophy is the idea that defects are avoidable, and that if the company removes the causes of defects, the defects will cease to occur. This may be true in manufacturing processes, but generally not true of service processes. Why not? Because of problems described in the Service Business Principles of the last few units. Customer content makes even the most well-thought-out and well-executed service process subject to occasional "defects." In this unit we will consider issues surrounding defect management.

Unit reading... The following reading pertains to Service Business Principles included in this unit. The instructor will let you know which of the readings you are responsible for studying.

Fitzsimmons2 chapter 10 on Service Quality.

Preparation for the next Service Business Principle (13a)

To consider... Before proceeding, consider the following and write thoughts and ideas below:

When a manufacturer identifies a product defect, often the product can be "reworked," meaning that the defect is corrected. Rework costs in terms of time and other resources. However, once a product is sufficiently reworked, it is as though the defect never occurred. Customers are not aware of how many times a product had to be reworked prior to the time it was sold. (The only rework customers are concerned about are those that take place *after* the customer has purchased the product.) Rework is not such a simple matter in service processes—even after a defect is repaired, the repaired production continues to suffer the consequences of the defect. How might this be so?

_____

_____

_____

_____

_____

_____

_____

_____

Unit 13

Service Business Principle 13a:

THE UNFORGIVING PRODUCT SYNDROME

Service Business Principle	*"With services, the customer-product is averse to rework, and remembers any experience with inspection and rework."*

Why it occurs... THE UNFORGIVING PRODUCT SYNDROME occurs because customers are involved in production, by virtue of supplying inputs to the process. In most cases, customers are aware of the need for rework, and remember the defect even after it is repaired.

Details... Service Business Principles in this unit deal with "service recovery," which is the service equivalent of product rework. Before expounding on techniques for service recovery, it is important to understand the costs involved in assuring service quality.

There are three general categories of costs in quality assurance: prevention, inspection, and rework. Prevention costs are costs associated with implementing systems to avoid quality problems. Inspection costs encompass measurement or evaluation of what is produced, so that defects might be identified. Rework (or recovery) is the costs of repairing the service or product that is found to have a defect. Service providers may focus on any of the three in quality improvement efforts, but should consider the following:

- It is virtually impossible to inspect quality into a service. Customers resist being inspected (as covered later in SBP: *Resistance to Measurement*). A great portion of customers with defects will choose to "walk" rather than bring the problem to the service provider's attention.[34] The standardized production of manufacturing allows the inspector to "sample," which is to only inspect a small portion of each production run—but the nonstandard production of services makes sampling much less effective. Further, if a defect is found through inspection, it is often impossible to repair the problem without affecting the customer.
- Service recovery can be very costly, for reasons discussed later. (in SBP: *Rework Plus*)
- It is impossible to prevent all defects in service processes, but can be much more cost-effective to prevent defects than to recover from defects.

The reason defect prevention strategies are so appealing in service businesses is because they are often the only strategies that shield defects from customers. Defects that occur and are repaired have a lingering effect, due to the memory of the customer.

How it impacts decisions... Service providers must decide how to allocate resources among defect prevention, inspection, and recovery.

What to do about it... A key effort in making the shift from a recovery strategy to a prevention strategy is to have systems for assuring the problems that occur (and are recovered) are not repeated. This means that all quality problems which are discovered are documented

---

[34] A TARP study reports that only about *four percent* of customers with complaints actually report the complaints to the company. See: TARP. (1986). "Consumer complaint handling in America: An updated study." , The Office of the Special Advisor to the President for Consumer Affairs, Technical Assistance Research Programs, Washington, D.C.
TARP. (1979). "Consumer complaint handling in America: Final report." , U.S. Office of Consumer Affairs, Technical Assistance Research Programs, Washington, D.C.

and assigned to an employee who is responsible for the process and for assuring appropriate improvements are made. The assigned employee needs to be held accountable for any selected improvements, and that the improvements accomplish the prevention objective.

For example... A family member of mine had a dentist remove her wisdom teeth. At least that was what was supposed to have happened. Instead, the dentist removed one of her molars. A dental retainer was subsequently employed to rectify the resulting problem. Yet even with the teeth repaired, you can bet we would think twice before seeing that dentist again.

My wife and I went to a business dinner at a Florida location of an Italian restaurant chain that we previously thought well of. When the waitress brought the food, she informed my wife that they were out of what she had ordered, and asked if she would like to select something else. (But everyone else at the table already had their food.) Further, my pasta had a piece of cardboard in it, which they were happy to fix. Even though we ultimately were given food without cardboard, the memory of the experience influenced our ceasing to patronize that restaurant chain.

I once took my Honda Accord to the Charlottesville, Virginia Honda dealer to have a missing carburetor inlet tube replaced. The missing part cost about $24. In the course of the service department's pitch, I wound up agreeing to about $800 of additional preventative maintenance (including new tires). When I picked up the car a few days later I learned that they had charged for every minor detail, including $40 for tire installation, which would have been free had I bought the tires where they got them—from the Goodyear dealer next door. As I left, poorer but wiser, I stopped to check the carburetor inlet tube. It was not there! The service (and I use that term loosely) manager apologized and agreed to install it for free once it came it. (It took about 15 seconds to install.) They fixed the problem, but my dissatisfaction kept me from ever returning.

On another occasion, I took my Honda to a repair shop for some simple repairs. I told the employee to call me for approval if it was going to be more than $100. (And I wrote that on the service order above my signature.) When I came to pick up the finished vehicle, I learned that it was to cost somewhat more than $100. I reminded the employee about my request to be called. He said he was sure I would approve, so he went ahead and completed the repairs. (I had been near a phone, so would have received any call he had made.) I did not consider that adequate justification for ignoring my request. So he cut down his labor charges so that the total was just under $100. I paid but never returned (partially because the shop changed ownership not long after that).

My airline application... Airlines are usually eager to recover when they misroute a passenger's baggage. They have a van that will deliver the baggage as soon as it is sent to the correct destination. In some cases, the passenger is happy with the recovery. But, if the passenger is on a short business trip, and does not get the bags until halfway through the trip, he is likely to be put out. He may trust the airline a little less, and insist on more carry-on baggage on future trips.

Supplemental reading... Fitzsimmons2 chapter 10 pages 303-304 on Service Recovery.

How manufacturing differs from services...

With manufacturing, the production process has the luxury of being separated from the customer in both space and time. As a result, defects can be hidden from customers by repairing them prior to shipment.

Unit 13

SBP 13a: The Unforgiving Product Syndrome   Name (if turned in):_____

Analysis questions...   To help apply this Service Business Principle, consider and answer the following questions about your specific service business process. (❑Check here if you are going outside of your target service business.)

Service company/business:_____

The service process:_____
    ① What is an example of a "defect" in the service process?
    ② At what points in the service process are defects typically detected?
    ③ What is involved in correcting a defect?
    ④ What impact does the remedy have on the customer?

①_____

_____

_____

_____

_____

_____

_____

_____

_____

_____

_____

_____

_____

_____

_____

_____

Unit 13

Application exercise...   Also to help you apply this Service Business Principle, complete the following analysis with regard to your specific service business process, or another service process in your business. (☐Check here if you are going outside of your target service business, which was _____.)

Service company/business:_____

The service process:_____

Design a plan for assuring that quality problems which are discovered (a) are adequately remedied with the customer, and (b) are appropriately avoided in the future. Who in the service organization will administer the defect prevention efforts, assigning problems to appropriate service employees? How will the problem reports be tracked? In what time frame and manner will they be followed up on? How will it be determined if the defect prevention efforts are effective?

Preparation for the next Service Business Principle (13b)

To consider... Before proceeding, consider the following and write thoughts and ideas below:

When a manufactured product needs to be reworked due to a defect, the rework process is often much less efficient and more costly than the process step that produced the defect. Further, the longer it takes to identify a defect for rework, the more costly it becomes. (For example, it is more costly to disassemble a finished product to repair a defect than to repair the defect prior to final assembly.) Does service recovery also bring inefficiency costs? Does the timing of the recovery affect the cost required to fix the problem? What other major costs are involved in service recovery?

_____

_____

_____

_____

_____

_____

_____

_____

_____

Unit 13

Service Business Principle 13b:
REWORK PLUS

Service Business Principle	*"With services, "product rework" often involves more than just bringing the product into specifications. When the product is the customer, there is also a need to rework the customer's attitude, which is an uncertain specification."*

Why it occurs... REWORK PLUS occurs because the customer is involved in the production process, by virtue of supplying his self, belongings, or information as process inputs.

Closely related to...   SBP: *The Unforgiving Product Syndrome*
SBP: *Who is in Control* and discussion of when to "bail out"

Details... Service defects often damage the attitude of customers towards the service provider. The service defect itself can often be rectified by re-running the service process (such as by having the customer back again). Rectifying the customer's attitude and regaining good will is a much more complex issue. In some cases, the good will can be regained by refunding the customer's money or giving the customer free service. Sometimes, it does not even take that. For example, a major automotive service chain reported that as a policy, customers with problems were given a coupon book for discounts on future service. However, some customers who claimed they would never return were thrilled to receive the coupon book. So perhaps their claim of "permanent" attitude damage was easier overcome than one would think!

Nevertheless, in some cases even extravagant attempts to recover the customer's attitude will be ineffective. Companies who claim they will do "whatever it takes" to satisfy customers probably use that as more of a marketing slogan than an operational policy. Some customers may never give the company another chance.

How it impacts decisions...   Service providers need to decide on policy for service recovery. Will all customers with a particular type of problem be given the same service recovery, or will it depend on the extent of damage done to the customer's attitude?

What to do about it...   Estimating the extent of customer-attitude damage can be a difficult, divergent process. For this reason, it is sometimes good to rely on the judgment of more experienced employees, such as front-line managers. Since it can even be difficult for experienced employees to accurately assess the impact of a service failure on a customer's attitude, companies often employ customer compensation strategies that do not require that assessment.

The simplest service recovery strategy is to offer to not charge the customer if he or she is dissatisfied. This may takes the form of an "unconditional service guarantee" which states that the service will be free if the customer is dissatisfied for any reason. One risk is that customers with insignificant or pretended attitude damage will be overcompensated. Perhaps a greater risk is that customers who have significant attitude damage will consider free service as *inadequate* compensation, and will depart with the attitude damage intact.

This tradeoff of risks is similar to concepts of statistical quality control. In statistical quality control methodologies, we speak of "type 1" and "type 2" errors, which represent "producers' risk" and "consumers' risk." The producers' risk is that a product will be inspected as faulty and reworked, when in fact it had nothing wrong with it. The consumers' risk is that a product will be inspected as okay, and sold to the customer, when in fact it had a defect.

This risk tradeoff for products is summarized in the following table. The results of each inspection are either appropriate ☺ or inappropriate ☹, depending on congruence between the inspection and the actual product.

Product Inspection	When Product Was Actually Good	When Product Was Actually Bad
inspected as good no rework done	Result: ☺ since good product was shipped.	Result: ☹ since bad product got to customer (consumers' risk).
inspected as bad reworked	Result: ☹ since wasted rework efforts (producers' risk).	Result: ☺ since problem was fixed before product was shipped.

For example, the inspection process of computer disk drives does not identify every possible problem. If a customer gets a disk drive that passed inspection but was faulty, the customer is upset (consumers' risk). If the company scraps or repairs a drive that failed inspection but was actually okay, the company wasted money (producers' risk).

A parallel concept exists in service businesses. In this case, the customer is the inspector, and may or may not report the perceived service failure.

Service "Inspection"	When Service Actually Did Not Fail	When Service Actually Failed
no complaint reported no service recovery	Result: ☺ since a good service was delivered.	Result: ☹ since the customer left angry (consumers' risk).
complaint reported customer compensated	Result: ☹ since customer was undeserving of service failure compensation (producers' risk).	Result: ☺ since service failure was recovered to some degree.

There surely is some statistical method for calculating the proper balance between consumers' risk and producers' risk. However, I would say that service providers are better off favoring the avoidance of consumers' risk over producers' risk, for the following reasons:

- First, consumers' risk can be much more costly to the company than producers' risk! TARP[35] studies reported that the average customer who experiences a service failure tell nine or ten others about the failure. That word-of-mouth is extremely powerful marketing. Further, each customer potentially represents a *lifetime* of service purchases, making it difficult to judge the total impact of losing their business.
- Second, the likelihood of producers' risk is extremely low. TARP studies also revealed that only about 4 percent of customers with problems report those

---

[35] TARP. (1986). "Consumer complaint handling in America: An updated study." , The Office of the Special Advisor to the President for Consumer Affairs, Technical Assistance Research Programs, Washington, D.C.

TARP. (1979). "Consumer complaint handling in America: Final report." , U.S. Office of Consumer Affairs, Technical Assistance Research Programs, Washington, D.C.

problems as complaints. This implies that customers have a low propensity to complain, which would be especially true if there was no actual reason to complain.
- Third, we may not care whether or not a service failure *actually* occurred, but rather, if it was *perceived* by the customer to have occurred.

Thus, service providers should probably be more concerned about under-compensating complaining customers than over-compensating them.

Service providers that have concerns about producers' risk can simply track the customers who are given compensation for reported complaints. If a particular customer is repeatedly compensated for reported service failures, he or she might be politely encouraged to seek out the competitors for service.

Unconditional Service Guarantees

The above discussion implies that unconditional service guarantees can be inadequate for service recovery because simply redoing the service does not completely recover the problem. For example, a hair stylist may advertise "If within seven days you do not like your haircut for any reason, come back and we will cut and style it again without charge." (This recognizes that haircuts can look different after the customer has washed and styled it on his or her own.) The problem is that the customer still has to *come back*! It can be much less costly to grumble than to execute the service guarantee.

Nevertheless, one benefit of unconditional service guarantees is that the likelihood of hearing about complaints ("voiced" complaints) is higher than without a guarantee. Another benefit is that they reduce customers' perceived risk of trying a service provider they have not tried before.

If an unconditional service guarantee is used, Christopher Hart points out that to be effective it needs to be:
- unconditional, without exceptions,
- easy to understand and communicate,
- meaningful (valued by the customer),
- easy and painless to invoke, and,
- easy to collect.

For example...

Domino's Pizza box states "If you are not completely satisfied with your Domino's Pizza® product, or service, for any reason, we'll make it right or refund your money. Guaranteed." This is worded to limit the company's liability, since the company can select the least expensive of "make it right" or "refund your money." If a customer does not like the arrangement of pepperoni slices on the pizza, the company can rearrange them. If the effort to make it right is too costly, the company can refund the money. The problem is when a customer has twenty hungry visitors at her house, and the delivery person takes the order to a similar address in a neighboring town. "Refunding the money" does not seem adequate for attitude recovery. In such circumstances, the store manager must decide how important it is to regain that customer's good will.

Federal Express has had a delivery guarantee in which money is refunded for late deliveries. Some customers do not care if the delivery is late, so refunded money is over-compensation. Other customers might have important meetings waiting on the delivery, and the cost of a late delivery is many times the price paid to Federal Express. As a result, judging the extent of attitude damage control in service recovery is no simple matter.

My airline application... The practice of "overbooking" airline flights sometimes results in passengers not getting on their scheduled flight, even though they have a ticket. In such cases, airlines attempt to minimize the cost of attitude recovery. The following is a hypothetical procedure: First, they deny any airline employees who do not need to be on the flight (with the most expendable attitudes). Then, they ask for volunteers to take the next flight (with no attitude damage). Then, they offer coupons for free travel at a later time for waiting for the next flight (larger attitude damage). Then, if necessary, they might arbitrarily select passengers to go, such as those who have not yet boarded. (Probably, in most instances the free travel coupons gather sufficient volunteers with minimal attitude damage from being "bumped.")

Supplemental reading...   Fitzsimmons2 chapter 10 pages 300-301 on Unconditional Service Guarantee.

    article: "The Power of Unconditional Service Guarantees" by Hart, C. W. L., 1988, in Harvard Business Review, vol. 66, no. 4 (Jul/Aug 1988), pp. 54-62.

    article: "The Profitable Art of Service Recovery." by Hart, C. W. L., Heskett, J. L., and Sasser, W. E., Jr. 1990. Harvard Business Review, vol. 68, no. 4 (Jul/Aug 1990), pp. 148-156.

How manufacturing differs from services...

With manufacturing, the product can be reworked and the customer would never know that it previously failed to meet specifications.

Unit 13

SBP 13b: Rework Plus   Name (if turned in):_____

Analysis questions... To help apply this Service Business Principle, consider and answer the following questions about your specific service business process. (❏Check here if you are going outside of your target service business.)

Service company/business:_____

The service process:_____
 ① What are common ways the service product can fail to meet specifications?
 ② In the case of a failure, what does it take to meet the original specifications?
 ③ In the case of a failure, what might it take to rectify the customer's attitude? Does this depend on the customer?
 ④ If an unconditional service guarantee is appropriate, how might the guarantee be worded? How might it be executed by customers and employees?

① _____

_____

_____

_____

_____

_____

_____

_____

_____

_____

_____

_____

_____

_____

_____

_____

_____

Unit 13

SBP 13b: Rework Plus   Name (if turned in):_____

Application exercise...

Also to help you apply this Service Business Principle, complete the following analysis with regard to your specific service business process, or another service process in your business. (❑Check here if you are going outside of your target service business, which was _____.)

Service company/business:_____

The service process:_____

Create a flowchart of a service recovery procedure. The procedure should start with a step for "Customer reports a complaint about the service." Include decision steps in the flowchart which attempt to ascertain the extent of the service failure damage, and identify corresponding levels of compensation to the customer. Your procedure may include steps for determining when the front-line employee should handle the service recovery, and when the service recovery should be handed over to a manager. The procedure may also include a step or steps for identifying whether the service recovery was adequate.

Preparation for the next Service Business Principle (13c)

To consider... Before proceeding, consider the following and write thoughts and ideas below:

Manufacturing organizations have different inspection strategies. A common but foolhardy strategy is to only let the customer inspect the product after it is delivered. The cost of repairing defects after delivery can be huge. It is less costly to fix defects before the product is shipped, since the repairs can be done at the factory. It is even less costly to repair defects when they occur in the production process, but this requires much more frequent inspection throughout the process. Generally, though, the earlier the defects are identified, the less costly it is to fix them. (These concepts were discussed in the *Rework Plus* SBP.)

We previously learned that customer involvement makes inspection less effective for service organizations, since the customer is often likely to recognize the defect even if it is inspected and repaired. Customers, in fact, act somewhat as inspectors. Is it better to involve customers as inspectors early in the service process, or as late as possible? What would be advantages and disadvantages of each approach? How might customers be involved as inspectors earlier in the service process?

Unit 13

Service Business Principle 13c:
EARLY COMMUNICATION/EARLY RECOVERY

Service Business Principle	*"With services, communication with the customer throughout the service delivery process can decrease the magnitude and expense of service failures. Conversely, failure to communicate early in the service process can allow small customer concerns to grow into large problems."*

Why it occurs...   EARLY COMMUNICATION/EARLY RECOVERY occurs because quality is ultimately defined by customers, and the most valid service "inspection" requires communication with the customer. If service expectations between the customer and the service provider are not clear, it will be less effective to "inspect" the service production without consulting the customers.

Details...   Some service businesses are communicative in nature, thus requiring the customer and the employee to be in constant communication. An example is psychological counseling, where the service process is one of communication. In such cases it is quite likely that the service provider will be aware of a potential quality defect, such as not being able to meet the customer's needs.

In many other services, communication with the customer is only a small part of the service process. Hotel employees, for example, typically only interact with customers at the beginning and the end of a hotel stay. However, most hotel problems experienced by customers occur sometime between the beginning and the end of the stay. If an employee queries the customer at the end of the stay, "Was everything okay with your stay?" and there *was* a problem, it would be quite difficult and costly to fix it *at that late time.* Many customers who had a major problem will not report the problem at that point, but will just take a mental note not to stay in that hotel again, making service recovery impossible.

If, however, the hotel has a simple mechanism for customers to register complaints at the time they occur, the opportunity exists for recovery while the customer is still present. Recovery after the customer departs is not only difficult but less-effective. If complaints are resolved *in a timely manner,* 95 percent of the time the customer will return.[36]

This problem of late communication with customers is particularly costly in highly-customized services, such as consulting and custom home building. Customize-service providers can be tempted to collect customer specifications up front, ignore the customer for months while the service process progresses, and present the customer with the results when they are complete or nearly complete. But what do you think happens when the customer sees the results and exclaims, "That's not what I thought you were going to do!"? The cost of recovery is great, since it may require undoing or scrapping months of work in order to redo it right. Such costs could have been largely avoided if the custom-service provider would have communicated progress earlier in the process, allowing misdirection to be corrected before great effort was expended.

How it impacts decisions...   The service company must decide when and how to appropriately open communication with customers in the service process.

---

[36] TARP. (1986). "Consumer complaint handling in America: An updated study." , The Office of the Special Advisor to the President for Consumer Affairs, Technical Assistance Research Programs, Washington, D.C.
    TARP. (1979). "Consumer complaint handling in America: Final report." , U.S. Office of Consumer Affairs, Technical Assistance Research Programs, Washington, D.C.

What to do about it...

There are a number of ways that service companies can increase customer communication through the service process.

Service providers can *actively* solicit feedback by periodically asking customers what they think about how the service is progressing. In addition to spotting problems, this can help customers know that the company is sensitive to their needs and expectations. However, this approach can be time-consuming, particularly with customers who demand rework of nit-picky items (which usually does not happen).

Another approach is for service providers to offer a channel of communication that is open to customers throughout the service process. In this way, customers who have a problem can have someone in the company to tell, so that the problem might be rectified. Previously we talked about the hotel example. What some top-notch hotels do is have a "Assistant Manager" on duty 24 hours a day to handle customers' problems. These hotels will often place a sign in each room saying, "If you experience any problem with your hotel stay, call 5555 and report it to the Assistant Manager on duty."

For example...

Continuing that hotel example, one day I was staying in a nice hotel on the shore of Waikiki in Hawaii. While I was sitting at one of their outdoor restaurants with an important associate, I hung my sports jacket over a chair that happened to be the landing place for bird droppings. I noticed that the overhead beam served as a seagull perch. I was a bit upset, but it did not seem appropriate to complain then. However, I later spoke with an "Assistant Manager" that the hotel encourages guests to see when problems occur. This person had my jacket promptly dry-cleaned and delivered to my room. I left the hotel with a good feeling. However, if I had not communicated the problem until the end of my stay, the hotel would have been unable to easily fix the problem and I would have left with a bad feeling about my stay.

I once hired an engineer to do some design work for a home I planned to build. Our original agreement was that he would complete the work in three weeks. Every week or so I would call to get a progress report. The engineer reported having been working on the project, but having some difficulties. Two months later we determined that the engineer was not capable of completing the work, and he was relieved of his duties. The engineer wound up spending a lot of time on the project but only billing us for the small amount of work that was adequately completed. That great expense of time to both us and the engineer could have been avoided if we would have had better communication about the progress earlier in the process.

Unit 13

My airline application...

In October of 1997 I flew into the new Denver airport on my way to Dallas. I arrived at 8:00 a.m., and my connecting flight was scheduled to depart at 9:05 a.m., Delta flight 1066. I checked in at the gate, even though I probably did not have to. At the scheduled departure time an airline employee announced that the flight would be delayed about thirty minutes while a required sixth flight attendant was transported from the hotel. I impatiently waited with some other passengers. I had a bus to catch in Dallas to visit a factory, and was using up my buffer time. At 9:35, an airline employee announced that the flight attendant was in the airport, and that the plane would begin boarding shortly. The employee said, "I cannot apologize enough," but a couple of free tickets would have been good enough apology for me.

At 9:45 we were still waiting when an airline employee announced that our first drink on the plane would be complimentary. That was no consolation to me, since a cup of apple juice is always complimentary. At 9:50 it was announced that there should be no problems now, that we should be departing in about ten minutes, and that they were working on rebooking the connecting flights.

At 10:02 an airline employee announced an apology for miscommunication–that apparently the supervisor was arranging to pick up the flight attendant from the hotel, and that some "borrowed" flight attendant needed to return to her flight.

By now we were on the plane–an experience patterned after the prisoner torture chambers of World War II movies. They said they would try to make our wait as comfortable as possible, and put in a videotape of a "Home Improvement" TV episode. One passenger helped the mayhem by repeatedly clicking the call button.

At 10:17 they announced that the sixth flight attendant was on board, and they were just missing one passenger who may have left to place a phone call. At 10:20, they explained that a flight attendant did not show up for work, and apparently it was *the first time* it ever happened and they have no contingency plan. Unbelievable! Was that the first time a flight attendant did not show up *ever*, or the first time *on that flight*? At 10:28 we watched the flight safety video, and at 10:33 we departed.

The airline had made attempts to communicate with customers, but not early enough and not with accurate information. They surely knew there was a potential problem *before* 9:05, when the flight was originally scheduled to depart. It may have been prudent to inform customers then, allowing them time to make phone calls and connecting flight decisions. The delay was more costly to some passengers than others. (I wound up catching my bus in Dallas, but just barely.) The airlines might have made attempts to identify passengers with special problems resulting from the impending delay.

How manufacturing differs from services...

With manufacturing, the customer is not involved in the production process, therefore is not available to give feedback about how the product is developing. Even with custom manufacturing (see SBP: *The Custom-Manufacturing Oxymoron*) the customer seldom inspects the product until it is complete. The assumption is that the engineering specifications of the product completely capture the customer's expectations for the product.

SBP 13c: Early Communication/Early Recovery   Name (if turned in):_____

Analysis questions...   To help apply this Service Business Principle, consider and answer the following questions about your specific service business process. (❑Check here if you are going outside of your target service business.)

Service company/business:_____

The service process:_____
  ① At what point are customer preferences known?
  ② At what point is the service checked to see if it corresponds with customer preferences?
  ③ What might be an appropriate mechanism for facilitating communication about progress during the service process, and for correcting problems that surface?

①_____

_____

_____

_____

_____

_____

_____

_____

_____

_____

_____

_____

_____

_____

_____

_____

Unit 13

SBP 13c: Early Communication/Early Recovery   Name (if turned in):_____

Application exercise... Also to help you apply this Service Business Principle, complete the following analysis with regard to your specific service business process, or another service process in your business. (❑Check here if you are going outside of your target service business, which was _____.)

Service company/business:_____

The service process:_____
    List six to ten steps of the service *delivery* process, from the time the customer requests service until the service is completed. Identify and describe a problem that could occur *early* in the service delivery process that could go undetected by the customer until the end of service delivery. Describe the costs of service recovery if that problem is not identified until the *end* of the service process. Could the potential problem have been discovered earlier in the process? How? How might improved communication between the service provider and the customer have helped minimize the cost and occurrence of this or other such problems?

Part IV - Service Quality and Value
Unit 14:
MEASURING SERVICE QUALITY AND PRODUCTIVITY

Unit reading... The following reading pertains to Service Business Principles included in this unit. The instructor will let you know which of the readings you are responsible for studying.
Fitzsimmons2 chapter 10 on Service Quality.

Preparation for the next Service Business Principle (14a)

To consider... Before proceeding, consider the following and write thoughts and ideas below:

As the saying goes, "you cannot manage what you cannot measure" (or at least observe). As a result, an important part of any quality management effort will be methods for measuring quality. In manufacturing processes, measurements are taken by use of scales (for weight), micrometers and rulers (for sizes), oscilloscopes (for electrical pulses), lasers (for surface textures), and many other mechanical instruments. What are the instruments used to measure quality in service processes? Think about how to measure quality in retail service, at a law firm, or on public transportation. What types of things are measured to capture an idea of service quality?

_____

_____

_____

_____

_____

_____

_____

_____

_____

Unit 14

Service Business Principle 14a:
MEASURING CUSTOMERS

Service Business Principle	*"With services, we often measure quality by measuring customers. Unfortunately, customer measurement is often far from precise."*

Why it occurs...   MEASURING CUSTOMERS occurs because of variability in (a) customer-provided specifications, (b) customer-supplied inputs and (c) output which is heterogeneous.

Details...   How do we measure customers? We measure their perceptions of the service relative to company or customer-provided specifications. We measure the impact of the service process on their selves, their belongings and/or their information. We also measure affective outcomes—the impact of the service on customer's attitudes. The methods for taking such measurements are customer surveys or other types of customer feedback.

Why is customer measurement far from precise? The following are some Service Business Principles that explain the imprecision of customer measurement:

• **Subjective Rulers** - With services, customer measures of quality are generally subjective. Making a subjective measure numerical does not make it objective.

For example, asking customers "On a 5-point scale, how satisfied were you with the timeliness of service?" may get a numerical response, but even the meaning of each scale point is a subjective judgment.

• **Intrusive Measurement** - With services, the act of customer-measurement of quality can influence perceptions.

The idea that measurement influences outcomes was observed many years ago as the "Hawthorne Effect." For example, be careful about asking customers for complaints or problems with the service, since research has shown that such questions inspire negative thinking and can promote dissatisfaction that otherwise would not be recognized. It is justified to ask for complaints if the service provider is willing and able to appropriately act on them.

• **Resistance to Measurement** - With services, most customers do not consider quality measurement to be value adding, therefore resist providing measurements. This resistance increases as the customers' cost of providing measurement increases.

For example, many customers consider it a hassle to fill out customer satisfaction surveys. Giving thoughtful feedback to the company requires mental effort, which many customers are not willing to expend. As a result, response rates for customer satisfaction surveys may be no higher than 5 to 15 percent.[37]

---

[37] Sampson, S. E., 1996. "Ramifications of Monitoring Service Quality Through Passively Solicited Customer Feedback." *Decision Sciences*, vol. 27, no. 4.
    Sampson, S. E., and Weiss, E. N. (1993). "Merchant's Tire and Auto." , University of Virginia, Charlottesville, Virginia.

• **The Halo Effect** - With services, customers automatically combine individual components of quality into an overall quality perception. Attempted measurements of individual components may actually have more to do with the overall perception than the individual components.

Often, service providers desire to know *which components* of the service delivery process are in need of improvement and which are okay. Given the halo effect, the problem is that customers form overall opinions and bias their report of each component based on that overall opinion.

• **Self-Selected Sampling** - With services, customer-measurement makes it is possible to influence sampling, but very difficult to *control* sampling. When we control sampling we know how survey-responding customers (sampled) compare with customers in general. Strategies to increase response rates, such as awards or drawing for prizes, influence some types of customers more than others. Therefore, it is important to consider sample bias.

Sampling bias describes how customers for which we have measures compare with customers in general. How do we know if the customers who give opinions represent customers in general? The answer is "very often, we don't." Nevertheless, it is reasonable to assume that customer survey responses are biased, differing in some way from the attitudes of customers in general. For example, we may believe that customers in a hurry are less likely to give a quality evaluation than customers with time on their hands. Therefore, we wind up surveying a disproportionate number of those with time on their hands, under-representing the attitudes of customers in a hurry. The responses to questions like "Was our service fast enough?" would not capture what hurried customers think.

• **Interpreting the Interpretations** - With services, customer measurement requires the customer to interpret both their perceptions and the measurement scale. Two customers with identical perceptions might interpret the measurement scale differently, resulting in different measurements.

It is a common fallacy to think that two customers who mark "good" on a "excellent-good-fair-poor" scale have the exact same opinion. Some customers may consider "good" as sufficiently adequate, whereas others may consider "good" to be substandard. As with *Subjective Rulers*, it is presumptuous to think that a customer mark on a defined scale is a precise, comparable measurement.

Another problem with customer measurement is that even if we are able to gather data that is interpretable, that data will not likely tell us how to fix the problem. (As compared with what is experienced in manufacturing: If a part is measured as being too big, the solution is to make it smaller, etc.) A service survey that reveals customers are dissatisfied may reveal little about how to increase satisfaction. Often the data we collect is used to identify *if* a quality problem appears to be occurring, and perhaps generate some *suggestions* for how it might be addressed.

Unit 14

How it impacts decisions... Service providers must decide how they will measure quality, and how they will *analyze* and *use* the measurements.

What to do about it... Some measurements of services quality might be objective, which makes things much easier. For example, a measure of quality at an accounting firm is the ability to balance the books—either they balance or they do not. Or, a measure of quality at an investment bank is the ability to generate a high return on investment, which can have an easily calculated value.

However, for most services, quality measurement is more complex than that. It is usually good to gather multiple measures. Some measures are internal, describing the service performance based on company-defined standards. Other measures are external, involving gathering perceptions of quality from customers.

It is pointless to measure service quality and then do nothing with the data. It can also be ineffective to use the data in the wrong part of the organization. For example, some multi-location companies concentrate their customer feedback gathering at the corporate office, with the hope that useful information will "trickle down" to the various locations. Typically, it is a good idea for service quality measurement data to be employed at the location in the company where quality improvement can occur, which is often the front lines. It is therefore good if the quality measurements can be fed to the lowest decision points in the organization.

Appendix D contains the paper "An Empirically Derived Framework for Customer Feedback System Design." That paper discusses in detail the design of customer measurement systems, including data gathering, analysis, and use.

For example... Were the Department of Motor Vehicles (DMV) concerned about service quality, it could collect multiple measures. Examples of internal measures would be the number of forms submitted with errors, the number of times problems are solved on the first visit, and the number of customers waiting in line at any given time. Examples of external customer measures are clarity about DMV procedures, perceived courtesy and helpfulness of DMV employees, and overall satisfaction with the process. These latter measures could be ascertained through a survey form handed to customers as they depart, a comment card box by the DMV office door, or telephone surveys of recent customers.

My airline application... Airlines might be particularly concerned about the quality of the interactions between employees and customers. They may want to track the interactions over time, to identify when more training or attention to these interactions is needed. The airline might periodically survey passengers to gather quality data. Some airlines include a comment card in the seat pocket in front of the passengers, allowing self-selected customers to offer their opinions.

Supplemental reading... Fitzsimmons2 chapter 10 pages 274-280 on Measuring Service Quality.
article: "An Empirically Derived Framework for Designing Customer Feedback Systems," found in Appendix D.
case: Merchant's Tire & Auto (available from Darden Educational Materials Services, University of Virginia).

How manufacturing differs from services...

With manufacturing, measuring quality often involves measuring a standard product, which measurements are mostly objective.

Quantitative analysis... (covered at the discretion of the instructor)

Customer measurements of quality which are numerical can be analyzed using Statistical Process Control (SPC) techniques. For example, SPC can help identify when service quality is tending to drift in an upward or downward direction. (Fitzsimmons2 chapter 10 pages 289-296 discuss Statistical Process Control.)

The topic of comparing numerical service quality data across locations will be addressed in SBP: *Comparing Apples and Oranges.*

SBP 14a: Measuring Customers   Name (if turned in):_____

Analysis questions...   To help apply this Service Business Principle, consider and answer the following questions about your specific service business process. (❑Check here if you are going outside of your target service business.)

Service company/business:_____

The service process:_____
  ① Given an appropriate definition of quality, how might it be measured?
  ② What objective measurements are available? Are they valid and relevant to customer-defined quality?
  ③ What subjective measurements are available? Are they comparable, one measurement to another?

①_____

_____

_____

_____

_____

_____

_____

_____

_____

_____

_____

_____

_____

_____

_____

Unit 14

SBP 14a: Measuring Customers   Name (if turned in):_____

Application exercise...   Also to help you apply this Service Business Principle, complete the following analysis with regard to your specific service business process, or another service process in your business. (❏Check here if you are going outside of your target service business, which was _____.)

Service company/business:_____

The service process:_____
   Redraw the flowchart of your service process. What internal quality measures could be taken and at what
   locations in the process? What external quality measures would be useful to know? Design a customer comment
   card that gathers customer perceptions of quality. Design a simple procedure for collecting, analyzing, and using
   the data as part of a quality improvement effort.

Preparation for the next Service Business Principle (14b)

To consider...   Before proceeding, consider the following and write thoughts and ideas below:

If manufacturing organizations want to motivate employees to work harder, they simply reward hard work. Employees or teams of employees who can produce more can be paid more, which can be an effective incentive. It makes sense that service companies would also want employees to be productive. However, productivity-based pay is no simple matter in most service organizations. Why would that be the case? How would a hospital implement performance-based pay? Or a law firm? Or a dry cleaning company? Or a copy center? How does one motivate employees to be productive in such service businesses?

_____

_____

_____

_____

_____

_____

_____

_____

_____

Unit 14

Service Business Principle 14b:
A MEASURE OF MOTIVATION

Service Business Principle	*"With services, employee motivation will often deteriorate to the level at which employees are measured."*

Why it occurs...   A MEASURE OF MOTIVATION occurs because it is very difficult to measure or even define employee productivity. (See SBP: *Difficulty in Measuring Output*.) Since productivity is loosely defined, employees often base their behavior on how productivity is "defined" in terms of how it is measured.

Details... Employee productivity in service organizations can be difficult to measure. The measurement used can have a significant impact on employee motivation. The following are some examples of motivation that results from various kinds of productivity measurements.

If you measure customer volume, you get rapid service. This is the case with some call centers, where customer service agents are measured according to call count quotas. The result can be lousy service to individual customers.[38]

If you measure complaints, you motivate complaint-avoidance behavior. That might sound like a positive thing except for the limits it can place on employee creativity and initiative. There are few greater motivators for meritocracy than to punish any adverse affects of risk taking, such as by making a big deal of random complaints.

If you measure work attendance, you motivate punctual clock punching. When eight hours of low productivity measures the same as eight hours of high productivity, many employees will reserve their energy by choosing for the former rather than the latter.

Granted, there are some employees who are motivated independently of what is measured. Those employees are likely to leave the organization due to mismatch between their values and the company's apparent "values." Indeed, measurement systems are a primary signal of an organization's value system.

How it impacts decisions... Companies should be careful in selecting how employee productivity will be measured, and especially how those measurements impact employees. What is *convenient* or *easy* to measure does not always portray what is truly important to the success of the organization.

What to do about it... It is difficult to say what the "best" productivity measurement method would be, since service processes differ and service organizations have various objectives. The decision of which measurements to track should be rooted in the values of the organization, which should be part of a viable and well thought out strategy.

---

[38] Page E1 of the June 8, 1998 *Salt Lake Tribune* contained an Associated Press article with the following statements: "Many customers complain about how hard it is to call customer service centers, where they get long waits, little information and often a bad attitude from people answering the phones. No wonder, says the Radclyffe Group, a management consulting firm that found in a study of 130 call centers that employees work under difficult and stressful conditions. Problems include . . . requiring [specified] numbers of calls to be handled by each worker."

For example... Among the most explicit measurement systems seen is service organizations is tipping at restaurants. Customers measure employee performance directly in the form of tips. Restaurants that have a no-tipping policy must rely on other means to motivate good service by employees.

Measurements do not necessarily have to tie into pay to motivate employees. Just knowing they are being measured influences employees' motivation. This was discovered with the legendary Hawthorne Studies, involving lighting experiments at a General Electric plant. When the lighting was increased, productivity went up. When lighting was lowered, productivity went up. The researchers discovered that by simply measuring the productivity of employees, productivity was influenced.

My airline application... It is very difficult to measure productivity of airline employees. What is a productive pilot? What defines a productive baggage handler? How does the company identify productive stewards and stewardesses? For airlines without formal measurement systems, the default becomes counting complaints. How do employees respond? By complaint minimization. Consider the personableness level of most airline employees, especially when compared with how it was a dozen or more years ago. Personableness does not seem to be on the increase.

An exception would be Southwest Airlines, who surely has access to complaint information but usually stands up for employees. Legend has it that one way Southwest measures the potential of customer service job applicants is to ask them to tell a joke. Such measurement motivates and promotes the "fun" culture for which Southwest is known.

Supplemental reading...   case: AT&T Universal Card Services (HBS)

How manufacturing differs from services...

With manufacturing, productivity is relatively easy to define in terms of units of output per time period. As such, employee motivation is generally focused on what is rewarded, such as piece-rate pay motivating rapid production.

Unit 14

SBP 14b: A Measure of Motivation   Name (if turned in):_____

Analysis questions... To help apply this Service Business Principle. consider and answer the following questions about your specific service business process. (❑Check here if you are going outside of your target service business.)

Service company/business:_____

The service process:_____
    ① How is productivity measured in this organization?
    ② How do those measurements impact employee motivation? What types of behaviors are employees motivated to do? What types of behaviors are employees motivated to avoid?
    ③ Might employees "manipulate" the measurements to their advantage without correspondingly improving productivity? How? What can the company do to prevent this?
    ④ What do the measurements imply about what the organization values?

① _____

_____

_____

_____

_____

_____

_____

_____

_____

_____

_____

_____

_____

_____

_____

_____

Unit 14

SBP 14b: A Measure of Motivation   Name (if turned in):_____

Application exercise...

Also to help you apply this Service Business Principle, complete the following analysis with regard to your specific service business process, or another service process in your business. (❏Check here if you are going outside of your target service business, which was _____.)

Service company/business:_____

The service process:_____

List three behaviors that would define good productivity for a particular type of employee at your target service business. For *each* behavior, describe a measurement which would motivate employees to exhibit the desirable behavior. How valid are those measurements–in other words, how accurately do they correlate with actual productivity? Might employees produce high measurements without correspondingly high productivity? How? Describe what the company might do to improve the validity of the measurements.

Preparation for the next Service Business Principle (14c)

To consider... Before proceeding, consider the following and write thoughts and ideas below:

A useful purpose for gathering quality and productivity measurements is the ability to do comparisons over time and across production facilities. Companies hope that measures are improving over time. Also, by identifying outstanding producers within the company, the "secrets to success" can be shared throughout the company. In manufacturing companies, objective quality data can be compared throughout the company. For example, the production area with the minimum number of defects per thousand operations might be considered the "benchmark" that sets the standard for the other production areas. With services, comparing across multiple locations might not be as simple a matter. If one store has six complaints in a given month, and another store has only three, does that mean that the second has twice the quality of the first? How might multi-location service providers compare quality and productivity across locations?

_____

_____

_____

_____

_____

_____

_____

_____

Unit 14

Service Business Principle 14c:

COMPARING APPLES AND ORANGES

Service Business Principle	*"With multi-location service companies, varying clientele may make production difficult to compare across locations."*

Why it occurs...   COMPARING APPLES AND ORANGES occurs because of heterogeneous inputs from customers, and heterogeneous outputs to compare.

Details...   Multi-location service companies may desire to compare service quality and productivity across the various locations. Reasons might include:
- To identify outstanding locations to set as examples for the rest of the company.
- To motivate location managers to improve results by having the various locations compete for rewards or recognition.
- To identify locations with problems in need of management attention.

These are potential advantages for having objective ways to comparing across service locations. However, with service companies measurement comparison across locations needs to be done with caution. The comparison of numerical measurements may not accurately reflect the comparison of how the various locations are operating.

For example, which is a more productive law office, the one who has two attorneys who win three cases and lose two in a given month, or the one who has four attorneys who win five cases and lose six in a given month? You may say the first, since it has more wins per attorney. However, the second has handled more cases. But, the first has a greater success rate. Yet, the second probably has more billable hours per attorney. Further, we have no idea of the complexity of each case, or the quality of the inputs (the client's position). Some cases are easy, and others are not. The bottom line is that comparisons of service quality and productivity can be very difficult.

How it impacts decisions...   Service providers should decide how to define quality and productivity, especially if employees or offices are given bonuses or other rewards based on superior quality and productivity.

What to do about it...   There is no general rule for establishing comparative measures of quality and productivity. However, measures should normally adjust for environmental factors beyond the control of the service employees. One technique for doing this is known as Data Envelopment Analysis (DEA). DEA considers the various inputs into a service process and the resulting outputs. It uses a mathematical procedure to evaluate outputs adjusted according to inputs, and can tell which service locations tend to get more (or better) outputs for fewer inputs.

For example...   A 114-location automotive service chain desired to improve customer service by rewarding store managers and other employees based on customer satisfaction ratings. The company developed a complex system for gathering customer satisfaction data, including in-store surveys, telephone surveys, complaint and compliment letters, and "mystery shopper" inspections by employees posing as customers. The challenge they found was that some stores received higher ratings than others for reasons other than how well the employees were providing customer service. For example, some stores sold mostly tires, which is a low-risk and easily satisfiable interaction with customers. Other stores sold mostly mechanical service, which is a highly divergent process subject to greater variability in satisfaction. Also, some stores were located in highly competitive areas, whereas others were in more rural regions. The result was that it was difficult to compare the customer satisfaction ratings to identify stores providing truly superior quality.

My airline application... Airlines have locations in numerous cities, called stations. How easy would it be to compare quality and productivity across the locations? The environment of each location certainly varies, including the availability of passengers and competition. Also, the design of airports might limit the ability to provide service quality. (What is an airline to do about cramped gate waiting areas?) Major hubs are likely to have higher overall traffic. Commuter routes are likely to have higher customer loyalty. Regional (i.e. smaller) airports are likely to have sporadic demand, more difficult planning of capacity, therefore lower utilization.

Supplemental reading... Fitzsimmons2 chapter 4 page 74 on Data Envelopment Analysis.
case: Merchant's Tire & Auto (available from Darden Educational Materials Service, University of Virginia).

How manufacturing differs from services...

With manufacturing, quality and productivity are generally measured in objective terms, allowing easier comparisons.

Quantitative analysis... (covered at the discretion of the instructor)

As mentioned, Data Envelopment Analysis (DEA) is mathematical a method for comparing numerical results across service locations. Details will not be discussed here, but are described in Fitzsimmons2 chapter 14 Supplement on pages 451-458.

The advantage of DEA is that it considers not just the output of a service process, such as in terms of quality or productivity, but also considers the process inputs. A service location that has high outputs but also consumes a large amount of inputs may not be doing as good of a job as a location that has medium outputs but consumes small amounts of inputs.

One type of input that might be considered is the competitive environment of the service location. Two service locations with the same quality and productivity measurements may compare differently when one is in a highly competitive environment and the other is in a location without competitors.

Unit 14

SBP 14c: Comparing Apples and Oranges   Name (if turned in):_____

Analysis questions...   To help apply this Service Business Principle, consider and answer the following questions about your specific service business process. (❑Check here if you are going outside of your target service business.)

Service company/business:_____

The service process:_____
     ① Is this a multi-location service company?
     ② Is production standardized across locations?
     ③ Do customer inputs vary across locations?
     ④ Do the management challenges vary across locations?
     ⑤ On what basis can the various locations be compared?

①_____

_____

_____

_____

_____

_____

_____

_____

_____

_____

_____

_____

_____

_____

_____

_____

Unit 14

SBP 14c: Comparing Apples and Oranges   Name (if turned in):_____

Application exercise...   Also to help you apply this Service Business Principle, complete the following analysis with regard to your specific service business process, or another service process in your business. (☐Check here if you are going outside of your target service business, which was _____.)

Service company/business:_____

The service process:_____
   Design a bonus system for rewarding employees based on service quality and/or productivity. What measurements would you use? How would you account for environmental factors, including variations in customer inputs and requirements? Comment on the advantages and disadvantages of your system.

Appendix Contents

Appendix A: Using the Workbook Website: http://sampson.byu.edu/workbook
Accessing the Website
Registering a Course on the Website
Registering a Student on the Website
Submitting Application Exercises Electronically
The FlowViewer Flowcharting Language
Running Simulation Exercises
Interpreting Simulation Exercise Results
Submitting Simulation Exercises Electronically
Downloading Simulation Exercise Software
Updates to the Workbook Website

Appendix B: Flowcharting Service Processes
Basic Flowchart Elements
Service Blueprinting
Using Service Blueprints
The FlowViewer Flowcharting Language

Appendix C: Quantitative Tools
The Use of Quantitative Analysis
Quantitative Topics Covered in this Appendix
    Forecasting Analysis: Basic Time-Series Methods
        (used with SBP 2a: *Simultaneous Production and Consumption*).
    Capacity Scheduling Analysis: The Critical Fractile Rule
        (used with SBP 2b: *Time-Perishable Capacity*).
    Location Planning Analysis: The Center of Gravity Method
        (used with SBP 2c: *Customer Proximity*).
    Labor Planning Analysis: Forecasting with Seasonality
        (used with SBP 2d: *Labor Intensity*).
    Optimization Analysis: Linear Programming
        (used with SBP 2e: *Perishable Output Illusion*).
    Queuing Analysis: Analytical Queuing Theory
        (used with SBP 3a: *Customers in Inventory*).
    Inventory Theory Analysis: The Economic Order Quantity and Safety Stock Approaches
        (used with SBP 3b: *Intangibility Myth*).
    Project Scheduling Analysis: The Critical Path Method (CPM)
        (used with SBP 3c: *Heterogeneous Production*).
    Facility Layout Analysis: Process Layouts
        (used with SBP 3d: *Difficulty in Measuring Output*).
    Statistical Process Control (SPC) Analysis: Control Charts for Variables
        (used with SBP 3e: *Difficulty in Maintaining Quality*).

Appendix D: Other Readings

mini-case: Christmas at UPS
reading: An Empirical Derived Framework for Designing Customer Feedback Systems

Appendix A:
Using the Workbook Website: http://sampson.byu.edu/workbook

The following is basic information about using the workbook website. Additional information is available on the website itself.

☞ Accessing the Website ☜

As with any portion of the World Wide Web, accessing the website requires having a computer with an Internet connection and a web browser. The workbook website is best when viewed with the latest versions of viewers such as Netscape® Navigator (Communicator) or Microsoft® Internet Explorer. However, most features of the website can be viewed from prior versions of web browsers.

When your web browser is running, simply enter "http://sampson.byu.edu/workbook" on the location (URL) line, or select Open... from the File menu and enter that address.

Anyone can access the public portions of the workbook website. Public information includes updates of workbook information, files for use with the Simulation Exercises, and a general workbook discussion group.

Other information on the workbook website is password-protected, and only accessible to students and instructors of courses which are registered on the website. An instructor of a registered course can post announcements on a web page that is only viewable to students in his or her course. Students can submit assignments electronically and view scores and grades as decided by the instructor. Student assignments can include graphical flowcharts with the FlowViewer on-line software. Students and instructors can participate in a course-specific discussion group, allowing course interaction over the Internet.

☞ Registering a Course on the Website ☜

Registration involves a small fee, which helps cover the costs of setting up and maintaining the workbook web server (including hardware, software, and paying the webmaster). Instructors wishing to register their courses on the workbook website should see http://sampson.byu.edu/workbook/course/register.htm for information. Current features and availability of course registration are described there.

☞ Registering a Student on the Website ☜

Once a course has been registered on the workbook website, each student will need to register on the course website. This is a simple process involving entering information such as a student ID number and e-mail address, and selecting a password. To register, see http://sampson.byu.edu/workbook/student/register.htm on the workbook website.

After you have registered, you will have access to the course home page. There you can see announcements and reminders posted by your instructor, submit assignments, view grades posted by your instructor, etc.

After you register, it is important that your remember your username and password. That information will be used to log on to the course home page on the workbook website. You will also need to know your courseID, which your instructor will tell you or which you can look up on the website.

Please do not share your username and password with other people, and avoid writing it down where others can see it. With that information someone could fraudulently submit assignments in your behalf and could view any of your grades that have been posted on the course site.

Apx A

If your instructor has not elected to register your course on the workbook website, you obviously cannot register on your course website. Registering a course on the workbook website is a decision left to each instructor.

☞ Submitting Application Exercises Electronically ☜

At the instructor's option, you may be allowed to submit Application Exercises electronically from your Course Home Page on the workbook website. After selecting which Application Exercise you are submitting, you will be given a form to enter your answer. You may type your answer directly into the form, or may choose to "cut and paste" it from your word processor. (The advantage of the latter is the opportunity to spell-check, which is not available in the form.) You can even enter graphical flowcharts by using the FlowViewer language described below. By clicking a button you can view your exercise formatted similarly to what you would have in your workbook. You can print it out to insert it in your workbook. When you are ready, you can click a different button to electronically submit your Application Exercise answer to your instructor. A confirmation will be e-mailed back to you for you to archive.

It is absolutely essential that each student keep a backup copy of submitted Application Exercise answers. As reliable as web servers and Internet networks are, they are not indestructible. Great effort has been taken to make the systems reliable; nevertheless, the responsibility for making the system fail-safe ultimately rests with each student, who should keep a backup copy of all of his or her work. This way, if there is a system failure, the work will not have been lost.

☞ The FlowViewer Flowcharting Language ☜

Application Exercise answers sometimes involve descriptions of service processes. A good way to depict service processes is with flowcharts. (Appendix B discusses service flowcharting.) When Application Exercises are submitted electronically, students can include flowcharts by entering information in the FlowViewer flowcharting language. This language takes simple text statements and renders them as graphical flowcharts. The following is a simple example of the FlowViewer language:

```
#imply eol
#begin flowchart
#heading Hotel Check-In Process
      (start)
          !
 [Greet customer.]
          !
<Does customer have reservation?>-no-><Is a room available?>-yes->(ok)
         !yes                                     !no
[Look up reservation information.]    [Explain and suggest competitor.]
         !<-------(ok)                            !
  [Register customer.]                         (stop)
          !
[Give customer room key.]
          !
       (stop)
#end flowchart
```

When this information is rendered for viewing or printing, the flowchart looks like the following:

Apx A

Details about the FlowViewer language are at http://sampson.byu.edu/workbook/viewer/instructions.htm on the workbook website. Basic elements of the FlowViewer language are summarized in Appendix B.

☞ Running Simulation Exercises ☜

The Simulation Exercises are part of the Quantitative Analysis material in Units 2 and 3. Simulation Exercises are computer models that run with simulation software.

To run Simulation Exercises you will need to have a computer running Microsoft Windows® 95, 98, or NT. You also must have a Web browser installed on the computer, such as Netscape Navigator® or Microsoft Internet Explorer®. Web browsers come pre-installed on most computers these days, or are commonly available for free download over the Internet. The web browser that is installed as your default browser will be started by the software as the means of viewing your exercise results.

The "Downloading Simulation Exercise Software" section below describes how to obtain the files necessary for running Simulation Exercises.

Information about specific Simulation Exercises is given in Units 2 and 3, units which tie in to Appendix C. General instructions for running Simulation Exercises are at found at http://sampson.byu.edu/workbook/simulation/instructions.htm on the workbook website.

☞ Interpreting Simulation Exercise Results ☜

Simulation Exercises have a numerical, not a verbal, result. The "result" is described with each simulation exercise, and may be something like "profits generated" or "minutes customers wait."

Each Simulation Exercise will determine a "target" value for the results, which is a value that is theoretically (although not always practically) the perfect value for the results of that exercise. You do not have to achieve the target value in order to have done well on the exercise. For some exercises, achieving a reasonable fraction of the target value will be good.

The combination of the result and the target value produces a "score." The score indicates how well you did at the exercise relative to how well might have been done.

For some Simulation Exercises, the target value will be different for each student and each time you run the simulation. This is because random elements are built into each exercise to allow students to repeat exercises for additional practice. The calculation of scores serves to "level the playing field" by adjusting results according to appropriate targets.

For some Simulation Exercises it is difficult or impossible to have a perfect score. How do you know if you did a good job on that exercise? If you submit your Simulation Exercise results electronically, you will be able to see how your score compares with scores submitted by other students (although you will not see the names of the other students). That way, you can see if your score is high or low relative to what other students have realized.

☞ Submitting Simulation Exercises Electronically ☜

As mentioned previously, running Simulation Exercises requires having a default web browser installed on the computer. To submit Simulation Exercises electronically, you will also need to have an Internet connection and your course must be registered on the workbook website.

After you have completed a Simulation Exercise, you will have the opportunity to provide your username, password, and courseID, so that the results will be submitted. If you are connected to the Internet, or if the default browser establishes an Internet connection, the electronic submission can occur. If you are not connected to the Internet, you can simply print out your results and score.

☞ Downloading Simulation Exercise Software ☜

Information about obtaining the files to accompany the Simulation Exercises in Appendix C: Quantitative Tools, can be found on the workbook website. At universities which have a computer network accessible to students, the instructor may choose to load the Simulation Exercise files onto the network so that students can access them there. Also, the files can be individually run on students' personal computers.

Information about obtaining the software is found at http://sampson.byu.edu/workbook/simulation/files.htm on the workbook website. Instructors should check the website about software availability prior to the start of each semester. Software development dictates that versions of the software may or may not be available for download at different times.

At the present time, the Simulation Exercises only run under Microsoft Windows operating systems (95, 98, or NT). If the software becomes available for other operating systems, the information will be posted on the workbook website at http://sampson.byu.edu/workbook/simulation.

As you might imagine, it is virtually impossible to foresee every possible configuration of computers that may be used to attempt to run the simulation software. Even though the software has been tested on different computer configurations, there is always the possibility that the software will not run on some other particular configurations. The workbook author, the workbook publisher, the software authors, and the software publisher do not individually nor jointly provide any warranties for the software, either expressed or implied. Also, the availability of versions of the software will vary over time. Check http://sampson.byu.edu/workbook/simulation on the workbook website about current simulation software availability.

☞ Updates to the Workbook Website ☜

As new editions of this workbook become available, the website will be changed to reflect the workbook updates. Instructors are always encouraged to use the latest edition of the workbook in their courses. The descriptions of workbook website functionality found in prior editions of the workbook (including descriptions in this second edition when the third edition becomes available) will be superseded by descriptions found in the latest edition.

Apx A

Appendix B:
Flowcharting Service Processes

(Note: This appendix gives the student a basic introduction to flowcharting with particular descriptions of a technique known a service blueprinting. Students with flowcharting experience may skim over the first portion, but should study the parts on blueprinting.)

Very often when we analyze service businesses it is helpful to consider the various steps in the process. The process can be written out as series of numbered steps, such as the following:

The Carpet Cleaning Process
1. Go to first room.
2. Move furniture away from walls.
3. Steam clean behind furniture.
4. Move furniture back to original positions.
5. Steam clean remainder of carpet.
6. Go to next room.
7. Repeat at step 2.

Lists of steps works fine for relatively simple processes, and even for some complex processes. Other processes are divergent, involving conditional steps that change the sequence of steps based on particular conditions. For example, consider the process of setting a customer up on a fitness program at a health club.

The Fitness Program Set-up Process
1. Gather basic information about the customer's health and fitness history.
2. Has customer been on a fitness program recently? If not, skip to step 4.
3. Review the prior fitness program.
4. Has customer had health problems that may limit a fitness program? If not, skip to step 7.
5. Advise customer to get a physical checkup before beginning the fitness program.
6. Schedule a follow-up consultation (for after they have a checkup). Stop.
7. Create a list of exercises appropriate for the customer's age and weight.
8. Show customer how to do each exercise, having them do each.
9. Does the customer appear to have physical discomfort with the exercises? If no, then go to step 13.
10. Does the discomfort result from too strenuous of exercises? If no, go to step 5.
11. Reduce the intensity of the program.
12. Go to step 8.
13. Schedule a follow-up consultation. Stop.

That is not a very complex process as described, but the various questions and branches makes it a bit confusing to follow. The process would be easier to follow with a flowchart, such as the one shown on the following page.

Apx B

The Fitness Program Set-up Process

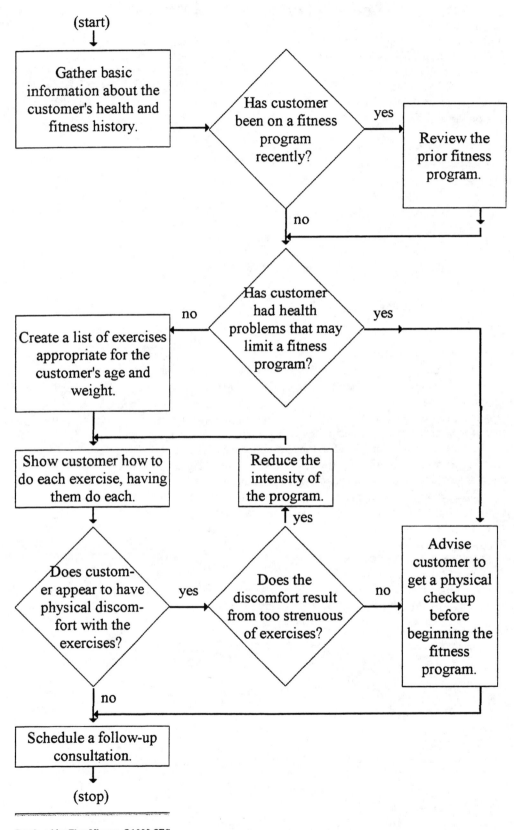

Basic Flowchart Elements

The example on the prior page illustrates some simple flowchart elements, which will be described below.

The most basic flowchart element is a **statement**, which is a step in the process to perform. Flowcharting conventions place statements in rectangles.

> *This is a statement.*

> *Greet the customer.*

> *Calculate the total.*

Statements are connected with **arrows**, which show the flow from one step to another.

> *First step.*
>
> ↓
>
> *Second step.*
>
> ↓
>
> *Third step.*

Decisions are represented by diamonds. Some decisions have dichotomous (two possible state) outcomes, such as yes or no.

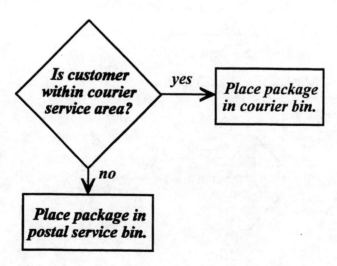

Apx B

Other decisions may have hundreds of possible outcomes. These decisions may also be placed in a diamond.

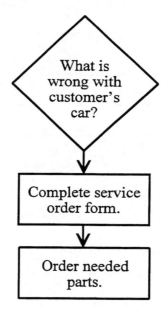

Sometimes we need to branch to a different **point** on the flowchart. Referenced points in a flowchart are often represented by circled words. Common example are the points at which a flowchart starts and ends

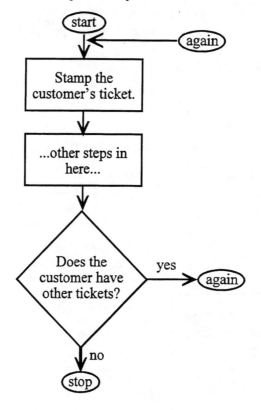

Triangles are used to represent various things in different types of flowcharts. A critical element to manage in service processes is customer or employee **waiting**. Triangles are a good way to represent waiting.

These were just a few simple examples of flowcharts using the basic elements. More flowchart examples can be seen at http://sampson.byu.edu/workbook/viewer/examples.htm on the workbook website.

Apx B

Service Blueprinting

Service blueprinting is a special type of process flowcharting. Service blueprinting involves layers of steps, with each layer representing a different proximity to the customer, or different functional areas. The original method of service blueprinting is attributed to Lynn Shostack.[39] Also, much of the following information is adapted by the article "The ABCs of Service System Blueprinting" by Jane Kingman-Brundage.[40]

The metaphor for a service blueprint is an architectural blueprint. One way to specify the design of a building is by listing all of the desired features, such as number and sizes of rooms, locations of light fixtures, etc. A more complex task would be to enumerate the steps of construction. A more practical way to specify the design of a building is through a blueprint. Blueprints show various aspects of a building and how they interrelate. Blueprints help identify potential problems, such as improperly placed support (load bearing) walls or inefficient walking paths through the building.

Likewise, a service blueprint shows the interrelationships between the various elements of a service process. In particular, service blueprints help us identify potential problems such as inefficiencies, unacceptable customer wait, and need for coordination between customers, contact employees, and support personnel.

A simple service blueprint may involve two layers, a "front office" and a "back office." The front office, called by some the "front stage," is those parts of the service process that are "visible" to the customer. Activities in the front office may include greeting the customer, taking the customer's order, operating on the customer's ingrown toenail, etc. Note that some of these activities can be performed over the telephone, and are thus part of the front office. "Visible" to the customer means that the customer is aware of how the process is going.

The back office, or "back stage," involves those parts of the process that are not "visible" to the customer. Generally, everything that takes place in a restaurant's kitchen is back-office. Customer inputs are likely to be involved in back-office processes, but the customers themselves are not.

In a service blueprint, the front office is separated from the back office by a "line of visibility." Think for a moment: Do we manage the front office differently than we manage the back office? As stated in Fitzsimmons2, page 86, "The front office is where the customer contact occurs, with concern for ambiance and effectiveness being necessary" and, "The back office is hidden from the customer and often operated as a factory for efficiency." The front office and back office have different roles, and need to complement each other.

More complex service blueprints may have more layers than just a front and back office. For example, the front office may be divided into three parts, one involving customer taking action on his or own own, one involving customer *interaction* with employees, and the third involving customer *observation* but not interaction. Further, the back office may be divided according to who does the work: the contact (front-line) employees, the support staff, the management, or outside service suppliers. These various layers of the process are depicted in the following diagram[41]:

---

[39] Shostack, G. L., 1984. "Designing Services That Deliver." *Harvard Business Review*, vol. 62(January-February 1984): 133-139.
Shostack, G. L., 1987. "Service Positioning through Structural Change." *Journal of Marketing*, vol. 51, no. 1(January 1987): 34-43.
[40] Kingman-Brundage, J. 1989. "The ABSs of Service System Blueprinting" In: M. J. Bitner and L. A. Crosby, Eds.), *Designing a Winning Service Strategy*, American Marketing Association, Chicago.
Reprinted in Lovelock, C. H., 1992. *Managing Services: Marketing, Operations, and Human Resources*, Prentice Hall, Englewood Cliffs: New Jersey, pp. 96-102.
[41] Somewhat adapted from ideas discussed by Jane Kingman-Brundage in "The ABCs of Service System Blueprinting" In: M. J. Bitner and L. A. Crosby, Eds.), *Designing a Winning Service Strategy*, American Marketing Association, Chicago, 1989.

	Layer of Service Process	Who Performs Process Steps	Where
line of independence→	Customer Action	customers (self-serve)	Front office
line of interaction→	Customer Interaction	contact employees & customers	Front office
line of visibility→	Customer Vision	contact employees	Front office
line of internal interaction→	Backstage Preparation	contact & support employees	Back office
line of implementation→	Support Functions	support employees	Back office
company boundary→	Management Functions	management	Back office
	Outside Service Suppliers	outside supplier	External

Architectural blueprints can be rendered with different amounts of detail, focusing on different parts of the system. One set of blueprints may describe the overall structure, another may describe the support beams sizes, and another may outline the electrical wiring plan. The details on a blueprint depend on the intended use.

Similarly, service blueprints can be created at different levels of detail, from different perspectives. It is not necessary to include *all* of the various layers in a blueprint for it to be useful. Some blueprints may include all seven layers described above, but they will probably be quite large. Blueprints should include just those layers that are necessary to capture the perspective of the process.

Ultimately, the detail of a service blueprint will depend upon the focus of analysis. And like an architectural blueprint, a service process can be represented from a number of different perspectives in various service blueprints.

The following pages contain simple service blueprints: one for a sit-down restaurant process and another for a baggage handling process. The restaurant blueprint is drawn from the perspective of a waiter, and includes layers for customer actions, interactions, and the "back office." The airline baggage handling blueprint considers the arrival of a passenger's bag, and the transportation of that bag either by the airline or by an inter-carrier airline. These are given as simple examples. Other examples, including more detailed examples, are found at http://sampson.byu.edu/workbook/viewer/examples.htm on the workbook website.

Apx B

The Sit-Down Restaurant Process: Waiter Perspective

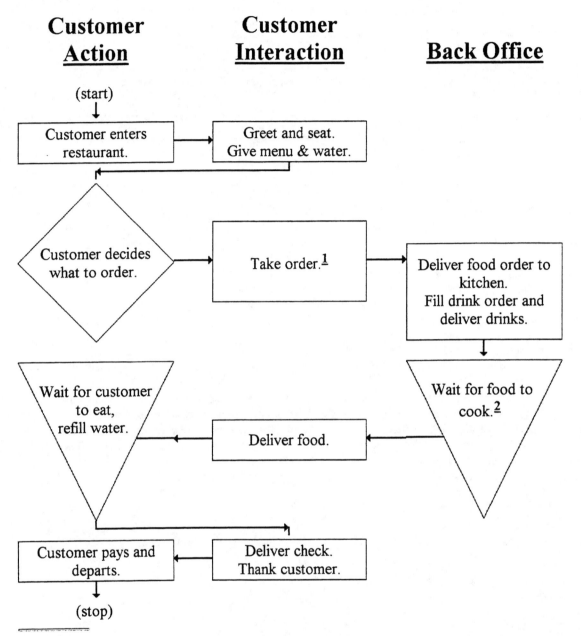

Customer Action

Customer Interaction

Back Office

(start)

Customer enters restaurant.

Greet and seat. Give menu & water.

Customer decides what to order.

Take order.[1]

Deliver food order to kitchen. Fill drink order and deliver drinks.

Wait for customer to eat, refill water.

Wait for food to cook.[2]

Deliver food.

Customer pays and departs.

Deliver check. Thank customer.

(stop)

[1]. Possible fail point: Mistakes in taking order are difficult to recover. Good to confirm order.
[2]. Fail point if wait is too long. Waiter should watch time.

Rendered by FlowViewer, ©1999 SES

The Airline Baggage Handling Process

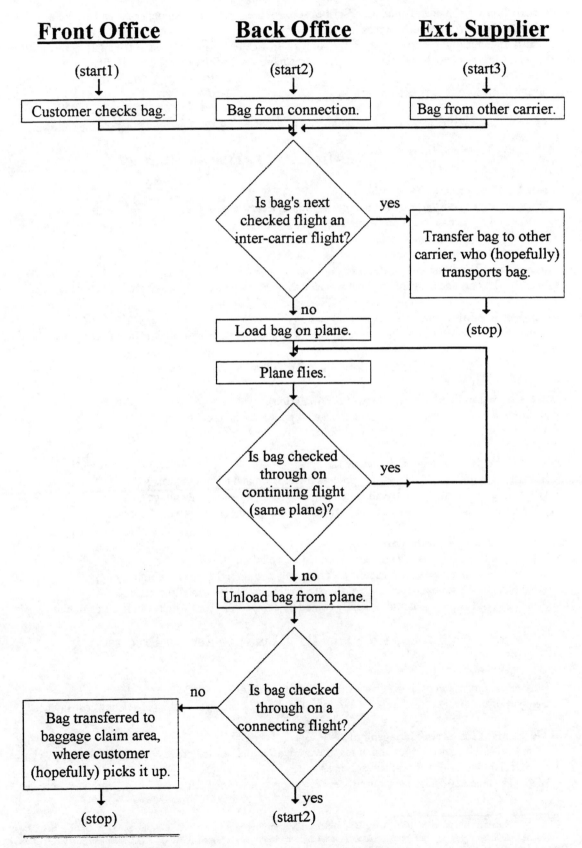

Front Office   Back Office   Ext. Supplier

(start1)   (start2)   (start3)

Customer checks bag.   Bag from connection.   Bag from other carrier.

Is bag's next checked flight an inter-carrier flight? — yes → Transfer bag to other carrier, who (hopefully) transports bag. → (stop)

no → Load bag on plane.

Plane flies.

Is bag checked through on continuing flight (same plane)? — yes →

no → Unload bag from plane.

Is bag checked through on a connecting flight? — no → Bag transferred to baggage claim area, where customer (hopefully) picks it up. → (stop)

yes → (start2)

Apx B

Rendered by FlowViewer, ©1999 SES

Using Service Blueprints

In her article, Jane Kingman-Brundage describes some of the ways service blueprints can be used by different individuals in the organization, such as in strategy formulation, marketing, and human resources[42]. That list can be expanded dramatically by observing how the study of service blueprints can assist the analysis of issues presented *each unit* of this workbook. (Some analysis requires more detailed Service blueprints than others, and sometimes service blueprints need to be redrawn from a different perspective: customer's perspective, front-line employee's perspective, manager's perspective, etc.)

Services Management issues that can be addressed by studying service blueprints include the following:

Issues from Part I - Fundamentals

Unit 1: Unified Services Theory Basics
- What are the key customer inputs that define this as a service process?
- Where in the process do customer inputs enter?
- How are the customer inputs processed?

Unit 2: Services Fundamentals: Planning
- What are key production elements that we need to be concerned about in service process design?

Unit 3: Services Fundamentals: Execution
- What are key elements in the process that should be the focus of day-to-day management?

Issues from Part II: Service Business Strategy

Unit 4: Understanding Non-Services (manufacturing)
- Besides customers, who are our non-customer suppliers to the process?
- What is our relationship to our goods suppliers? Would a partnership be appropriate?

Unit 5: Identifying Strategic Opportunities
- In what ways does/might our service process differ from that of competitors?
- Where in the process should we allocate resources for competitive advantage?
- What parts of the service process would need to change if the process were exported?

Unit 6: Identifying Strategic Threats
- What parts of the process can customers do just as well on their own?
- What parts of the process must customers practically count on the service company to provide?
- What parts of the service process are visible to customers and possibly to competitors?
- What parts of the process could be easily copied by competitors, and which would be difficult to copy?

Issues from Part III - Managing Service Processes

Unit 7: Cost Issues
- How might process steps in the "back office" be run more efficiently?
- Can part of the "front office" process be shifted to the back office to realize efficiency cost savings?

Unit 8: Human Resources Management
- What key skills are needed for new hires to work with in the service process? communications? clerical? decision making and problem solving? others?
- Who makes the key decisions about process direction? the service employee? the customer? company policy?

---

[42] Kingman-Brundage, J. 1989. "The ABSs of Service System Blueprinting." In: M. J. Bitner and L. A. Crosby, Eds.), *Designing a Winning Service Strategy*, American Marketing Association, Chicago. Reprinted in Lovelock, C. H., 1992. *Managing Services: Marketing, Operations, and Human Resources*, Prentice Hall, Englewood Cliffs: New Jersey, pp. 96-102.

Unit 9: Marketing in Services

- Can the customers learn about the quality of the process without actually experiencing it? How? Can the key features of the process be adequately described in print or other media?
- At what service process steps do employees have the opportunity to encourage customers to repurchase or purchase other services?
- What process steps are most costly to the service provider? most valuable to the customer? How does this influence the appropriate price to charge for the service?
- Where in the process do or can customers be given a physical "take away" from the process?

Unit 10: Production and Inventory Control

- Where does most of the waiting take place in the process?
- How might the negative effects of customer waiting be mitigated by changing the process during the waits?

Issues from Part IV - Service Quality and Value

Unit 11: Defining Service Quality

- Where in the service process are customer expectations molded?
- What are the key steps where customer expectations are met or not met?
- Where is service failure most likely to occur?
- What steps can be added to make foolproof key parts of the service process?

Unit 12: Challenges in Delivering Service Quality

- At what point in the service process should customer suggestions and comments be solicited?
- What is the process for acting on customer suggestions and comments?
- Where in the process could inadequate customer inputs cause problems?
- What steps can be included to assure that customer inputs are adequate?

Unit 13: Service Recovery

- What is the service recovery procedure? Who is responsible for resolving service problems?
- What are the steps of the decision process for determining how much to compensate customers experiencing service problems?
- Where in the service process is communications with customers used to assist early detection of possible service problems?

Unit 14: Measuring Service Quality and Productivity

- Where in the service process is quality measured?
- If quality is measured by customer surveys, what process steps are used to gather the survey responses?
- How are quality measures used to help motivate employee attention to crucial elements of the service process?

These are just some examples. Obviously, it would be overwhelming to study all of these issues in one sitting. That is why each unit of this workbook focuses on a particular element. In some units of this workbook you are instructed to create a flowchart (or service blueprint) as part of an Application Exercise. However, the exercise of revisiting your service blueprint for process insights can be valuable in all of the units.

Apx B

The FlowViewer Flowcharting Language

The FlowViewer flowcharting language allows you to graphically produce flowcharts over the Internet. If your course is not using electronic submission of Application Exercise or is not using course workbook website features, you may skip this section.

A detailed description of the FlowViewer language, a tutorial, and many examples are found at http://sampson.byu.edu/workbook/viewer/ on the workbook website. One of the best ways to learn how to use FlowViewer is to consider the examples there and practice with your own examples.

This section contains only a brief introduction the FlowViewer language. Topics which will be discussed include:

Entering FlowViewer Statements

FlowViewer flowcharts can be created in any Application Exercise that is being entered via the website. Further, from your course home page (for registered courses) you can access a FlowViewer practice page. At that page simply enter the FlowViewer statements in the text box and click "View." The rendered flowchart will then be displayed.

Alternatively, you may want to enter your FlowViewer statements in a word processor or in a spreadsheet, then "cut and paste" them into the Application Exercise web form or FlowViewer practice page. One advantage of these methods is that you can spell-check your flowchart before submitting it. If using a word processor or spreadsheet, you probably want to select a fixed-width font such as Courier to help your statements line up nicely on the screen.

Spreadsheets are probably the best method to enter *complex* flowcharts, since you can put different flowchart elements in adjacent rows and columns, and can easily shift things by moving spreadsheet cells. Using spreadsheets for this purpose can be helped by taking advantage of alignment and word-wrap features built in to spreadsheet programs. For more information about using spreadsheets to enter FlowViewer statements, including examples, see http://sampson.byu.edu/workbook/viewer/spreadsheetentry.htm.

Of course, you can always enter FlowViewer statements simply by typing them directly into the Application Exercise web form or FlowViewer practice page. That should be sufficient for all the simple examples listed in this appendix section.

Nevertheless, even simple flowcharts may contain lines that are longer than the width of your screen. This is true of both electronically submitted Application Exercise and FlowViewer commands you enter in the practice page. It is important to understand "word wrap," which is also a feature of most word processing programs.

Word processing programs wrap text that is longer than a page line so that it does not extend beyond the right margin–you do not have to press enter but the word wrapping is automatic. When you press "Enter" in your word processing document, a marker code is inserted indicating the end of a paragraph. "Enter" produces a "hard-return," whereas word wrapping produces a "soft-return." A "soft-return" is equivalent to a space.

In electronically submitted Application Exercise answers and FlowViewer statements, you certainly may have lines that wrap beyond the end of a line. When you look at the screen, you will not be able to tell the difference between a wrapped line and a line that ends with an "Enter." The way you mark the end of an *actual* line is by ending the line with a pound character #. The "#" character at the end of a line signifies a "hard-return." A "#" character anywhere except the end of a line is not a "hard-return"but is simply a "#" character. A return (line-break) that is not preceded by a "#" marker is simply treated as a space.

Therefore, the following text:
```
The quick brown fox jumped over the lazy dog.#
```
is equivalent to:
```
The quick brown
fox jumped over
the lazy dog.#
```

As another example, you might electronically submit the following as part of an Application Exercise answer:

```
The following is an example of a very simple flowchart.#
#begin flowchart#
     (start)#
        !#
<Does the amount on the bank statement equals the amount on the register?>-no-
>[compare each item]#
        !yes#
     (stop)#
#end flowchart#
What do you think?#
```

When the instructor receives it, it might have word-wrap like this...

Apx B

```
The following is an example of a very simple flowchart.#
#begin flowchart#
     (start)#
        !#
<Does the amount on the bank statement equals the amount on
the register?>-no->[compare each item]#
        !yes#
     (stop)#
#end flowchart#
What do you think?#
```

...or like this...

```
The following is an example of a very
simple flowchart.#
#begin flowchart#
       (start)#
          !#
<Does the amount on the bank
statement equals the amount on the
register?>-no->[compare each item]#
          !yes#
       (stop)#
#end flowchart#
What do you think?#
```

It does not matter which of those ways it wraps: It will graphically render the same either way. FlowViewer will concatenate (combine) all lines that do not end with the end-of-line (eol) mark "#".

If you do not care about entering and seeing end-of-line markers (#), then type "#imply eol" (but without the quotes) as the *very first statement* of your Application Exercise answer or FlowViewer practice commands. FlowViewer will then *imply* that a "#" should go at the end of each line, without you entering the "#" markers or seeing them as you are editing.

In the following example, the "#" end-of-line markers are not necessary since none of the lines wrap: (the various flowchart commands will be described below)

```
#imply eol   ;imply the # end-of-line markers without me entering them.
#begin flowchart
(start)
    !
[This is a simple flowchart.]
    !
  (stop)
#end flowchart
```

That example is equivalent to the following:

```
#begin flowchart#
(start)#
    !#
[This is a simple flowchart.]#
    !#
  (stop)#
#end flowchart#
```

When using the "#imply eol" command at the start of an electronically submitted Application Exercise answer, the system implies that it will automatically insert the # characters at the end of each line before sending it to the instructor. This is necessary because some e-mail systems do funny things with word wrapping. Having the "#" end-of-line markers will make it possible for the instructor to graphically view the submitted answer even if the e-mail system does its own word wrapping.

Starting and Ending a Flowchart

FlowViewer flowcharts start with the statement:
```
#begin flowchart#
```
and end with the statement:
```
#end flowchart#
```

Any text between "#begin flowchart#" and "#end flowchart#" is treated as FlowViewer statements. Any text outside of those two markers is rendered as the default browser text. This allows you to have multiple, separate flowcharts in a single Application Exercise answer, as in the following example:

```
I will now present my first flowchart:#
#begin flowchart#
(start)#
    !#
[This is the first simple flowchart.]#
    !#
 (stop)#
#end flowchart#
Which is followed by my second flowchart:#
#begin flowchart#
(start)#
    !#
[This is the second simple flowchart.]#
    !#
 (stop)#
#end flowchart#
And this is simply some text in my Application Exercise answer.
```

Note that in the following section, the "#begin flowchart#" and "#end flowchart#" were not listed for many of the small examples, but must be entered if you want to view the flowchart.

FlowViewer Elements

The following is a brief summary of how to represent the various flowchart elements that were described earlier in this appendix:

- Place process step statements in [brackets]
- Place decision steps in <less-than greater-than symbols>
- Place points in (parentheses)
- Place wait steps in \slash symbols/
- A down-arrow to connect a step with one below is represented with an exclamation point ! (think of it as a line pointing down)

When the FlowViewer commands are rendered (viewed graphically), the process steps appear in rectangles, decisions in diamonds, wait steps in triangles, and the arrows appear as arrows. Due to present technical limits, points appear in parentheses, as an oval with the top and bottom open.

Here is a simple example of a FlowViewer flowchart:
```
#start flowchart#
    (start)#
        !#
[Do something.]#
        !#
    (stop)#
#end flowchart#
```

You can have as much "white space" (spaces or tabs) before or after any FlowViewer elements. The white space is ignored.

In the following subsections, examples of pieces of flowcharts will be given. The #begin flowchart and #end flowchart were omitted from the partial examples, but must be included for flowcharts to render (display graphically).

Decision Alternatives

The outcome of decisions diamonds can be handled in a number of ways.
One outcome can be a point in the next column:
```
<Broken?>-yes->(fix procedure)#
```

The outcome can be a statement or diamond in the next column:
```
<Broken?>-yes->[fix it]#
```
or
```
<Broken?>-yes-><Under warranty?>-yes->[Send it in]#
```

One of the decision outcomes can be listed below:
```
<Broken?>-yes->[fix it]#
    !no                !#
[use it]<----------/#
```

Headings

You can add headings to your flowchart:
```
#heading This is the heading of the flowchart#
```

If you have multiple headings on the same line, separate them by semicolons:
```
#heading First column heading; Second column heading; Third column heading#
```

These column headings will be aligned above separate columns–the topic of the next subsection. If you are not using columns headings, and do not have any semicolons on the heading line, the heading will be the full width.

If you want a heading to span more than one column, enter the number of columns and a colon immediately before the heading text, as in the following example:
```
#heading 2:Two-column heading; 3:Three-column heading#
```

Columns

FlowViewer allows you to place flowchart elements in various columns. By default, each column is approximately 250 pixels wide, so the number of columns viewable on your browser will depend on the resolution of your graphics adapter, or your printer. (If you try to fit more columns on the screen or printed page than supported by your hardware, you will get funny results–in particular, the various columns will not line up properly. You can print more columns with a landscape printer setting than with a portrait setting.)

A good use of columns is to represent the various layers of a service blueprint. You can identify the individual columns with headings:
```
#heading Front office; Back office#
```

If you want the front office steps to be in the first two columns, put a blank heading in column 2:
```
#heading Front office;;Back office#
```
or have the first heading span two columns:
```
#heading 2:Front office; Back office#
```

A more complex example is:
```
#heading Customer interaction; Customer visibility; Front-line employees;
Support staff; Management; Outside suppliers#
```

If you have more than one element on a line, the elements will show up next to each other in adjacent columns:
```
[One step] [Another step]#
```

As mentioned before, you are free to put as much "white space" as you care to before or after any separate element. "White space" is created with spaces and/or tabs.

```
[One step][Another step]#
```
renders the same as
```
[One step]         [Another step]#
```
which renders the same as
```
      [One step][Another step]#
```

If you want all of the statements below to begin on a different column, you can put "#to" statements.
```
#to column 2#
#to next column#
#to prior column#
```

All statements in the flowchart after these statements will start in the designated column. To return to the first column, enter:
```
#to column 1#
```

To have only the current line skip a column, use the double semicolon (;;) column spacer:
```
#to column 1#
[this statement appears in column 1]#
;; ;; [this statement appears in column 3]#
;;[this statement appears in column 2]#
```

Connectors Between Columns

You can connect statements in one column to statements in another column in a number of ways. In most cases, the results look very good. Occasionally, there may be gaps in connectors due to way browsers display FlowViewer results. (This typically occurs when connectors are on the same line as statement elements.) If your connectors do not connect in the manner you would like them to, do not be discouraged. With a little creative effort there is always a way to represent a flowchart that looks great.

The following are some basic connectors.

To connect to the column to the right, use:
```
[column 1 statement]    [column 2 statement]#
        \-------------------->!#
;;                    [another column 2 statement]#
```

To connect to the column to the left, use:
```
[statement]    [statement]#
    !<------------/#
[another]#
```

To connect more than one columns to the left, include spaces in the line
```
[column 1 statement]    ;comment in column 2; [column 3 statement]#
        \------------------- --------------------->!#
;;                      ;;                  [another column 3 statement]#
```

Apx B

You may have noticed by now that you only use down arrows (!) to connect to statements below the current line. To connect to statements above the current line, you should normally use (points).
```
[initial statement]#
    !<-(again)#
[statement]#
    !#
<repeat?>-yes->(again)#
    !no#
  (stop)#
```

An alternate way to connect to statements above is with up-arrows, depicted by the carat ^ symbol. The use of the carat symbol for this purpose does not look very good in text (non-rendered) form, but looks better on the screen. To connect an up-arrow to the left, use

```
<-------\#
```

and to connect an up-arrow to the right, use

```
/-------->#
```

To simply place a vertical line, use "|" which is a split-vertical-bar on most keyboards. One nice thing about this symbol is that it automatically adjusts its height based on the height of other statements on the same line.

The following is an example of some of these elements:

```
  (start)#
     !#
[initial statement]#
     !#
[statement]<------\#
     !          ^#
[another one]    |#
     !           |#
<repeat?>-yes->[prepare to repeat]#
     !no#
  (stop)#
```

To connect both an up-arrow and a down-arrow, use:

```
<-------|#
```

or

```
|-------->#
```

as in the following example:

```
  (start)#
     !#
<question?>-yes->[statement]#
     !no              !#
[statement]<----------|#
     !                ^#
<question?>-yes->[statement]#
     !no#
  (stop)#
```

Or to connect four ways, use "+", as in:

```
;;                                  !#
[Check signature.]<-credit-<Payment method?>-check->[Check driver's license]#
       \----------------------->+<---------------------------/#
;;                                  !#
;;                            [Give receipt]#
```

You need to be careful when using "/" and "\" connectors that you do not confuse them with wait symbols. That confusion only rarely happens, but you should be aware of it. For example,

```
[prepare to wait]----->\wait/#
```

may not render properly because the characters

```
----->\
```

render as a right arrow that turns down. The way to get the wait box to render properly is to separate the right arrow from the wait box with one or more spaces:

```
[prepare to wait]-----> \wait/#
```

Comments

You can put comments on a line with other statements by enclosing the comments in semicolons.
```
[This is a statement];comment about that statement;#
```

Actually, if the statement is the last element on a line, then the closing semicolon can be omitted.
```
[This is a statement];comment about that statement#
```

However, if the comment is not the last element on a line, both opening and closing semicolons need to be included[43]:
```
[First statement];comment about first statement;[Second statement]#
```

If you put a semicolon comment inside of an element, it will simply appear as typed.
```
[This is a statement;comment about that statement;]#
```

To put a comment inside of a flowchart element, you can use a footnote as described below.

Non-Rendering Comments

Comments that you do not want to appear on the rendered flowchart can be enclosed in {braces}:
```
[This is a statment]{I need to remember to spell check this flowchart}#
```

The braces can be used to temporarily comment out parts of the flowchart on a line:
```
[statement to display]{[statement to comment out]}#
```

To comment out an entire line so that it does not display, start the line with "#rem" for remark:
```
#rem [commented out statement]->[another statement commented out]
```

The #rem command can also be used to record notes about an exercise answer that you are still working on. When you electronically submit an Application Exercise answer to your instructor, any non-rendering comments in the answer will be included (unless you delete them before submitting it).

Footnotes

FlowViewer allows the inclusion of footnotes by enclosing footnote text in the ~tilde~ symbol. Footnotes are a good way to comment about specific portions of a flowchart, since they take up little space in the body of the flowchart. Footnotes are also a good way for the instructor to give feedback to students about what they have submitted. Unlike regular comments (with semicolons), footnote markers can appear inside of any element and even outside of the "#begin flowchart#" and "#end flowchart#" markers.

For example:
```
[Tell the customer to go fly a kite~Is this a good idea?~]#
```

The footnote text will appear below in the rendered document, with hyperlinks to and from the location of the reference. If you want footnotes to appear earlier in the rendered document, enter
```
#place footnotes#
```
at the location of the footnotes. Note that this command will only place whatever footnotes have been encountered *up to that point*. Any footnotes that have not been placed by the bottom of the document will be placed at the bottom.

---

[43] If desired, you can specify how much horizontal space to take up by the comment by entering a number followed by a colon at the start of the comment. Unlike with headings, the number is not the number of columns, but the number of *parts* of columns (roughly 3 parts per column). The following is an example:
```
#[statement];1:narrow comment;[statement];4:wider comment;[statement]
```

Thick-border Elements

To emphasize some element borders, use multiple adjacent markers. For example:
```
[this is a regular statement box]#
[[an emphasized statement box]]#
[[[[[this is an extremely emphasized statement box]]]]]#
```

Actually, all FlowViewer is counting is the number of "[" statement markers, and ignores multiple closed markers. That last statement will render the same as this one:
```
[[[[[this is an extremely emphasized statement box]#
```

Due to graphical limitations, thick borders are not available for every flowchart element, and the amount of thickness is limited. (For [statements] the limit is quite large since the thickness is the border width, but for other elements each available thickness requires separate graphic images.) If you are wondering if thick borders are available for a particular element, simply try to render that element with extra markers. For example, a thicker arrow can be created with multiple bars:
```
     !         ;a regular connecting arrow#
     !!        ;an emphasized arrow#
     !!!       ;a more emphasized arrow#
 !   !!!       ;a regular arrow in one column, and a thick arrow in the next#
```

More examples of thick borders are at the workbook website (http://sampson.byu.edu/workbook/viewer).

Formatting Flowcharts with HTML

(This section is a bit technical, for which I apologize. It is necessary because of the way FlowViewer uses HTML to render flowcharts. **Feel free to skip this section and continue with the next section: Entering and Finding Mistakes.**)

In some ways the appearance of flowchart elements can be changed by using features of HTML, the HyperText Markup Language. This includes tags, special character codes, and element attributes.

HTML Tags

HTML tags can be used to modify the appearance of text. They can be included inside *or outside* of the `#begin flowchart#`...`#end flowchart#` markers. For example, to bold a phrase use the `<b></b>` tags:
```
This is <b>very important</b> to remember.#
```

Within flowchart statements, HTML tags could be confused with decision diamond markers. To prevent that problem, within flowcharts proceed all HTML tags with an underline.

```
#begin flowchart#
<Are there fewer than _<b>3_</b> customers waiting in line?>#
    !_<b>no_</b>#
#end flowchart#
```

Pretty much any HTML tag can be used. Examples include:
```
_<i>italics_</i>
_<font size=+2>bigger font_</font>
_<font color=Red>red text_</font>
_<h1>first level heading font_</h1>
_<h2>second level heading font_</h2>
_<ul>_<li>list_<li>of_<li>items_</ul>
_<ol>_<li>numbered_<li>list_<li>of_<li>items_</ol>
_<p>paragraph of text_</p>
```

Just remember when using HTML tags with flowchart statements, precede each tag with an underline symbol.

HTML Special Character Codes

You can insert special symbols in a flowchart by taking advantage of HTML special character codes. HTML character codes start with an ampersand "&" and end with a semicolon ";". For example the HTML code for the temperature degree symbol is "°" which can be inserted in any text.

```
<Is the temperature greater than 32&deg; Fahrenheit?>-no->(freezing)#
```

For that question, it may be desired to use the greater-than symbol ">" instead of "greater than." That could be a problem, because > would mark the end of the decision text. A solution is to use the HTML character code for "greater-than," which is >

```
<Is the temperature &gt;32&deg; Fahrenheit?>-no->(freezing)#
```

The less-than symbol is represented with <

```
<How many customers in line?>-2 or more->[open another cash register]#
    !&lt;2#
```

One particularly useful HTML character code is ­ which produces a soft hyphen. Browsers let the word after the soft hyphen wrap to the next line if necessary. (Minus signs "-" are generally non-breaking.)

```
[Join the book&shy;of&shy;the&shy;month club.]#
```

Spaces in text will be a line break if at the line needs to wrap. To prevent a space from breaking at the end of a line, use   as the non-breaking space symbol:

```
[Move from location A to location B]#
```

Other characters can be used by entering &#n; where n is a decimal ANSI codes (many ASCII codes will also work). At this writing, a big list of such symbols and codes is at http://www.cs.hks.se/html/iso-entities.html. For example, to enter a tilde ~ character use "~" to avoid confusion with a footnote mark. The code "`" produces an underline symbol, in case you need to put one right before a <decision marker>. Or a minus sign can be entered with "-" which can be used to avoid confusion with a horizontal line:

```
<Is it positive or negative?>-&#45;->(negative)#
```

Word-Wrap in Flowchart Viewing

The previous section titled "Entering Flowchart Commands" discussed word-wrap at the time commands are entered or e-mailed. This section is about how words wrap when they are graphically displayed (rendered).

Text that fits within rendered elements will wrap to multiple lines if necessary in your browser. Presently, browsers do not automatically hyphenate words. If you do not like the way the text is wrapping inside of a flowchart element, you can use the "­" soft-hyphen symbol described above. Or, you can force a hyphen in a word by inserting "-_
" which is a hyphen followed by an HTML line "break" tag.

```
<Do we appreciate the manner in which this text wraps?>#
```
might become
```
<Do we apprec-_<br>iate the man-_<br>ner in which this text wraps?>#
```

Apx B

However, since different browsers can have different font settings, the best looking hyphenation on one browser might not look good given a different font. Most browsers have the capability to enlarge or reduce the font. If you change the font you may need to change any hyphenation.

The
 HTML tag can be useful in a number of contexts, such as headings:
```
#heading This is such a long_<br>heading that we want_<br> it to appear
on multiple lines.#
```

Changing Element Size and Alignment

FlowViewer renders (graphically displays) most basic flowchart elements in a space that is 200 pixels (screen points) wide. The height of flowchart elements can vary somewhat. For example, a statement with a little text:
`[Fix it]#`
will be shorter than one with much text:
`[Repair the broken part by replacing the outside fitting]#`
which will likely wrap.

However, the vertical space occupied by multiple elements on a line will be the height of the tallest object on the line. The following example will render in a space as tall as the largest element:
`[Fix it]--->[Repair the broken part by replacing the outside fitting]#`

In particular, default-sized decision diamonds and wait triangles are 200 pixels tall (the default), even if they only contain a small amount of text. As such, any decision statements that appear on a line with a <decision> or \wait/ element will need to also be 200 pixels. In the following example, the "fix it" statement will be 200 pixels tall, due to the 200 pixel tall decision on the same line:
`<Broken?>-yes->[Fix it]#`

It is harder for FlowViewer to know how tall a [statement] should be when it appears with other larger statements, such with `[Fix it]` in this example:
`[Fix it]--->[Repair the broken part by replacing the outside fitting]#`
The height of the larger statement will depend on the font settings of your browser.

To force a statement to be a certain minimum height, enter {`set height=n`} *inside* of the statement markers, where *n* is the number of pixels tall. For example, to make `[Fix it]` 90 pixels tall, enter:
`[{set height=90}Fix it]--->[Repair broken part by replacing outside fitting]#`

You can actually set the `width` of some statements as well, if you do not want the 200 pixel default.

Points in (parentheses) are only as big as the display font. Therefore, a point on the same line with a tall element may have a lot of space around it. FlowViewer attempts to position points in the space so that they look good. For example, with
`<Broken?>-yes->(fix)#`
the (`fix`) point will be show near the arrow. However, when points are attached to elements on different lines, FlowViewer may be unable to provide nice alignment.

```
<Broken?>-yes-><Can it be fixed?>-no->[buy a new one]#
   !no                !yes                    !#
(continue)    <Is it under warranty?>-no->(pay)#
```

With this example, there will be two points, (`continue`) and (`pay`) on the same line as a 200 pixel tall decision. FlowViewer aligns both in the vertical middle of the 200 pixel space. The (`pay`) point aligns with the arrow to the left of it, but not the arrow coming down from above. If pay were a statement element it would be near both arrows. The (`continue`) point will have extra space between it and the "no" arrow from the <`Broken?`> decision above. It would be better if the (`continue`) point were vertically aligned at the top of the space taken by that row. This can be accomplished by entering {`set valign=top`} as a hidden comment *inside* of the (`continue`) point marker (valign stands for vertical alignment):

```
<Broken?>-yes----------------><Can it be fixed?>-no->[buy a new one]#
    !no                                !yes                    !#
({set valign=top}continue)      <Is it under warranty?>-no->[pay]#
```

Values for valign can be top, middle, or bottom. You can also specify the horizontal alignment with {`set align=left`} or {`set align=center`} or {`set align=right`}. (The default is often center.) Multiple settings should be separated by a space, such as {`set valign=middle align=right`}.

For more information about these advanced formatting features, see the viewer section of the workbook website.

Entering and Finding Mistakes

If you enter a statement that FlowViewer does not recognize, the results will simply show up as text. Click the "Back" button on your browser and correct the statement.

To help you find problems in your FlowViewer statements, you can direct FlowViewer to show the source text for each line it is about to render:
```
#show text#
```

The text you entered to create each line of your flowchart will display just before it is rendered.

To turn the show text feature off part way through a flowchart, enter:
```
#stop showing text#
```
or
```
#hide text#
```

Feel free to experiment with FlowViewer statements. If there is a feature you think it would be nice for FlowViewer to have, or if you experience a bug in FlowViewer, send a note to webmaster@sampson.byu.edu.

Entering Wide Flowcharts

As mentioned in the "Entering FlowViewer Statements" section above, probably the best method to enter complex flowcharts is by using a spreadsheet. Your flowchart can be entered in a spreadsheet, then it can be "cut and pasted" into the Application Exercise web form or to the FlowViewer practice page.

If you choose to use a spreadsheet to enter your flowchart, you may want to take advantage of spreadsheet features such as word wrap, spell checking, column widths, and cell alignment. Those features can make the flowchart look good in the spreadsheet, and then look even better when rendered by FlowViewer. For information and examples about using these types of spreadsheet features when entering FlowViewer statements see http://sampson.byu.edu/workbook/viewer/spreadsheetentry.htm on the workbook website.

Keep in mind that even though you can view a wide flowchart, whether you can print it or not depends on the printing capabilities of your web browser. Some browsers will truncate or scrunch flowcharts that are wider than the printed page. You may need to scale your flowchart to get it to fit on a printed page. Information about scaling the size of a flowchart is found at http://sampson.byu.edu/workbook/viewer/scaling.htm on the workbook website. Printing flowcharts is the topic of the next subsection.

Printing FlowViewer Graphics

The following are some basic hints for printing flowcharts so that they look as nice on the printed page as they do on the screen. I apologize for the complexity of the following discussion. Unfortunately, working with printers is sometimes a complex process.

Apx B

Printing Multiple Columns

As just mentioned, when you use multiple columns in your flowchart, all of the columns may show up on your screen, but may be "scrunched" on your printed page, unless you reduce the size of your flowchart. If you print in landscape mode you can print more columns. Landscape mode is a function of your printer properties (or settings). From your browser's "File" menu, select "Print" or "Print Setup." Select the printer property or settings. Each printer driver has its own way to select landscape printing–but it is usually pretty clear.

Printing Diamonds and Triangles

When you render (i.e. view the graphical results of) FlowViewer statements, decision and wait symbols appear with text on top of a shape symbol. The best way this is accomplished depends on what web browser you are using. Decision and wait symbols can be rendered one of two ways:
- as background graphics, or
- as layers.

Most recent versions of Netscape® Navigator® and Microsoft® Internet Explorer® will display background graphics, but only the latest versions will allow them to print background graphics. (A background graphic is a graphic that appears behind a table's contents.) Old browsers may not even display background graphics, meaning decision diamonds and wait triangles will not appear on the screen–you will either have to draw them in or upgrade your browser.

With the latest versions of Netscape Navigator (or Communicator), you can print background graphics by selecting "Page Setup" from the "File" menu. One of the Page Options is "Print backgrounds." If you check that option then the backgrounds will print. (Be careful if that setting resets from one session to the next. I have noticed that the program sometimes does *not* print background graphics unless I clear then re-set the setting–a Netscape Navigator bug that will probably be remedied in versions after 4.06.)

With the latest versions of Microsoft Internet Explorer, you have the opportunity to select options (such as by selecting "Internet Options" from the "View" menu.) Way down the list of "Advanced" options is a choice for printing, including "Print background colors and images." Check that option to print the flowcharts. (Also be careful that the setting does not reset between sessions.)

FlowViewer attempts to detect what browser you are using and likely defaults to rendering diamonds and triangles with background graphics. If FlowViewer attempts to render diamonds and triangles some other way, you can force it to render them using background graphics by placing the statement:
`#use background graphics#`
right after the `#begin flowchart#` command.

If for some reason your browser does not support printing background graphics, you can still print decision diamonds and wait triangles if your browser supports layers. The layers feature allows shapes and text to be stacked on one another on the screen and on the printed page. One advantage of layers is that they allow decision diamonds and wait triangles to be scaled, such as:
`<{set height=100}This diamond is 100 pixels tall>#`

For more information about scaling the size of your flowchart, see
http://sampson.byu.edu/workbook/viewer/scaling.htm on the workbook website.

To render a flowchart using layers, place the statement:
`#use layers#`
right after the `#begin flowchart#` command.

The one drawback of layers is that the alignment of diamonds and triangles on the screen may be different than on your printer. This is because text on the screen automatically comes with a small left margin, but layers have no left margin. Therefore, a document that looks well-aligned on the screen may look slightly misaligned when printed. To remedy this problem, enter the statement:
`#to print#`
right after the `#use layers#` command. The `#to print#` command does not compensate for the screen left margin, making the screen flowchart look slightly misaligned. However, it should look okay when printed. If you have problems using layers or want more information see http://sampson.byu.edu/workbook/viewer/layers.htm.

If your browser supports layers and your flowchart is rendered using layers, then the diamonds and triangles should print without changing any print settings. If your browser does not support layers, and you attempt to

`#use layers#`, then diamonds, triangles, and possibly other graphics will not appear on the correct positions on the screen.

At this writing, Netscape Navigator 4.07 and Microsoft Internet Explorer 4.0 are both available *for free* at each company's website. Those browsers support both layers and printing background graphics, allowing you to choose how you want diamonds and triangles to render. So, if you do not like the way flowcharts print from your current browser, then get a new browser.

The other symbols (besides decision diamonds and wait triangles) and text used in flowcharts will print with most any graphical browser. Although diamonds and triangles will not print with older browsers, they will appear correctly on the screen.

Other FlowViewer Commands

One advantage of the FlowViewer command language is that we can continually add new commands and features which are immediately available to everyone who uses FlowViewer on the system. You can read about other features that have been added to FlowViewer at http://sampson.byu.edu/workbook/viewer on the workbook website.

For example, at this writing work has begun to develop a matrix viewer that will allow two-dimensional matrices to be created as part of Application Exercises. Information about that and other future features will be posted at http://sampson.byu.edu/workbook/viewer on the workbook website.

If you have a suggestion about how to enhance FlowViewer, send your idea to the workbook website webmaster at webmaster@sampson.byu.edu.

Apx B

Summary of Basic FlowViewer Commands

```
[statement]    ;Process steps in brackets.
    \wait/     ;Process wait steps in slashes.
<decision?>    ;Process decisions in less-than greater-than symbols.
    (point)    ;Process points in parentheses.
       !       ;Down arrow is an exclamation mark.
       ^       ;Up arrow is a carat symbol.
       |       ;Vertical bar is a (split) vertical bar symbol.
/----/, \-----!, etc.        ;Various symbols show column change in different directions.
;comment;      ;Enclose comments in semicolons.
            ;Comment to end of line do not need closing semicolon.
{text}                 ;Comments in braces do not display when rendered.
~footnote text~    ;Enclose footnote text in tilde symbols.
#place footnotes#  ;Location for any footnotes encountered up to that point.  Default is at bottom.
```

```
#begin flowchart ;name=beach.flo#
#heading 3:The Natural Tanning Process#
\wait until Saturday/<-no-<Saturday?>-almost->[think about beach]#
        !                      !yes                        !#
        \---- ---->[go to the beach]<------------/#
;;                         !#
;;                  \bask in the sun/<-----------\#
;;                         !                          ^#
[go to pharmacy]<-burnt-<tan enough?>-no->[turn over~apply lotion~]#
        !                         !yes#
[get sunburn lotion]---->[go home]----->(stop)#
#end flowchart#
```

Miscellaneous Commands

```
#begin flowchart#            ;Marks the start of some FlowViewer commands.  (Text may precede.)
#end flowchart#              ;Marks the end of those FlowViewer commands.  (Text may follow.)

#heading (what)#             ;Print a heading.
#heading 2:two-column heading; 3:three-column heading#

#to column 1#                ;Statements below to appear in column 1.
#to next column#
#to prior column#
;;[statements...]#           ;Double-semicolon tabs current line to next column.

#show text#                  ;Show each line before it is rendered; helps check for mistakes.
#hide text#                  ;Stop showing each line before it is rendered.
#use background graphics#        ;Use background graphics for diamonds and triangles.
#use layers#                 ;Use browser's layers feature to display diamonds and triangles
#to print#                   ;If using layers, aligns diamonds and triangles relative to left of printed page.

#imply eol   ;"#" end-of-line markers will not be typed, but must be implied.  This *must* be first line if used.
```

Other commands and examples are at http://sampson.byu.edu/workbook/viewer on the workbook website.

Appendix C:
Quantitative Tools

This section goes with the Quantitative Analysis sub-sections in Units 2 and 3. Each of the Service Business Principles in Units 2 and 3 can be used to introduce specific types of quantitative analysis. This appendix introduces the student to one or more quantitative tools that can be used to help make decisions in service operations planning or execution.

The student should read the Service Business Principle section in Unit 2 or 3, and should have a try at the Simulation Exercise *before* reading the corresponding information in this section. This helps the student explore the potential challenges in resolving operational decisions, and understand more how the quantitative analysis contributes to the decision process.

The Use of Quantitative Analysis

Quantitative tools are often used to *assist* in making decisions, but you as the manager makes the ultimate decisions. Effective use of quantitative techniques requires understanding the inherent assumptions and correctly interpreting the results. I have often said in class that companies are better off hiring operations analysts who are confessedly ignorant at quantitative analysis methods than hiring those who know quantitative techniques but ignore the assumptions.

Quantitative Topics Covered in this Appendix

Related to Service Business Principle

Forecasting Analysis: Basic Time-Series Methods . . . . SBP 2a: *Simultaneous Production and Consumption*

Capacity Scheduling Analysis: The Critical Fractile Rule . . . . SBP 2b: *Time-Perishable Capacity*

Location Planning Analysis: The Center of Gravity Method . . . . SBP 2c: *Customer Proximity*

Labor Planning Analysis: Forecasting with Seasonality . . . . SBP 2d: *Labor Intensity*

Optimization Analysis: Linear Programming . . . . SBP 2e: *Perishable Output Illusion*

Queuing Analysis: Analytical Queuing Theory . . . . SBP 3a: *Customers in Inventory*

Inventory Theory Analysis: The Economic Order Quantity
      and Safety Stock Approaches . . . . SBP 3b: *Intangibility Myth*

Project Scheduling Analysis: The Critical Path Method (CPM) . . . . SBP 3c: *Heterogeneous Production*

Facility Layout Analysis: Process Layouts . . . . SBP 3d: *Difficulty in Measuring Output*

Statistical Process Control (SPC) Analysis:
      Control Charts for Variables . . . . SBP 3e: *Difficulty in Maintaining Quality*

Apx C

Forecasting Analysis:
Basic Time-Series Methods

*Read this in conjunction with **SBP 2a: Simultaneous Production and Consumption**.*
(You should complete the SBP 2a Quantitative Analysis section before proceeding here.)

There are many ways to forecast demand. The following are some examples:
- Judgement methods, such as expert opinion.
- Counting methods, where we count the number of people who *say* they will be future customers. A market survey is an example of a counting method.
- Time-series methods, where we take prior demand date (a "time series") and project it into the future.
- Causal models, where factors which relate to demand are used to predict demand. For example, a ski resort may determine that the number of customers on a given weekend is a function of the amount of snow.

Here we will consider a few time-series methods.

The most simple time-series method is *naive extrapolation*. We "extrapolate" when we take a series of past data and project it into future. Naive extrapolation can be accomplished by simply using the last period of actual data as the forecast for the future. This is to say that the forecast for a given period (t) is the actual from the prior period (t-1). This is mathematically represented as: $F_t = A_{t-1}$.

The prior period may have random "noise" in it, which decreases its value as a forecast. One way to overcome some of the noise is to have the forecast be a function of the prior few periods of actual data. An example is a *moving average*. A three-period moving average has the forecast being the average of the prior three periods of actual demand data. In general, an *n*-period moving average is:

$$F_t = \frac{\sum_{i=1}^{n} A_{(t-i)}}{n}$$

You will note that each of the prior *n* periods has equal weight in calculating the forecast. It might be desirable to have more recent period have more weight, which can be accomplished with a *weighted moving average*, which is represented by the following equations:

$$F_t = \sum_{i=1}^{n} W_i A_{(t-i)} \quad where \quad \sum_{i=1}^{n} W_i = 1$$

For example, if $W_1 = 0.5$, $W_2 = 0.25$, and $W_3 = 0.25$ then the prior period would have twice the weight of the actual values from 2 and 3 periods ago.

A technique called *exponential smoothing* also bases a forecast on prior data, giving the most weight to the most recent period. If we a forecast and an actual value for the prior period, then we can calculate a forecast as:

$$F_t = F_{t-1} + \alpha(A_{t-1} - F_{t-1})$$

Therefore, the forecast for a given period is the forecast for the prior period adjusted by alpha (α) times the **error** from the prior forecast, which is $A_{t-1} - F_{t-1}$. When that error is positive then we under-forecasted in the prior period. When that error is negative then we over-forecasted. When $\alpha=1$ then we add all of the error back in, causing the forecast to be simply the prior actual. This can be an over-reactive forecast, that naively follows any noise in the data.

When $\alpha=0$ then we completely ignore the error, and the forecast is simply the same as the forecast for the prior period. This naive approach ignores the change in the past period from its forecast.

Alpha values between 0 and 1 each possess a degree of sensitivity to changes in the actual data time series. As a rule of thumb, α values should be selected in the range of 0.1 to 0.3.

One nice thing about exponential smoothing is that calculating a forecast only requires knowing the past period's forecast and actual value. All of the prior forecasts are captured in the current forecast.

Exponential smoothing is somewhat like a weighted moving average. You will note that the prior period's actual data (A_{t-1}) has a weight of α in calculating the forecast, with the remaining $(1-\alpha)$ weight going to the prior forecast. That prior forecast includes a weight of α for the actual of the period before that (A_{t-2}). Therefore, the effective weight of A_{t-2} on F_t is $\alpha(1-\alpha)$. Likewise, we could calculate that the effective weight of A_{t-3} on F_t is $\alpha^2(1-\alpha)$, and the effective weight of A_{t-4} $\alpha^3(1-\alpha)$, etc. That is why the technique is called exponential smoothing: because the effective weight of each prior period of actual data is an exponential function of the number of periods ago of the actual data.

One issue with using the exponential smoothing forecasting technique is that at some point you need to come up with a starting forecast. There is usually no forecast available for the very first period of your prior data. For the second period of prior data, you can use the first period actual as the forecast. This naive extrapolation gets the forecasting started. Then, you can use the exponential smoothing equation to calculate the forecast for the third period and for all subsequent periods.

Other Reading

The following is reading about Forecasting from other texts, which you may be using in your course. Your instructor will inform you which if any of this reading you are accountable for, and may assign problems or other exercises from that reading.

- Fitzsimmons2 chapter 16 on Forecasting Demand for Services.
- Chase8 chapter 13 on Forecasting.
- Stevenson6 chapter 3 on Forecasting.
- Heizer5 chapter 5 on Forecasting.

Simulation Exercise

You should re-run the simulation *autoshop.mod*. Again, print your final results and submit them as directed by your instructor (either on paper, or electronically if your course is registered on the workbook website). Hopefully your results will be improved by the use of analytical methods described above. The following is a hint about how to run the simulation with improved results:

Redo the simulation exercise using a time-series forecasting technique.

Applying Forecasting in Your Target Service Business

How might Forecasting analysis be applied in your target service business? Consider the following questions with regard to your target business:

① If a time-series forecasting technique is used, how easy would it be to gather historical demand data? (Keep in mind that there can be a big difference between *sales* and *demand*. Sales are usually observable, but demand often is not.)
② What factors might make historical data unreliable in predicting future demand?
③ What other types of information might be helpful in determining accurate forecasts?

Apx C

Increasing the Simulation Challenge (Levels)

Simulation Exercises can be run at higher "levels" for students interested in a more challenging problem. The following is how higher levels effects the *autoshop.mod* simulation: When you select higher levels, the data being forecasted becomes increasingly complex.

Capacity Scheduling Analysis:
The Critical Fractile Rule

*Read this in conjunction with **SBP 2b: Time-Perishable Capacity**.*
(You should complete the SBP 2b Quantitative Analysis section before proceeding here.)

If the costs of insufficient capacity are the same as the costs of excess capacity then it makes sense to plan capacity to exactly meet the best forecast we have for demand. If the costs are different, then it makes more sense to use an analysis technique such as the "Critical Fractile Rule" to plan capacity.

The Critical Fractile Rule is also called the "Perishable Inventory Model" or the "Newsperson" problem. The newsperson sold newspapers on the street corner in a busy city. He was trying to determine how many newspapers to order for the next day. He paid 30¢ for each newspaper, and charged each customer 50¢. Therefore, if he did not have enough newspapers he could not get any more papers, so lost the 20¢ profit for each additional customer (the cost of under-ordering, or c_u). If he had too many newspapers, he would have to throw them out at the end of the day, thus losing the 30¢ he paid for each paper (the cost of over-ordering, or c_o). Since the cost of over-ordering was greater than the cost of under-ordering, it made sense to bias his order on the low side.

If the newsperson has a forecast that is a probability distribution, called $\tilde{d}$, he can use the Critical Fractile Rule to determine the optimal number of newspapers to order. The Critical Fractile is calculated as
$$C.F. = c_u/(c_u+c_o)$$

First, our newsperson needs to calculate a cumulative probability distribution, which is the probability that demand is less than a certain amount. The cumulative probability distribution for a normal distribution is found at the back of most text books involving statistics. Alternatively it can be calculated using a spreadsheet function. For example, in Quattro Pro the spreadsheet function is @NORMINV(cf,mean,sd) where cf is the computed critical fractile percent, mean is the mean of the normal distribution, and sd is the standard deviation of that distribution.

The newsperson would select the number of newspapers equal such that the cumulative probability distribution equals the critical fractile. For example, if the newsperson forecasted sales of 100 newspapers with a standard deviation of 25 papers, normally distributed, and a critical fractile of 20/(20+30)=0.4, then he should order the number of newspapers for the 0.4 point on the cumulative distribution. A cumulative normal distribution table shows a z-value of 0.345 at the 0.4 probability level. That z-value table has a mean of 0 and standard deviation of 1. Therefore, to convert to a mean of 100 and standard deviation of 25 we multiply the z value by the desired standard deviation and then add the desired mean, or: (0.345 x 25)+100 = 108.625 newspapers. For simplicity we simply round to the nearest newspaper, and order 109 newspapers.

Relevance to Services Planning

The critical fractile rule is also called the Perishable Inventory Model because it is applicable in product ordering situations where the product is perishable, with reduced value if it is not immediately sold. The critical fractile rule is useful in services capacity planning because–according to this Service Business Principle–capacity is often time-perishable. Answering the important question of how much capacity to plan for is greatly helped by analyzing the costs of over capacity and the costs of under capacity.

Other Reading

The following is reading about Capacity Scheduling from other texts, which you may be using in your course. Your instructor will inform you which if any of this reading you are accountable for, and may assign problems or other exercises from that reading.

- Fitzsimmons2 pages 369-372 on the Single-Period Model for Perishable Goods.
- Fitzsimmons2 chapter 13 on Managing Capacity and Demand (critical fractile is discussed on pages 392-395).
- Chase8 chapter 7 on Strategic Capacity Planning.

- Stevenson6 chapter 5 on Capacity Planning (beginning on page 208). Stevenson6 contains a supplement to chapter 2 on Decision Making, which includes capacity planning decisions.
- Heizer5 chapter 7 on Process Strategy and Capacity Planning.

Simulation Exercise

You should re-run the simulation *bakery.mod*. Again, print your final results and submit them as directed by your instructor (either on paper, or electronically if your course is registered on the workbook website). Hopefully your results will be improved by the use of analytical methods described above. The following is a hint about how to run the simulation with improved results:

You might use the critical fractile rule to determine how many cakes to bake each day.

Applying Capacity Scheduling in Your Target Service Business

How might Capacity Scheduling analysis be applied in your target service business? Consider the following questions with regard to your target business:

① In planning capacity, how would the cost of under-capacity (c_u) be estimated? (Some of the costs may be easily quantified, others may not.)
② How might the cost of over-ordering (c_o) be estimated?
③ Is there reason to believe that the distribution of demand is *not* normally distributed? What factors or events might cause demand to be some random distribution other than normal? (The critical fractile can still be calculated for non-normal distributions, but it can be a little more complex.)

Increasing the Simulation Challenge (Levels)

Simulation Exercises can be run at higher "levels" for students interested in a more challenging problem. The following is how higher levels effects the *bakery.mod* simulation: When you select higher levels, the cost values and sales data make the problem increasingly challenging.

Apx C

Location Planning Analysis:
The Center of Gravity Method

*Read this in conjunction with **SBP 2c: Customer Proximity**.*
(You should complete the SBP 2c Quantitative Analysis section before proceeding here.)

One technique to assist in making location decisions is the "center of gravity" method. With this method, the coordinates for the optimal location are chosen as an average of the coordinates of the various neighborhoods which are weighted according to the number of customers expected from each neighborhood.

For example, imagine there are three neighborhoods: Applegate, Barstow, and Canterberry. We might draw a grid over a map of the area with horizontal and vertical coordinates, and find Applegate is centered at (5,3) meaning 5 coordinate points horizontally and 3 coordinate points vertically. Barstow is centered at (4,2) and Canterberry is centered at (3,6). The average of the horizontal, also called the x-axis, coordinates is (5+4+3)/3 = 4.0. So, we might assume that it would be good to centrally locate the fitness club we would put it at 4.0 on the horizontal axis. However, this fails to consider that there may be many more customers coming from one neighborhood than from another. Imagine that Applegate contains 200 potential customers, Barstow contains 75, and Canterberry contains 25. We would probably want to be nearer to Applegate than to Canterberry. Therefore, we use the customer counts as weights, recognizing that of 300 total potential customers, 200/300 = 66.6% come from Applegate. The weighting can be accomplished by multiplying each coordinate value by the corresponding customer forecast, summing across all customer locations, and dividing by the sum of the customer forecasts. For this example, the optimal horizontal coordinate is:

$$x = \frac{(5 \times 200) + (4 \times 75) + (3 \times 25)}{(200 + 75 + 25)} = 4.58$$

Therefore, the optimal horizontal coordinate is 4.58 on the grid. So also, the vertical (y) coordinate can be calculated:

$$y = \frac{(3 \times 200) + (2 \times 75) + (6 \times 25)}{(200 + 75 + 25)} = 3.00$$

Locating the fitness club at exactly (4.58, 3.00) on the coordinate system may not be possible, since there may not be any available land at that location. The decision maker may choose a location that is feasible and near that location. Recall that the calculation is simply based on estimates on number of customers, which may vary in accuracy. Also, the distances to the neighborhoods are more than a function of map coordinates, since roads may be direct or may wind around. Also, the center of gravity method does not consider the subjective factors listed above. However, this method does provide useful information that can help make the location decision.

When is the Center of Gravity technique appropriate? As with all quantitative analysis techniques, the results are only as good as the assumptions inherent in the model. The Center of Gravity technique inherently assumes that the "cost of inconvenience" for each customer is proportional to the square of the Euclidean distance to the service location. (The Euclidean distance is the distance in a strait line, "as the bird flies.") For example, it is four times as inconvenient to travel to a service location that is two miles away than one which is only one mile away.

Is this a reasonable assumption? In many cases it is. For one thing it captures the commonly accepted idea of "increasing marginal costs," which is that the incremental cost increases the farther from the target (of zero travel). The use of Euclidean distances is not always appropriate, such as in areas where road layouts prevent direct travel between locations. In such cases "brute force" analysis may be needed, such as enumeration of all possible service locations. Nevertheless, in many situations, the Euclidean distance is as good of a distance estimate as can be easily calculated.

Other Reading

The following is reading about Location Planning from other texts, which you may be using in your course. Your instructor will inform you which if any of this reading you are accountable for, and may assign problems or other exercises from that reading.

- Fitzsimmons2 chapter 7 on Service Facility Location.
- Chase8 chapter 9 on Facility Location.
- Stevenson6 chapter 8 on Location Planning and Analysis.
- Heizer5 chapter 8 on Location Strategies.

Simulation Exercise

You should re-run the simulation *fitness.mod*. Again, print your final results and submit them as directed by your instructor (either on paper, or electronically if your course is registered on the workbook website). Hopefully your results will be improved by the use of analytical methods described above. The following is a hint about how to run the simulation with improved results:

Use the center of gravity method to calculate the optimal location. The competitor will not choose the same location that you choose, but will attempt to select a good location.

Applying Location Planning in Your Target Service Business

How might Location Planning analysis be applied in your target service business? Consider the following questions with regard to your target business:

① Is distance to the service an important factor in whether customers select a company in your target service business?

② Would Euclidean distances be an appropriate way to estimate the distance from customers to the service location? Why or why not?

③ Besides distance to customers, what other major factors will influence whether customers select a particular company in your target service business?

Increasing the Simulation Challenge (Levels)

Simulation Exercises can be run at higher "levels" for students interested in a more challenging problem. The following is how higher levels effects the *fitness.mod* simulation: When you select higher levels, the competitor becomes increasingly aggressive in attempting to take your business.

Apx C

Labor Planning Analysis:
Forecasting with Seasonality

*Read this in conjunction with **SBP 2d: Labor Intensity**.*
(You should complete the SBP 2d Quantitative Analysis section before proceeding here.)

Forecasting techniques such as simple exponential smoothing or even linear regression do not do a good job when seasonality is present. A good way to forecast prior sales data that is known to have seasonality is to deseasonalize the data first. To *deseasonalize* data is to temporarily remove the seasonal behavior of the data. The resulting data can then be forecasted with usual techniques, such as exponential smoothing.

To deseasonalize sales data we first need to calculate seasonality indices for each period within the seasonal cycle. A seasonality index is calculated as the average for a particular period within the seasonal cycle divided by the average of all seasonal cycles. As an example, consider the following quarterly sales data for a home painting service that has an annual seasonal cycle:

	Prior Sales				
Quarter	1996	1997	1998	Average	SI
I	47	43	44	44.67	0.91
II	49	55	43	49.00	0.99
III	53	58	58	56.33	1.14
IV	44	48	49	47.00	0.95
	Average			49.25	1.00

The first quarter seasonality index (SI) of 0.91 indicates that during the first quarter sales tends to be 91 percent of average quarter sales. In other words, sales during that quarter is 9 percent below the overall average. That 0.91 is equal to 44.67/49.25, and the 44.67 is simply the average of the first-quarter sales in the data, and 49.25 is the average of the sales data for all quarters.

It is interesting, but not surprising, to note that the average of the seasonality indices is 1.00, which means that on average, the quarterly sales is 100 percent of the average.

Once we have calculated seasonality indices, we can deseasonalize the prior sales data by dividing each one by its corresponding SI.

	Prior Sales Data				Deseasonalized Data		
Quarter	1996	1997	1998	SI	1996	1997	1998
I	47	43	44	0.91	51.82	47.41	48.51
II	49	55	43	0.99	49.25	55.28	43.22
III	53	58	58	1.14	46.34	50.71	50.71
IV	44	48	49	0.95	46.11	50.30	51.35

A forecast can be generated from the deseasonalized data by using any standard time-series technique. Continuing with the example, we arbitrarily forecast using exponential smoothing with alpha of 0.3:

Year	Qtr.	A_t	F_t
1996	I	51.82	-
1996	II	49.25	51.82
1996	III	46.34	51.05
1996	IV	46.11	49.64
1997	I	47.41	48.58
1997	II	55.28	48.23
1997	III	50.71	50.34
1997	IV	50.30	50.45
1998	I	48.51	50.41
1998	II	43.22	49.84
1998	III	50.71	47.85
1998	IV	51.35	48.71
1999	I	?	49.50

We now have a deseasonalized forecast of 49.50 for the first quarter of 1999. Since we want a forecast for all of 1998, we will arbitrarily use that 49.50 as a forecast for each quarter of 1999. (Another alternative would be to estimate a trend that would continue throughout 1999.)

Would we really expect quarterly sales through 1999 to be 49.50? We are not done yet, for we have not accounted for the expected seasonality. We need to *reseasonalize* the forecast, by multiplying in each corresponding seasonality index. The reseasonalized forecast is what we would then use to plan our labor resource requirements.

Year	Qtr.	deseas. forecast	SI	reseas. forecast
1999	I	49.50	0.91	44.89
1999	II	49.50	0.99	49.25
1999	III	49.50	1.14	56.62
1999	IV	49.50	0.95	47.24

Therefore, we would expect third-quarter sales for 199 to be 56.62, which is equal to 49.50 times 1.14. (If we round numbers it is best to wait until the end to avoid losing precision.) The house painting company may thus want to hire some temporary help during the third quarter to meet the extra demand.

This entire process of deseasonalizing demand data through reseasonalizing the forecasts is a form of *time series decomposition*. An extension of this will also account for trend or other factors.

Other Reading

The following is reading about Labor Planning from other texts, which you may be using in your course. Your instructor will inform you which if any of this reading you are accountable for, and may assign problems or other exercises from that reading.

- Fitzsimmons2 chapter 16 on Forecasting Demand for Services discusses Exponential Smoothing with Seasonal Adjustment (beginning on page 499). That approach is a little different than the deseasonalize-reseasonalize approach described above.
- Chase8 chapter 13 on Forecasting has a section on Decomposition of a Time Series (beginning on page 520). That section includes a discussion of also accounting for trend.

Apx C

- Stevenson6 chapter 3 on Forecasting has a section titled Techniques for Seasonality (beginning on page 106), which refers to seasonality indices as "seasonality relatives."
- Heizer5 chapter 5 on Forecasting has a section titled Seasonal Variations in Data (beginning on page 161).

Simulation Exercise

You should re-run the simulation *pizza.mod*. Again, print your final results and submit them as directed by your instructor (either on paper, or electronically if your course is registered on the workbook website). Hopefully your results will be improved by the use of analytical methods described above. The following is a hint about how to run the simulation with improved results:

You may want to use time-series decomposition or other analysis technique to determine your daily labor schedule.

Applying Labor Planning in Your Target Service Business

How might Labor Planning analysis be applied in your target service business? Consider the following questions with regard to your target business:

① Even if you can reliably forecast changes in demand over time, are there costs or restrictions that limit the potential for changing capacity according to changes in demand?
② Are there other ways to adjust capacity for seasonal changes in demand besides changing staffing levels?

Increasing the Simulation Challenge (Levels)

Simulation Exercises can be run at higher "levels" for students interested in a more challenging problem. The following is how higher levels effects the *pizza.mod* simulation: When you select higher levels, the seasonality of the demand becomes increasingly complex.

Optimization Analysis:
Linear Programming

*Read this in conjunction with **SBP 2e: Perishable Output Illusion**.*
(You should complete the SBP 2e Quantitative Analysis section before proceeding here.)

With mathematical programming, we usually attempt to minimize or maximize a certain objective subject to various constraints. A *decision variable* is a variable we are attempting to solve for. A *solution* consists of values for all decision variables. An *objective function* is a equation that tells the "goodness" or "badness" of a particular solution. A *constraint* is an inequality or equality equation that tells if a particular solution is *feasible*, or acceptable. If a constraint is not satisfied for a particular equation, then the solution is *infeasible*, and should no be considered.

The following is an example of solving a labor scheduling problem with a spreadsheet. When we discussed labor scheduling in the *Often Labor Intensive* Service Business Principle, we ignored the assumption that employees may need to work on shifts of specific durations.

Imagine that a restaurant has the following forecast for demand (customer groups) for each hour of the day:

Hour	11	12	1	2	3	4	5	6	7	8
Groups	4	24	16	4	4	12	24	40	32	20

This data might be represented by an array variable D, where D_t is the forecasted demand for period t in number of groups of customers. (For clarity, we will use t=1 for the 11:00 a.m. hour, t=2 for the noon hour, etc.)

If each server can handle 4 customer groups per hour, how many employees will we need during each hour. This question is complicated by the fact that our employees either work part-time 4 hours per day or full-time 8 hours per day. (For simplicity we will not presently consider break times, which is an interesting problem in itself.) Imagine that full-time employees are paid $6 per hour, and part time employees are paid $8 per hour, according to union rules.

Let us define a decision variable set F_t which tells how many full-time employees will start at period t. Also, let us have a decision variable set P_t that will tell the number of part-time employees starting at period t.

Our *objective function* will be to minimize the total cost of labor (to have enough for demand). This is as follows (since full-time employees work 8 hours at $6 per hour and part-time employees work 4 hours at $8)
   Minimize:

$$48\sum_{t=1}^{10} F_t + 32\sum_{t=1}^{10} P_t$$

Now we will consider the *constraints*, which define acceptable solutions. In particular, the number of employees starting at any time period must be at least one-forth of the number of groups to arrive. For the first period, this is as follows:

$$4F_1 + 4P_1 \le D_1$$

Since this is a *constraint*, we will only consider solutions in which this constraint is met. By convention, we typically put the terms containing decision variables on the left side of the inequality sign, and the constant terms on the right side of the inequality sign. The left-hand-side of the inequality sign is referred to as the "LHS," and the right-hand-side is referred to as the "RHS."

For the second hour we still have the servers from the first hour, plus the servers who started the second hour:

$$4F_1 + 4F_2 + 4P_1 + 4P_2 \le D_2$$

For the fifth hour we have the full-time employees who started the first five hours, plus the part-time employees who started hours 2, 3, 4, and 5 (the part-time employee who started in period 1 has left by then):

$$4F_1 + 4F_2 + 4F_3 + 4F_4 + 4F_5 + 4P_2 + 4P_3 + 4P_4 + 4P_5 \leq D_3$$

In general, this constraint is represented as:

$$4\sum_{i=0}^{7} F_{t-i} + 4\sum_{i=0}^{3} P_{t-i} \geq D_t \qquad \forall t = \{1..10\}$$

That notation at the far right means that we need one of these constraints "for all ($\forall$) values of t from 1 to 10." We assume with this notation that any variable with a subscript that evaluates less than zero will not exist, and would be ignored.

A final constraint we need is for the number of employees of any type starting at any time period to be greater than or equal to zero. Otherwise, a computer solver may attempt to schedule a negative number of employees, earning $6 or $8 for each of them. The overall formulation, including this non-negativity constraint, is as follows:

Minimize:

$$48\sum_{t=1}^{10} F_t + 32\sum_{t=1}^{10} P_t$$

Subject to (s.t.):

$$4\sum_{i=0}^{7} F_{t-i} + 4\sum_{i=0}^{3} P_{t-i} \geq D_t \qquad \forall t = \{1..10\}$$

$$F_t \geq 0, P_t \geq 0 \qquad \forall t = \{1..10\}$$

Linear Programming with a Spreadsheet

In ancient computing days, prior to the 1980's, the software for solving linear programs were cryptic and difficult to use. For a period of time, linear programming was available an add-in for spreadsheet software, but now it is standard. Both Microsoft Excel and Corel Quattro Pro have an "optimizer" built in for easily setting up and solving linear (and non-linear) programs.

(This discussion of linear programming with a spreadsheet assumes some basic working knowledge of either Excel or Quattro Pro. Basic knowledge includes copying cells, inserting rows, etc.)

The procedure for setting up a linear program on a spreadsheet involves (1) designating cells to contain the decision variables, (2) entering an equation in a cell to calculate the objective function, and (3) specifying the cells for constraints.

(1) Decision Variables

For the restaurant staffing example above, we simply start with spreadsheet cells that tell for each hour of the day (*t*), how many customer groups are expected to arrive (Dt). Next to that, we might create columns for the number of full-time servers starting that hour (Ft), and the number of part-time employees starting that hour (Pt).

	A	B	C	D
1	t	Dt	Ft	Pt
2	1	4	**0**	**0**
3	2	24	**0**	**0**
4	3	16	**0**	**0**
5	4	4	**0**	**0**
6	5	4	**0**	**0**
7	6	12	**0**	**0**
8	7	24	**0**	**0**
9	8	40	**0**	**0**
10	9	32	**0**	**0**
11	10	20	**0**	**0**

Since we do not yet know how many servers will start each hour, I have entered a bolded zero in each decision variable cell.

(2) Objective Function

It is a simple matter to sum the number of full-time and part-time employees. We can then multiply those values by the costs of each, the sum of which is the total cost we desire to minimize:

	A	B	C	D
1	t	Dt	Ft	Pt
2	1	4	**0**	**0**
3	2	24	**0**	**0**
4	3	16	**0**	**0**
5	4	4	**0**	**0**
6	5	4	**0**	**0**
7	6	12	**0**	**0**
8	7	24	**0**	**0**
9	8	40	**0**	**0**
10	9	32	**0**	**0**
11	10	20	**0**	**0**
12		sum	0	0
13		cost	48	32
14		min	0	

Where equation cells are as follows:
- C12=@SUM(C2..C11)
- D12=@SUM(D2..D11)
- B14=C12*C13+D12*D13

Cell B14 is the objective function to be minimized.

(3) Constraints

First, let us look at the constraints on the server requirements to meet demand. Let us begin by calculating the number of servers available during the last hour (t=10) and work backwards. The number of servers available during hour 10 is any full-time servers who *arrived* between hours 3 through 10, plus any part-time servers who arrived during hours 7 through 10. In our spreadsheet we could enter this in cell E11 as @SUM(C4..C11)+@SUM(D8..D11). If we then copy cell E11 to cell E10, we find that for period 9 we have @SUM(C3..C10)+@SUM(D7..D10) servers, which is exactly what we wanted.

Apx C

Now, we may encounter a problem when we copy the sum formula from cell E10 to cells above E8. That is because we are summing the prior 9 periods of full-time employees, but no time periods existed prior to period 1. The avoid a possible error, we will create some dummy cells above period 1 that we will set to zero.

	A	B	C	D	E	
1	t	Dt	Ft	Pt		
2			0			
3			0			
4			0			
5			0			
6			0			
7			0	0		
8			0	0		
9	1	4	0	0	0	←@SUM(C2..C9)+@SUM(C7..C9)
10	2	24	0	0	0	←@SUM(C3..C10)+@SUM(C8..C10)
11	3	16	0	0	0	←@SUM(C4..C11)+@SUM(C9..C11)
12	4	4	0	0	0	←@SUM(C5..C12)+@SUM(C10..C12)
13	5	4	0	0	0	←@SUM(C6..C13)+@SUM(C11..C13)
14	6	12	0	0	0	←@SUM(C7..C14)+@SUM(C12..C14)
15	7	24	0	0	0	←@SUM(C8..C15)+@SUM(C13..C15)
16	8	40	0	0	0	←@SUM(C9..C16)+@SUM(C14..C16)
17	9	32	0	0	0	←@SUM(C10..C17)+@SUM(C15..C17)
18	10	20	0	0	0	←@SUM(C11..C18)+@SUM(C16..C18)
19		sum	0	0		
20		cost	48	32		
21		min	0			

In the above example, the equation that is entered in any of the cells in column E can be copied to the location for the other sums. To create the LHS (left-hand-side) of the constraints we simply multiply each cell in column E by 4. The RHS (right-hand-side) of each of these constraints is simply Dt, the expected demand for each period.

	A	B	C	D	E	F	G	H
1	t	Dt	Ft	Pt		LHS		RHS
2			0					
3			0					
4			0					
5			0					
6			0	0				
7			0	0				
8			0	0				
9	1	4	0	0	0	0	≥	4
10	2	24	0	0	0	0	≥	24
11	3	16	0	0	0	0	≥	16
12	4	4	0	0	0	0	≥	4
13	5	4	0	0	0	0	≥	4
14	6	12	0	0	0	0	≥	12
15	7	24	0	0	0	0	≥	24
16	8	40	0	0	0	0	≥	40
17	9	32	0	0	0	0	≥	32
18	10	20	0	0	0	0	≥	20
19		sum	0	0				
20		cost	48	32				
21		min	0					

Note that the inequality symbol ≥ does *not* need to be entered in the spreadsheet, but is placed there simply as a reminder.

We can now enter the optimizer and tell the spreadsheet program where the objective function and constraints are located. In Quattro Pro this is likely done by selecting Tools|Numeric Tools|Optimizer from the menu. Remember that it is possible to re-configure the menu, and that different versions of the program may have menu items in different locations, so you might need to consult the help screen.

Quattro Pro's optimizer asks for the "Solution Cell," which is the objective function. For this example C21 should be entered as the Solution Cell. You need to be sure and specify "Min" in order to minimize that solution cell. The "Variable Cell(s)" are the decision variables, and should be specified as C9..D18. Those cells will be modified by the optimizer to maximize the objective function.

Constraints are added in Quattro Pro by clicking the "Add..." button. The "Add Constraints" dialog box asks for the "Cell" (LHS), the "Operator" (an inequality, equality, or integer specification), and the "Constant" (RHS). Fortunately, we can add a block of constraints at one time. For the demand constraints, enter F9..F18 as the "Cell," select ≥ as the "Operator," and enter H9..H18 as the "Constant." Each of the LHS equations will be automatically paired up with the corresponding RHS value.

We almost forgot about our constraints that our decision variables (Ft and Pt) are all non-negative. This is easily done. Click the "Add Another Constraint" button and enter the decision variable range, C9..D18, as the "Cell." Select ≥ as the "Operator" and enter 0 as the constant. This indicates that all of the decision variables must be greater-than or equal-to zero.

For one last constraint, let's also specify that the decision variable values must be integers. It does not make sense to have a fraction of an employee start work during a given hour. By specifying that the decision variables are integers, we are entering the realm of "Integer Programming," which can be more complicated than simple linear programming, but is not more complicated when using a spreadsheet optimizer. Click "Add Another Constraint" then enter C9..D18 again as the "Cell." This time select Integer as the "Operator." We are now done adding constraints, so click "Ok."

In the solver dialog box you should now see three constraint sets. If any are missing, click "Add..." again and add them.

At the dialog box simply click "Solve" to solve the integer program. After the solution is reached, the optimizer may tell you that the result is within the specified tolerance limits. You can click "Close" to close the optimizer dialog box and look at the solution.

Other Reading

The following is reading about Optimization from other texts, which you may be using in your course. Your instructor will inform you which if any of this reading you are accountable for, and may assign problems or other exercises from that reading.

- Fitzsimmons2 chapter 18 on Linear Programming Models in Services.
- Chase8 supplement to chapter 7 on Linear Programming.
- Stevenson6 supplement to chapter 5 on Linear Programming.
- Heizer5 quantitative module B on Linear Programming.

Simulation Exercise

You should re-run the simulation *ski.mod*. Again, print your final results and submit them as directed by your instructor (either on paper, or electronically if your course is registered on the workbook website). Hopefully your results will be improved by the use of analytical methods described above. The following is a hint about how to run the simulation with improved results:

Formulate a linear program to calculate the best speed for the ski lift to maximize profit. Profit is **(Runs × RunFee) - (LiftSpeed × LiftSpeedCost)**. The linear program will probably have two decision variable: **LiftSpeed** and **Runs**, both of which can be considered continuous variables that are greater than zero. In addition,

the linear program will probably have five constraints: one for the maximum LiftSpeed, one for the minimum LiftSpeed, one for the maximum number of runs when skiers are waiting (**LiftSpeed × Skiers × 30 / LiftDistance**), one for the maximum number of runs when skiers are not waiting (**Runs -**
LiftSpeed × ChairSeats × 60 / ChairSpacing ≤ 0), and one for the maximum number of runs a skier will ski in an hour (**Runs ≤ Skiers × MaxRunsPerHour**).

After you formulate your linear program, rerun the simulation *ski.mod*. The program will give you values for all of the parameters, and you will need to calculate the optimal **LiftSpeed**. Solve the linear program either graphically or with a spreadsheet. Enter the calculated **LiftSpeed** into the computer and resume the simulation.

Applying Optimization in Your Target Service Business

How might Optimization analysis be applied in your target service business? Consider the following questions with regard to your target business:

① What are a few examples of operational factors that it would be good to optimize, so that they are not too high and not too low? (Examples might involve speed of production, quantities of machines, customer scheduling intervals, number of tasks assigned to each employee, etc.)
② What information (problem parameters) would you need to know in order to determine the optimal levels or amounts of those factors? (Examples might be costs incurred for various factor levels, or limits to factor values.)
③ How difficult would it be to mathematically represent the relationships between the various problem parameters and the factors being optimized?

Increasing the Simulation Challenge (Levels)

Simulation Exercises can be run at higher "levels" for students interested in a more challenging problem. The following is how higher levels effects the *ski.mod* simulation:

Queuing Analysis:
Analytical Queuing Theory

Read this in conjunction with **SBP 3a: Customers in Inventory**.
(You should complete the SBP 3a Quantitative Analysis section before proceeding here.)

Let us return to the factors that influence the amount of waiting that customers are subjected to, namely:
  • the rate at which customers arrive,
  • how fast the servers serve, and,
  • the way the service system is configured.

The first two items can be expressed mathematically as probability distributions.

Customer Arrivals

Customer can arrive in many ways. They can arrive individually or in groups. They can arrive at a steady rate on in spurts. They can arrive and then depart because the expected wait is too long, which is called *balking*. Other customers may arrive and wait for a while, only to be frustrated and leave, which is called *reneging*.

We may characterize random customer arrivals by a probability distribution. The most common distribution used for arrivals is the Poisson distribution. The Poisson distribution is a *discrete distribution*, meaning that only certain numerical values will come from the distribution. The values that come from the Poisson distribution are whole numbers greater than or equal to zero. A value from the Poisson distribution represents a number of customers arriving in a particular time period. We assume that only whole numbers of customers arrive–no fractional customers.

The probability density function for the Poisson distribution is as follows:

$$P_T(n) = \frac{(\lambda T)^n e^{-\lambda T}}{n!}$$

Which is interpreted to mean that the probability that exactly *n* customers will arrive during a time period of length T will be $P_T(n)$. The parameter λ is called *lambda*, and represents the average number of customers arriving per single time period. (Recall from your statistics class that e is a constant of approximately 2.718, and $n! = n \times (n-1) \times (n-2) \times ... \times 2 \times 1$.)

For example, if a single time period is defined as one hour, and an average of 4 customers arrive each hour, then $\lambda=4$. Note that lambda is a "rate," which is expressed in units (i.e. customers) per time period. If the arrival of customers is random according to a Poisson probability distribution, then the probability that exactly 3 customers will arrive in a one-hour time period is $P_1(3) = (4 \times 1)^3 e^{-4 \times 1} / 3! = 0.1954$, or a 19.54% probability.

Perhaps a more insightful way of looking at the arrival of customers is by considering the average time between any two customers arriving. If one customer arrives at exactly 10:03 and the next customer arrives at exactly 10:25 then the time between those arrivals is 22 minutes. The time between adjacent arrivals is called the *interarrival time*. It is important to note that the average arrival rate is simply the inverse of the average interarrival time.

If the arrival rate, expressed as customers per time period, is random and follows an Poisson distribution, then the interarrival time is also random and follows a *negative-exponential distribution* (sometimes just called an exponential distribution). The exponential distribution is *continuous*, meaning that values from the distribution can be on any real number. In fact, the amount of time between arrivals can be any real number, it could be 3 minutes, 3.2 minutes, 3.21 minutes, 3.21958382349438234823 minutes, etc.

Apx C

The mean of the negative exponential distribution is $1/\lambda$ and is in units of time period. For example, if the average time between customer arrivals is 2 minutes then lambda is ½. Note that this corresponds with the Poisson mean of

½ of a customer per minute. In this sense, lambda in the Poisson distribution is the same lambda in the corresponding exponential distribution.

The probability density function for the exponential distribution is:

$$f(t) = \lambda e^{-\lambda t}$$

This probability density function only has relative interpretation, and the $f(t)$ value does not directly represent the probability of occurance. For example, if lambda equals 4 then $f(1)=0.0733$, which does *not* mean a 7.33% probability of the interarrival time being exactly 1. In fact, since there are an infinite amount of unique real numbers then the actual probability of the interarrival time being any particular real value is zero. (Technically, the plim or probability limit is zero.)

What we might be interested in is the probability that an interarrival time will be in a given range of values. For example, we may desire to know the probability that a customer will arrive in the next five minutes, give that a customer just arrived. This value comes from the cumulative probability distribution for the exponential distribution:

$$F(t) = 1 - e^{-\lambda t}$$

If the average interarrival time is 4 minutes then lambda equals 0.25. The probability that the next customer will arrive in the next 5 minutes is $F(5) = 1-e^{-4 \times 5} = 0.7135$ or a 71.35 percent probability.

Now, lets imagine that no customer arrives in the next 5 minutes (which has a 28.65 percent probability of occurring). At that point, what is the probability of a customer arriving in the *next* 5 minutes? Is it greater than or less than the original 71.35 percent probability? Some people would argue that it is less, since customers must be generally delayed. Others would argue that it is more, since we need more customers to reach our average of 4 minute interarrival times (a concept called "regression to the mean"). Rather than speculate, we can calculate the probability.

If we assume interarrival times follow the exponential distribution, and 5 minutes have passed, then we can calculate a new F(t) function that starts at t = 5. This new F(t) will be the same as the old F(t) except that it will be "normalized," meaning that it will be scaled by a factor so that the probability of a customer arriving between t=5 and t=∞ will be 100 percent. This must be, since it means that the interarrival time will be *some* value. (Ignoring the possibility that no customer will ever arrive.)

The probability of a customer arriving between t=5 and t=∞ from our original function was 28.65 percent. So, to scale that to 100 percent we simply subtract 0.7135 from the original F(t), since no customer arrived during that period, and multiple the remaining value by 1/0.2865. The resulting cumulative probability function is:

$$F_{t+5}(t) = (1 - e^{-\lambda t} - 0.7135)\frac{1}{0.2865}$$

You will note that $F_{t+5}(5) = 0$, since we already know that no customer arrived in the first 5 minutes. What we are interested in knowing is the probability of a customer arriving in the *next* 5 minutes, given that no customer arrived in the first five minutes. That is simply $F_{t+5}(10)$ which, when accounting for rounding error, is (0.9179-0.7135)/0.2865=0.7135. Amazing! What that means is that the probability of a customer arriving in the second 5 minutes given that no customer arrived in the first 5 minutes is *exactly* the same as the original probability of a customer arriving in the first 5 minutes! The passage of time has absolutely no impact on the probability distribution of future interarrival times. This is known as the *memoryless* property of the distribution.

The memoryless property indicates that the probability of a customer arriving in the future is *not* a function of when customers arrived in the past. If each customer arrival is independent of each other customer arrival, the memoryless property makes perfect sense. It is a common assumption that customers exist independently of one another, and arrive at the service provider when they please.

In summary, if customer arrivals are completely independent then the memoryless property makes sense. The exponential distribution is a good distribution to assume, since it possesses the memoryless property (although it is not the only one that does). If we assume an exponential distribution for interarrival times, then we are inherently assuming a Poisson distribution for arrival rates. This is an important assumption that we will come back to later.

Service Rates

The "service rate" is the average rate at which customers can be served, and is expressed as *customers per time period*. This is different from the "service *time*," which is the average amount of time it takes to serve one customer. We can easily calculate one from the other by inverting the value.

It makes sense that is servers serve faster then customers will have to wait a shorter time to be served. How long does it take to be serve a customer? Sometimes the service rate is constant as are rates in many manufacturing processes. In other cases, service times vary based on variations in customer inputs and variations in service requirements. For example, we might assume that service rates also follow a Poisson distribution. This implies that the time between completing the service for individual customers follows an exponential distribution.

Recall that we used lambda to represent the average arrival rate. We will use μ (spelled mu and pronounced "m-you" like the sound of a cat) to represent average service rate. When the service rate is constant, then μ is that service rate.

Converting Times to Rates and Rates to Times

As just mentioned, service *rates* can be converted to or from service *times* by inverting the value. For example, if we have a service *time* of 2 customers per minute, then the service *rate* would be ½ minutes per customer. Note that we invert not only the numbers, but also the units of measure. For this example we inverted "customers per minute" to come up with "minutes per customer."

As another example, if we have a service *time* of 20 minutes per customer, then we have a service *rate* of 1/20 customer per minute. What is 1/20th of a customer? That means that on average we are able to complete 1/20th of a customer's service in one minute. It would probably be more clear to express this service rate in customers per *hour*. This conversion is simply done by recognizing that 60 minutes/hour is a unity, since the top and the bottom of the fraction are equal (60 minutes = 1 hour). Therefore, we can multiply our service rate by the time conversion unity:

$$rate = \frac{1}{20}\frac{customer}{minute} \times \frac{60}{1}\frac{minute}{hour} = 3\frac{customer}{hour}$$

You will observe that the equation has "minute" in the numerator and in the denominator, so the "minutes" cancel.

I recommend that when doing time unit conversions you *always* include the units of measure in the conversion. If the units of measure do not convert properly, you have probably made a mistake. The following is an example of a mistake while trying to convert a service time of 5 minutes per customer to hours as the time unit:

$$5\frac{minutes}{customer} \times 60\frac{minutes}{hour} = 300\frac{minutes^2}{customer \times hour} = ???$$

You will note that the minutes do not cancel because they are both in the numerator. A correct way to do that conversion is:

$$5\frac{minutes}{customer} \times \frac{1}{60}\frac{hour}{minute} = \frac{1}{12}\frac{hour}{customer}$$

where the "minutes" cancel because they are both in the numerator and in the denominator.

Recall that the average arrival rate is simply the inverse of the average interarrival time. This discussion about converting service rates to or from service times also applies to converting average arrival rates to or from average interarrival times.

Some important things to remember about service times and rates:
- Times are different than rates. If you have an equation that calls for the service rate, and you use the service time instead, it will produce erroneous results. You must invert the time first.
- Be careful about units of measure. If you have an equation that asks for both the service rate and the arrival rate, then they must both have the same units of measure. Using a service rate in "customers per minute" with an arrival rate in "customers per hour" will cause problems.

Queuing System Configuration

There are a number of ways of characterizing a queuing system.

- **Queue configuration**. There might be one queue feeding multiple servers, or each server having its' own queue.

- **Queue discipline**, or the way the next customer is selected from the queue to be served. A common queue discipline is first-in-first-out (FIFO) which is the same as first-come-first-served (FCFS). Hospital emergency rooms take patients based on urgency of need, which is often not FIFO. Restaurants and hair solon may serve customers with reservations first, based on the time of their reservation.

- **Queue size limits**. Some queues will hold a limited number of customers. Others will only hold a fixed number of customers, after which subsequent customers will be turned away.

- **Number of service phases**. Some services have the customer wait for a single service. With others, the customer waits to see the first server, then may wait to see another server, and perhaps a third, etc. For example, at some fast food restaurants the customer waits to place an order, then gets in cashier line to wait to pay for the order.

- **Number of servers**. There could be one server who serves all of the customers, or multiple servers. In some situations, such as self-serve, there are as many servers as there are customers (since each customer is a server). Each server who provides essentially the same service to customers at a given phase of the service process is called a "*channel*." If three servers serve customers waiting in a single queue, then we have a three-channel system.

Modeling with Queuing Theory

"Queuing theory" is an analytical method for estimating the performance of a queuing system under certain assumptions. System performance may include length of the queue in terms of time or number of customers, utilization of workers which is the percentage of the time they are busy serving customers.

Herein we will only consider a relatively simple set of assumptions. For more complex systems you will need to see supporting reading. We may make the following assumptions:
- Customers arrive independently from one another according to a Poisson distribution with average arrival rate of λ. This average arrival rate is stable throughout the time period under consideration.
- The service *rate* is from any general distribution (e.g. normal, uniform, etc.) with a mean of μ. Note that the average service *time* is $1/\mu$. The standard deviation of the service time is σ (which is "sigma"), and the variance of the service time is σ^2.
- There is a single phase of service and a single channel (server) at that phase.
- The queue has infinite capacity, and the queue discipline is FIFO.
- $\mu > \lambda$.

These assumptions define what is known as a **M/G/1** queuing system. M means there is an exponential arrival process, G means there is a general probability distribution for the service process, and 1 means there is one server.

If we make those assumptions, then we can calculate the following:
- The "traffic intensity," identified by ρ or "rho," is calculated as λ/μ. For a single-server system like this rho is the average utilization of that server.

- The average number of customers waiting in the queue, called L_q, is $(\lambda^2 \sigma^2 + \rho^2)/(2(1-\rho))$, where σ^2 is the variance of the service time, as described above.
- The average amount of time a customer waits in the queue, called W_q, is L_q/λ

We might also define the "system" to include the queue and the server station. Therefore, the number of customers in the system include the customers waiting in the queue and any customer being served.

- The average number of customers waiting in the system, called L_s, is $L_q + \rho$
- The average amount of time a customer waits in the system, called W_s, is L_s/λ

With all of these equations, it is essential that you use consistent units of measure. If, for example, your lambda is in customers per minute and your mu is in customers per hour, the resulting calculations will be meaningless. (To convert customers per minute to customers per hour multiply by 60.)

A Special Case: Constant Service Times

A special case of the M/G/1 model is the M/D/1 model, which shares all of the same assumptions *except* for now assuming that the service time is a constant amount, not varying from one customer to the next. (The "D" stands for *deterministic*, which is that the service time has no randomness.) A constant service time simply implies that there is no variance in the service time, which is that $\sigma^2 = 0$. If we substitute $\sigma^2 = 0$ to the M/G/1 equations above we get the **M/D/1 queuing equations**:

- The traffic intensity, ρ, is still as λ/μ.
- The average number of customers waiting in the queue, L_q, is $\rho^2/(2(1-\rho)) = \lambda^2/(2\mu(\mu-\lambda))$
- The average amount of time a customer waits in the queue, W_q, is $L_q/\lambda = \lambda/(2\mu(\mu-\lambda))$
- The average number of customers waiting in the system, L_s, is again $L_q + \rho$
- The average amount of time a customer waits in the system, W_s, is again $L_s/\lambda = W_q + (1/\mu)$

These equations may be helpful in solving the carwash simulation where only the only service is washing cars. If multiple services are offered and customers randomly choose different services of different service times, then it would probably be necessary to use the M/G/1 equations.

How can their be a line when $\mu > \lambda$?

If the average service rate, μ, is greater than the average arrival rate, λ, will customers still wait in line? Initially we may think that we are serving customers faster than they are arriving, so customers will not have to wait, but that is incorrect. The fact is, λ and μ are *average* rates. During some time periods, more than λ customers will randomly arrive, and it is possible that some customers will take longer than $1/\mu$ to be served. Over time, this random nature of arrivals and service means that the average line length will be greater than zero.

If, on the other hand, arrivals were not random but occurred exactly λ per time period, and if the service rate was exactly μ all the time, then customers would not have to wait. But, how often does that situation occur? Barring appointments, how would customers even know when to arrive so that the arrival is constant.

Other Reading

The following is reading about Queuing from other texts, which you may be using in your course. Your instructor will inform you which if any of this reading you are accountable for, and may assign problems or other exercises from that reading.

- Fitzsimmons2 chapter 17 on Queuing Models and Capacity Planning.
- Chase8 supplement to chapter 5 on Waiting Line Management.
- Stevenson6 chapter 19 on Waiting Lines.
- Heizer5 quantitative module D on Waiting Line Models

Apx C

Simulation Exercise

You should re-run the simulation *carwash.mod*. Again, print your final results and submit them as directed by your instructor (either on paper, or electronically if your course is registered on the workbook website). Hopefully your results will be improved by the use of analytical methods described above. The following is a hint about how to run the simulation with improved results:

Assume that customers arrive randomly according to a Poisson distribution with an average rate (λ) of ArrivalRate, which is given at the start of the simulation. Also assume that the other assumptions of a M/D/1 model are satisfied.

In the simulation you will need to specify WashTime. Your objective might be to specify a WashTime so that the AverageWait will be close to TargetWait.

Recall that the W_q equation will tell us the average wait that can be expected to occur given problem assumptions. If we set W_q=TargetWait we can solve for μ, the average service rate, which can be used to solve for WashTime.

For the M/D/1 model you will recall that $W_q = \lambda/(2\mu(\mu-\lambda))$. Using simple algebra to solve for μ we have:
$$W_q (2\mu(\mu-\lambda)) = \lambda$$
$$2 W_q (\mu^2 - \lambda\mu) = \lambda$$
$$\mu^2 (2 W_q) - \mu (2 W_q \lambda) - \lambda = 0$$
You may recognize this as a simple quadratic equation that we are solving for μ. As a brush-up from your algebra class, if we have a quadratic equation in the form:
$$ax^2 + bx + c = 0$$
where a, b, and c are constants, then the solution for x is:

$$x = \frac{-b \pm \sqrt{b^2 - 4ac}}{2a}$$

which is the *quadratic root equation*. So, we can use that equation to solve for the appropriate μ, with
$$a = 2 W_q$$
$$b = -2 W_q \lambda$$
$$\text{and } c = -\lambda.$$

The quadratic root equation contains the plus or minus symbol "$\pm$" which implies that you can calculate two values for μ. One of those values is likely to be negative, so should not be used: it is impossible to have a negative service rate.

Once you calculate the target value for μ, you can then calculate the optimal WashTime. Recall that the service time is the inverse of the service rate. To be precise, the service time includes WashTime and PullUpTime. Therefore, we have:

$$\mu = \frac{1}{serviceTime} = \frac{1}{PullUpTime + WashTime}$$

$$\frac{1}{\mu} = PullUpTime + WashTime$$

$$WashTime = \frac{1}{\mu} - PullUpTime$$

That is the WashTime that, give the assumptions of the M/G/1 model, will tend to produce an average wait time of W_q. It is important to note that W_q will occur asymptotically, after an infinite amount of time. It is possible and even likely to have a value of W_q different from the average wait time for shorter periods of time. However, your calculated WashTime is still your best bet to produce the desired AverageWait which is near TargetWait.

Applying Queuing in Your Target Service Business

How might Queuing analysis be applied in your target service business? Consider the following questions with regard to your target business:

① The cost of idle capacity can often be easily estimated. How might we estimate the cost of customers or customer inputs waiting to be served?
② What assumptions of the queuing models described in this section are most likely to *not* be met?

Increasing the Simulation Challenge (Levels)

Simulation Exercises can be run at higher "levels" for students interested in a more challenging problem. The following is how higher levels effects the *carwash.mod* simulation: When you select higher levels, you provide more services. The advantage of offering more services is that we customers who select more services are can be charged more.

At the start of the simulation you are asked how many services to provide (the levels). Previously, you select 1 service, which was to wash cars. The second service that is available is to wax a car, which is to spray it with a protective wax. The third service is to buff the car, in which the machine rubs the car surface with a soft brush makes the wax shine more. Thus, there are three types of customers based on the service they select: wash only, wash/wax, and wash/wax/buff.

The wax process always takes exactly WaxTime minutes, and the buff process always takes exactly BuffTime minutes, which are given to you at the beginning of the simulation. Customers selecting only a wash will be completed in PullUpTime + WashTime minutes from when it is their turn to receive service. Wax customers will take PullUpTime + WashTime + WaxTime minutes to complete service and cars subjected to wash/wax/buff with thus take PullUpTime + WashTime + WaxTime + BuffTime minutes to be completed.

You will also be told the fraction of these customers who are expected to want a wash only (WashFraction), the fraction who are likely to want wash/wax (WaxFraction), and the fraction who want the whole shooting match (BuffFraction). If BuffFraction=0.50 then 50 percent of the customers will select the wash/wax/buff service. Note that WashFraction + WaxFraction + BuffFraction = 1.00.

Hints for Higher Levels

With this simulation the service time is no longer deterministic, but random based on the combination of services that the customer selects. Therefore we will need to use the M/G/1 model, which is slightly more complex.

First, let us calculate μ as a function of our TargetWait, which we will use for W_q. As described above, the M/G/1 equation for W_q is:

$$W_q = (\lambda^2 \sigma^2 + \rho^2)/(2(1-\rho))/\lambda$$

and since $\rho = \lambda/\mu$ we have

$$W_q = \lambda(\sigma^2 + 1/\mu^2)/(2-2\lambda/\mu)$$

We can now solve for μ as a function of W_q (i.e. TargetWait), λ, and σ^2. We already have the first two, but will need to calculate σ^2, which is the variance of the service time. A standard way of calculating variance is:

$$\sigma^2 = var(t) = E(t^2) - E(t)^2$$

where $E(\bullet)$ is the expectation operator. $E(t)$ is simply the average t value. If t is the time of service, then $E(t)$ can be calculated as:

$$E(t) = AverageTime = PullUpTime + WashFraction \times WashTime$$
$$+ WaxFraction \times (WashTime + WaxTime)$$
$$+ BuffFraction \times (WashTime + WaxTime + BuffTime)$$

This works because WashFraction, WaxFraction, and BuffFraction each represent the probabilities that the service time will be WashTime, WashTime+WaxTime, or WashTime+WaxTime+BuffTime, respectively. PullUpTime is a separate term because *all* customers have to pull their cars into the machine.

One problem is that this E(t) is a function of WashTime, which we do not have but are solving for. This can be easily handled by recalling that the variance of any set of numbers is equal to the variance of those numbers with the same constant added to each. This is to say that the variance of all customers' service times is equal to the variance of all customers service times minus WashTime. Likewise, we can also eliminate PullUpTime from the variance calculation. Therefore,

var(t) = var(t−PullUpTime − WashTime)

$\qquad$ = E((t−PullUpTime − WashTime)^2) − E(t−PullUpTime − WashTime)^2

We can calculate

E((t−PullUpTime−WashTime) ^{2}) = WaxFraction × WaxTime^2 + BuffFraction × (WaxTime + BuffTime)^2

and

E(t− PullUpTime−WashTime) = (WaxFraction × WaxTime) +BuffFraction × (WaxTime + BuffTime)

The difference between the first of these calculations and the second squared is:

$\qquad$ σ^2 = WaxFraction × WaxTime^2 + BuffFraction × (WaxTime + BuffTime)^2

$\qquad\qquad$ − (WaxFraction × WaxTime +BuffFraction × (WaxTime + BuffTime))^2

That equation can be simplified a little, but not much. Note that σ^2 is a function of parameters which you are given at the start of the simulation. It is important to note that for this problem σ^2 is *not* a function of WashTime, which is good since it is what we are solving for.

Now that we have σ^2, λ, and W_q, we can solve for μ and then calculate the desired WashTime. Let us solve for μ:

$$W_q = \lambda(\sigma^2 + 1/\mu^2)/(2- 2\lambda/\mu)$$

Multiplying both sides by (2-2λ/μ)) gives us:

$$W_q (2- 2\lambda/\mu) = \lambda(\sigma^2 +1/\mu^2)$$

Further multiplying out terms to eliminate produces:

$$2W_q - 2W_q \lambda/\mu = \lambda\sigma^2 + \lambda/\mu^2$$

Moving everything to one side reveals:

$$2W_q - \lambda\sigma^2 - 2W_q \lambda/\mu - \lambda/\mu^2 = 0$$

Multiplying everything by μ^2 produces a quadratic equation with the variable μ:

$$\mu^2(2W_q - \lambda\sigma^2) - \mu(2W_q\lambda) - (\lambda) = 0$$

Recall that we can easily calculate the root of a quadratic equation aμ^2+b μ+c=0 by:

$$\mu = \frac{-b \pm \sqrt{b^2 - 4ac}}{2a}$$

In this case, a = $(2W_q - \lambda\sigma^2)$, b = $- (2W_q \lambda)$, and c = $- (\lambda)$.

After we calculate the target μ, we can then easily calculate the corresponding value for WashTime. Recall that if the average service rate is μ, in customers per hour, then the average service *time* is 1/μ, in hours per customer. If we want an average service time in *minutes*, we simply multiply that value by 60, or 60/μ. From calculations above we have:

$\qquad$ 60/μ = AverageTime = WashFraction × (PullUpTime + WashTime)

$\qquad\qquad$ + WaxFraction × (PullUpTime + WashTime + WaxTime)

$\qquad\qquad$ + BuffFraction × (PullUpTime + WashTime + WaxTime + BuffTime)

By combining WashTime and PullUpTime terms we have:

$\qquad$ 60/μ = PullUpTime + WashTime + (WaxFraction × WaxTime) +BuffFraction × (WaxTime + BuffTime)

Now we can simply solve for WashTime, in minutes, which is:

$\qquad$ WashTime = 60/μ − PullUpTime − (WaxFraction × WaxTime) − BuffFraction × (WaxTime + BuffTime)

This is the WashTime that will lead to an AverageLength which is equal to TargetLength, given an infinite number of customers. In practice, when we do not have an infinite number of customers, the AverageLength will vary somewhat due to the random nature of the system.

Inventory Theory Analysis:
The Economic Order Quantity and Safety Stock Approaches

*Read this in conjunction with **SBP 3b: Intangibility Myth**.*
(You should complete the SBP 3b Quantitative Analysis section before proceeding here.)

In this section we will consider two common approaches to inventory management. The first approach attempts to minimize costs of ordering inventory and keeping inventory. The second considers the costs of not being able to satisfy customers because of insufficient inventory.

(1) The Economic Order Quantity Approach

Perhaps the most popular and notorious inventory model is the Economic Order Quantity, or EOQ. The EOQ model makes a number of assumptions that are rarely met in actual situations, such as:

- Demand is constant, meaning it does not vary over time.
- The product in inventory is considered homogeneous, meaning one unit of inventory is the same as the next.
- The item in inventory can be stored from one period to the next, but with a "holding cost" that is constant per item per time period. For example, the cost to keep a television set in inventory for one year would include warehouse space, insurance, etc.
- We can order at any desired interval (i.e. we are not restricted to ordering only once per month, etc.).
- The cost to place an order and receive a shipment is constant.
- The only costs we are concerned about are holding cost and ordering cost.

If those assumptions are met, then we can take the following values:
    D = demand in units per year
    S = the ordering cost in $ per order
    H = the holding cost in $ per unit per year

$$EOQ = \sqrt{\frac{2DS}{H}}$$

The EOQ value is theoretically the order quantity (Q) which minimizes the total cost (TC) defined as

$$TC = \frac{SD}{Q} + \frac{HQ}{2}$$

The first term of TC is the annual ordering cost, and the second term is the annual holding cost. You will see that if you take the first derivative of TC and set it equal to 0, solving for Q, the result will be the EOQ. So, in fact, the EOQ value does minimize TC *given the various assumptions*. Despite the fact that the assumptions are rarely met (in either manufacturing or service environments), the EOQ model is useful in simply illustrating how costs tradeoffs might be analyzed.

Apx C

(The EOQ is technically a fixed-quantity system, since the EOQ amount is a fixed amount. However, since we are inherently assuming that demand is constant–an unrealistic assumption–the EOQ is winds up being a fixed-period system as well.)

(2) Safety Stock Approach

Perhaps a more relevant inventory management approach for services is based on a calculation of *safety stock*, which is inventory that is kept just in case demand is higher than expected.

Typically, the safety stock is based on the uncertainty in demand from the time one order is placed until the next order arrives. This requires understanding the concept of *lead time*, which is the amount of time from when an order is placed until when it arrives. The lead time might be represented by LT, which might be in days, weeks, month, etc. In the following time line, lead time is 2 weeks and an order is placed every 6 weeks...

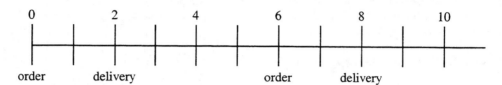

Imagine that demand is estimated to be 10 units per time period, with a standard deviation of 5 units. At week 0 we place an order that will arrive at week 2 and will last us until week 8. Therefore we need to order 6 weeks of demand, or 60 units. However, the safety stock needs to cover from the order date, week 0, up through the next order delivery, week 8. The safety stock needs to include 8 periods of uncertainty.

If demand for each period is independent–meaning that the random demand at a given period is not a function of demand from prior periods–then we can calculate the uncertainty in demand using a simple formula. We denote the standard deviation of demand for a single period as σ_1. The standard deviation of demand for n periods is:

$$\sigma_n = \sqrt{n \times \sigma_1^2}$$

This is based on the idea that the variance, σ^2, for n periods is n times the variance for one period. (It is inappropriate to add standard deviations, which is the square root of the variance. Also, for simplicity we are ignoring the fact that when a stockout occurs before the current order arrives the variance of *sales* temporarily becomes zero.)

For the above example, the uncertainty is 5 units per week, and the time from the initial order to the delivery of the subsequent order is 8 weeks. The standard deviation of demand over that 8 weeks is 14.14, according to the above formula.

Besides knowing the standard deviation of demand up through the subsequent delivery date, we also need to know the probability distribution of that demand. It is often safe to assume that random demand comes from a normal distribution. (Based on the concept known as the "central limit theorem" which states that the average of values from any given distribution approaches a normal distribution when many samples are averaged.) This distribution will be useful in using the critical fractile rule to calculate the safety stock.

"Service Level" Calculation of Safety Stock

One approach to calculating safety stock is to set safety stock according to a desired "service level." The "service level" is the percent of the time we want to avoid a stockout, or being out of an item when a customer want it. A service level of 80 percent would mean we do not want to be out of the item more than 20 percent of the time.

The safety stock is calculated by multiplying the standard deviation of demand by a z-value, which tells how many standard deviations are needed for a given service level. We can look up a z-value in a standard normal distribution table, or using a spreadsheet function. For example, the z-value for an 80 percent service level is 0.8416, which is the Quattro Pro spreadsheet function @norminv(0.8,0,1) or the Microsoft Excel function =NORMINV(0.8,0,1), either of which returns 0.8416.

Once we have the z-value, we can calculate safety stock as $z \times \sigma_n$ where n is the number of periods from the current order time up until the delivery date for the subsequent order, or 8 in the example above. That example would have safety stock of $14.14 \times 0.8416 = 11.90$. As such, the company would probably order 12 units of safety stock.

Can safety stock be negative? Yes, if the service level is less than 50 percent. However, most products will have a service level of perhaps 60 to 90 percent.

One common problem with the service level approach to setting safety stock is that companies choose the desired service level somewhat arbitrarily. Service levels are often set arbitrarily high, without regard for the impact on inventory levels and corresponding costs. A critical fractile approach uses costs to calculate an appropriate service level.

Critical Fractile Calculation of Safety Stock

Recall that the critical fractile calculation requires knowing the cost of under-forecasting, c_u, and the cost of over-forecasting, c_o. The cost of under forecasting is the cost of a stockout, or not having the item when a customer arrives to pick it up. This may include the profits which are lost because the sale was not made, and the cost of good will with the customer.

The cost of over forecasting is the cost of having unneeded inventory during the order period. This is typically the holding cost, which may include the cost of tied up capital, shrinkage (product disappearing), insurance, space requirements, etc.

Once we have estimates for those costs, we can calculate the critical fractile as c.f. $= c_u/(c_u+c_o)$. The c.f. value tell us the probability level on a cumulative normal distribution at which to set the safety stock.

For example, imagine that we have a product that costs the retailer $50 and sells for $60. We might therefore set c_u = $10, or the profit that would be lost with a lost sale. Imagine that the cost of an excess unit of inventory from one order to the next is $4, which is c_o. The critical fractile is $10/(10+4) = 0.714$, which is like a z-value. Again, the critical fractile is the point in the cumulative probability distribution which minimizes total expected cost, which point corresponds to a specific service level. Again, we need to identify the point on the cumulative normal distribution which is corresponds to the critical fractile. The spreadsheet approach is the simplest. For example, using Quattro Pro you would type @norminv(0.714,0,1) which returns 0.5651. This value can be multiplied by the standard deviation of demand in order to calculate the safety stock.

From the example above, recall that the standard deviation of demand from the present order to the delivery of the subsequent order is 14.14 units. Therefore, safety stock should be $14.14 \times 0.5651 = 7.99$. The company should therefore order 8 units of safety stock.

In addition to the safety stock, how much should the company order of the given item. Since the time between two subsequent deliveries is 6 weeks, they should order for 6 weeks of demand. In the example above, that would be $6 \times 10 = 60$ units. Add to this the safety stock, and subtract any inventory already on hand. Imagine that the company has 3 units on hand at the start of week 0. Based on the above calculations, we would order $60+8-3=65$ units.

Other Reading

The following is reading about Inventory Theory from other texts, which you may be using in your course. Your instructor will inform you which if any of this reading you are accountable for, and may assign problems or other exercises from that reading.

Apx C

- Fitzsimmons2 chapter 12 on Managing Facilitating Goods.
- Chase8 chapter 15 on Inventory Systems for Independent Demand.
- Stevenson6 chapter 13 on Inventory Management. For example, page 589 discusses the critical fractile rule under the heading of The Single-Period Model.
- Heizer5 chapter 12 on Inventory Management.

Simulation Exercise

You should re-run the simulation *shoe.mod*. Again, print your final results and submit them as directed by your instructor (either on paper, or electronically if your course is registered on the workbook website). Hopefully your results will be improved by the use of analytical methods described above. The following is a hint about how to run the simulation with improved results:

Now you have the opportunity to use the calculation analysis just covered, or any other analysis, to assist your decision making.

Applying Inventory Theory in Your Target Service Business

How might Inventory Theory analysis be applied in your target service business? Consider the following questions with regard to your target business:

① What is a facilitating good that is kept in inventory and needs to be replenished on a regular basis?
② What are the decision rules for determining when and how much to replenish?
③ How big of a problem would it be if the service provider ran out of that facilitating good? Would a sale be lost, or could a substitution be made?

Increasing the Simulation Challenge (Levels)

Simulation Exercises can be run at higher "levels" for students interested in a more challenging problem. The following is how higher levels effects the *shoe.mod* simulation: When you select more advanced levels of the simulation, lead time and order cycle, and inventory ordering system may vary to make the exercise more challenging.

Project Scheduling Analysis:
The Critical Path Method (CPM)

Read this in conjunction with **SBP 3c: Heterogeneous Production.**
(You should complete the SBP 3c Quantitative Analysis section before proceeding here.)

The objective of project scheduling analysis is to determine (a) when each activity of a project needs to begin and end, and (b) what alternative schedules may be used in case of unforseen project difficulties.

An *activity* is a task that needs to be accomplished as part of a project. Throughout projects, we also have *events*, which are points in time such as the starting or completion of a particular activity.

Each activity has a *duration*. Sometimes the activity duration is known precisely. Other times it may be random according to some probability distribution. There is always the possibility that an activity will be delayed from the originally expected start time or duration. Part of project scheduling analysis will be to determine what the best course of action is when an activity is delayed.

Project scheduling can be enhanced by creating a *graph*, which is a graphical representation of the project activities. (Another name for a project graph is a project *network*.) The graph technique that will be shown here is called *activity-on-node*. A *node* is a point or circle on a graph that represents an event. Activity nodes are connected by a directed line called an *arrow* or an *arc*.

The following *graph* example includes four activities: A, B, C, and D.

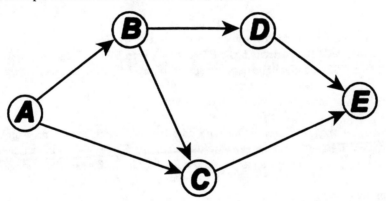

The most valuable thing about a project graph is that it depicts the *precedence relationships* between the various activities. Some activities have predecessors, which are activities that must be completed before the current activity is started. An *immediate predecessor* (I.P.) is an activity that comes *immediately* before a given activity on a graph.

In the example above, activity A is an I.P. for activity B, and has an arrow showing this precedence relationship. Other immediate predecessors are as follows:

Activity	I.P.
A	(none)
B	A
C	A, B
D	B
E	C, D

Apx C

The opposite of a predecessor is a successor, which is an activity that cannot be started until the current activity is completed. With the activity-on-node method, we place arrows on the graph pointing from activities to their *immediate successors* (I.S.). In the above example, activity B is an immediate successor of A.

Often we create a node that marks the start of the project called a *start node*. The start node has zero duration, and has arrows pointing to all activities that have no immediate predecessor. (The start node is their immediate predecessor.) It is also common convention to create an *end node* with zero duration that has all activities without immediate successors pointing to it. In the above example, activities B, C, and D might be actual activities, and A and E might be the start node and end node, respectively.

It is useful to write the estimated activity durations on the graph by each node. This information will be useful in determining the project schedule. For the present we will assume that the activity durations are known as a fixed value (t).

The first thing we want to do is determine a schedule of the earliest each activity can begin. As just stated, we always start project schedules with a "dummy" activity of 0 duration called the start node. The start node always begins at time 0, which marks the beginning of the project.

(For simplicity, we will assume herein that each time period is a day. However, this does not necessarily have to be the case. A time period can be a week, an hour, or some other period.)

Any activities without any immediate predecessors have an arrow pointing to them from the start node. These activities will all have an early start date, or ES, of 0. The early start date is the first day an activity can start if there are no delays. Once you have calculated the ES for any given activity you can immediately calculate the early finish date, or EF, as:

$$EF = ES + t$$

where t is the given activities duration (which is sometimes denoted by d). Note that EF actually calculates as the day *after* the activity is completed. If an activity has a ES=5, a t=2, then EF=7. That activity will start at the beginning of day 5, will take 2 days, and will be done just prior to day 7 (at the earliest).

All activities that have ES days should also have EF days calculated.

At this point, some activities in the graph may not have ES days yet. Any such activity for which *all immediate predecessors* have EF days will have the ES day equal to the *maximum* EF day for all immediate predecessors. The maximum is used because the given activity cannot be started until *all* immediate predecessors are completed.

This process of determining ES and EF days is repeated throughout the graph until they are calculated for all activities. Again, by convention, all activities in the project that have *no* immediate successors have an arrow pointing to a *end node*, which is a zero-duration activity that signifies the completion of the project. So, of course, the end node has an ES and EF day equal to the maximum EF day of the graph.

This process of calculating ES and EF days is called the *forward pass*.

The overall completion of the project, which is the EF of the end node, is generally denoted T. T represents the number of days it will take to complete the project if everything goes exactly as planned in this schedule.

The fact is, things seldom go as planned. Activities are delayed or other problems arise.

One important question may be how many days can an activity can be delayed from its early start day before delaying the entire project. This can be determined by doing a *backward pass* of calculations.

We begin the backward pass by calculating the late finish, or LF, of the end node, which is the latest that activity can be completed without delaying the entire project completion. Of course, the latest the end node can be completed is T, the overall project duration. Once we have the LF for any given activity, we can immediately calculate the late start, or LF, for that activity by:

$$LS = LF - t$$

where, again, t is the activity's duration.

Any activity for which all immediate successors have LS days calculated will have a LF value equal to the *minimum* of the LS values for all immediate successors. It is the minimum because the given activity *has* to be finished before *any* of the immediate successors begin.

This process, the backward pass, is repeated until LS and LF days are calculated for all activities of the project. If it is done correctly, then you will find that the LS of the start node will be 0, indicating that then entire project cannot be delayed from the start without delaying the entire project at the end.

The question is, how much an each specific activity be delayed without delaying the entire project. This possible delay amount for each activity is called the *slack* (although some people call it *float*). The total slack, or TS, for a given activity is calculated as:

$$TS = LS - ES$$

which is mathematically equivalent to

$$TS = LF - EF.$$

(Sometime total slack is simply denoted S.) All activities that have a slack which is greater than 0 can be delayed up to TS periods without delaying the entire project. (However, this may not be true if any predecessor activities have been delayed, which can consume some of the slack.) The cost of delaying an activity with sufficient slack can be effectively zero.

Any activities that have a slack of exactly 0 are on the *critical path*. These activities cannot be delayed even one day without delaying the entire project. The cost of delaying any critical path activities will at least include the cost of delaying the entire project, unless the duration of other critical path activities can be reduced. The significance of the critical path is why this analysis approach is called the *critical path method*, or *CPM*.

When faced with a choice between delaying a critical path activity or delaying a non-critical path activity, it us probably best to delay the latter. Other analysis methods, such as *PERT/Cost*, help us to determine which activities to "crash," or complete on an accelerated schedule to recover lost time.

With the simple example of a graph above, imagine that activity A is the start node, E is the end node, and activities B, C, and D have durations of 3, 2, and 4 respectively. The following are the forward pass calculations for this project:

Activity	I.P.	t	ES	EF
A	(none)	0	0	0
B	A	3	0	0+3=3
C	A, B	2	max(0,3)=3	3+2=5
D	B	4	3	3+4=7
E	C, D	0	max(5,7)=7	7+0=7

The overall project duration is the EF of the end node, in this case 7. That means that the project could possibly be completed in 7 days. That 7 becomes the LF value for the end node, then we work backwards in the backward pass and calculate LF and LS values:

Apx C

Activity	I.P.	t	ES	EF	I.S.	LS	LF
A	(none)	0	0	0	B, C	0–0=0	min(0,5)=0
B	A	3	0	3	C, D	3–3=0	min(5,3)=3
C	A, B	2	3	5	E	7–2=5	7
D	B	4	3	7	E	7–4=3	7
E	C, D	0	7	7	(none)	7–0=7	7

We can then calculate activity slack time as LS–ES (or LF–EF):

Activity	I.P.	t	ES	EF	I.S.	LS	LF	TS
A	(none)	0	0	0	B, C	0	0	0–0=0
B	A	3	0	3	C, D	0	3	0–0=0
C	A, B	2	3	5	E	5	7	5–3=2
D	B	4	3	7	E	3	7	3–3=0
E	C, D	0	7	7	(none)	7	7	7–7=0

The activities that have a slack of zero are on the critical path, meaning that if they are delayed from their ES times, the overall project will be delayed. In this example, activities A, B, D, and E are on the critical path.

Activity C has a non-zero slack of two, meaning that it can be delayed up to two periods from the ES time without delaying the overall project.

This was an extremely simple example, just for illustration. With more complex projects it is important to recognize that activities can possibly share slack times, so that if one activity uses up some slack, then later activities may have less slack than they did, and some new activities may join the critical path. The way to know this is to recalculate the values for the portion of the project remaining to be completed.

Other Reading

The following is reading about Project Scheduling from other texts, which you may be using in your course. Your instructor will inform you which if any of this reading you are accountable for, and may assign problems or other exercises from that reading.

- Fitzsimmons2 chapter 8 on Managing Service Projects.
- Chase8 chapter 3 on Project Management.
- Stevenson6 chapter 18 on Project Management.
- Heizer5 chapter 16 on Project Management.

Simulation Exercise

You should re-run the simulation *home.mod*. Again, print your final results and submit them as directed by your instructor (either on paper, or electronically if your course is registered on the workbook website). Hopefully your results will be improved by the use of analytical methods described above. The following is a hint about how to run the simulation with improved results:

This time, you might use CPM or some other analysis technique to calculate the optimal schedule, and to make decisions about rescheduling various activities. Remember that when an activity is delayed, future activities may lose slack.

Applying Project Scheduling in Your Target Service Business

How might Project Scheduling analysis be applied in your target service business? Consider the following questions with regard to your target business:

① Think of a project that may be involved with your target service business. How many separate activities might be involved in the project?

② Besides precedence relationships, are there other factors that might prevent some activities from being scheduled simultaneously, such as requiring the same resources? (For example, two activities that must be done by the same person, but can be done in any order.)

③ What are some project activities that would be easy to predict the activity duration?

④ What are some project activities that it would be very difficult to predict their duration in advance?

Increasing the Simulation Challenge (Levels)

Simulation Exercises can be run at higher "levels" for students interested in a more challenging problem. The following is how higher levels effects the *home.mod* simulation: When you select more advanced levels of the simulation, the penalty structure will change making the exercise more challenging.

Apx C

Facility Layout Analysis:
Process Layouts

*Read this in conjunction with **SBP 3d: Difficulty in Measuring Output.***
(You should complete the SBP 3d Quantitative Analysis section before proceeding here.)

Unfortunately, there is no simple way to determine a guaranteed optimal solution to a process layout problem. We can, however, determine some solutions which are better than other solutions. This is done by creating alternate layouts, and then calculating a "total travel distance" value for each. Those values can be compared, with the lower values indicating less expected travel distance.

The total travel distance value is calculated by multiplying each value from the station distance matrix by the corresponding value from the expected number of trips matrix. Each of these products are then added together to produce the total travel distance value.

The following is an example. Imagine a law firm that has three offices for staff employees. The offices are numbered 1, 2, and 3. Office 1 and 2 are relatively near one another, but 3 is farther away. We might have a **distance matrix** as such:

	office 1	office 2	office 3
office 1	0	3	7
office 2	3	0	4
office 3	7	4	0

As an example, each number in the distance matrix might indicate tens of feet between offices.

We have three employees that need to be assigned to those offices. These employees with each other to conduct business with the following approximate daily frequencies (the **trips matrix**):

	employee A	employee B	employee C
visits employee A	-	5	8
visits employee B	3	-	2
visits employee C	5	2	-

If employee A were assigned to office 1, employee B to office 2, and employee C to office 3, then we could multiply each element of the distance matrix above with the corresponding element of the trip matrix above, then add those products together, to get the overall "cost" of the layout. In this case we would have $(3 \times 5) + (7 \times 8) + (3 \times 3) + (4 \times 2) + (7 \times 5) + (4 \times 2) = 131$. What does that 131 mean? It means that given the projected trip frequencies in the trip matrix, the employees would walk 1310 feet to conduct business. That figure will be useful if we want to compare this to an alternate layout, or assignment of employees to offices.

An alternate layout may be to swap the office assignments of employees A and B. With that swap, we simply create a new trip matrix with the order of employees corresponding to the order of the offices:

	employee B	employee A	employee C
visits employee B	-	3	2
visits employee A	5	-	8
visits employee C	2	5	-

Again, we can calculate an overall cost of this layout by multiplying each element of the revised trip matrix with the corresponding values in the distance matrix. We now have $(3 \times 3) + (7 \times 2) + (3 \times 5) + (4 \times 8) + (7 \times 2) + (4 \times 5) = 104$. This projected total travel distance is a 20 percent reduction from the previous layout. Therefore, swapping employees A and B could reduce the unproductive overhead time spent traveling between offices.

How do we come up with alternate layouts?

You will note in the above process layout problem, no hard-fast rules were given for coming up with the optimal layout. In fact, finding the optimal layout can be a trial-and-error process–try a number of layouts and pick the best.

Common sense indicates that we should put stations involving frequent trips next to one another. This is a simple problem given three-location problems like the example above, but much more difficult with problems involving tens or hundreds of locations. Software exists to solve more complex process layout problems. However, that software does not guarantee optimal solutions in all cases, but does come up with solutions that are pretty good.

Your calculation of the total cost of a layout can be simplified somewhat by using a spreadsheet. If you have a distance matrix and a trips matrix entered such that the corresponding elements line up, you can use the @sumproduct(•) function to calculate the overall cost. For example if the distance matrix is in cells B2 through F6, and the trips matrix is in cells H2 through L6, then the overall cost could be calculated with the function @sumproduct(B2..F6,H2..L6). In Excel that function would display as =SUMPRODUCT(B2:F6,H2:L6).

Of course, this type of numerical analysis is simply one factor to help make decisions. The fact is, office 1 may have a big window, office 2 may have new carpet, and office 3 may be near the water cooler. A combination of factors should be considered in layout decisions or any operational decisions.

Other Reading

The following is reading about Facility Layout from other texts, which you may be using in your course. Your instructor will inform you which if any of this reading you are accountable for, and may assign problems or other exercises from that reading.

- Fitzsimmons2 chapter 6 on The Supporting Facility. Particularly, pages 128-136 are on Layout.
- Chase8 chapter 10 on Facility Layout.
- Stevenson6 chapter 6 on Facilities Layout.
- Heizer5 chapter 9 on Layout Strategy.

Simulation Exercise

You should re-run the simulation *hospital.mod*. Again, print your final results and submit them as directed by your instructor (either on paper, or electronically if your course is registered on the workbook website). Hopefully your results will be improved by the use of analytical methods described above. The following is a hint about how to run the simulation with improved results:

You might consider a few layouts (assignments of departments to wing-floors) and calculate the overall travel cost of each using the procedure described above.

Apx C

Applying Facility Layout in Your Target Service Business

How might Facility Layout analysis be applied in your target service business? Consider the following questions with regard to your target business:

① Does employee and/or customer travel within the service facility influence productivity or customer satisfaction?
② How might travel between various parts of the service facility be estimated?
③ How might that travel be reduced besides reorganizing the service facility?

Increasing the Simulation Challenge (Levels)

Simulation Exercises can be run at higher "levels" for students interested in a more challenging problem. The following is how higher levels effects the *hospital.mod* simulation: When you select higher levels, the size of the hospital building increases, with more departments to assign.

Statistical Process Control (SPC) Analysis:
Control Charts for Variables

Read this in conjunction with **SBP 3e: Difficulty in Maintaining Quality**.
(You should complete the SBP 3e Quantitative Analysis section before proceeding here.)

One way to investigate this is with *Statistical Process Control*, or SPC. SPC allows us to make assumptions about data to help separate simple random variation–also called *natural variation*–from variation that is caused by changes in the process–called *assignable variation*.

The foundation of Statistical Process Control is the central limit theorem, which states that the sum (or average) of a number of measurements from any single given probability distribution will approximate a normal distribution. This holds true regardless of the distribution of the individual measurements. How close the sums (or averages) approximates the normal distribution depends on how many measurements are in a sample, which number is called the *sample size*.

The two general types of quantitative quality measures are *attributes* and *variables*. An attribute is dichotomous, meaning that it takes on the values of "acceptable" or "unacceptable." Unacceptable represents a quality defect. An example is a bank transaction, which is either correct or is not correct.

Herein we will consider variables, which are continuously scaled. In theory, a variable can take on any value within a given range, although they are often measured at specific intervals. The cookie ratings from the simulation exercise are variables, since they can take on any value between 0 and 10.

There are two things we are concerned about with our sample measurements. One is that the mean of the measurements is statistically in *control*. To be in *control* means that the process merely contains random variation, not assignable variation. One way to analyze the control of a process is with a *control chart*. To test for statistical control of the variable mean we would use an x-bar control chart.

The term x-bar, denoted $\overline{X}$, represents the mean of a sample of measurements. Each measurement in a sample is an X value, i.e. X_1, X_2, X_3, etc. If the sample size is n, then n of the X value measurements are averaged to calculate an x-bar value. (The bar denotes "mean of values.")

An x-bar chart is a line graph with each plotted point being the x-bar value for a sample of measurements. We also plot a line on the chart which represents the mean of our x-bar values. The mean of x-bar values is, as you might imagine, called x-bar-bar, denoted $\overline{\overline{X}}$. X-bar-bar is the mean of a group of x-bar values.

For example imagine that we have the following measurements:

Day	Five Measurements					X-bar	R
1	48	45	45	45	50	46.6	5
2	45	48	46	50	46	47.0	5
3	47	51	46	49	45	47.6	6
4	41	40	42	41	42	41.2	2
5	47	46	48	48	44	46.6	4
6	46	44	45	43	42	44.0	4
7	43	40	52	48	49	46.4	12

Apx C

Note that the sample size is five. The sample size is *NOT* seven, which is the number of samples.

The x-bar values are calculated as the mean of the measurements in each sample. The column labeled R contains the sample range values. The range of a sample is simply the maximum measurement in the sample minus the minimum measurement in the sample. These R values will be used later.

We can calculate x-bar-bar to be 45.63 as the average of the x-bar values. Of course, we would expect some of the x-bar values to be above the x-bar-bar value, and some to be below it. If there is just natural variation, then we would expect a random distribution above and below the mean. If we plot the data we see the following:

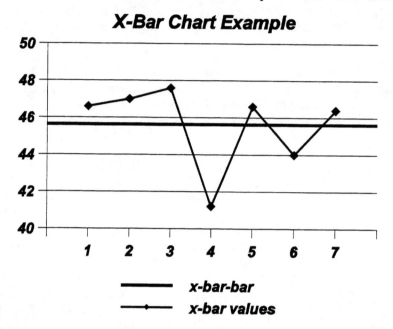

We observe that the first three points are above the mean line, but that otherwise, the data seems to be randomly dispersed above and below the mean. The movement around the mean line in this example appears to be natural variation.

Another thing it would be good to know about the x-bar values is how dispersed they are. In particular, we would like to know if a particular x-bar value was outside of a reasonable range. The x-bar values are going to vary somewhat simply due to natural variation. Unusual variation may indication that there is a *special cause*, or a specific reason, for variation. That special cause may be a problem that needs to be addressed.

Statistically, we can calculate a range of reasonable variation in the x-bar chart. That reasonable range is bounded by *control limits*. The *upper control limit* indicates the maximum value that is statistically reasonable, and the *lower control limit* indicates the minimum reasonable value. By "reasonable" we mean being likely to occur given natural variation. This is different from "acceptable" in terms of acceptable quality. It is up to management, employees, and customers to decide what is acceptable in terms of quality measurements.

The upper and lower control limits are calculated from some equations based on the central limit theorem, which was mentioned previously. To simplify the required calculations, tables are available which contain control limit factors. The following is a three-sigma factor table.

Three-sigma Factor Table

sample size	A-factor	B-factor	C-factor
2	1.880	0	3.268
3	1.023	0	2.574
4	0.729	0	2.282
5	0.577	0	2.114
6	0.483	0	2.004
7	0.419	0.076	1.924
8	0.373	0.136	1.864
9	0.337	0.184	1.816
10	0.308	0.233	1.777

(Source: *Quality Control Handbook*, J.M. Juran, editor. New York: McGraw-Hill, 1979.)

This is called a three-sigma factor table because it place control limits three standard deviations from the mean. From the normal distribution we know that 99.7 percent of all random values will be within three standard deviations of the mean. In other words, it is quite unlikely that natural variation will cause recurring values outside of three-sigma control limits.

The A-factor from the table pertains to x-bar charts. The other two factors will be used in a different chart. (Some text books call these factors by different names, such as A_2, D_3, and D_4.) The sample size is the number of measurement in each sample. Be careful to not confuse the sample size with the number of samples. The sample size is *not* the number of samples in the chart! It is the number of measurements *within each sample*.

Although you can construct a control chart with a sample size of 2, it is probably not the best. The bigger the sample size, the more statistically representative will be your control chart values. A sample size of 5 or 6 is probably okay. Larger sample sizes are the best, but they often take more effort to gather.

The upper control limit (UCL) for an x-bar chart is calculated as

$$UCL_{\bar{X}} = \bar{\bar{X}} + A\bar{R}$$

where r-bar is calculated as the average of the sample range values, as discussed previously. The lower control limit (LCL) for an x-bar chart is similarly calculated as

$$LCL_{\bar{X}} = \bar{\bar{X}} - A\bar{R}$$

Since the factors were from a three-sigma factor table, we expect that three standard deviations of x-bar values will be between the LCL and the UCL. The central limit theorem shows that the x-bar values tend to follow a normal distribution. Three standard deviations from the mean of normal distribution includes 99.7 percent of the probability density. This means that 99.7 percent of the time, a random number drawn from a normal distribution will be within three standard deviations from the mean. It is quite unlikely that values would fall outside of that range on a regular basis.

Apx C

From the data above, we can calculate control limits for the example x-bar chart as LCL=45.63–0.556×5.43=42.50 and UCL=LCL=45.63+0.556×5.43=48.76 . We plot these control limits on our control chart, as follows:

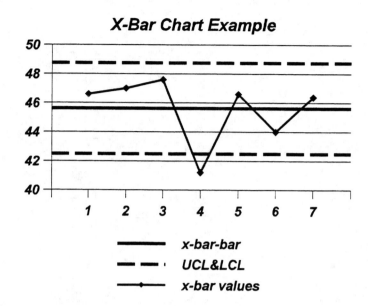

X-Bar Chart Example

——— x-bar-bar

— — ' UCL&LCL

———— x-bar values

In this data we conclude that something peculiar might have happened in period 4, since the x-bar value is below the lower control limit. Keep in mind that it is *possible* that the x-bar value for period 4 is a random occurrence. We need to be careful about jumping to conclusions that something is definitely wrong with the process. However, such a x-bar value is not very likely to occur without a special cause. (Since only 0.3 percent of truly random values will be outside of the three-sigma control limits.) Therefore, it would be good to investigate the situation further.

An x-bar chart tells us if the central tendency (i.e. mean) of the samples appears to be in control over time. Another chart, the *R-chart*, tells us if the variance within each sample tends to be in control over time. It is certainly possible for the sample means to be in control over time, yet the sample variance is getting worse and worse.

An R-chart is created similar to how we create an x-bar chart except for the following:
- the points which are plotted are the R, or range, values calculated above.
- the central line is the R-bar value, which is the mean of the R values.
- the upper control limit, LCL_R , is simply the B-factor times R-bar.
- the lower control limit, UCL_R , is simply the C-factor times R-bar.

Again, since we are using three-sigma factors, we would expect the R values to fall within the control limits 99.7 percent of the time.

For the data from the example above we calculate LCL_R =2.115×5.43=11.48, and LCL_R =0×5.43=0. Note that lower control limits for R-charts are bounded by zero, since it is impossible to have R values less than zero.

The control chart is as follows:

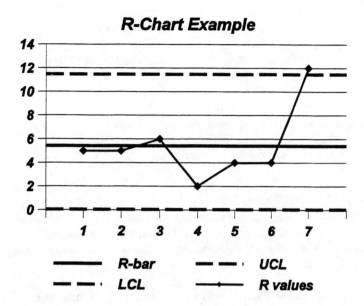

We see that in period 7 the range of values appears to have gone up beyond what is statistically common. It is interesting to note that the x-bar value for that sample was fine, meaning that on average the measurements in the sample were in control. However we had more variance in that sample that we might have usually expected, so we should investigate for special causes or changes in the process.

Do we care if an R value is at or below the LCL? (Assuming we have a non-zero LCL) It seems that less variance would be better. In fact it might be good to investigate *improvements* in the process so that they can be assured to continue in the future.

Summary of Things to Look For

What are we looking for in a control chart that might cause us to suspect the process has changed? The following are some examples:
- An unusual tendency for the sample values to be above or below the x-bar-bar or R-bar line. "Unusual" might mean five or more in a row.
- An unusual tendency for the sample values to be near a control limit. Here, "unusual" might mean two or more values that are very near the control limit.
- Values that appear outside of the control limits. If three-sigma control limits are used, then it is quite unusual for even one value to appear outside of the control limits.
- Other peculiar patters in the data, such as erratic fluctuations above and below the mean, or patterns that repeat over a fixed number of samples.

Again, with each of these occurrences we *investigate* for special causes. Such patterns of behavior can happen with mere natural variation, but they are not likely.

Updating Control Limits

Apx C

Once you have constructed a control chart based on currently available data, you can construct a control chart. It is probably a good idea to have at least five to ten samples of data to construct your control chart. Then, as you collect more samples of data, they can be appended to the control chart. As long as the process appears to be in control, it is usually not necessary to recalculate the control limits and central line with each new sample–just use the ones you originally calculated. However, if it is determined that the process has changed, then it would be good to gather measurements from the new process as the basis for re-calculating control limits.

Other Reading

The following is reading about Statistical Process Control (SPC) from other texts, which you may be using in your course. Your instructor will inform you which if any of this reading you are accountable for, and may assign problems or other exercises from that reading.

- Fitzsimmons2 pages 288-298 on Service Process Control.
- Chase8 supplement to chapter 6 on Statistical Quality Control Methods.
- Stevenson6 chapter 10 on Quality Control.
- Heizer5 chapter 4 supplement on Statistical Process Control.

Simulation Exercise

You should re-run the simulation *cookies.mod*. Again, print your final results and submit them as directed by your instructor (either on paper, or electronically if your course is registered on the workbook website). Hopefully your results will be improved by the use of analytical methods described above. The following is a hint about how to run the simulation with improved results:

This time you might use a control chart or charts to help you determine if your process is in control.

Applying Statistical Process Control (SPC) in Your Target Service Business

How might Statistical Process Control (SPC) analysis be applied in your target service business? Consider the following questions with regard to your target business:

① What are a few examples of measurements it would be useful to track in the service process?
② How difficult or costly would it be to gather adequate samples of those measurements? How would the measurements be taken?
③ Why might we expect *natural* variation to occur in those measurements, even if the process is in control? (This emphasizes the need for caution in not overreacting to variation in the measurements.)

Increasing the Simulation Challenge (Levels)

Simulation Exercises can be run at higher "levels" for students interested in a more challenging problem. The following is how higher levels effects the *cookies.mod* simulation: When you select higher levels, the number and types of oven breakdowns potentially increases.

Appendix D:
Other Readings

This appendix contains readings which, at this writing, are not available from another published source. With this edition this includes two readings by the author:

- "Christmas at UPS," a mini-case by the author that can be used with Unit 10, specifically with the *Customer Inventory Cost* Service Business Principle.

- "An Empirically Derived Framework for Designing Customer Feedback Systems," an article by the author that provides guidance for designing customer comment cards and other customer feedback systems. This article is a reading good reading for Unit 12 (SBP: *Everyone Thinks They're an Expert*) and Unit 14 (SBP: *Measuring Customers*). The reading will be particularly helpful in completing the Application Exercise associated with those Service Business Principles.

At this writing the latter article is under review with a journal, and is published here with the written permission of the journal editor.

Apx D

Christmas at UPS
An Exercise in Queuetility

December 13, 1994

My story is real--at least as far as perception is reality. It seems like it happened just yesterday. Actually, it did.

This year, all I have wanted from Santa Claus was a particular electronic music keyboard. I had purchased the keyboard from a local electronics store for $20 a month or so earlier. I have seen similar keyboards in stores for $200, and mail order for $178. I had considered budgeting one for months, but had not. When I saw this one, I knew it was the one for me. It was used. It was a little beat up. I love buying useful things that are used and a little beat up, because they are cheap, like me. The salesperson told me it somewhat worked. They had plugged it in earlier—it made a clicking sound. Being the incorrigible tightwad that I am, I ventured. For 30 bucks I got the keyboard and a big box of used A/C adapters (do any of you need a spare adapter?).

The keyboard actually worked fine as long as you played the key of G. I don't mean play a musical selection in the key of G, but rather every 13th key that was a G. Pressing the other keys did not result in what one would term pleasing sounds. This probably would not have been a problem except for the fact that I am not aware of any songs that only require G keys. So, I carefully tore the thing apart, hoping to find one wire loose that would fix it. (Which actually happened to my great-uncle who bought a broken car from the government which he fixed by re-arranging the spark plug wires.) I narrowed the cause of my keyboard's problem down to the circuit board, which represents just about everything complex about the device. After lying torn apart on my desk for a few weeks, I concluded that if it wasn't going to fix itself I was going to have to send it in.

On this particular day, yesterday, my wife picked me up from the office to go to lunch. Our two boys were already sound asleep in their car seats, which meant we may have a peaceful, although drive-in lunch. We drove west, with our eye out for a drive-in restaurant that did not serve junk food. I hoped we would not find one too soon, since the UPS office was on far west side of town. I wanted to go to UPS, because my keyboard was in the trunk. Affixed to the keyboard was a mailing label and a return authorization number. The company had agreed to fix/replace the keyboard for $60, even though I had purchased it as-is.

The day before I had called the UPS toll-free number listed in the phone book for information. I was please to learn that UPS indeed has an office in Tallahassee, and further delighted to learn that it was not all the way out near the airport. I was told the hours of business. A few days before, the Bruno's grocery store, which accepts packages for UPS shipment, refused my package because "it is not wrapped in brown paper." I asked the UPS person on the phone if brown paper was necessary. He responded, "No, in fact don't wrap it in brown paper since it gets torn." Great!

After we finished our Subway sandwiches in the parking lot, we were a short distance from the UPS office. The UPS phone person not only told me the address, but how to get there. This was amazing, since he was clearly at some central office far from Tallahassee. My wife was driving, so I navigated.

Sure enough, there it was. The first driveway was marked with a "customer entrance" sign pointing to the driveway on the other side of the building. As we drove by, we saw a large open building with people lined up into the parking lot. When we came to the next driveway, my wife drove right on by. "Where are we going?" I asked. "You saw the waiting line, didn't you?" was her response. "Oh, I don't know. Maybe it is not as bad as it looks." Besides, the kids were still asleep. We drove back.

I hopped out and got my box out of the trunk. Then, I surveyed the situation. There were clearly two lines reaching into the parking lot, but the lines began about five feet inside the building. (See the diagram at the end.) The lines were only four or five people deep! Even though it was a cold day, a short wait outside would be no problem.

Being the operations management minded person that I am, I quickly analyzed the situation and decided to take the line at the left. The lines seemed to have the same number of people, but the line on the right had a guy with a cart with probably five large packages on it. Who knows how long that will take to process.

I noticed the people in front of me had a similar paper in their hands. There were no signs or display boxes containing forms, so I looked to the table at the front of the line. There were the papers, AND a pen, which I had not brought. By now, there was a gentleman behind me in line. But I needed that paper and pen, and did not want to lose my position in line. So, I walked up, picked up the paper and pen, and walked back to my position, glancing at the gentleman to make sure he was not upset that I wanted to reclaim my place. No problem. All was well.

I filled out the form using the back of my box as my tablet. Meanwhile, the gentleman behind me realized he needed the same form. But I was using the only pen that was up there. Fortunately, he was able to borrow one from the young man in front of me. I thought, "That young man is prepared." So I thought.

By now, it did not seem the slightest impropriety to walk up and put the pen back on the table, and then reclaim my place in line. We had socially developed as a line. We were in this together, and intended to maintain order. There were now three or four people behind me in line.

At least five minutes had passed, and our line had not moved an inch. The other line was moving. I knew this because I kept politely moving out of the way to let people from the other line pass to the area at left where packages are weighed. (See diagram at end.) The man with the cart of boxes was at the front of the other line.

There was something wrong at the front of my line. The area was seeping with confusion. People were having conversations, which is not normally acceptable at the front of a line.

The man with the cart was processed in no time flat. The end of the other line was no further back than where I was (which is where I started). Should I switch lines? I looked behind me and saw that there were more people behind me than in front of me. Why should I switch to the **end** of the other line when I was **more than halfway** up in the line I was in. I stayed.

People that joined the other line proceeded through their line. Amazingly, that line never increased in length, although our line was picking up a new person now and then. Every minute or so I thought "I should switch lines." But no--the ultimate frustration would be switching lines and having the right line stop just as the left line started moving. We have to start moving soon. So I stayed.

"Do I even need to be in this line?" I asked myself. Perhaps I should just walk over to the weighing area, where UPS employees were standing idle. No, there must be some reason why we have to wait in this line first--why else would we be here.

Succinct conversations had started at the back of our line, which of course is acceptable and is a sure sign that we had been together long enough to have developed socially as a group. "It looks like the packing tape is free," one person commented, observing that the primary activity at the front of theses lines was UPS employees putting tape over people's boxes that already looked sealed.

The gentleman behind me commented "This is the slow line." "Yes, it is," I responded. I felt slightly comforted, knowing that the answer to "Is it just me, or is this the slow line," was a resounding "It's not just me."

Finally after another five or 20 minutes, our line began moving. The bottleneck lady moved to the lineless weighing area, where she began a conversation with other UPS employees.

The next few people in our line were slowly processed. Meanwhile, the weighing area became bottlenecked, and for the first time, a half-dozen people were waiting to have their packages weighed. I thought, "I guess it is now all right that I am in a slow line, since otherwise I would just have to be waiting to have my packages weighed." Somehow that made me feel better.

Apx D

Finally, the young man with the pen who was in front of me wheeled his hand-truck and three boxes to the front of the line. I was almost there! He put the top box on the table. The UPS employee responded "All of that masking tape has got to go." The young man furiously started yanking masking tape off of the second box. Should I help him. I didn't want to meddle, or reveal my great impatience. The first box was not even closed. Who is this guy. One of his boxes had some company name on it. The other boxes had no names on them at all. What's going on here?! Doesn't this guy know UPS will not ship things without addresses?! Clearly not, as revealed by the conversation. The UPS employee, an older man, sternly said to him "When you ship things in used boxes like this you need to cross out the old writing and labels, and leave the mailing address." The young man, still working on his boxes, mumbled "Well, some of us don't know what we were supposed to do." Amen to that.

The UPS man brought up a big roll of brown paper. Oh no, he's not going to wrap these things is he?! He instead started tearing off large pieces of paper and stuffing them in the empty top quarter of young man box #1. What service. I wonder if they would wrap my Christmas presents for me if I brought them by.

Please keep in mind that this is a true story. I probably would have written a more incredible story if I were to take creative liberties. But then again, maybe not.

After some additional confusing discussion, the UPS man handed the young man a marker, which he used to start writing addresses on his boxes. The UPS man waved his hand for me to come to the other side of the table. Finally a breakthrough! I am glad I was prepared. I will be the example of speed and efficiency. No conversations out of me! Just please don't ask me to wrap the thing in brown paper.

I placed my keyboard box on the table carefully so that the address would be facing the man, a simple act, but a contribution to the cause of efficiency. The address was preprinted by the repair company, so was clearly legible. I gladly presented the UPS man with my completed form. Things were going great! "I need your return address on the box here," he said, pointing to a place on the box. Oh no! I thought the return address had been preprinted on the label. Well, I am not going to make this into a major incident, but the place where I left the pen was now covered by young man box #3. The UPS man graciously offered me a pen that did not work. He then generously exchanged it for one that worked, and I scribbled my address, abbreviating my first name so as to not take any more time than necessary--hopefully recovering a small portion of efficiency.

He looked carefully at the ends of my box. Ha, no masking tape here. I used only genuine 3M packing tape. "Is this corrugated cardboard?" he asked. What the heck is corrugated cardboard? Isn't that the stuff that is a wavy layer sandwiched between two flat layers? I have no idea. Think, think. The keyboard repair company sent me instructions recommending that I ship it in this original container with UPS as the preferred shipper. I could not imagine them recommending this if UPS had any problem with that type of box. If corrugated cardboard was a UPS requirement, I deduced, then logically this box <u>must</u> be corrugated. "Yes," I quickly responded. He was happy about that, I hoped.

He took a marker and made a large circle around my mailing label, and wrote "To" at the top. I felt a little more confident it would get there now. "Do you want a tracking number?" he finally asked. I had seen numerous UPS advertisements about the great benefits of their new tracking system, but I had no idea the tracking number was optional. They are not optional with Federal Express. Perhaps this whole line was optional! I shivered at the thought. Well, by golly, I didn't wait in line for somewhere between 15 minutes and 2 hours just to have him check my box for return addresses and cardboard type. "Sure," I responded. After slapping on a tracking sticker, he concluded our conversation with, "Take this over to the weighing area."

There was a mere one person waiting to have her small package weighed. I recognized her as someone from the back of the fast line who had arrived 15 minutes after I got there. She was standing in front of a device that looked like a scale, but presently without an operator. A UPS employee down the table at a different scale (one with rollers on top) took her package and weighed it. She then looked on a chart taped to the table to determine the charge, which she wrote on the shipping form. It was my turn! I glanced back at the long slow line I came from, feeling some sympathy for those poor souls. It was a cold day.

The weigh lady checked the keyboard package weight - 12 lbs. "Is this going to a business or a residence." "A business," I said, "but which is cheaper." "Business." That made sense, since the UPS truck has to go more out of its way to visit residence. She wrote the fee on my paper.

The weigh lady now appeared to have a moment of free time on her hands. She turned around to watch a small package on the conveyer belt that delivered packages up into some big dark abyss. I don't know how that package got there, since I did not see her weight it. Perhaps there was some other easier way to get one's packages on this important conveyer belt. She turned the package on its side to either check something or make the contents more comfortable, and then turned back around to wait for the next weighing customer.

Suddenly, a lady from near the back of the slow line I had come from walked up and asked the weigh lady, "Do I need to wait in that line? My packages are already taped." She had been smart enough to leave her packages holding her place in the slow line. "Do you have your shipping form?" the weigh lady queried. "Yes," to which the weigh lady conceded with a subdued "Sure, bring them up." Minimal conversation--it was marvelous. She got her packages and brought them up. I admired this woman greatly. She **deserved** a short wait! I did not, since I was a gutless conformist. I did not care to observe the grimace on the faces of the others in the slow line upon seeing this development. I could see the light at the end of the tunnel, and was not looking back.

All that was left for me was to pay. I had my wife's wallet, with cash, checks, and a credit card. I preferred to use a check. There were two or three people between me and the cashier station. Again, some conversation, which is not a good sign. I thought, "I will be prepared, so as to recover some efficiency in this confusing process." "Do you take checks?" I asked the weigh lady, as if she would have any idea, being of a different job function. "Yes," she responded. She sounded confident enough to warrant starting to complete a check. Everything except the amount. "Is this the amount," I asked the weigh lady while pointing to the fee amount she had written on my paper, "or is tax added?" I suspected no tax was added, but she unconfidently responded that she thought tax was to be added.

I was now two people away from being served by the cashier. I noticed that the lady in front of me had a company check, also with only the amount to be filled in. She would not slow things down. However, the lady at the cashier was having problems. She was writing a check, when she spontaneously engaged in conversation with the quite cheerful cashier. This could be a problem, so I listened in. The cashier said that normally they do not take checks that do not have the persons name and address pre-printed on them. Oh, please don't let this completely ruin an otherwise dismal experience. Please, take this lady's check, or at least move her to the line for people without their names and addresses preprinted on their checks (which did not exist since there was only one cashier). I had my name and address on my checks, and was ready to go. All the two of us needed was the final amount.

The cashier quickly processed the next lady's company check, and then took my shipping paper as the first lady continued to write information on her check. This shows that there is mercy and occasional efficiency in properly staffed queues. The cashier rung me up on the register and announced the amount. I started filling in the amount on my check. It was seven dollars and something. I could not see the cash register display, so said "How much was that again?" "Seven eighty-four," which, by the way, did not include any tax.

In a jiffy I tore out my completed check and plopped it on the table. "Could I see your driver's license?" Now, this is not a fair question. How does she know that I have a driver's license. Perhaps I have some physical condition that prevents me from driving. Perhaps I want to save our dear environment and not contribute to the air pollution automobiles produce. The drivers license question is unfairly discriminating. Besides, I left my driver's license in the glove box of my other car.

Now, I am not going to make this an incident either. I did not balk, nor threaten to sick the EEOC or some other rights advocacy group on them. Instead I carefully placed my wife's drivers license on the table.

The cashier placed her nose a foot above the license to get a careful view. It didn't matter, since my wife's picture does not look like me even from ten feet away. She is a redhead, and I have a mustache. "This doesn't look like you," the cashier brilliantly deduced. Now, given lighter circumstances I would made some a comment such as, "That was taken before my plastic surgery." But, this was not the time nor the business environment for such a comment.

Apx D

"That," my dear cashier, "is my wife who is **right there** with our two sleeping kids in the car," I declared as I pointed to our car that has been parked in a fire zone for somewhere between 20 minutes and 3 hours. "Did she sign this check?" was the response. "No. I did," I said with a slight air of defiance.

Perhaps it was because the cashier has kids or grandkids that sometimes sleep in the car. Perhaps it was because in some strange way the "S" of UPS stands for service. Perhaps, like the brilliant lady who skipped the slow line, the cashier also understands that for every policy is an equal and opposite anti-policy (i.e. exception). Perhaps it was because if she did not take my check, her station would turn into the bottleneck. Or perhaps it was because Christmas was only two weeks away. Whatever the reason, she turned the check over and wrote my wife's name and drivers license number on the back. I was happy, but would hate to think of what would happen if someone stole my wife's checkbook and attempted to ship a bunch of really heavy packages to Singapore via UPS.

I was outa there! The kids were still asleep, but woke up about a mile down the road. They probably woke up due to our discussion of the educational value of my experience. We decided that I needed to document the experience for educational use—if for no other reason than to justify my poor judgment in sticking to the queue at UPS.

Epilogue

Upon arriving home that evening, I discovered that a box from UPS had arrived for me. It was a pair of binoculars that a repair company should have shipped to my father-in-law in Utah instead of to me in Florida. Last August I attempted to fix them for him, but only made them worse, so I decided to send them in to the repair company. How much can a pair of binoculars weight? In other words, how many postage stamps would it take to mail them to Utah. The post office _is_ right on my way to work.

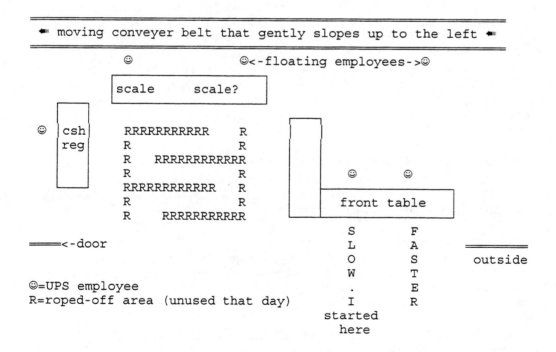

rev2/14/94

An Empirically Defined Framework for Designing Customer Feedback Systems

by Scott E. Sampson
December 18, 1997

ABSTRACT

Crosby and others have pronounced that "quality is free." (Crosby 1979) Of course, this supposition is contingent on the ability for investments in quality to generate a return. Up front investments in quality can result in returns in the form of reduced rework costs, increased productivity, increased sales and market share, etc. (see e.g. Evans and Lindsay 1993, p. 19) Any idea that "quality is merely an expense" is surely antiquated given enlightened views—improvement investments are expected, even required, to generate acceptable returns.

This paper applies the same return requirement to customer feedback systems. Collecting and analyzing customer feedback costs money, but often the return or impact on the bottom line is not clear. After discussing the customer feedback investment, we will present a framework for utilizing customer feedback to advance quality at various parts of an organization—consistent with the total quality idea. That framework describes potential goals and objectives for customer feedback. Within the framework, we will present illustrations coming from our extensive field study of feedback instruments.

KEY WORDS

customer-driven quality, customer feedback, information gathering, TQM

Introduction

Many companies collect feedback from customers, yet surprisingly few expect or require the collection effort to bring substantial benefits to the organization. Although customer feedback systems have the potential for promoting customer-driven quality, they are commonly utilized for little more than a complaint management. As such, the only "return" that is hoped for is the complaining customers, with only minor impact on the overall organization. In fact, there is no reason that customer feedback systems should not be considered an investment that requires an adequate return throughout the organization.

This article describes means of designing customer feedback systems that are tied to real business needs. The framework is the result of a seven-year study of customer feedback systems including analysis of hundreds of customer feedback instruments. It is not the purpose of the present article to describe the data collection and analysis, but rather to describe the overall framework for system design which comes from analysis and observations. As will be described, this overall framework starts with specific goals and objectives, which form the basis for customer feedback solicitation efforts and data use. Examples from the instrument data will be cited to illustrate effective and ineffective methods for gathering customer feedback. Various feedback system design issues will be discussed and options will be enumerated.

Is Customer Feedback "Free?"

The phrase *customer feedback* can be broadly defined. It includes any solicited or unsolicited information received from customers during or after the delivery of a service or product. Examples of unsolicited information are complaint letters, tips for the waiter, or comments made to employees. Such unsolicited feedback can be useful and yet limited in scope. Many companies extend the scope of feedback they receive by soliciting the feedback, such as through comment cards or customer surveys.

It is easy to believe that there is inherent value in collecting customer feedback. What is not so easily understood is that customer feedback is a *resource*—just like labor, capital, inventory, and so forth—that comes with a *cost*. It costs to collect feedback. It costs to analyze the feedback. It costs to act on the feedback. How costly might this be? Technical Assistance Research Programs, Inc. (TARP), in a study of 22 large "customer-driven" companies, found that the companies spent a median of $1 million and employed the equivalent of 13 full-time professional staff per year on customer feedback systems.[1] These are not trivial costs.

What is also not generally understood is that expenditures in customer feedback should be considered an investment. Why should it be otherwise? Companies consider expenditures in new technologies an investment and

Apx D

expect a return. So also do they expect a return for investments in plant and equipment, research and development, and marketing campaigns. Enlightened mangers even consider inventory to be an investment—and if inventory costs cannot be justified by impact on the bottom line, inventories should probably be reduced or eliminated.

Likewise, expenditures in customer feedback systems should be required to contribute to critical business processes, but often they do not. After studying those customer-driven companies, the TARP researchers report that "many of these companies have little to show for their investment" in customer feedback systems. Why is there such little return from customer feedback system investments? The TARP researchers conclude that the problem is not in gathering the data, but in putting the data to use. Other researchers report meager attempts to use customer feedback data. For example, Gilly and Hansen [2] report that 44 percent of complaint letters sent to businesses received no response whatsoever, and it seems unlikely that these companies took any other action except perhaps to reprimand someone. Hart, Heskett, and Sasser [3] report that more than half of all company responses to customer complaints actually *reinforce* the customers' negative reactions.

Evidence indicates that even companies that *solicit* feedback often do little with the information they receive. Customer feedback often sits in an in-box until it is filed (or "round-filed") after little more than a casual perusal. Only when glaring problems are revealed in the feedback— such as one area of the company generating numerous complaints—is action taken. Not-so-glaring problems are often overlooked. Harvesting value from *positive* feedback is rarely seen.

Few companies do a good job of assuring a good return on investment from customer feedback systems, yet many companies continue to invest in them. Consumer products have toll-free numbers on the labeling. Comment cards are particularly prevalent in service industries. For example, in our survey of 456 unique hotel properties, more than 200 were currently distributing customer comment cards. Retail, education, banking, and many other service industries likewise invest highly in collecting customer feedback. Yet we have seen that few companies ever evaluate these efforts as an investment which is justified by an adequate return.

We certainly do not propose that investments in customer feedback be simply abandoned. What we do recommend is that companies insist on a return commensurate with the investment.

Using Customer Feedback in a Total Quality System

There are a number of possibly reasons why companies do not get an adequate return on their customer feedback. The personnel assigned to handle customer feedback systems could be inexperienced. Management might think the company is technology driven, not market driven. Management might consider customer feedback unimportant, and only collect data to give the *appearance* of concern. Even companies that claim to have "customer focus" make meager attempts at tying customer feedback into real quality improvement.

Our research indicates that a core reason good companies fail to harvest value from customer feedback is because they *start* by gathering customer feedback. Isn't that what they are supposed to do? Can they act on the data if they don't first have the data? Well, no. Neither can they act on the data if they do not have data that is actionable. And it is unlikely that they will act on the feedback if there is no system in place for putting the feedback to work. How can they have a effective system if it is not tied to functional areas of the organization.

A key idea behind total quality is that it "...works horizontally across functions and departments...." (Gamble 1992) Therefore, it seems, using customer feedback in a total quality system will require identifying how the information can be used throughout the organization, not just in the marketing department (as is often the case). Identifying where to use the feedback is one of the questions that need to be answered before an effective customer feedback system can be put in place. Also, before gathering customer feedback, every company should start by carefully defining the objectives of customer feedback in the quality improvement process. Therefore, a total quality approach to applying customer feedback system should start with the following issues:
- defining *where* information is needed and *who* will use the customer feedback,
- specifying *what* the goals and objectives for the feedback will be (or *how* the feedback will benefit the company), and
- using these goals and objectives to determine *what* feedback should be collected, *how* it should be collected, and *how* it should be analyzed and used.

In other words, a key to harvesting quality improvement value from customer feedback is understanding how the information can be used *throughout* the organization. The following sections describe a framework which will help address these *where*, *who*, *what*, and *how* issues.

● Using Feedback Across the Organization

An early question that total quality companies should ask themselves is, "Where can customer feedback benefit the company and who is going to use it?" There are four functional areas of the company where customer feedback can be of particular value. These are:

- Design - Those responsible for determining what services or products will be offered and what the systems will be for production and delivery.
- Marketing - Those responsible for attracting new or previous customers and providing them with pre-purchase information.
- Operations - Those responsible for actually producing and delivering the service or product.
- Customer Support - Those responsible for providing support to customers. Generally, this support comes *after* they have purchased the service or product. This support function should arguably involve design, marketing, and operations. However, in many companies, customer support is assigned to a specific group of employees.

Of course, there are other departments where customer feedback can provide a return to total quality efforts. However, these four are critical, and are the focus of this research.

Concurrent with defining where feedback will be used is specifying *what* the goals and objectives for the feedback are. This will identify *how* the information will benefit the designated functional area(s)—how it will help them do their job(s) better. There are a variety of goals and objectives to which feedback can contribute.

The following four sections describe sample goals that are relevant to each of the four functional areas just listed. With each goal, examples are given for how actual companies collect information towards that goal. These examples are from our study of customer feedback instruments of more than 600 service-sector companies. Although our examples come from service companies, the goals can be relevant to manufacturing companies as well.

Consistent with this generality, we will use the phrase "service product" to refer to the output of both service and manufacturing companies. The service product can be the service offered by a service company, and since manufactured goods serve a customer's need, a manufactured product can also be considered a service product.

● 1. Goals Relating to Service Product Design:

Ascertain customer needs. Customer needs form the basis for service product features. Knowing which needs are most important can help the company decide what service product features to offer. One hotel assesses customer-need importance with the following question: "Which of the following is your most important reason for visiting Colorado Belle? ○Gambling Atmosphere/theme ○Room Quality ○Dining ○Entertainment ○Parking ○Pricing ○Location ○Know someone." Survey results can help determine which features to focus on.

Also, customer feedback can help you understand potential needs which could be met. One home improvement retailer (Lowe's) identifies product needs not currently being met by asking customers, "What other products should Lowe's carry?" The Bucksaw Point Resort in Clinton, Missouri gathered facility design information from experts—their current customers—by asking what needs they would like to have met: "We are planning on building additional cabins. What changes can we make to answer your needs?"

Develop the service product. Development should be an ongoing process, whether we are dealing with new or old products. By asking specific questions, companies can get specific information. For example, Jefferson National Bank (JNB) asks customers, "Where else would you like to see a JNB 24-Hour Teller machine?" Other companies seek more general service product development information. One retailer asks customers, "Of our weaker points, which one or two would you like to see us correct first?" That may not be the best question format, since it may have negative connotations. Perhaps a better approach to the same issue is the question asked by Hahn Shoes store: "Briefly describe one area where we could improve our store."

Benchmark versus competition. Valuable information can be gained from studying competing companies. One retailer asks, "Is there any merchandise that you buy from our competitors that we don't carry? if so what is it?" Another simply wants to know how it compares on a rating scale: "Compare Famous Brands Housewares Outlet to Competition... (Excellent) A B C D E (Poor)."

2. Goals Relating to Marketing:

Identify customers. Feedback can help us know who our customers are. Hahn Shoes asks this relevant identifying question: "Shoe size___," which can help spot if complaints about selection are occurring with specific sizes. Cotton Ginny, a Canadian clothing store, asks customers, "How often do you go to the movies? ❑Weekly ❑Monthly ❑Rarely. Do you own a car?_____ Use public transportation?_____" This information can help the company more accurately target its marketing efforts. The Alexander Hotel in Miami directly asks, "What was the deciding factor in choosing The Alexander?" The answer may not be obvious to the customer, however, since there might have been a variety of factors that entered into the selection decision. Quality Inn gives the customer a list of possible reasons when it asks: "You decided to stop at a QUALITY HOTEL because: (list of nine options, including 'other...')."

Promote service product. Feedback itself can be used as a marketing tool. An automotive-service chain uses positive customer feedback to market quality improvement initiatives within the company. Many companies have used positive customer feedback in advertising in the form of "testimonials." An art museum asks, "Would you recommend this exhibition to a friend? Why?" The responses can help the museum "recommend" the exhibit in its marketing media.

Generate sales leads. Feedback is one way to get leads for repeat business. The clothing retailer Raleighs has as the final check-box on its comment card: "I would like to open a Raleighs Charge." Other companies ask on comment cards if the customer would like information about other products. Comment cards can even be used to generate leads to other potential customers. For example, the Cranwell Conference Center in Lenox, Massachusetts, asks customers to list "Other groups you feel might be interested in our facilities and services."

3. Goals Relating to Operations:

Measure specification conformance. Operations managers need to know if employees are producing the service product that was designed to be produced. With manufactured goods, production may be inspected prior to the time it is shipped. Customer feedback can be a second line of defense against process drift.

Services often involve simultaneous production and consumption, which means that the customer receives the service at the same time it is being produced. As such, it may be impossible or impractical to inspect for defects. Customer feedback can provide the needed check on production. The following are some examples:

- Talbots (women's clothing retailer) asks, "Do you have a Talbots Charge? If not, did the sales associate offer you a Talbots Charge application?" (This implies that offering a charge might be a standard operating procedure.)
- Thom McAn (shoe retailer) asks, "Did the salesperson offer to measure your feet? ❑Yes ❑No."
- The San Francisco Music Box Co. (retailer) asks "Were you told we can change the tunes in some items? ❑yes ❑no ❑don't remember."
- Eastern Mountain Sports (outdoor equipment retailer) asks: "Was our service cheerful, helpful and quick? ❑Yes ❑No If not, why not?____" (The "why not" may be better answered by the employees. Perhaps what the company should have asked was "If not, in what way was it lacking?")
- Alaska Airlines asks its customers to rate the *cockpit announcements* according to "Content..." and "Clarity..." (each on a five-point scale).
- A Marriott Courtyard hotel asks, "Was everything in working order? ❑Yes ❑No *If not*, what was the problem(s)?"

Compare across organization. If the company has multiple sites, such as a restaurant chain or auto-service chain, or multiple departments, such as a library or a department store, customer feedback can provide a basis for comparing operations results across the organization. This requires that the feedback identify the specific location within the company about which the customer is commenting. This information is generally available: approximately three-fourths of the comment cards we studied identified the location of service. Some cards ask the customer to write the location on the card. Where appropriate, it can be more reliable to stamp a location identifier on the cards before presenting them to customers, which is often done.

With the location of service identified, customer feedback can be compared across locations. For example, a corporate Hilton Hotels comment card asks "How likely would you be to return to this Hilton if in the area again?" (on a seven-point scale), which is a measure of potential loyalty to the *specific* property. The results from various Hilton properties can then be compared. A challenge in such comparisons, though, will be interpreting results in light of operational and environmental differences across locations. For example, a hotel in a highly competitive environment may garner different loyalty results than a property with little competition in the area (implying that in a competitive environment, the employees may need to work a little harder). Nevertheless, the comparative data can help identify properties with potential problems, or properties that have discovered means to operational excellence that should be shared throughout the company.

Increase employee involvement. Feedback can help employees take ownership for the production process and its outcomes. The retailer Target tells customers, "When a store team or an employee does 'something special,' tell us about it. We'll forward your report along with our personal commendations and praise. After all, good customer service deserves to be recognized."

Of course, this implies we can identify the employee. A Hyatt Hotels' comment card makes this difficult by asking, "During your stay, did you encounter an employee who provided exceptional Hyatt service? ❑Yes ❑No" — but it does not ask *who* the exceptional employee was. A Marriott hotel card asks, "Were any of our associates especially courteous or helpful?" which may imply that the customer will identify the employee. Day's Inn identifies the employee for the customer with a comment card that says, "Welcome.. Your Room Has Been Prepared By: (name of employee listed). Your Comments Are Welcome."

In this area of employee recognition and reward, beware of *gaming*, which is inappropriate manipulation of feedback results by employees. For example, at some universities, faculty admit to limiting productivity in the classroom out of fear of poor student evaluations. An industry example of gaming is employees who encourage happy customers to give feedback directly to management (such as on a comment card) but keep complaining customers from receiving the standard feedback form (by not leaving a card for them to complete).

4. Goals Relating to Customer Support:

Evaluate customer satisfaction. Feedback can help take the "pulse" of our customers. A JC Penny catalog questionnaire asks, "Please tell us what was disappointing or not as expected." Such questioning can be rephrased more positively. The clothing retailer Petite Sophisticate asks for an evaluation of the clothing sold: "The merchandise is: ❑Versatile and exciting! ❑Needs pizzaz. ❑Mediocre at best!" Such questions are written with the target market in mind. Another clothing retailer, August Max Woman, asks, "Our service was... ❑Wonderful ❑Just OK ❑Needs help ❑What service." and "Store appearance... ❑Looked great ❑Looked good ❑Neat & Clean ❑Poorly organized ❑A disaster."

Assure repeat business. Feedback can assist in the companies' customer-retention efforts. Crestar Bank asks customers, "Have you experienced any problems with Crestar that you would like us to look into? If so, please describe the problem(s)." A challenge is that generally customers with a problem want speedy resolution; they do not want to wait for the company to "look into" it. The retailer Target addresses this timing issue by stating on their card, "Need immediate attention? Ask a Target employee to page the manager on duty *or* Drop this card at the customer service desk *or* give it to a cashier."

Provide sounding board. Customer focus requires being able to communicate with customers, particularly when the customers want to communicate. Hampton Inns has a comment card that starts with "Dear Ray" and has several blank lines that are followed by "Sincerely," with room for the customer's name and address. A card from the women's clothing retailer Audrey Jones simply states, "Audrey Jones is your store so call me anytime at 1-800-(phone number)." This allows for two-way feedback, which sometimes is desired and sometimes is not. One retailer leaves this up to the customer by including a check box with the statement: "✓ if you wish to receive acknowledgment of your comments."

Short- and Long-Term Objectives

The above described goals are listed in Table 1 according to their functional areas. For each goal, a short-term and a long-term objective pertaining to the goal is listed. Short-term objectives primarily address a *current* need or situation; they typically point to the resolution of an immediate problem or question. The short-term benefits are realized as long as the feedback system is in place and functioning properly; if the feedback flow stops, the short-term benefits typically cease.

>>> *See Table 1 (Customer Feedback System Options) at end of this paper* <<<

The long-term objectives of Table 1 more generally focus on *future* needs and functional requirements. The feedback investment return might not be immediately realized, but it will come through the advancement of the firm, including the firm's processes, products, and reputation. In fact, feedback received today may take months to be acted upon, and it may take even more time to harvest its value.

How might one choose whether to focus on short-term or long-term objectives? Typically, if a problem or immediate need is present and the feedback objective can help rectify the situation, then consider the short-term objectives. If the organization's focus is on establishing future development opportunities, then consider the long-term objectives. Very often the customer feedback system will address some combination of objectives of both types.

Once the goals and objectives of the customer feedback system have been decided on, the actual design of the system directly follows. This includes determining (a) *what* feedback to collect (survey questioning and response types), (b) *how to use* the feedback data (including the type of analysis), (c) *how to collect* the feedback (including

Apx D

the type of solicitation), (d) *when* to collect the feedback, and (e) *where* the feedback will go through the organization (called "channeling"). These five major design issues (a) through (e)—and important related issues—will be addressed in the next four sections. The start of each section will identify the specific issues which are discussed in the section. All of the design issues will be summarized in Table 2 at the end of this article. We begin with design issues (a) and (b).

Questioning, Response Type, and Analysis

Issues discussed in this section include:

(a)	questioning	*The type of questions to ask customers, including wording.*
	response type	*The format of the question responses.*
(b)	data use	*How the collected feedback can be appropriately analyzed and used.*
	bias sensitivity	*Whether the data use is sensitive to response bias.*

For each objective listed in Table 1, examples of the type of corresponding questions are listed in the "Survey Question Examples" column. Specific examples from actual surveys were described previously. Nevertheless, the feedback survey designer needs to consider carefully the choice of questions, including wording and response type, for a couple of reasons. First, the space on customer feedback survey instruments can be very expensive in terms of response rate: If customers see the survey form before completing it, more questions or more complex questions will result in fewer responses. The response-rate issues will be discussed further below.

A second reason for carefully considering the questioning is the well-documented "Hawthorn Affect," which is that simply measuring people influences their responses. The implication here is that poorly worded survey questions can lead to inaccurate responses. Books on survey design discuss considerations pertaining to question wording.

Also listed in Table 1 are the response types typical for the survey question examples. The response type is the format the customer is given for response. Some responses are structured, allowing for numerical analysis, and other responses are unstructured, which requires qualitative analysis. The following are general response types employed, listed from the most structured to the least structured.

- Dichotomous — or two choices, such as "yes or no."
- Scale — rating scales with typically five or seven points; they come in many varieties. Any book on survey design will include general guidelines on scale selection. Some crucial issues to consider are discussed in the paper appendix "Interpreting Rating Scales."
- List (to check) — alternatives in which the customer is instructed to select one or more, such as "What did you like most about our cruise ship? ❑entertainment ❑food ❑sports..."
- Field (or Fill-in-the-blank) — typically a question followed by a short blank line for a brief (few-word) response. Examples of field questions include "Who was your server?" or "What do you consider the most exceptional feature of this product?"
- Open-ended — typically represented as blank lines on the survey form preceded by a statement such as "Please tell us what you think" or "Comments?"

Also, for some of the questions listed in Table 1, the "Name/address/phone" response type is specified, which is a special Field type. By requiring the customer to identify him- or herself, we violate anonymity, which may lower response rates and increase bias (since those who cherish anonymity are unlikely to respond). If customer identification is listed as "optional," the company can expect about half of the customers to omit addresses, limiting the ability to send replies.

The response types listed in Table 1 are typical for the corresponding question examples listed in that table. However, questions can be worded to allow for different response types. The selected response type should certainly be consistent with the question wording. An example of dichotomous questions mismatched with a scale response type is a restaurant's actual comment card that states, "Please rate the following with #5 as the highest and #1 as the lowest," followed by "Was an appetizer suggested? 5 4 3 2 1" and "Dessert was suggested. 5 4 3 2 1." (A dichotomous response type would have matched those items.)

Further, the response options need to be adequate for the type of feedback. List-type responses should include all high-frequency responses and often an "other" response. Rating-scale questions should allow for "no opinion" or "not applicable" responses if the customer may have no experience with that portion of the service or product. Even open-ended questions need to be adequate in design. For example, the comment card of a major photography chain states, "Please tell us about your experience at Glamour Shots," which is followed by two 3-inch

(8 cm) lines an eighth-of-an-inch (3 mm) apart. That is an extremely small response space matched with a big-response question.

In addition, the selection of response type will have implications for the customer completing the survey and for the data which is received. As described in Figure 1, response types that tend to be the easiest to respond to are those whose responses are the least flexible. Also, the response types that allow for the greatest variety of feedback data to be collected are not readily analyzed by quantitative means.

>>> *See Figure 1 (General Implications of Response Type) at end of this paper* <<<

Some companies set the response type to make the survey computer readable. However, that only reduces the time to enter the feedback in the data base, not the time to complete the survey. For example, a comment card received some time ago at the Anaheim Hilton and Towers was partially computer readable, but it had 40 rating questions, one list question, three dichotomous questions, four field questions, and one open-ended question. The company was probably poised to quickly analyze submitted comment cards with the computer, but probably relatively few cards were submitted, given the extent of questioning. Fairfield Inn, on the other hand, uses computer technology at the front desk to simplify the process of customers giving feedback at checkout: customers only have to push a few buttons in response to on-screen questions. Fairfield Inn's response rates have been above 50 percent, which is outstanding.

As Figure 1 shows, the data use is directly tied to the response type. More important, the data-use requirements should correspond with the particular goal and objectives of the feedback. The second-to-last column of Table 1 describes how the data might typically be used towards accomplishing the goal. The descriptions in the table are, of course, quite brief and certainly do not cover the variety of ways feedback data can be put to use towards the goal. The important issue is that the feedback use is goal and objective oriented, which requires that the feedback have a positive impact on the organization.

Active or Passive Feedback Solicitation

This section discusses feedback solicitation type and related issues:

(c)		
solicitation type	*How the feedback should be solicited (active or passive).*
extent of questioning	*How intense to make the questioning.*
feedback incentive	*What incentives are given to customers for feedback.*
visibility	*What percent of customers think a solicitation is directed at them.*

Solicitation of feedback is the type of appeal the company gives the customer to encourage feedback. *Active solicitation* involves a direct, personal appeal for feedback, such as by telephone surveys or "exit surveys" (stopping customers as they depart the establishment). *Passive solicitation* does not involve a direct, personal appeal, but largely requires that customers initiate the feedback, such as by picking up a comment cards displayed at an establishment or calling a toll-free telephone number printed on product packaging. A primary difference between the two solicitation types is the ability to control response bias.

Some uses for feedback data are sensitive to response bias, as indicated in the final column of Table 1. *Response bias* is the condition that the feedback received is not representative of the customer population in general. A common example is *extreme-response bias*. This occurs when customers with extreme opinions—delighted or enraged—are more likely to respond to some surveys than customers who are simply satisfied. If extreme-response bias occurs and one out of every ten comment cards comes from an angry customer, then we *cannot* say that ten percent of the customers are angry. An angry customer may be many times more likely to reply than a customer with no complaint.

In some situations, response bias can hinder the feedback goal and objective from being accomplished. For example, if we are trying to identify our customers, yet our responses are biased, then the collected data will not represent the customers in general. Perhaps customers of some age groups are more likely to respond than other age groups—the calculated means and histograms of feedback would include that bias.

When response bias is a problem, suggested by a "Y" in the last column of Table 1, often the only remedy is to resort to *active feedback solicitation* and *controlled sampling*. Active solicitation can be quite costly in terms of labor and communication expense. Therefore, a relatively small portion (perhaps only five percent) of the customers are selected to be surveyed, which is called the "sample." This sample of customers who are surveyed is typically either randomly selected (with the same likelihood for any given customer being selected) or selected so that the chosen customer sample represents the overall customer population in ways that are known (as in "stratified sampling"). (For more information on active solicitation sampling, see any marketing research textbook.)

Apx D

To avoid biases in the results (such as "non-response" bias), it is important that the active solicitation *response rate* (the percent of surveyed customers who actually respond) be quite high —as much as 80 to 90 percent for personal interviews[4] and 50 percent for mail surveys.[5] The push for high response rates can increase the intensity of the solicitation—and the cost. Besides monetary costs for labor and communications, intense active feedback solicitation can also incur a cost in terms of customer goodwill. One company we studied refers to their customer-survey phone calls as "courtesy calls" to minimize the negative impression of being called by a surveyor. Yet whatever the survey is called, many people do not like to be pushed to give feedback.

In those cases where response bias is less of a concern, which includes most of the objectives from Table 1, a better alternative can be *passive feedback solicitation*.[6] With passive solicitation, the company presents the customer with the opportunity to submit feedback, but the actual feedback effort is primarily initiated *by the customer*. A common example of this is a comment card left where the customer will see it. The card may have "Please give us your comments" printed on the front, which is a much more passive solicitation than someone calling up the customer to ask for comments. We must rely on the customer to pick up the card and complete it.

A more recent example of passive feedback solicitation is customer response forms on the World Wide Web.[7] Customers (and others) complete an on-screen form which is electronically submitted to the company's feedback database. Some companies even allow the customer to specify where they would like such feedback to be routed to at the company. For example, Bell South's Web-based feedback form included six different "submit" buttons, allowing the responding customer to select the department that will receive the feedback.

Response rates for passive solicitation will be much lower than for active solicitation— perhaps only five to ten percent of all customers—and response bias will typically be quite high. However, in some cases response bias can actually be a good thing. For example, if we are trying to use feedback to motivate employees or reclaim dissatisfied customers, being *more likely* to hear from customers with strongly positive or negative opinions can be a good thing.

A great advantage of passive solicitation is that the solicitation costs are a great deal lower than for active solicitation, which is largely because the effort to initiate response is primarily left to the customer. One major implication of this is that it is usually cost effective to passively solicit feedback from *every customer*, whereas active solicitation (e.g., phone surveys) of every customer is likely to be cost prohibitive. In addition, *every customer* may be passively solicited *every time* he or she repurchases, which is accomplished by a *continual collection of feedback data*. (Active solicitation, such as market studies, often only occur over a finite period of time, after which the feedback collection stops and the data is analyzed.)

Perhaps the greatest disadvantage of passive feedback solicitation is that the response rate is extremely sensitive to the extent of questioning (which includes the number and complexity of questions on the feedback form). Active solicitors can often get away with 20 or 30 questions and still have an adequate response rate, and as one expert stated, "A general rule of thumb is that a mail questionnaire should not exceed six pages in length." [4] The response rate for a passive solicitation that involves six pages of questions will likely be near zero. As a different rule of thumb, including more than five average-complexity questions on a comment card will adversely affect the response rate.

One way to simplify the questioning and allow for more effortless feedback is to change the question and response type. For example, some years ago the Disneyland Hotel had a comment card with 55 distinct rating-scale questions. It asked about everything from the telephone operators to the tram service—apparently Disney was interested in detailed responses. However, if they were simply looking for extreme responses, an alternative questioning could be "What was exceptional?" and "What needs improvement?" with a field response type and possibly some options listed in parentheses.

Another way to simplify the questioning is to ask each customer only a few of the possible questions. For example, the Fairfield Inn feedback system cited previously includes six questions; however, each customer is only asked to respond to four of the six. This allows the company to increase the scope of questioning without adversely affecting response rates.

If the response bias inherent in low response rates is *somewhat* of a problem (i.e. if the feedback received needs to somewhat represent general customer sentiment), and if passive solicitation is used, response rates can be further improved by

- offering incentives, such as a drawing or a reward for submitting feedback;
- increasing the solicitation "visibility," which represents the percent of customers who see the passive solicitation and consider it to be *directed at them*; or
- making a personal appeal for feedback, such as having an employee encourage the customer to complete a comment card (as is done at some restaurants and hotels).

This last method makes the solicitation semi-active and can result in improved response rates at a relatively low cost. It is important to recognize that while each of these approaches can improve the response rate, if not well managed, they can present additional forms of response bias. For example, one auto-service company entered responding customers in a drawing for a free set of tires, which would bias the results against people who just purchased new tires. Another example of introducing bias involves visibility: An industrial clothing cleaning company required employees to place a comment card in the pocket of each garment that was returned to a customer to increase visibility of the solicitation. However, some employees were omitting the cards for customers known to be dissatisfied. The customer-response statistics were used as the basis for employee bonuses, but the responses received were clearly not representative of customers in general. A similar bias effect will occur if employees are instructed to personally ask each customer to please complete a comment card, but then the appeal is "forgotten" when it is known that the customer has reason to be disgruntled.

In summary, the choice between active or passive solicitation largely comes down to whether the objective for the feedback is sensitive to response bias. If response bias is not a problem, the cost advantages are clearly in favor of passive solicitation.

In-Process or Ex-Post Solicitation

Next, we consider the feedback solicitation timing issue:

(d)	temporal frame	*When the feedback should be collected.*

This feedback-system design issue is whether to collect the feedback *in-process* (during production and delivery) or *ex-post* (after-the-fact). An example of in-process solicitation of feedback is placing a small plastic card by the phone in a hotel to encourage guests to dial "444" for the assistant manager if a problem arises. A common example of ex-post solicitation is providing comment cards that are addressed back to the company for the customer to submit at his or her convenience. One computer superstore had a card that provided both in-process and ex-post solicitations: half was a business reply mail comment card that could be submitted later, and the other half was a "Do you need immediate help?" card on which the customer would write his or her name, give the card to a cashier, and the manager on duty would be immediately paged.

One factor that can influence the appropriate timing of feedback collection is the detail of feedback desired. If a college professor wants student opinions about specific class sessions, then during-the-semester (in-process) feedback solicitation is probably necessary, because people tend to forget details with the passage of time. If, however, that professor simply desires to know students' overall impressions of the course or to know what the most memorable highlights were, an end-of-semester (ex-post) solicitation would be easier to administer and less costly in terms of data collection and analysis. In fact, the students may not have enough information to give overall impressions partway through the semester.

Another advantage of ex-post solicitation is that it can be tied to an event. A hotel might solicit feedback *in-process* by placing a comment card in the customers' rooms on a desk. An *ex-post* alternative is for the hotel to attach comment cards to customers' bills when they are slipped under their door before checkout or handed to them at the front desk. This latter method may result in a better response rate, since the feedback solicitation is at a time when the hotel briefly has the customers' attention. Soliciting feedback at the time the bill is received can also work for other services, such as auto repair, restaurants, and retail.

One disadvantage of ex-post solicitation, relating to the loss of feedback about service details, is an increased "halo effect." The *halo effect* occurs when customers respond to various questions based on an overall impression about the service, even if the questions are about specific details. As an illustration, one professor reported that one or two students who did not like his class answered the "Was the instructor punctual?" question negatively, even though the professor was perfectly punctual. Often, the halo effect is not so blatant, but it occurs nonetheless.

Regardless whether the feedback is gathered in-process or ex-post, it is essential that the feedback be acted upon appropriately and in a timely manner. This may include a rapid response or acknowledgment to the customer. In an attempt to be *systematic* about this feedback response, be careful not to portray impersonal insincerity. For example, the author had two different experiences with Kinko's copy centers that prompted submitting feedback. In both cases the exact same "canned" response was received, which had nothing to do with any of the feedback. This seemed inconsistent with Kinko's comment card stating "What you have to say is important to us." A similar experience happened when giving electronic feedback to members of Congress—with *different* members of Congress providing the *exact same* canned reply.

Apx D

Feedback Channeling

This is the last of the major feedback-system design issues:

(e)	channeling	*Where the feedback goes in the company, and who responds.*

The matter of who "owns" the feedback and is thus responsible for its appropriate use was defined previously when the functional area(s) to benefit from the feedback were determined. Certainly those targeted to benefit should have the feedback channeled (i.e., directed) to them. The feedback may initially be submitted to a central location. For example, 77 percent of comment cards we studied were addressed for return mail (87 percent of which are postage paid). It is interesting to note that 52 percent of the preaddressed comment cards supposedly go to the president or other high officers in the companies. In many cases, this is window dressing: The president does not actually give attention to each submitted card. However, having feedback gathered at a central location can help economize the cost of any recording and processing of the data, and it can minimize the gaming that can occur if feedback is first reviewed by employees whom the feedback is about. A critical condition for the success of centralized feedback collection is being able to *quickly* channel the feedback to those who are to act on and benefit from the data. This channeling of feedback to responsible parties must usually be done daily. If these parties are required to report back on the action taken responding to customer feedback, which is a good idea, this reporting needs to also be done in a systematic and timely manner.

Final Step: Use and Review

The final steps in harvesting feedback are to collect and use the feedback as planned and to periodically review the feedback objectives and corresponding system. This is not truly "final," since customer feedback systems should evolve over time. The objectives and needs in the organization are going to change over time, and thus the direction and implementation of the customer feedback system should correspondingly change as necessary. A well-planned customer feedback system may provide a good return for six months to a year. However, within that time frame it would be good to evaluate appropriate changes. The changes may be simple, such as re-wording a question on a comment card, or complex, such as switching from passive to active feedback solicitation. Often, parts of the feedback system will remain the same for many years, such as a question asking for customers' overall impressions, so that the response trends can be accurately compared over time. What is important is that the feedback system evolve as necessary in response to the organization's evolution and changing functional needs.

Summary

Table 2 summarizes the process of harvesting value from customer feedback by designing the feedback system around business needs and objectives. Note that by starting with the goals and objectives, many of the decisions about the feedback system can be readily answered.

>>> See Table 2 (Major Issues in Designing a Customer Feedback System) at end of this paper <<<

~

Paper Appendix: Interpreting Rating Scales

There has been much debate over the years about the correct interpretation of responses to rating scales. To understand the debate, one needs to consider the two major types of rating scales: interval and ordinal.

Interval scales are represented by a distance or numerical value. The distance between any two points on the scale is equal to the difference between the numbers ascribed to the points. The following is an example:

How would you rate our service overall? (5 is best)
1　　2　　3　　4　　5

The various points of the interval scale do not need to be discretely defined, as in the example above; and in fact, the scale can be continuous, like the following:

Draw an "X" on the line where you consider our service:
poor————————————————excellent

The numerical value for this scale is determined by measuring the distance between the left end of the scale and the customer's "X."

The main problem with interval scales is that many people do not normally consider their attitudes and opinions in numerical or graphical terms. Even though it is quite easy for the company to interpret the scale, many customers may find it difficult to ascribe precise meaning to the points on the scale. They are more accustomed to describing their views and feelings semantically (verbally), as is typical of ordinal scales.

For **ordinal scales**, we merely assume that the items on the scale are in some order (such as from worst to best). A commonly used example is this:

> How would you rate our service overall?
>   poor   fair   average   good   excellent

That is actually a bad example of an ordinal scale, since it presupposes that "average" (the mean value) is less than good. If the service at such establishments in general is considered "good," then "good" might be average. A better example would be this:

> How would you rate our service overall?
>   poor   fair   good   very good   excellent

The scale points are in order and do not seem to overlap. The scale points are adjectives, which should bode well with most customers. (Although some may ascribe different meanings to the word "good," etc.) However, for analysis we are *not* justified in saying that good is halfway between poor and excellent. In other words, it is generally *inappropriate* to assign poor=1, fair=2, good=3, etc., so that the responses from various customers may be averaged. Such assigning of numerical values would assume that the differences between each adjacent scale adjective are equal, which is generally not true. Thus, ordinal scales can be more difficult to analyze than interval scales, since statistics such as means and standard deviations are not appropriate. Below is a meager attempt to create a hybrid interval-ordinal scale.

> How would you rate our service, overall?
>   poor   fair   good   very good   excellent
>   1   2   3   4   5

Such a scale will probably just makes things worse, since many customers will answer according to the ordinal scale, while the company will interpret the response by the interval scale. And as just described, the two are not likely to coincide.

So how might ordinal scale responses be appropriately analyzed? Some "non-parametric" statistical procedures can be applied. However, the most common appropriate way to analyze ordinal responses is to count the number of responses in each category and create a histogram (bar chart) that shows the frequencies. The frequencies can then be compared against response goals, such as a certain percentage of customers reporting "very good" or "excellent."

A suggested alternative for an ordinal rating scale is the following (versions of which are currently used by companies in various industries):

> How would you rate our service overall?
>   excellent   satisfactory   needs improvement

One advantage of this scale is that the objectives for frequencies are inherent in the scale: maximize "excellent" and minimize "needs improvement" responses. Further, the actions for responses are inherent in the scale: for "needs improvement," find out what was wrong and fix it, and for "excellent," find out why and promote it. Finally, since there are only three scale points, the representation of customers in each category can be sufficient to draw statistical conclusions, even when the overall response rate is relatively low.

Paper References

1. J. Goodman, D. DePalma, and S. Broetzmann, "Maximizing the Value of Customer Feedback," *Quality Progress*, volume 29, December 1996, pp. 35-39.

2. M.C. Gilly and R.W. Hansen, "Consumer Complaint Handling as a Strategic Marketing Tool," *Journal of Consumer Marketing*, volume 2, Fall 1985, pp. 5-16.

Apx D

3. C.W.L. Hart, J.L. Heskett, and W.E. Sasser, Jr., "The Profitable Art of Service Recovery," *Harvard Business Review*, volume 68, July-August 1990, pp. 148-156.

4. W.G. Zikmund, *Business Research Methods*, Fourth ed. (Chicago: The Dryden Press, 1994), p. 208-209.

5. P.L. Erdos, *Professional Mail Surveys* (New York: McGraw-Hill, 1970), p. 144.

6. S.E. Sampson, "Ramifications of Monitoring Service Quality Through Passively Solicited Customer Feedback," *Decision Sciences*, volume 27, 1996.

7. S.E. Sampson, "Gathering Customer Feedback over the Internet: Instruments and Prospects," *Industrial Management and Data Systems*, 1999.

Paper Tables and Figure

Apx D

Table 1: Customer Feedback System Options *(continued on next page)*

Functional Aim of Feedback				Question Response Type*		Sensitive to Response Bias?	
Goal	Objective	Short- or Long-Term Objective	Description of Objective	Survey Question Examples		How to Use the Feedback	
Ascertain Customer Needs (DESIGN)	Assess	S	Determine the strength of various customer needs being met.	How important are each of the following product features...	S	Means and histograms. Use to help prioritize service product improvement efforts.	Y
	Probe	L	Determine important needs potentially addressed by the service product.	What features are important for this type of service product? What other needs we might serve?	F O	Use as a discussion topic for focus groups with customer groups.	N
Develop Service Product	Check	S	Assure that the service product is meeting the objectives it was designed to meet.	How would you rate us according to the following objectives...	S	Means and histograms. Identify service product weaknesses or fail points.	Y
	Prescribe	L	Identify ideas for future features or service products.	Suggestions? Possible improvements?	O	Use as seed ideas in the design process.	N
Benchmark Versus Competition	Compare	S	Determine how our company is viewed relative to the competition.	How would you rate us relative to the competition...	S	Means and histograms. Can help identify where we need to study the competition.	N
	Borrow	L	Determine ways in which the competition provides a superior service product.	What do you particularly like about our competitors?	O	Use as guidance for studying competitors' service products.	N
Identify Customers (MARKETING)	Describe	S	Determine what type of people our customers are.	Age? Income? (other demographic questions)	L F	Means and histograms. Assist in targeting and advertising.	Y
	Trace	L	Discover why/how our customers came to be our customers.	How did you select us? What features were major selling points?	L o r O	Analyze effectiveness of various advertising and sales efforts.	Y
Promote Service Product	Impress	S	Give the perception that the company cares about customers and quality.	(any questions about perceived quality and meeting customer needs)	A	Respond to feedback, when possible (i.e. have name and address or phone).	N
	Publicize	L	Collect exceptional service product reviews for future publicizing.	Comments about our company? Anything you consider exceptional?	O	Publish excerpts in company and other publications.	N
Generate Sales Leads	Push	S	Invite customers to repurchase.	Which of these (service products) can we send you more information about?	L N	Forward to sales department.	N
	Enroll	L	Encourage customers to join a frequent purchase club or mailing list.	Would you like to join our (membership club or mailing list)?	D N	Forward to sales department.	N

*Question response types: Dichotomous (e.g., yes/no), Scale (e.g., 1 to 7), List to check, Field (Name/address/phone), Open ended, Any.

Table 1 (continued)

Functional Aim of Feedback		Short- or Long-Term Objective		Question Response Type*		Sensitive to Response Bias?	
Goal	Objective	S/L	Description of Objective	Survey Question Examples	Type	How to Use the Feedback	Y/N
Measure Specification Conformance (OPERATIONS)	Inspect	S	Determine if the service product performed to formal specifications.	Did (such-and-such service product feature) occur?	D	Feed failure information back to employees responsible for providing that feature.	N
	Track	L	Track areas of potential variance to assure the process remains in control over time.	Rate the following features we provide...	S	Use standard control-chart analysis to identify if and when the process goes out of control.	Y
Compare Across Organization	Focus	S	Help focus management on company sites or departments in need of attention.	What department/location did you visit? Comments? (look for problems) How do they rate...?	F O S	Summarize data by department/location, looking for patterns, outliers, and high variance.	N
	Baseline	L	Develop performance standards based on best practices occurring in the organization.	What department/location did you visit? How did they do in these areas...	F S	Summarize data and distribute to each department/location, highlighting top results.	Y
Increase Employee Involvement	Motivate	S	Provide the basis for rewarding or punishing employees for the service product they provide.	Ratings for... (employees or their work). Employee to nominate for recognition? Why?	S F O	Recognize or reward employees for top ratings or significant nomination by customers.	N
	Empower	L	Direct employees in development of their area of responsibility.	How might we improve... (specific aspects of the service product)	O	Direct the feedback to employees, who then report how it is handled.	N
Evaluate Customer Satisfaction (CUSTOMER SUPPORT)	Reassure	S	Receive assurance that customers are generally satisfied.	Did we meet your expectations? How do we rate overall?	S	Means and histograms. Compare with target rating values.	Y
	Protect	L	Watch for customer problems that could potentially become serious (such as legal liability).	Complaints? Comments? (focusing on complaint responses)	O	Investigate complaints, especially reoccurring. Resolve problems before they turn serious.	N
Assure Repeat Business	Recover	S	Attempt to reconcile and reclaim dissatisfied customers.	Any problems with...? Were you satisfied with...?	D N	Contact customers when possible and offer apology and remuneration.	N
	Retain	L	Determine reasons customers defect to prevent future defections.	What might cause you to choose the competition? How likely is that to occur?	O	Build checks into the service product to assure defection-inducing problems are avoided.	N
Provide Sounding Board	Hear	S	Allow customers the opportunity to speak their minds.	Comments?	O	When possible, thank customer for feedback. Apply other objectives as appropriate.	N
	Communi-cate	L	Provide the opportunity to interact with customers.	Questions or comments? Would you like a response? Name and address?	O D N	Tell the customer how you acted on the feedback, and possibly ask for more feedback.	N

*Question response types: Dichotomous (e.g., yes/no), Scale (e.g., 1 to 7), List to check, Field (Name/address/phone), Open ended, Any.

Apx D

Table 2: Major Issues in Designing a Customer Feedback System

Items to determine: (from the first five columns of Table 1)

functional target	*Where will the feedback be used in the company? (e.g., design, marketing, operations, customer support)*
feedback goal	*What is the ultimate purpose(s) of gathering feedback? (This is based on needs of the company.)*
objective frame	*Is the objective to serve an immediate need (S) or long-term (L) objective?*

Which then specifies... (from last four columns of Table 1)

(a)	questioning	*The type of questions to ask customers, including wording.*
	response type	*The format of the question responses (dichotomous, scale, list, fill-in-the-blank, open-ended).*
(b)	data use	*How the collected feedback can be appropriately used (quantitative analysis, qualitative analysis, seed ideas, etc.)*
	bias sensitivity	*Whether the data use is sensitive to response bias.*

Response bias sensitivity then guides...

(c)	solicitation type	*How the feedback should be solicited. Response bias sensitivity usually requires "active" solicitation; otherwise "passive" solicitation is much less costly.*
	extent of questioning	*How intense to make the questioning. The response rate will be inversely related to the extent of questioning.*
	feedback incentive	*What incentives are given to customers for feedback. Incentives may be tangible (such as a drawing for prizes) or intangible (such as promise for response, if desired).*
	visibility	*What percent of customers "see" a passive feedback solicitation, and perceive that it is directed at them.*

Data requirements and use determine...

(d)	temporal frame	*When the feedback should be collected (in-process or ex-post).*
(e)	channeling	*Where the feedback goes in the company, and who responds.*

Figure 1: General Implications of Response Type

Implications for the responding
customer

Demands*:	Flexibility:	Response Types:
low	*inflexible*	Dichotomous
↑	↑	Scale
⋮	⋮	List
↓	↓	Field
high	*flexible*	Open-ended

Implications for the feed-back data	**Variety:**	*limited*	←— — — — — — — — — — —→	*wide*
	Analysis:	*quantitative*	←— — — — — — — — — — —→	*qualitative*

*Demands in terms of time and effort to respond.

Apx D

References from Introduction Section

Ammer, C., and Ammer, D. S. (1984). *Dictionary of Business and Economics*, The Free Press, New York.

Bannock, G., Baxter, R. E., and Reese, R. (1982). *The Penguin Dictionary of Economics*, Penguin Books, Ltd., Harmondsworth, Middlesex, England.

Castells, M., and Aoyama, Y. (1994). Paths towards the informational society: Employment structure in G-7 countries, 1920-90. *International Labour Review*, 133(1).

Chase, R. B. (1978). Where Does the Customer Fit in a Service Operation? *Harvard Business Review*, 56(6), 137-142.

Dilworth, J. B. (1993). *Production and Operations Management: Manufacturing and Services*, Fifth Edition, McGraw-Hill Inc., New York.

Eiben, T., and Davis, J. E. (1995). The New 500 For the New Economy. *Fortune*, 166.

Fitzsimmons, J. A., and Fitzsimmons, M. J. (1998). *Service Management: Operations, Strategy, and Information Technology*, Second Edition, Irwin / McGraw-Hill, New York.

Fornell, C., Johnson, M., Anderson, E., Cha, J., and Bryant, B. (1997). The American Customer Satisfaction Index: Nature, purpose, and findings. *Journal of Marketing*, 60(4), 7-18.

Gonçalves, K. P. (1998). *Services Marketing: A Strategic Approach*, Prentice Hall, Upper Saddle River, New Jersey.

Hackett, G. P. (1990). Investment in Technology-The Service Sector Sinkhole? *Sloan Management Review*, 31(2), 97-102.

Henkoff, R. (1994). Service is everybody's business. *Fortune*, 129(13), 48.

Hill, T. P. (1977). On Goods and Services. *The Review of Income and Wealth*, 23(4), 314-339.

Kelly, R. F. (1997). A New Perspective of Trade Policy for Services: Interdependence and Relationships (speech given September 13, 1996). *Vital Speeches of the Day*, 63(6), 175-178.

Levitt, T. (1972). Production-Line Approach to Services. *Harvard Business Review*, 43.

Murdick, R. G., Render, B., and Russell, R. S. (1990). *Service Operations Management*, Allyn and Bacon, Boston.

Pearce, D. W. (1981). *The Dictionary of Modern Economics*, The MIT Press, Cambridge, Massachusetts.

Productivity.Indexes. (1988). Multiple Input Productivity Indexes. , American Productivity & Quality Center, Houston.

Riddle, D. (1985). *Service-Lead Growth*, Praeger Publishing, New York.

Schmenner, R. W. (1995). *Service Operations Management*, Prentice Hall, Englewood Cliffs, New Jersey.

Shostack, G. L. (1987). Service Positioning through Structural Change. *Journal of Marketing*, 51(1), 34-43.

Sundbo, J. (1997). Management of Innovation in Services. *The Service Industries Journal*, 17(3), 432-455.

Thomas, D. R. E. (1978). Strategy is Different in Service Businesses. *Harvard Business Review*, 159.

United Nations. (1993). *Stastical Yearbook*, Department of International Economic and Social Affairs Statistical Office, New York.

van Biema, M., and Greenwald, B. (1997). Managing our Way to Higher Service-Sector Productivity. *Harvard Business Review*, 87-95.

Index

Full Table of Contents

T of C